Embodied Histories

Embodied Histories

NEW WOMANHOOD
IN VIENNA, 1894–1934

Katya Motyl

The University of Chicago Press CHICAGO AND LONDON

The University of Chicago Press, Chicago 60637
The University of Chicago Press, Ltd., London
© 2024 by The University of Chicago
Published 2024
Printed in the United States of America

33 32 31 30 29 28 27 26 25 24   1 2 3 4 5

ISBN-13: 978-0-226-83214-2 (cloth)
ISBN-13: 978-0-226-83216-6 (paper)
ISBN-13: 978-0-226-83215-9 (e-book)
DOI: https://doi.org/10.7208/chicago/9780226832159.001.0001

Library of Congress Cataloging-in-Publication Data
Names: Motyl, Katya, author.
Title: Embodied histories : new womanhood in Vienna, 1894–1934 /
Katya Motyl.
Description: Chicago : The University of Chicago Press, 2024. |
Includes bibliographical references and index.
Identifiers: LCCN 2023039951 | ISBN 9780226832142 (cloth) |
ISBN 9780226832166 (paperback) | ISBN 9780226832159 (ebook)
Subjects: LCSH: Body image in women—Austria—Vienna—History—
19th century. | Body image in women—Austria—Vienna—History—
20th century. | Women—Austria—Vienna—Identity—History—
19th century. | Women—Austria—Vienna—Identity—History—
20th century. | Urban women—Austria—Vienna—Social life and customs—
19th century. | Urban women—Austria—Vienna—Social life and
customs—20th century. Femininity in popular culture—Austria—
Vienna—History—19th century. | Femininity in popular culture—
Austria—Vienna—History—20th century.
Classification: LCC HQ1610.V5 M67 2024 |
DDC 306.4/6130820943613—dc23/eng/20230828
LC record available at https://lccn.loc.gov/2023039951

Contents

Introduction

On 21 January 1934, at two forty-five in the morning, forty-year-old Hedwig Patzl stood near the Café Royal on Margaretenstrasse in the IVth District of Vienna.[1] It was a relatively mild winter night, with dark clouds threatening a light dusting of snow.[2] The café was crowded with fun-seekers and revelers, and the seductive sounds of jazz poured out onto the winter streets. For a whole hour, Patzl loitered outside the café, while a police officer surreptitiously watched her. Finally, the officer approached Patzl and asked her why she was standing outdoors and for whom she was waiting. He had seen her trying to chat up the few men who had walked by, and he suspected she might be an unregistered sex worker. But Patzl would not be intimidated. She saucily responded that "she could stand where, when, and for however long she wanted." After all, she was on her way home and was "just listen[ing] to the music." She could, she insisted, engage in whatever practices she liked.

Embodied Histories: New Womanhood in Vienna, 1894–1934 is about these practices. It rewrites the history of the New Woman by looking at the performance of new womanhood—everyday embodied practices that constituted a form of gender subversion in Vienna from the fin de siècle to the interwar period. By loitering on the street that winter night, Patzl was a woman engaging in deviant behavior. The simple act of standing thus became an act of defiance, a challenge to normative womanhood. It was, in short, a practice of *new* womanhood, contributing to the transformation of what it meant to perform womanhood, and by extension, to *be* a woman. One of the central arguments of this book, then, is that everyday embodied practices, such as standing, play an important role in generating historical change. Changes in gender and sexuality occurred not only from the top down, but also from the ground up, and significantly, I argue, from the *body* up.

That Patzl stood near the Café Royal is significant. After all, cafés were the "site of urban modernity and cultural exchange," of spectacle and consumption.[3] Moreover, this particular café was the seat of the Viennese Film Exchange (*Filmbörse*), and for those looking to work in the film industry—an unambiguously modern industry—it was the obvious place to go. Vienna witnessed a cinema boom shortly before the First World War that continued well into the interwar period, with theaters opening their doors across the city. In the IVth District, there were six movie theaters in 1934; a few streets from the Café Royal was the Schikaneder Ton-Kino, which happened to be screening *Sehnsucht nach Wien* (*Longing for Vienna*) on the very day Patzl stood longingly on the streets of Vienna. The practices of new womanhood emerged within these spaces of urban modernity: cafés, cinemas, streets. *Embodied Histories* further argues that there is a dynamic relationship between the city and the body. Rather than consider the city, as both discursive and physical space, as containing the distinct body, I am proposing instead that we think of the city as being *of* the body, and by the same token, the body as being *of* the city. The city therefore affects the body just as the body affects the city. New city streets and cafés encouraged Patzl to stand, despite being a woman, but the practice of women standing outdoors also contributed to the further transformation of the city. This book therefore examines how new womanhood emerged in tandem with a distinctly *new* Vienna.

But even if the Café Royal was a site of urban modernity, it was also, most likely, a classic Viennese *Kaffeehaus* with a grand counter displaying trays of strudels and tortes, a billiard table, round tables with bentwood chairs, and a row of upholstered booths. Sitting in clouds of cigarette smoke, patrons would read local newspapers attached to bent-cane holders while stirring small cups of coffee, most likely a *mélange*, served on metal trays with small glasses of water. At night, the café would lure locals with dancing and live music, wine and beer, and, if the mood struck, a *Gspusi* (fling). The space of the Viennese *Kaffeehaus* was to be savored with the entire body and all its senses. If the modern city brought with it new opportunities for the practices of new womanhood, then Vienna's culture of corporeality—embodied by its *Kaffeehaus* culture—made these practices legible.

But who was the New Woman, exactly? And was Patzl such a woman?

In Search of the New Woman

Thirty years before Hedwig Patzl stood near the Café Royal, the New Woman was frequently shown standing in the pages of novels and magazines, and on the stage. Images depicted her standing on chairs, giving up her seat on the tramway, or taunting a male pedestrian from across the street.[4] She stood as she adjusted her cycling hat, smoked a cigarette, or attended the races, for she was more interested in betting on men than on horses.[5]

A neologism coined by the English feminist and novelist Sarah Grand (1854–1943), and then capitalized by Ouida (the nom de plume of Marie Louise de la Ramée [1839–1908], the prolific author of romantic stories) in 1894, the New Woman was a caricature popularized by the fin-de-siècle media to such a degree that she acquired a visual iconography that was easily identifiable across the globe.[6] In Britain and America, the New Woman "cavorted through the pages of *Life*, *Puck*, *Punch*, and *Truth* perched on bicycles and smoking cigarettes; she looked learned in judges' wigs and academic gowns and athletic in riding pants and football helmets."[7] In France, she was "alternatively envisioned as a gargantuan *amazone* or an emaciated, frock-coated *hommesse*."[8] By the 1920s, the New Woman—known alternatively as the Modern Girl, flapper, *moga*, or *garçonne*—became even more widespread, her iconography consisting of "bobbed hair, painted lips, provocative clothing, elongated body, and open, easy smile."[9] While contemporaries typically identified the New Woman "with reform and with social and political advocacy," the Modern Girl was associated "with the 'frivolous' pursuit of consumption, romance, and fashion."[10]

A similar iconography appeared in fin-de-siècle Vienna, though filtered through a local idiom. In Grete Meisel-Hess's 1902 novella, *Fanny Roth*, Viennese readers would have immediately recognized the eponymous character as an "emancipated woman," a New Woman.[11] In addition to being an avid composer and violinist, Fanny is a reader of Friedrich Nietzsche and Henrik Ibsen, an admirer of the Vienna Secession, and a foe of the corset.[12] And she rides a bicycle. In the late 1890s and early 1900s, in the midst of an emergent cycling craze, the New Woman was almost always imagined and depicted as a cyclist, dressed in sporting attire and a hat (see fig. I.1).[13] Even if she did not ride the bicycle, it was always shown nearby, symbolizing her literal and figurative freedom—from stasis on the one hand, and from convention on the other.[14]

Antifeminist media portrayed the New Woman as a towering Amazon who was typically dressed in a top hat and/or pants and carried a walking stick, thereby embodying a potent, even virile feminine beauty. She was always stronger than her male counterpart, who was often shown as smaller than her, effeminate, and beholden to her gaze and chivalry. In one alpine-themed caricature from 1907, a tall, buxom New Woman was shown hiking through the mountains, dressed in *Lederhosen*, with an axe slung

FIGURE I.1. The New Woman was frequently depicted on a bicycle. From the top, left to right: (1) "The woman cyclist has the motto: 'The bike is under my control.'" (There is a play on words, here, since *unter der Haube* literally means "under the hat," which is appropriate insofar as the woman wears a hat. It also means "to have under control," or "to be married." In this way, the woman cyclist expresses not only her mastery over the bike, but also her preference for a bike over a husband.) (2) "The bicyclist races and wants a victim." (3) "At home, you steer me with advice and force, and yet, you are unable to [steer] this little bike." (4) "Two hearts and one bicycle." (5) "He: 'Do stay longer, all of that riding is dangerous.' She: 'Not biking is even more dangerous. . . .'" (6) "'Oh my God, did something happen to you?' 'If you did not see anything—no!'" (7) "All's unwell!" From "All' Heil," *Der Floh*, 8 July 1894, 5. ANNO/ÖNB.

over her shoulder, as her male guide scrambled weakly behind her (see fig. I.2).[15] Although he was the mountain guide—the leader or *Führer*—she was clearly the one leading *him*. The New Woman, it seemed, was posing a threat to the masculinity of men.

At other times, the New Woman was imagined as not only acting masculine, but looking it as well. Neither tall nor Amazonian, she was envisioned as either muscle-bound and stocky or dandyish and wraith-like. Sometimes referred to as a "Man-Woman" (*Mannweib*)—in French, an *hommesse*—she looked, dressed, and acted like a man, perhaps even, some believed, *was* a man with male desires. Writing in 1903, the Jewish-Austrian writer Otto Weininger even argued that "a woman's demand for emancipation and her qualification for it are in direct proportion to the amount of maleness in her," suggesting that the New Woman was physiologically partly male.[16]

Antifeminist contemporaries believed that the New Woman's "manly" and noticeably foreign "lifestyle" were the cause of her "unwomanly" behavior—a logic used especially in the 1910s to explain the rioting suffragettes.[17] In one advertisement for a coffee substitute, foreign products such as strong tea, whiskey, and hot and spicy food (presumably Hungarian paprika) were decried for making women "nervous, angry, eccentric" (see fig. I.3).[18] The New Woman posed a threat not only to the masculinity of men, then, but also to the particularly Viennese femininity of women, thereby leading to what contemporaries called "degeneration" and sexual crisis.[19]

By the 1920s, the New Woman underwent yet another transformation. Recalling the Amazon of the 1900s, this New Woman, known occasionally as the "Modern Woman" (*moderne Frau*), was tall in stature, slender, and androgynous. While her slim physique contributed to her androgyny, it was her haircut—the pageboy or *Bubikopf*—that was viewed as especially boyish, prompting an outcry among conservatives who feared its degenerative effects.[20] The *Bubikopf* became such a cause célèbre that the haircut became *the* signifier of the New Woman at this time; in fact, if the bicycle was the New Woman's prop in the 1890s, then by the 1920s it was the *Bubikopf*, with the result that the New Woman was sometimes even referred to *as* a *Bubikopf*.[21] In addition to symbolizing a freewheeling boyishness, the *Bubikopf* also signified frivolity, free love, and sensuality.[22] A woman sporting the haircut appeared uninterested in marriage and children, looking instead for sexual adventure or a "comrade and soul friend."[23] In a caricature from 1924, a "modern woman" sporting a zippy *Bubikopf* lounges comfortably on a plush armchair, her arms draped over its spine while her top calf is crossed loosely over her knee (see fig. I.4).[24]

FIGURE I.2. A 1907 caricature of the New Woman as a towering Amazon hiking through the Alps. Her male guide exclaims, "Freedom lives in the mountains!" To which she responds: "With whom?" From "Ihre Frage," *Wiener Caricaturen*, 14 July 1907, 1. ANNO/ÖNB.

FIGURE I.3. In this advertisement for Imperial Fig Coffee, a chaotic group of unruly New Women are rounded up by the police. Two gentlemen stand on the sidelines, wondering, "How is it that suffragettes behave in such an unwomanly manner?" The reason is because they "follow a manly lifestyle." "If they drank Imperial Fig Coffee like the Austrian and Viennese housewife," the gentlemen insist, "they would likewise be the loveliest and most good-natured ladies." From "Imperial-Feigen-Kaffee," *Illustriertes Familienblatt: Häuslicher Ratgeber für Österreichs Frauen* 28, no. 2 (1913): 14. ANNO/ÖNB.

A gentleman bends stiffly toward her, promising, "My dear madam, if you will be with me, I will never leave you!" Meanwhile, the woman peers skeptically at him and replies, "But that is precisely what scares me."

It was not just the antifeminist media that propagated this image. In 1926, a new magazine appeared in circulation, *Die moderne Frau* (*The Modern Woman*), that targeted a range of different "modern" women, including the "beautiful and chic woman who finds her life's purpose in fashion, society, and flirtations."[25] Another women's magazine, *Moderne Welt* (*Modern World*), featured spreads of androgynous women's fashion, with occasional caricatures poking fun at the anxiety generated by the

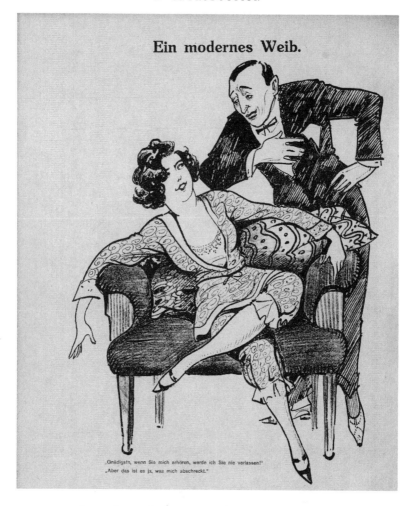

FIGURE 1.4. In a caricature from 1924, a modern woman with a *Bubikopf* hesitates after receiving a proposal from her beau. After he tells her that he "will never leave [her]," she responds, "but that is precisely what scares me." From "Ein modernes Weib," *Wiener Caricaturen*, 1 May 1924, 8. ANNO/ÖNB.

new style.[26] Finally, women themselves sometimes drew on New Woman imagery. In a personal ad from 1926, two women—"one, plump, the other, a slim, blond *Bubikopf*, not boring, thank God"—were looking for "two fun friends" for the occasional night on the town.[27]

Finally, the Social Democratic Workers' Party (SDAP), which governed Vienna for most of the 1920s, also conjured up a version of the New Woman, "the female part of the 'neue Menschen'" who would revitalize Viennese society.[28] Like the Modern Woman, the socialist version was "youthful, with a slender-garçon figure," "[made] supple by sports, with bobbed hair and non-constraining garments," and a "fearless, open, and relaxed" temperament.[29] And yet, unlike the frivolous *Bubikopf*, she was neither an avid shopper nor a single good-time girl. Not only was the SDAP's New Woman frugal, as well as committed to rational dress and sensible shoes; she also saw herself, first and foremost, as a mother whose job it was to manage the triple burden of housework, wage work, and child-rearing.[30]

✳

Scholarship on the New Woman has often focused on the figure's representation in popular culture, attributing her ubiquity to contemporary antifeminist anxieties or feminist fantasies about women's emancipation.[31] Debora Silverman, for example, situates the *Femme Nouvelle*/New Woman of fin-de-siècle France within the context of the burgeoning women's movement, French women's access to higher education and professional careers, and a declining birth rate after 1889, to explain how the figure came to symbolize anxieties about the decline of the bourgeois family.[32] Meanwhile, in *Civilization Without Sexes*, Mary Louise Roberts argues that the 1920s' *Femme Moderne*/Modern Woman "served as a symbol of rapid change and cultural crisis" in the wake of the First World War.[33] And, according to Carroll Smith-Rosenberg, the New Woman in Victorian America was a "condensed symbol of disorder and rebellion."[34]

But who were the actual new women to whom the New Woman referred? *Were* there even new women? Most scholars agree that the term has many limitations, for few women identified themselves as new women to begin with; moreover, the image rarely corresponded to the reality on the ground.[35] As Helmut Gruber points out, Vienna's "working women were light years removed from that attractive image of the new woman projected in socialist literature."[36] In fact, the term is mostly used by historians as an analytic category or heuristic device to make sense of changes in gender and sexuality in the late nineteenth and early twentieth centuries.[37]

Some scholars have used the term to study those women who moved beyond the so-called private sphere of the home to the public sphere of politics and society. These were university graduates, medical women, white-collar workers, and women who had acquired independence and new opportunities to earn a living.[38] They were also theater actors, performers, and journalists, sex workers, leisure-seekers, and consumers.[39] In Vienna, these new women were active in the burgeoning women's movement and organizations, including the General Austrian Women's Association (*Allgemeiner Österreichischer Frauenverein*, AÖF, founded in 1893), the League of Austrian Women's Associations (*Bund Österreichischer Frauenvereine*, BÖF, founded in 1902), or the Women's Right to Suffrage Committee (*Frauenstimmrechtskommitee*, founded in 1906).[40] They were the women involved in the sex reform movement and the League for the Protection of Motherhood and Sexual Reform (*Bund für Mutterschutz und Sexualreform*, founded in 1907).[41] They were often Jewish women pursuing higher education degrees and careers.[42] They were the women who were involved in the modernist art movement or who worked in theater or film.[43] They worked as sex workers or labored outside the home, a trend that began in the 1860s and continued into the interwar period.[44] They served as nurses during the First World War and participated in the war effort.[45] And, after the introduction of women's suffrage in 1918, they were the women who voted or became involved in politics.[46] In short, they were women who consciously transgressed into the "public" sphere.

But the separate spheres paradigm has many limitations, given that the spheres were never mutually exclusive in the first place. Scholars have thus come to think of new women not just in terms of entering new spaces but also in terms of engaging in new *acts* in both new and old spaces. In *Disruptive Acts: The New Woman of Fin-de-Siècle France*, Mary Louise Roberts argues that the new women of fin-de-siècle France engaged in "disruptive acts" that "play with gender norms by embracing both conventional and unconventional roles."[47] Similarly, Liz Conor describes the new women in 1920s Australia as engaging in "techniques of appearing," while the Modern Girl Around the World Research Group similarly argues that "being seen was a quintessential feature of the Modern Girl."[48] Finally, although she is mostly concerned with the discursive New Woman, Lena Wånggren nevertheless observes that even this figure is "often connected not only with ideas or concepts, but with specific tools, technologies and practices"—in short, with acts.[49]

Embodied Histories shifts the focus from the New Woman/new women to the acts or performances of new womanhood. It argues that, while most Viennese women did not identify as new women per se, many of them performed new womanhood by engaging in everyday embodied practices that subverted and defied normative femininity. Set in modernizing Vienna from the fin de siècle to the interwar period amid its "corporeal turn," the book traces the emergence, proliferation, and consolidation of these embodied practices and details how they came to transform womanhood for years to come.

To return to Hedwig Patzl: it is doubtful that she identified as a new woman. She may not even have been sympathetic to the feminist movement. And yet, she engaged in a practice of new womanhood: she stood outside for over an hour in the middle of the night. She did not just transgress into public space, she *stood* in that space. To understand just how radical this simple act was, let us examine it from a theoretical perspective.

Embodied Practices, Embodied Subjects

In 1925, a Viennese magazine observed that "a new gender is emerging that wants to be understood in the context of its time."[50] New womanhood, this book argues, was that new gender expression. Judith Butler famously argued that gender constitutes a bodily performance, a series of repeated gestural iterations and citations that give shape and substance to gendered subjectivity.[51] Although Butler observed that performativity is always constrained by hegemonic norms, subversion or "gender trouble" is also possible. This book partially draws on Butler's idea of performativity while reframing new womanhood in terms of practices. Like Butler, I focus on how bodily practices shaped gendered subjectivities, including *new* gendered subjectivities, and attempt to answer the question of how the practices of new womanhood generated possibilities for a different kind of woman, a new woman.

But *Embodied Histories* deviates from Butler's work in significant ways. For Butler and many performance studies scholars, the subject "performing" gender does not exist. Rather, the performances of gender are what give coherence and materiality to the subject, creating the illusion of a stable sexed performer. Although this book acknowledges the instability and contingency of subjectivity, it does not deny the subject's existence, even as my understanding of the subject differs significantly from the traditional liberal view. New womanhood may have been practiced absentmindedly at times, but there really were existing subjects doing the practicing. *Embodied Histories* claims that these subjects, these practitioners of new womanhood, were *embodied women*.

By "embodied women" I do not mean people who are genetically female and/or endowed with female reproductive organs. Rather, I mean people who lived everyday lives as women-in-the-world.[52] This book draws on the more recent "material turn" in history, as well as on the paradigm shift in feminist history and theory that considers gender as lived and embodied and rethinks the body as endowed with its own agency.[53] It uses feminist phenomenology, which takes the position, following Simone de Beauvoir, that consciousness is embodied, so that being a woman means embodying her in space. De Beauvoir argued that, within Western society, women are reduced to immanent body-objects and denied the transcendent subjectivity of men. From childhood onward, women are socialized to conform to and embody this immanence: "Games and daydreams orient the little girl toward passivity," de Beauvoir observed, "but she is a human being before becoming a woman; and she already knows that accepting herself as a woman means resigning and mutilating herself."[54] Thus, for de Beauvoir, normative womanhood constitutes a kind of physical resignation or mutilation. More recently, feminist phenomenologists such as Iris Marion Young and Susan Bordo have argued that normative femininity involves the process of making bodies smaller and more burdensome.[55]

Embodied Histories shows that a normative, hegemonic performance of womanhood, which was synonymous with upper-class, white, Catholic, German-speaking femininity, existed in late nineteenth- and early twentieth-century Vienna.[56] While it was certainly different from the normative femininity described by de Beauvoir and others, it too was immanent and burdensome. The book then traces the emergence of a new womanhood specifically defined by its performative *deviance* from or *subversion* of normative femininity.[57] If normative femininity involved the practice of physical restraint, for example, new womanhood was marked by its deviation from physical restraint via practices of dynamism and expression. If normative femininity was defined by sitting, new womanhood—as practiced by Hedwig Patzl—involved its subversion via standing. And it is precisely because new womanhood defined itself in reference to and deviation from the practices of normative femininity that it could still be described as a kind of womanhood, *even as* a new gender expression.

The embodied practices that *Embodied Histories* examines are ordinary and quotidian, the kind one may engage in today without much thought. These include but are certainly not limited to practices of walking, body-shaping, emoting, desiring, and seeing/knowing. Further, given their nature, many of these practices may have been done absentmindedly, a product of "regulated improvisation" instead of conscious will.[58] At other times, they may have been done more consciously as what Michel de Certeau would describe as a tactic, a practice of everyday resistance.[59] Despite their ordinariness, these embodied practices had powerful effects: not only were they identified and perceived as deviant, leading to outrage and backlash; they also came to transform what it meant to act as and to be a woman. Ordinary embodied practices, this book insists, are the site of quiet revolution, the locus of agency, and the generators of historical change.

Although the practices of new womanhood were not viewed as unified at the time, we can, retrospectively and analytically, understand them as part of the same new womanhood phenomenon. I take inspiration from David Halperin's genealogical approach in *How to Do the History of Homosexuality* to show that, like modern homosexuality, new womanhood was also the result of historical processes of "accumulation, accretion, and overlay"—that it has, in other words, no single history, but rather multiple histories of multiple practices (hence my book's title).[60] In *Embodied Histories*, I trace the individual histories of these embodied practices and show how they were consolidated over time, thereby displacing older articulations of femininity.

While anyone could engage in the practices of new womanhood, these practices only acquired significance—and visibility—when done by embodied women.[61] I take an intersectional approach and examine the experiences of a wide range of embodied women. These include women unknown today, such as Magdalene W. and Hilde R., locally known women such as Mathilde Hanzel-Hübner, and world-famous women, such as the composer-muse Alma Mahler-Werfel and the Jewish actor Elisabeth Bergner. While many were bourgeois women, others belonged to the working class, including sex workers, migrants, factory workers, and domestic servants. New womanhood was not limited to the bourgeoisie; it was performed by bourgeois and working-class women alike, operating as a visible erasure of class difference. And while most of these women may appear white to us today, many of them—Jews and Slavs from eastern Europe—were seen as anything but that by German-speaking gentiles. In fact, what made new womanhood so radical, I argue, was its diverse class, ethnic, linguistic, and religious origins.

Was new womanhood—in its performative deviance from and resistance to normative, hegemonic femininity—always and completely transcendent, whole, and liberating? Not necessarily. In fact, one of the central points of *Embodied Histories* is that while new womanhood was often viewed in this way by feminist contemporaries, this was not always the case. After all, just because a practice of new womanhood, such as standing on the street, may *feel* liberating does not necessarily mean that *it is* liberating. This book therefore challenges whiggish narratives of women's emancipation by revealing that there is no straightforward teleology from immanence to transcendence. The history of gender and sexuality does not follow a logical trajectory, nor does it necessarily end in liberation. It is, in the words of Dagmar Herzog, syncopated: meandering and unpredictable.[62]

An Urban History

How does one account for the emergence of these embodied practices? *Embodied Histories* argues that they arose in tandem with the modernizing city of late nineteenth- and early twentieth-century Vienna. Hence, this book's unique chronology from 1894, when Vienna's urban transformation was in full swing and the term "New Woman" was first coined and capitalized, to 1934, when both the city and (new) womanhood were undergoing further transformation as the threat of Austro-Fascism became a reality. "The city in its particular geographical, architectural, and municipal arrangements is one particular ingredient in the social constitution of the body," observes the feminist phenomenologist Elizabeth Grosz.[63] Specifically, "the form, structure, and norms of the city seep into and affect all the other elements that go into the constitution of corporeality," including how we see each other, our understanding of space, our comportment and orientation, and our corporeal exertion. By the same token, the body "transforms, reinscribes the urban landscape according to its changing (demographic) needs."[64] *Embodied Histories* thus situates the embodied practices of new womanhood within and as part of Vienna's urban history. It shows that, as the city transformed into a modern metropolis, its residents, including their gendered embodied practices, changed as well.[65] One of the central arguments of the book is that there exists a dynamism and interrelatedness between bodies and cities, and more specifically, between gendered embodiment and urban modernity.

On the most basic level, the modern city inspired new metropolitan self-identification and self-fashioning, as well as participation in a cosmopolitan, interurban community.[66] These included new habits, as well as the "routinised rituals of transportation and clock watching, factory discipline and timetables," a new "culture of time and space," and new sensory experiences derived from the "carnivalesque" and "spectacularized" elements of urban life.[67] Some scholars even suggest that the modern city reorganized the cultural hierarchy of the senses by giving primacy to vision.[68] Finally, the city was also the site of new sexualities, even gender expressions.[69] Thus, "despite its bureaucratic conformity," observes Elizabeth Wilson, "at every turn the city dweller is also offered the opposite—pleasure, deviation, disruption," including the possibilities of gender subversion, as well as (this book argues) new womanhood.[70] For Hedwig Patzl, it meant standing outside in the early morning, listening to music in a city that was in some ways a part of her. Vienna was a part of her because it encouraged her to engage in a practice that many ladies would never have dreamed of doing: standing in the street. But it was also a part of her because, by

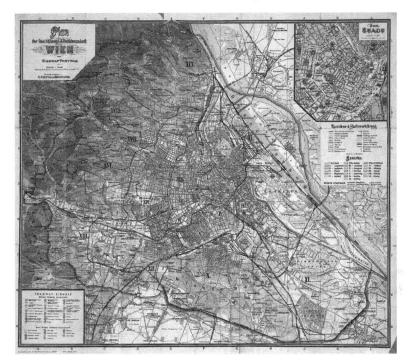

FIGURE I.5. A map of Vienna from 1898–1899 that provides information about the city's modern train lines, tramways, footpaths, roads, and parks. From "Plan der Reichshaupt und Residenzstadt Wien" (Vienna: Verlag G. Freytag & Berndt, later Kartogr. Anstalt G. Freytag & Berndt, 1898–1899, Reproduction: 2000, Production: 1898–1899, Draft). Wien Museum Inv.-Nr. 249875, CC0.

standing in the street, Patzl contributed to the further transformation of Vienna into a modern urban space.

Between the late nineteenth century and the interwar period, Vienna underwent a massive metamorphosis (see fig. I.5). At the fin de siècle, it was the capital of the multiethnic and multilingual Dual Monarchy of Austria-Hungary, a city that was in dialogue with the urban centers of central Europe and that modeled itself after western European cities such as Paris and London. In fact, as Allan Janik and Stephen Toulmin write, "on the entire continent of Europe, Francis Joseph's Vienna could be compared as a city only to Paris. This was the physical setting of a Vienna that rapidly became not just a city, but the symbol of a way of life."[71] And, like Paris during "haussmannization," Vienna experienced extensive rebuilding starting in 1857: the city walls were razed, and in their place emerged the magnificent tree-lined Ringstrasse; new, grid-like streets replaced the meandering network of medieval alleyways; imposing public buildings, such as the Opera (1869) and the University (1877–1884), dotted the urban landscape; the suburbs were incorporated into the city as outer districts; the number of buildings increased from 12,000 in 1880 to 41,000 in 1910.[72] Despite the stock market crash of 1873, the Austrian economy grew steadily in the late nineteenth century, with Vienna witnessing growth in the machine, electrical, textile, and clothing industries.[73] New factories attracted labor migrants, including many women, from outside of Vienna, often from Bohemia and Moravia.[74] Vienna's population and physical footprint grew exponentially, so that by 1910 it became the fourth largest European city after London, Paris, and Berlin.[75]

As the city expanded, so too did its network of infrastructure and communication, including its streetcars and a city railroad (*Stadtbahn*), as well as telegraph and postal systems. Under the leadership of Karl Lueger, the Christian Social (CSP) mayor of Vienna from 1895 (or 1897) to 1910, Vienna continued its transformation into a metropolis.[76] The charismatic and deeply antisemitic "*schöner Karl*" (handsome Karl) implemented a program of municipal socialism, which included the erection of gas works in 1896–1899 and an electrical power plant in 1900, the rechanneling of the Vienna River in 1904, and the construction of new schools, hospitals, cemeteries, and parks. New sanitation projects provided Viennese residents with clean drinking water, a sewage system, efficient trash collection, and paved streets.

Fin-de-siècle Vienna also witnessed the emergence of a culture of consumption, as evidenced by the proliferation of shops and glitzy department stores selling the newest fashions, as well as a mass culture that included "the 'sensation technologies' of the prater (carrousel, big dipper, ghost train, great wheel, etc.), the 'imagination technologies' of cinema and football, or 'narcotic technologies' such as alcohol and tobacco."[77] With the aid of new technologies and an increase in literacy rates, print media flourished and the number of tabloids, newspapers, magazines, and books mushroomed by century's end and continued into the interwar period.

The years of economic growth came to a halt with the First World War. Vienna suffered from widespread food shortages and witnessed the arrival of thousands of desperate refugees fleeing the hostilities of the Eastern Front.[78] With the death of Emperor Franz Joseph in 1916 and the Allied victory in 1918, the Habsburg monarchy was reduced to a small Austrian rump state, "a mutilated torso bleeding from all its arteries."[79] Vienna became both the capital of the First Republic and a separate province and, under the leadership of the Social Democratic Workers' Party

(SDAP), which secured control of the municipal government thanks to universal suffrage in 1919, a bastion of reform aimed at creating a proletarian counterculture with New Men and New Women. Indeed, despite economic decline and inflation, interrupted by a brief period of recovery starting in 1925 and ending with the stock market crash of 1929, interwar Vienna witnessed the construction of four hundred communal housing blocks for workers (*Wiener Gemeindebauten*), and was the site of social welfare projects, public health services, education reform, even sexual reform.[80] Economic recovery also meant more cinemas, shops, and cafés and cabarets—such as the Café Royal—playing American jazz.

But "Red Vienna," as it was known among its critics, was a dot of red in a sea of Black: the national government was in the hands of the Christian Social Party, with Ignaz Seipel named chancellor of Austria in 1922.[81] The tensions between the parties and the polarization within society would, in combination with the economic hardships precipitated by the Great Depression, come to define the politics of the interwar period. When, by 1927, the working classes of Vienna lost faith in the SDAP after a clash with the police at the Palace of Justice, the peculiar version of authoritarianism known as Austro-Fascism began its rise.[82] In 1932, Engelbert Dollfuss became chancellor; he suspended parliament in 1933, crushed a working-class uprising in 1934, and was assassinated by Nazis later that year. His successor, Kurt Schuschnigg, guided the increasingly fragile Austrian state until the Anschluss with Germany in 1938.[83]

Embodied Histories considers how different processes of urban modernity in Vienna—including its urban renewal projects (chapter 1), growing consumerism and the practice of modern total war (chapter 2), mass culture (chapter 3), print culture (chapter 4), and modern medicine and hygiene initiatives (chapter 5)—created opportunities for new embodied practices and, as a result, new womanhood, and how these practices in turn further changed the contours of the city. In this way the book underscores the interrelationship between body and city. Insofar as it views the period from the 1890s to the early 1930s as defined by urban modernity on the one hand, and new womanhood on the other (indeed, the images of the New Woman continued to be circulated during all this time), the book reveals continuities between two periods that have often been viewed as distinct, separated by the no man's land of the Great War. But the war, this book argues, while significant in its effects on gender and sexuality, only accelerated changes that were already taking place *before* 1914 at the fin de siècle. This book, then, is a story of change *and* continuity. While each one of its five chapters considers a different practice of new womanhood, *Embodied*

FIGURE I.6. According to the Austrian Jewish writer Stefan Zweig, Vienna was an "epicurean city," known for its "sensuous pleasures," including its many cafés. From "Wien 1, Ring-Café," photograph (Vienna, 7 July 1915). BAA/ÖNB.

Histories always subscribes to this chronology of continuity, locating the roots of the practice in a fin-de-siècle urban transformation, tracing its development over the course of the First World War and after, and describing its proliferation and effect on the city in the late 1920s and 1930s.

Vienna's Culture of Corporeality

Only in a setting with a culture of corporeality could embodied practices become visible and laden with meaning. Early twentieth-century Vienna was just such a setting. In *The World of Yesterday*, the Austrian Jewish writer Stefan Zweig recalled this culture in rich detail. "Proud and magnificent, with shining avenues and glittering emporiums," Vienna was, according to Zweig, "the city of music," of "Gluck, Haydn and Mozart, Beethoven, Schubert, Brahms and Johann Strauss," of military marches and *Burgmusik*. It was also "an epicurean city," for "the people of Vienna were gourmets who appreciated good food and good wine, fresh and astringent beer, lavish desserts and tortes," which they would consume in the city's many cafés (see fig. I.6). He recalled how the Viennese loved their "sensuous pleasures," "indulged themselves, ate well, enjoyed parties and the theatre, and made excellent music." "The entire city was united in this sensitivity to everything colorful, musical and festive," recalled Zweig, "in this delight in theatrical spectacle as a playful reflection of life, whether on the stage or in real space and time." This "theatrical mania" extended even to the city's Catholicism and its unique culture of death, for "a genuine Viennese turned even his death into a fine show for others to enjoy."[84]

In his groundbreaking *Fin-de-Siècle Vienna: Politics and Culture*, Carl Schorske characterized Viennese fin-de-siècle culture as anything but corporeal. A product of the alleged crisis of Austrian liberalism on the one hand, and the emergence of an irrational "politics of a new key" on the other, Viennese modernism, Schorske argued, involved an escapist retreat from everyday life. This culture was the domain of "homo psychologicus," the psychological human disillusioned with politics and committed to an aesthetic *Gefühlskultur*. Hence, according to Schorske, Hugo von Hofmannsthal's writings cultivated an "irrational force of feeling," while Sigmund Freud's *Interpretation of Dreams* was a "voyage interieur," an exploration of the "world of instinct" in response to liberal-rationalist, academic orthodoxy and aggressive antisemitism.[85] This was a culture divorced from the body.

Despite its resilience, Schorske's paradigm has also come under scrutiny.[86] Most recently, scholars have critiqued the paradigm's characterization of fin-de-siècle modernism as only psychological and divorced from the body. Nathan Timpano, for example, argues for the centrality of "hystero-theatrical gestures" in Viennese cultural production.[87] Alys X. George suggests that the irrational and psychological were rooted in a "corporeal turn" that emerged with the scientific materialism of the second Vienna medical school and extended into the interwar years. George also considers the impact of this culture of corporeality on Viennese modernism, which came to view the body as "a kind of somatic and semiotic utopia," "offer[ing] answers to pressing questions in an era of unsettling change."[88]

The body, however, was central not just to Viennese modernism, but also to its culture and society more broadly conceived. Although few scholars have made this point explicitly, the body's presence in many recent histories of Vienna is striking. These include, but are certainly not limited to, Wolfgang Maderthaner and Lutz Musner's urban history of "the other side" of fin-de-siècle Vienna; Peter Payer's urban histories of the senses; Scott Spector's study of sexual and criminal deviance; Nancy Wingfield's history of prostitution in Imperial Austria; Maureen Healy's social history of the First World War; Lisa Silverman's history of the cultural codes of

Jewishness; Britta McEwen's history of sexuality and emotion in interwar Austria; and Michaela Hintermayr's study of suicide.[89] This scholarship makes clear that Viennese culture—whether fin-de-siècle, wartime, or interwar—was hardly just psychological and solipsistic. It was *in* the world and *of* the material world.

Embodied Histories contributes to this new revisionist history by considering various aspects of Vienna's culture of corporeality. Perhaps even more important, it considers how this particular Viennese culture shaped gender: new womanhood may have been a global phenomenon, but it took on a particular expression in Vienna. In fact, my justification for writing a history of new womanhood in Vienna is this: where better to study gender-as-embodied-practices than in a city that was fascinated with the body?

New Methodologies

During the initial stages of my research, I assumed that the performance of new womanhood would have consisted of grand, public gestures, such as screaming at the front lines of a suffrage rally, giving a speech, or going on a hunger strike. I soon realized, however, that far more common but no less subversive were more pedestrian embodied practices that are easier to overlook. In fact, my first encounter with a practice of new womanhood was a mode of walking that I describe in chapter 1 as *flânerie*. I encountered this practice while conducting research in the Viennese archives because of the controversy (and paperwork) it generated, for flânerie was not only deemed unwomanly by many contemporaries, but also considered criminal. My search for new womanhood thus led me to focus on infractions in which women behaved badly by engaging in seemingly trivial practices that were deemed subversive precisely because they deviated from normative femininity.

The focus on infractions led me to the archives of institutions with disciplinary or punitive aims: the police department, courts of law, the hospital or sanatorium. But these archival documents, by virtue of having been generated by those in power, only told part of the story. In fact, they rarely explained what exactly made a practice controversial in the first place. Although I was able to understand that it had to do with the practice's unwomanliness, I had to probe further to understand *why* and *how* it was unwomanly. Nor did the archives tell me how a practice was perceived and what cultural or social meanings were attributed to it. Moreover, I could not know what motivated a woman to engage in it in the first place, where she learned it, and what it meant for her. And, finally and crucially, the archives did not tell me what the embodied practice looked or felt like. How could I write a history about embodied practices without knowing how they were embodied?

To answer these questions, this book employs innovative methodologies from gender, cultural, and urban history. First, it draws on a range of different types of sources in conjunction with the above-mentioned archival documents, including periodicals, films, photographs, advertisements, novels, travelogues, advice literature, musical scores, ego documents such as diaries and personal letters, maps, and the very city of Vienna itself. I read these disparate sources together and against one another, between the lines, and against the grain. I also read for silences because what is not said is often especially significant.

Second, I turn to my own body and embodied experience.[90] In the conclusion to her book on domestic service in late eighteenth-century England, Carolyn Steedman observes that it is "with [physical activity] either depicted or undertaken, that you may find yourself in the greatest closeness with the dead and gone."[91] Despite the two hundred or so years separating Steedman from her laboring domestic subjects, she shares with them a similar way of cooking: "I chop (anyone cooking chops) an onion, scrape a nutmeg on a grater, in the same way. . . . Physical activity carries the past and something of everyone who has ever sliced a lemon in half for squeezing, stripped the yellowing leaves from a Savoy cabbage, or come to their own conclusion that the best way to peel a parsnip is to boil it first." And while some of these practices certainly changed over time, "there is something here about the extraordinarily limited ways you can cut a lemon, given the shape of the fruit and the existence of carbon steel knives," that makes these practices relatable even to us modern readers. This idea can be extended to many of the embodied practices considered in this book. It is the limited ways you can stand or walk given the physiological capacities and limitations of human legs and feet that makes the practice—despite its foreignness—also intelligible in a fundamental and physical way. Thus, in trying to understand these practices, I too tried to undertake some of them in the very spaces in which they emerged. Thus, I practiced standing on the very spot where Patzl stood. The café was no longer there, but with the help of old photographs, I could imagine it.

Finally, this book engages in historical imagination, the method of informed, research-based speculation that considers how something *could have been* and thereby attempts to fill the lacunae between established facts. Imagination and speculation may seem anathema to historical practice today, but that is to a large degree due to convention.[92] In fact, I would argue that most historians, by virtue of being humans living in the

historical present, must engage in some form of imagination and speculation in order to construct a narrative involving motives, reasons, desires,
and emotions. But the relevance and utility of historical imagination are
also a matter of definition. If we define history as a positivist enterprise
that seeks to uncover the Truth, then imagination and speculation would
appear to have no place in historical practice. But if, instead, history involves the reconstruction of multiple and partial narratives that sometimes
exist in contradiction with one another, then imagination and speculation
are fundamental to it. I subscribe to the latter definition, which shares similarities with what Caroline Bynum calls "history in the comic mode."[93]
"In comedy, the happy ending is contrived," writes Bynum. "Thus, a comic
stance toward doing history is aware of contrivance, of risk. It always ad-
mits it may be wrong. A comic stance knows there is, in actuality, no ending (happy or otherwise)—that doing history is, for the historian, telling
a story that could be told another way."

Throughout the book, and particularly when describing an embodied
practice of new womanhood, I periodically engage in historical imagination. Because these practices are crucial to the book's argument but also
elusive to the historian, historical imagination proved to be the most effective tool to bring them to life. Thus, I "historically imagine" by drawing
on the above-mentioned sources, coupled with my own embodied experience, and translating them into a comic stance that dwells on the possible
and probable.[94] I also consider those witnessing the practice and their
possible point(s) of view. Finally, I try to conjure up the discursive and
physical space and place of Vienna, to elucidate how the modern city was
inextricably linked to the performance of new womanhood. In this way,
historical imagination manages to reveal how practices that were ordinary
and may appear trivial to our modern sensibilities were actually filled with
radical possibility. Additionally, and perhaps most significantly, historical
imagination helps readers understand the practices not only intellectu-
ally, but also physically and in their own bodies as a form of historical
proprioception. After all, as the Viennese novelist and dramatist Hugo von
Hofmannsthal insisted in 1911, the "expressive possibilities of the body are
far greater than the language of words."[95]

The Body of the Book

Embodied Histories is organized into five chapters, each of which excavates
the history of an embodied practice of new womanhood. Insofar as the
book attributes big changes in gender and sexuality to everyday embodied
practices, each chapter begins with an originally researched, thickly de-

scribed microhistory that delves into a particular moment in a Viennese woman's everyday life and explores how a certain embodied practice she engaged in subverted and expanded categories of womanhood, thus leading to an infraction of some sort. The book further situates each embodied practice within the long history of Vienna, considering its urban modernity and cosmopolitanism on the one hand, and its distinct corporeality on the other. In this way, although the chapters are related to one another, they are also self-contained histories.

Chapter 1, "New Moves: *Flânerie*, Urban Space, and Cultures of Walking," begins on an evening in 1916, when the artificial-flower maker Magdalene W. and her adult niece were falsely apprehended on the streets of Vienna for clandestine prostitution. They were arrested, I argue, because of the way they walked through urban space: they engaged in a leisurely and expansive form of movement that resembled the streetwalking of sex workers. At a time when the police force was making a concerted effort to crack down on unregistered, or clandestine, prostitution, the arrest made sense. But what prompted the two women to "streetwalk" in the first place? The chapter shows how streetwalking became widespread with the emergence of flânerie. The transformation of the urban landscape, as encapsulated by the construction of the elegant Ringstrasse, encouraged the new practice of walking leisurely. Flânerie was originally the domain of the *Gigerl*, the Viennese equivalent of the Parisian *flâneur*, who not only consumed urban spectacle, but also produced it with his outlandish costumes and affected gait. Soon, however, flânerie came to be appropriated by others, including women. By using police reports, documentary films, photographs, travel guides, newspapers, and advertisements, I employ historical imagination to reconstruct several instances of women engaging in flânerie well before the incident in 1916. The chapter concludes with a consideration of flânerie in feminist phenomenological terms and of how it subverted conventional feminine movement and thus became a practice of new womanhood. Whether consciously or not, by strolling through the street that evening, Magdalene W. and her niece were new women.

As new women appropriated the walk of the *Gigerl*, it seemed that they started to look like him, too. Chapter 2, "New Shapes: The Masculine Line, the Starving Body, and the Cult of Slimness," begins in 1932, when a cis woman, Gisela Piowati, was misgendered as a man wearing women's clothing. What contributed to this misgendering? I argue that it had to do with Piowati's silhouette, specifically her body's shape, which conformed to what contemporaries understood as a "masculine" appearance. This chapter draws on fashion illustrations, print media, memoirs, intellectual treatises, advertisements, and wartime police reports (*Stimmungsberichte*) to trace how women's bodies, specifically their shape, underwent a transformation in the early twentieth century. At the fin de siècle, the world of fashion was turned upside down when a new "masculine line" came to replace the hourglass ideal of the previous century. Although the French fashion designer Paul Poiret, who traveled to Vienna in 1911, was best known for this silhouette, Viennese dress reformers emphasized a similar shape. During the First World War, the linear silhouette made its way from clothing to the body: on the Viennese home front, people were starving, and their bodies became weaker and thinner as a result. After the war, fashion and diet culture continued to emphasize the slim linear silhouette, rebranded as the "modern line," in which many women, in an effort to maintain and care for their bodies in the wake of a starvation war, actively partook via body-shaping practices. The chapter concludes by returning to the case study with which it started and engaging in historical imagination to envision Piowati's body—most likely a linear, "masculine" body—as the body of a new woman.

Another dimension of new womanhood was the embodied expression of emotion, in particular that which entailed translating the "inner" feelings of the "self" into "outer" expression on the body and face. Chapter 3, "New Expressions: Emotion, the 'Self,' and the (Kino)Theater," opens in April 1920, when the Jewish actor Elisabeth Bergner checked herself into the Steinhof sanatorium, where she was diagnosed with nervousness, or hysteria. A few years later, Bergner would become a famous silent-film actor known for her hysteric performances on the silver screen. This case study is emblematic of two central questions in this chapter. First, was hysteria an early mode of emotional expression that many women, living in an emotionally restrained society, could draw on? And second, was the theater—whether the cinema or the stage—the means through which these modes of emotional expression were conveyed?

This chapter uses diary entries, performance reviews, musical scores, libretti, films, and film fan magazines in conjunction with feminist theories on spectatorship to reveal how modern theater exposed the public to an embodied vocabulary of emotion, including hysteria, that went against the bourgeois conventions and codes of feminine emotional behavior. Viennese theater underwent a transformation at the fin de siècle, eschewing language in favor of bodily modes of expression, including physical acting techniques, pantomime, and (significantly) modern dance. The American modern dance pioneer Isadora Duncan's "free dance" technique was particularly influential in Vienna: it helped introduce an emotional body language that was kinetic and affectual, moving spectators to feel with the performer. With the emergence of silent film—the successor to modern dance—this body language became more varied and nuanced. Further-more, the industry's celebrity culture encouraged its spectators not only to feel with performers, but also to emulate their emotionality outside the theater in order to express "themselves." While actors such as Bergner practiced new womanhood on the silver screen, spectators feeling and liv-ing through her—and later, emulating her emotionality—practiced it, too.

Like the embodied expression of emotion, the feeling of desire in the body came to play a significant role in the definition of new womanhood. Chapter 4, "New Sensuality: A Sexual Education in Desire and Pleasure," begins in 1926, when a young married woman, Hilde R., wrote to an advice column to complain about her "cold" marriage. To cope, she admitted to reading romance novels for pleasure. Many sex reformers derided such novels for being sexually repressive and regressive. Why, then, did Hilde R. and women like her derive so much pleasure from reading them? This chapter argues that romance novels were part of a larger body of "bad books" that emerged at the fin de siècle as a scandalous form of early sexual education and knowledge, even though they were not necessar-ily intended to be read that way. Women read these books—including the Italian sexologist Paolo Mantegazza's *Physiology of Love* (1874), the German author E. Marlitt's romance novel *Goldelse* (1866), and the Aus-trian women's rights activist Grete Meisel-Hess's *Fanny Roth* (1902)— not for "facts" about sexuality, but to learn about their personal desire: to recognize and experience it in their bodies as well as to feel pleasure. While bourgeois morality conceived of desire as being opposite to love, this literature effectively framed it as being part and parcel of love and of woman's subjectivity. Although the full-fledged sex reform movement that emerged in Vienna by the interwar period made "objective" sexual knowledge more accessible to women, it encouraged them not only to recognize and experience their subjective, personal desire, but to pursue and fulfill it with their spouses. Unsurprisingly, even though bad books did not emphasize that desire be pursued and fulfilled with the body of another and therefore seemed old-fashioned or even sexually repressed, new women such as Hilde R. continued reading them, precisely because, I suggest, such books enabled them to find pleasure in something that both sexological tracts and the reform movement ignored: the personal experience of desire.

With this experience of desire came a new sense—and vision—of reproductive embodiment. Chapter 5, "New Visions: Reproductive Em-bodiment and the Medical Gaze," opens in 1927, when a young housemaid named Julianne Schneeberger was convicted of abortion. Instead of plead-ing not guilty, Schneeberger admitted that she had deliberately undergone the procedure to terminate her pregnancy, demonstrating a striking medical literacy rooted in a new way of seeing/knowing the body. Instead of relying on folk medicine and body feelings as women had done before, Schneeberger viewed her body much like a physician would: that is, as a medical object in need of diagnosis and treatment. Drawing on abortion trial records, state sanitation papers, medical texts, and advertisements, this chapter traces the development of this internalized medical gaze. The nineteenth century witnessed the emergence of a new medical paradigm, the displacement of midwives by physicians, and the proliferation of a bourgeois language and culture of hygiene, including the widely popular hygiene exhibitions in London (1884), Vienna (1906), and Dresden (1911). In Vienna, the city known for its dissections and culture of death, the result was that many ordinary people learned to internalize the medical gaze—this new vision—as evidenced by venereal disease prevention efforts and regimens of menstruation hygiene. But the medical gaze could also be a source of agency, a practice of new womanhood. For Schneeberger, the medical gaze rendered her body pregnant and gave her the tools to take matters—as well as her own matter—into her own hands.

The epilogue, "Are There Even Women?" explores how these histories and practices of new womanhood crossed and converged to produce what came to be known and remembered as the figure of the New Woman. Furthermore, it describes the emergence of a *new* new womanhood in the 1930s that was often viewed as reactionary inasmuch as it arose within the reactionary politics of the decade. The epilogue concludes by considering the following problematic: if womanhood is always being displaced by a new womanhood and a newer womanhood, then, to quote Simone de Beauvoir, "Are there even women?"

New Moves

On 18 September 1916, at about a quarter to eleven in the evening, Police Agent Franz Schneider observed two women walking on Mariahilfer-strasse, a large shopping street in Vienna.[1] The women, Magdalene W. and her adult niece, strolled in a leisurely manner, occasionally peering into shop windows. Schneider approached them to ask what they were doing on the street past the ten o'clock curfew. After "an excited exchange of words," he accused them of being unregistered sex workers and handed them over to a watchman, who escorted them to the police station.

But Schneider was mistaken. These women had not been sex workers. Two years into the First World War, the Vienna police mistook two non-sex workers for sex workers. Why? Although historians often answer this question by pointing to transgression into public space, I argue that it had to do with the *way* they walked through space.[2] By strolling through the city that evening, these women cited the deviant streetwalking of sex workers, thereby subverting normative femininity as well as re-embodying it in the process. For the duration of their walk, Magdalene W. and her niece practiced new womanhood, even if they were unaware of doing so.

This chapter examines how moving through urban space became part and parcel of new womanhood. Using the 1916 incident as a reference point, the chapter begins with an examination of how streetwalking came to signify sex work within Imperial Austria's system of regulation, so that any woman walking the street risked being arrested for prostitution. It then continues with an exploration of streetwalking's resemblance to the Parisian walking practice of *flânerie*, which in fin-de-siècle Vienna was practiced primarily by the foppish dandy known as the *Gigerl*. And yet, as evidenced by Magdalene W. and her niece, women engaged in forms of flânerie as well. In fact, as demonstrated by a series of arrests between 1899 and 1901, in which non-sex workers were mistaken for sex workers, many Viennese women, enticed by the city's transformation of urban space as well as by a burgeoning culture of walking, started appropriating flânerie well before the First World War. The chapter then considers flânerie in feminist phenomenological terms, as an embodied practice that subverted conventional feminine movement in favor of something more expansive, continuous, and—significantly—new. Finally, it shows how flânerie became, by the interwar period, mainstream enough that a growing consumer market emerged dedicated to urban walking.

Ultimately, this chapter emphasizes the two main points of this book: First, that everyday embodied practices such as flânerie constituted a tactic of gender subversion, which ushered in the transformation of womanhood. Second, that these practices emerged in tandem with a changing urban landscape, suggesting, in the words of Elizabeth Grosz, that "the form, structure, and norms of the city seep into and affect all the other elements that go into the constitution of corporeality," including gendered embodiment.[3]

Regulating Prostitution, Immobilizing the Streetwalker

Most states in nineteenth-century Europe did not criminalize prostitution, but tolerated it by subjecting it to a system of regulation that was based on the Napoleonic Code of 1804. At a time when venereal disease was believed to be a grave public health issue, regulation promised to protect the bodies of male citizens, particularly soldiers, by ensuring the availability of healthy sex workers. As Nancy Wingfield has written in *The World of Prostitution in Late Imperial Austria*, such regulation appeared later in Vienna than in other European cities as a result of the vocal opposition of the Roman Catholic Church, which sought to abolish prostitution altogether. Then, in 1873, the same year that Vienna hosted the World Exhibition that attracted thousands of visitors from the empire and abroad, regulation was implemented in the imperial capital through a series of ad hoc and oftentimes contradictory measures.[4] The result was a system that consisted of the so-called voluntary registration of sex workers with the police, the distribution of health books (*Gesundheitsbücher*), and biweekly medical examinations. Twelve years later, the vagrancy law (*Vagabundengesetz*) of 24 May 1885 formalized some of the system's provisional measures in its Paragraph 5.[5] Specifically, police became more vigilant about cracking down on unregistered, or "clandestine," prostitutes and had the right to arrest any woman suspected of prostitution if she could not provide evidence of registration or occupation, as well as to force her to submit to an internal examination for venereal disease. And despite efforts to reform the system in 1911, the practice of arresting suspicious women continued into the First World War, especially with the help of civilian denunciations against all perceived enemies on the home front.[6]

Significantly, roughly 90 percent of sex workers in Vienna did not register with the police.[7] That so many women practiced clandestine prostitution is telling because it reveals just how fraught with complexity the system of regulation happened to be. Regulationists, as defenders of the system came to be called, viewed prostitution as a necessary supplement to marriage that aimed to satisfy what was believed to be the relentless sex drive of men. Because the system was based on a sexual double standard (*Doppelstandard*) that placed the burden of health and morality solely on women (men were not subjected to medical examinations), many prostitutes were reluctant to register with the police. In fact, once they registered, sex workers, now branded as "lost girls" or "fallen women," would be forced to endure relentless harassment, isolation, even homelessness.[8] As Keely Stauter-Halsted has put it, police registration could be viewed as "a permanent category, one from which a woman would be hard-pressed to return to the moral mainstream."[9]

But perhaps the most important reason that so many prostitutes failed to register with the police was that many of them did not pursue commercial sex full-time, engaging in it sporadically or as a supplement to other low-income work. It is important to underscore that prostitution was neither a stable type of employment nor a fixed identity. As Wingfield has observed, "the category 'prostitute' was not self-evident, but contingent," precisely because "women moved between the two categories [of tolerated and clandestine prostitution] as well as in and out of the trade during their working lives."[10] This movement is highlighted in this chapter; it also serves as one of my main interventions in the prostitution literature. While historians such as Wingfield have identified prostitution in Vienna as a figurative type of movement—a movement into and out of sex work—this chapter focuses on prostitution as a literal and (crucially) embodied movement in the form of streetwalking. The crackdown on clandestine prostitution, then, can be understood as the attempt to manage and ultimately stop this movement, to stabilize the category of "prostitute" on the one hand, and immobilize the mobile streetwalker on the other.

In the next section, I explore the mechanics of streetwalking-as-movement in greater detail. I then discuss how non-sex workers, such as Magdalene W. and her niece, came to practice this type of movement. In fact, for these non-sex workers, streetwalking was a type of flânerie—a leisurely walking practice that became popular in Vienna at the fin de siècle. Significantly, flânerie subverted the conventions of womanhood, thereby constituting a practice of new womanhood. What begins as a story about prostitution, then, quickly turns into a story about walking practices and the new women engaging in them.

Streetwalking

Streetwalking was one way Viennese police identified clandestine sex workers, precisely because they regularly walked through city streets in search of clients. In his memoir, *The World of Yesterday*, the Austrian Jewish novelist Stefan Zweig recalled the "countless girls for sale trying to pick up customers on the street . . . said in Vienna to be 'on the line' [*auf den Strich*], because the police had divided up the street with invisible lines, leaving the girls their own patches in which to advertise." These women walked through city streets "day and night, well into the hours of dawn," "endless[ly] wander[ing] from place to place," so that they came to be known as being not only *on* the street, but *of* the street.[11] They practiced their trade in parks, near bridges, on streets and alleyways, even in public gardens.[12] "In the Volksgarten," wrote Joseph Schrank, the police physician and president of the Austrian League to Combat Traffic in Women, "the so-called Alley of Sighs is generally known as a rendezvous spot for those in need of love [*Liebesdürftige*]."[13] Streetwalkers also wandered in proximity to train stations, mirroring the itinerancy of streetwalking itself. A man writing to the police department in 1918 recalled meeting an "extremely pretty, tall, very well-dressed lady, blonde," at a train station, with whom he spent an afternoon in an "hourly" hotel (*Stundenhotel*), only to be infected with syphilis.[14]

That it was not uncommon to encounter streetwalkers near train stations was partly because many of them were migrants from the Habsburg east, particularly Bohemia and Moravia. They would often arrive in Vienna at the Nordbahnhof train station and then find a room to rent in the nearby working-class and predominantly Jewish district of Leopoldstadt.[15] The home of the Prater, Vienna's largest park and "love market," the IInd District became infamous for rampant prostitution and streetwalking.[16] "While in other districts after midnight it has already become quite peaceful," observed a Viennese tabloid, "in Leopoldstadt, especially in the Praterstrasse and on Praterstern, there still reigns an active hustle and bustle." "Here, a whore quarrels with her pimp, there, two drunkards fight, and on every corner, some run-down street whore attacks a colleague with her umbrella."[17] But streetwalking frequently occurred in other parts of the city as well, including the working-class districts of Hernals and Brigittenau (the XVIIth and XXth Districts, respectively), the more bourgeois Landstrasse (the IIIrd District), and even in the posh

Ist District, which was, incongruously, home to both the Kaiser and many brothels.[18] In this way, streetwalking defied spatial logic; it occurred in working-class, middle-class, and upper-class districts alike.

Streetwalkers often meandered through parts of the city closed to them, such as public squares and busy boulevards and streets, and in proximity to churches and schools. The Graben, the imposing street at the center of Vienna's Ist District, had long been a popular site for street-walkers, even though it was technically off limits to them.[19] As Schrank recalled, "Oftentimes the Vienna police tried to keep the Graben-nymphs out of the [Graben], but it never lasted long and [it] went back to being the playground of the Viennese demimonde."[20] Likewise, the elegant Kärntnerstrasse, which began at the Opera and ran perpendicular to the Graben, came to be known as the "racetrack of venal sex," where street-walkers competed with "'lavender' lads" for male attention.[21] According to Michel de Certeau, a city's "spatial order organizes an ensemble of possibilities (e.g., by a place in which one can move) and interdictions (e.g., by a wall that prevents one from going further)," so that "a walker actualizes some of these possibilities." At the same time, "he invents others, since the crossing, drifting away, or improvisation of walking privilege, transform or abandon spatial elements."[22] By meandering through the city as they pleased, taking shortcuts through "corners of remote streets, especially side streets" and alleyways, Vienna's streetwalkers actualized, subverted, and invented new spatial possibilities.[23]

In addition to engaging in this "pedestrian promiscuity," streetwalk-ers also took part in a particular kind of movement, which consisted of a slow-paced "roaming" and "strolling," "spreading themselves out on the street" in the process.[24] According to a police report, it was typical for "six or more prostitutes" to "promenad[e] at a distance of three to five steps from one another, often in the middle of the street and always without a hat."[25] Sometimes the women would walk back and forth on a street in a repetitive, "conspicuous" fashion. One letter writer complained to the police that, "on some evenings, ten to fifteen girls promenade [around the Ist District's fashionable Tuchlauben], resulting in such scandals that one wonders why no watchman comes."[26] Police reports often referred to streetwalking as a "hanging about" (herumtreiben), indicating the languid pace of this type of movement.[27] Meanwhile, a Viennese tabloid color-fully described streetwalkers as "the servants of Venus vulgi vaga," of the vagrant goddess of love, suggesting that streetwalking was itself a form of vagrancy.[28]

While this leisurely form of movement served as one indicator of sex work, another was the interruption of movement, including "standing by the front door," "lingering [*das Verweilen*] on the street in the company of other prostitutes, as well as loitering [*das Stehenbleiben*] or walking around [*das Umhergehen*] night cafés or bars."[29] A hat manufacturer in the Ist District complained that streetwalkers would often loiter around his shops, ruining business: "It is frequently the case that our shop windows are essentially besieged [by streetwalkers], so that ladies from bourgeois circles shy away from looking at our window displays."[30] As a contemporary newspaper put it, "some eager watchman may only see—even during the day—a woman stand on a spot for a long time or walk back and forth, maybe even look around, and he will arrest her for 'luring passersby or conspicuous behavior.'"[31] For example, Gisela Pocs, a twenty-five-year-old "dancer from Budapest," was arrested for clandestine prostitution in 1914 for "standing" (*stehen bleiben*) on the corner of the busy Kärntnerstrasse, "looking around" (*umschauen*), and "smiling at men."[32] Pocs also dared to raise her skirt with her elbows protruding, exposing a gold anklet that "sparkled with every step."

Walking in Wartime Vienna

Let us return to the 1916 incident with which this chapter began. Police Agent Schneider acknowledged that one reason for his apprehending Magdalene W. and her niece was that "they had walked slowly."[33] Drawing on what we know about streetwalking, we can employ historical imagination to visualize this scene in detail. Insofar as one of the central points of this book is to highlight the subversive power of ordinary embodied practices, the method of historical imagination allows us to sidestep the authority of the archive by closely examining women engaging in a practice—in this case, walking slowly—that would normally have been overlooked. The archive might make passing reference to walking, but it does not elaborate on what it may have looked or felt like; in fact, most sources pay little attention to such practices, if any. Meanwhile, it may be difficult for modern readers to imagine why walking slowly could be perceived as subversive enough to warrant arrest. Historical imagination remedies this by allowing us to resurrect practices that would otherwise have been overlooked or forgotten and make sense of them according to contemporary logic. But more than making sense of these practices, historical imagination invites modern readers to embody them as well. If the Latin root of the word "imagination" is *imaginare*, "to picture oneself," then one of the goals of historical imagination is self-reflexive: it encourages us to picture ourselves engaging in these practices—in short, to feel

FIGURE 1.1. A 1913 postcard of Mariahilferstrasse, a large shopping street dividing the VIth and VIIth Districts in Vienna. From Paul Ledermann (photographer), "Maria-hilferstraße. Haydn-Monument" (Vienna: 1913, production; 1916, application). Wien Museum Inv.-Nr. 206945, CC0.

our bodies moving through space via proprioception. For what better way is there to truly understand an embodied practice than through the body itself?

On an evening in late summer, two women promenaded down a darkened Mariahilferstrasse (see fig. 1.1), chatting with each other and taking in the view of the moon glowing as a waning crescent in the overcast sky.[34] According to Magdalene W.'s testimony, she and her niece were returning home from a wine cellar (*Volkskeller*), so they might have been somewhat inebriated as they ambled down the street, loudly giggling and taking up both physical and aural space. It is quite possible that these two "night enthusiasts" relished this break from the bleak realities of the home front: the stroll constituted a moment of freedom to breathe in the late summer air, to allow their eyes to wander, to linger in front of shop windows—such as the department stores Herzmansky and Gerngross, opened in 1863 and 1879, respectively—and to move through the city as they pleased.[35] Somewhere along the way Schneider espied them. Did he notice their excessive laughter? Did he wonder what they were doing outside their homes in the evening? We do not know. But we do know that their languorous gait aroused his suspicions: two women strolling along, seemingly aimlessly, could not just be enjoying the sights of the city. They could not just be walking. They had to be prostitutes.

Schneider's conclusion—and confusion—is understandable because streetwalking, as I discussed above, had traditionally signified prostitution. And yet, with the onset of the First World War, more women began walking the streets.[36] Of course, working-class women had been walking on the streets well before the outbreak of war. What changed was that the demand for unskilled labor grew and, as more men were enlisted to fight, the state came to rely on youth, prisoners of war, and (notably) women to continue the war effort. In this way, the war "sp[ed] up a transformation that was already under way," so that, by 1918, 53.4 percent of the Viennese labor force was female.[37] Women from all walks of life were forced to go out on the street and walk to their jobs as metalworkers, carpenters, blacksmiths, cobblers, uniform cutters, laboratory assistants, clerical workers, technicians, and telephone/telegraph operators. Other jobs, such as postal work or tram driving and conducting, required women to go outside physically and move through city streets. Although she was identified as an artificial-flower maker—a type of work that would decline drastically after the First World War due to changing fashions—Magdalene W. was most likely enlisted to contribute to the war effort and work at one of these jobs.

Food acquisition was another reason for women's greater mobility. Compared to other European capitals, Vienna's wartime food scarcity was especially severe, with the first ration cards issued as early as April 1915 for flour and bread (chapter 2).[38] In 1916, the rationing of sugar, milk, coffee, and lard was introduced; in 1917, of potatoes and marmalade; in 1918, of meat.[39] This breakdown of civil society on the home front literally moved women out of their homes to make ends meet. They walked to market squares and queued outside for long stretches of time. Riots often ensued. A police report written only a few days after Magdalene W. and her niece were apprehended observed that, at the market in the VIIth District, three hundred people left the potato stalls empty-handed, leading to a "mighty uproar."[40]

On their walk to and from work and market squares, Viennese women encountered streetwalkers, and sometimes they turned to streetwalking themselves. According to an article published shortly after the war, "while in the past, the biggest contingent [of prostitutes] was made up of vagrant servant girls, waitresses, or low-paid workers, today a large part consists of clerks and other female office workers, daughters of respected civil servant families, who look for and find employment this way mostly out of necessity and less out of frivolity or addiction to luxury."[41] For some women, walking the streets was, in fact, the most effective way to meet

FIGURE 1.2. By the First World War, more Viennese women appeared to engage in pleasurable walking practices, as evidenced by these ladies walking a dog along the shop-lined Graben, near Habsburgergasse, in 1915. From Rudolf Pichler (photographer), "Wien I, Graben 21/22," photograph (Vienna, 8 July 1915). BAA/ÖNB.

clients: migrants, soldiers, prisoners of war, Red Cross officers, or men unable to fight.

But the war also changed the social rules governing Viennese society. Many women, like Magdalene W. and her niece strolling along the Mariahilferstrasse, began moving through the city as a pleasurable end in itself. Viennese women wandered from district to district, went into movie theaters and coffeehouses, visited parks and city beaches [*Strandbäder*], peered into shop windows, and enjoyed the city's newly constructed boulevards. They strolled, promenaded, and loitered. In one photograph from 1915, for example, two bourgeois women are captured walking a dog along the shop-lined Graben—the same street once known for its eponymous "nymphs"—as a young woman promenades past them (see fig. 1.2). It is to this more pleasurable walking practice that we now turn—a practice that, it turns out, had its roots well before the First World War, within the context of Vienna's late nineteenth-century urban transformation.

The Ringstrasse and the Gigerl's Flânerie

For contemporaries, the "aimless wandering" and leisurely "promenading" of streetwalking and walking the streets recalled the bourgeois walking practices that emerged in the nineteenth century, often in response to urban renewal projects that rearranged, broadened, and lengthened streets, and built new parks, public squares, and some ninety new streets.[42] Urban planning also meant spatial segregation of various urban functions, so that areas for walking and driving vehicles were differentiated.[43] In Vienna, it was the Ringstrasse, the newly constructed tree-lined boulevard built along the city's former walls, that encouraged the new practice. Built during the liberal *Gründerzeit* between 1857 and 1865 (some of its famous buildings would not be finished until later in the century, around 1888), the Ringstrasse magnified space horizontally instead of vertically, thereby emphasizing space and circular flow.[44] Unlike the dark and cramped alleyways of yesteryear—which, to Viennese liberals, mirrored the constraints of the *Vormärz* era—the Ringstrasse and boulevards encouraged the flow of people and, symbolically, of ideas. By the fin de siècle, Vienna was a city whose spaces inspired perambulation.

According to a travel guide from 1906, "The Ringstrasse must be taken as a whole, for though it is divided into a number of 'Rings,' it is generally viewed by visitors in the course of a single walk or drive."[45] It was while strolling across the boulevard's many rings, and especially past the illustrious Sirk-Ecke, named after the corner of the Ringstrasse and the Kärntnerstrasse where the fashionable Café Sirk reigned, that the bourgeoisie came to regard walking less as a means to an end—as a mode of transportation or as a dietetic practice to maintain or restore health—and more as a pleasurable and aesthetic end in itself. In this way, promenading became a ritualized activity, a routine with a conspicuous choreography.[46] On Sunday mornings, ladies with plumed hats and gentlemen with walking sticks would partake in the Ringstrassenkorso with an air of elegance and self-importance, greet friends and acquaintances, stop to admire the imposing architecture of their newly modernized city, and continue walking at a leisurely pace.

Although sociability was part and parcel of walking, the nineteenth century also gave birth to the practice of solitary urban walking. A bourgeois gentleman strolling by himself engaged in the socially accepted practice of flânerie—what Walter Benjamin, drawing on the work of Charles Baudelaire, described as the act of "botanizing of asphalt."[47] And unlike the solitary walking of the Romantics, who took to the wilderness in search of the sublime, flânerie found expression in the landscape of the modern city, among its phantasmagoria of sights and sounds, "the ebb and flow of movement, in the midst of the fugitive and the infinite."[48]

Flânerie could only be practiced by the flâneur.[49] Originally conceived of as a nineteenth-century city dweller who wandered along the arcades of Paris and, later, along the bustling boulevards constructed under the stewardship of Baron Georges-Eugène Haussmann—the "haussmanniza-tion" of Paris was, perhaps, one of the greatest urban renewal projects of nineteenth-century Europe—the flâneur came to epitomize, according to Benjamin, modern urban spectatorship, visually consuming the industrial-ized city, yet also resisting its speed and relentless production. (Benjamin even noted that, "around 1840, it was briefly fashionable to take turtles for a walk in the arcades. The *flâneurs* liked to have the turtles set the pace for them. If they had had their way, progress would have been obliged to accommodate itself to this pace.") Thus, in both compliance with and defiance of industrial capitalism, the flâneur would wander aimlessly and leisurely, delighting in the visual spectacle of the modern city. He would walk through the city as he pleased and map his own topography of urban space. He would linger and loiter on street corners, observing and catalog-ing every passerby. "The street becomes a dwelling for the *flâneur*," wrote Benjamin, "he is as much at home among the facades of the houses as a citizen is in his four walls."[50] On the street, he would "become one flesh with the crowd," feel at home in the anonymity and alienation that he could find there.[51]

But the Viennese flâneur did not exist in a wholly unencumbered space. Keith Tester examines the place of the flâneur in Robert Musil's 1930–1943 novel, *The Man Without Qualities*, which is set in Vienna before the First World War. In Musil's Vienna, streets are chaotic, cacophonous, and prone to collisions, with the result that "the idle and considerable strolling and observing which is the essence of *flânerie* has become doubtful."[52] Accord-ing to Tester, "Musil identifies three sources of the challenge to *flânerie*. First, there is the problem of traffic," and the possibility of an accident. "Second, *flânerie* and the profound intellectual activity it requires might become simply exhausted; the mysteries of the city could well become just banal and boring." And "third, *flânerie* is rendered less and less likely by the increasing domination of rationality and of an order which is imposed on the city as if by necessity."

Importantly, the Viennese flâneur not only managed to overcome these obstacles; in doing so, he asserted his unique individuality and was rec-ognized as doing so. And indeed, unlike the Parisian flâneur—the ideal type—the Viennese flâneur was often imagined as standing out from the crowd. Contemporaries referred to him as a *Gigerl*, the "clownish" dandy or fop "for whom," wrote the modernist architect Adolf Loos in 1898, "the sole purpose of clothing"—and of flânerie (in German, *flanieren*)—"is to make him stand out from his environment."[53] In a caricature from 1889, one *Gigerl* encounters another *Gigerl* walking along the Ring.[54] Both men look nearly identical: mustachioed, enjoying a smoke, holding gloves in one hand and walking sticks in the other, and dressed in top hats, patterned trousers, high-collared shirts, with ties and boutonnières. And yet, as soon as the first *Gigerl* notices the second *Gigerl*'s monocle-free face, he reproaches the latter for "promenading so nakedly on the Ring." Alarmed by his fashion faux pas, the second *Gigerl* instantly "jumps, horrified, into a carriage," indicating that on Vienna's Ringstrasse, flânerie involved not only the consumption of urban spectacle, but also its production—which the monocle, as a foppish corrective lens, embodied.

The *Gigerl* was at home on the Ringstrasse. Numerous caricatures depicted him in his natural habitat, sometimes in the company of a second *Gigerl*. (Was he, perhaps, more sociable than the Parisian flâneur?) He thus came to be known as being not only *on* but also *of* the Ring, for the person and the place seemed to coalesce and become one and the same.[55] Around 1895, the k. u. k. (Imperial and Royal) military bandmaster J. F. Wagner composed a "Gigerl March." The score's cover depicts two of these Viennese flâneurs walking on what is presumably the Ring, armed with walking sticks and monocles, both instruments of Viennese flânerie (see fig. 1.3).[56] Worth noting is their physical comportment mid-gait: their posture is stately, their gaze is pompous, their arms are elegantly arranged, and they move apart from the rest of the crowd. In short, the street belongs to them; they are at home on the street, in fact, they *are* the street, embodying its majesty and movement. And as a piece of music intended for military marching—arguably a type of movement that aims to assert dominion, as well as an extremely Habsburg form of movement—Wagner's "Gigerl March" translated the *Gigerl*'s flânerie and domination of the street—his very being—into sound.[57]

Feminist revisions of the flâneur have identified its gendered, masculine bias as well as its reliance on vision, insisting that the figure constitutes the very embodiment of the male gaze.[58] As Baudelaire put it: "He [the flâneur] gazes upon the landscape of the great city. . . . He delights in fine carriages and proud horses, the dazzling smartness of the grooms, the expertness of the footmen, the sinuous gait of the women, the beauty of the children. . . ."[59] The city's architecture, horses, working classes, women, and children are all uttered in one breath: the inanimate and animate, the animal and the human, the young and the old, they are all one and the same insofar as they are all the object of the flâneur's assertive and power-

FIGURE 1.3. On the cover of J. F. Wagner's "Gigerl March," two Viennese flâneurs, known as *Gigerl*, promenade along what appears to be the Ringstrasse, in the heart of the city. From J. F. Wagner, "'Gigerl' Marsch für Pianoforte" (Vienna: Rebay & Robitschek, ca. 1895). Image taken by author. Personal collection.

ful "eagle eye." In Vienna, the flâneur's counterpart was an "impressionist," to borrow William M. Johnston's term—a spectator of the transitory and the ephemeral as encapsulated by city life.[60] Solitary urban walking was, in short, a masculine domain.

And yet, unlike the Parisian flâneur, the Viennese *Gigerl* could also be, by virtue of being both consumer and producer of urban spectacle, the object of another's gaze. Returning to the cover of Wagner's "Gigerl March," we notice that, as the two dandies in the foreground survey the cityscape, a lady observes them from the background while her companion, another lady, turns her head toward her, as if engaged in conversation. Not only is a woman the bearer of the gaze, but masculinity is its object. Unsurprisingly perhaps, the *Gigerl*'s masculinity was frequently called into question by contemporaries, who mockingly referred to him as "the transformation of man into woman," the masculine counterpart to the new woman, and a "Jewish" wheeler and dealer.[61] (As Peter Andersson has observed, antisemitic commentators often equated the "strutting" on the Ring with Jewish social climbing.[62]) Thus, the *Gigerl*'s dominion of the street could also be broken. If the Viennese flâneur occupied a less consistent position of power than his counterpart in Paris, then Viennese flânerie itself must be understood as laced with even greater ambivalence.

Streetwalking indexed flânerie insofar as it, too, involved a leisurely pace, a peripatetic movement through urban space, as well as a loitering and looking. As Susan Buck-Morss puts it, "prostitution was indeed the female version of *flânerie*. . . . the *flâneur* was simply the name of a man who loitered; but all women who loitered risked being seen as whores."[63] The Viennese streetwalker (*Strichmädl*) was similar to the *Gigerl* in that she, too, was *of* the street, was both consumer and producer of urban spectacle, both bearer and object of the gaze, as well as a gender deviant (a "fallen woman" or "lost girl"). And yet, unlike the *Gigerl*, she could be apprehended for her flânerie. Seen in this light, Magdalene W. and her niece were arrested that late evening in September 1916 because they engaged in flânerie at a time in Vienna when streetwalking was the only version of flânerie understood to be available to women and flânerie, more generally, was viewed with ambivalence.

Women's Walking Practices

Inasmuch as streetwalking was the only version of flânerie available to women, a woman walking by herself had to follow a particular script. According to a contemporary etiquette book, such a lady was supposed to move with purpose instead of aimlessness and to follow only well-established paths and trajectories.[64] She was also encouraged to maintain a tidy, "uniform step, which must neither be too big nor too small," avoid "big movements," and keep her hands placed on her stomach or her arms extended alongside her skirt.[65] Although skirt-holding was generally frowned upon, given its necessity in certain situations on city streets etiquette manuals advised a woman to employ a "dress holder" accessory or a cord loop so that she would not have protruding elbows. In the event that she had no other choice, she was advised to hold her skirt at the front instead of at the side.[66] Another etiquette book included a section devoted to "The Street," specifying that "all conspicuous dress and behavior should be avoided."[67] And unlike the streetwalker who actively sought to meet the gaze of a client, a lady's "eyes may not wander"; nor could she "look in shop windows for too long."[68] Contemporary film footage confirms this: almost all the women seen walking in the 1906 Pathé Frères documentary, *Vienne en Tramway*, refrain from letting their eyes wander; their gaze is fixed downward on the path ahead.[69]

Although these instructions were meant for bourgeois women, a working-class woman followed a similar script insofar as she constantly "risked the danger of being mistaken for a prostitute" and, as such, "had to demonstrate unceasingly in her dress, gestures, and movements that she was not a 'low' woman."[70] Looking respectable often meant walking with her clasped hands hanging in front of her stomach or with one or both arms bent at a right angle with the forearm held across the waist. In public and in the presence of men, she too walked purposefully, though often at a quicker pace than her upper-class counterparts.[71] For example, toward the beginning of the 1906 Pathé film (0:54), a working-class woman holding a basket and a parasol, possibly a domestic servant, is spotted darting swiftly and purposefully across the Ringstrasse near the Burgtheater (see fig. 1.4). In short, a woman walking by herself had to convey the activity's purpose, move with respectability and physical restraint, and eschew any evidence of pleasure.

And yet, the 1906 documentary also depicts several instances of women walking in ways that were not prescribed for them. It is worth noting that the documentary was filmed from a moving streetcar whose route ran almost entirely along the Ringstrasse. Did the elegant, tree-lined boulevard studded with imposing neo-historicist buildings and green spaces entice others in Vienna to move in new ways? Put another way, was there a causal relationship between urban change and a new gendered embodiment? Four pieces of evidence from the film suggest that the answer is "yes."

First, the film shows that the trajectories people took through urban space were often haphazard and disorderly. Both men and women crossed streets whenever and wherever they pleased, carelessly darting through traffic and crisscrossing through crowds. Working-class women in particular were often seen ignoring fixed paths altogether, taking shortcuts, and running across busy thoroughfares in a panicked hurry. While many

FIGURE 1.4. Fin-de-siècle Viennese conventions of normative femininity dictated that a woman walking alone had to move in a purposeful way so as not to be mistaken for a prostitute. In this film still, a working-class woman does just that by crossing the street swiftly and with a clear aim in mind. From *Vienne en Tramway* (Pathé Frères, 1906). Collection Austrian Film Museum, Vienna.

women walked with a sense of purposefulness, they often did so by taking unconventional routes, moving through the city with pedestrian promiscuity.

Second, although women generally refrained from carrying walking sticks, they often held parasols in similar ways. For example, shortly after the above-mentioned domestic servant scurries by (1:01), a woman walking with a gentleman whose hands are clasped behind his back in a chivalrous manner is seen swinging her tightly furled parasol much like a *Gigerl* would swing a walking stick (see fig. 1.5). Although parasols were typically used as practical items meant to protect the woman carrier from rain or sun, Peter Andersson notes that they occasionally also served as "gender-transgressive accessor[ies]" that conveyed the same "relaxation, ease, and licensed immobility"—and mobility, I would add—of a walking stick.[72] In a fashion image from a magazine, an elegantly dressed lady holds her tightly wound parasol like a staff in a gesture of licensed immobility.[73] Meanwhile, in the above-mentioned moment in the film, the parasol, held casually, gives the woman license to be mobile; swinging it produces the momentum that propels the young woman forward. At several other moments in the film, women are seen wielding parasols in a similar way. On the Sirk-Ecke (2:00), a stout working-class woman wearing an apron is seen walking briskly down the street, her face looking down at her loosely furled parasol, which is pointed forward in a diagonal, forging the path ahead.

Third, despite prescriptions to refrain from moving their arms into peripheral space (as mentioned above, both bourgeois and working-class women often held their arms and hands alongside their torso, near their stomachs, or wrapped around their waists), the film depicts several women standing or walking in an expansive and assertive akimbo pose, which involved placing the hands on the hips and projecting the elbows outward. Near the opera house (1:37), for instance, a younger woman dressed in a dark color is seen waiting for the tram, her right hand holding an unfurled umbrella, which partially conceals her face, while her left hand rests on her hip in a gesture of defiance (see fig. 1.6). Although the akimbo pose was most frequently seen among working-class women and market stallholders, by the fin de siècle it had made its way to the upper classes as well.[74] Andersson identifies two main uses of the akimbo pose by women at this time: to express either semiconscious fatigue or conscious effrontery. In the above example, the woman at the tram stop appears to convey a combination of both; she seems fatigued from standing and waiting in the bright sun (she is holding a parasol, after all), but also irritated and willing to show it. The akimbo pose, however, also appeared when women held up their dresses and skirts in order to increase mobility—yet another example of physical transgression on the street. Despite recommendations to hold dresses from the front, women often held them from the side, raising the hem by pulling up the fabric near the upper thigh, so that

FIGURE 1.5. Many Viennese women started subverting existing gendered walking conventions by the fin de siècle, as demonstrated in this film still of a lady holding a parasol as if it were the gentleman's accessory, a walking stick. From *Vienne en Tramway* (Pathé Frères, 1906). Collection Austrian Film Museum, Vienna.

the elbow would jut out to the side. Near Schwarzenbergplatz (2:29), for example, a younger woman dressed in a lightly colored skirt and blouse hikes up her skirt as she walks behind a moving tram, her left hand clutching the fabric near her hip in a gesture reminiscent of the akimbo pose. Shortly afterward (3:02), near Praterstern, a working-class woman trudges wearily away from the camera, holding her skirt in a similar way. In both instances, raising a skirt not only increased mobility; it also produced peripheral space.

Finally, even though loitering was explicitly prohibited, there is one instance in the film (3:09) when a well-dressed woman wearing a light-colored blouse adorned with two large bows, a dark skirt, and an ornate hat stands with no clear sense of purpose in front of the monument to Wilhelm von Tegetthoff, a renowned mid-nineteenth-century admiral, at Praterstern (see fig. 1.7). She stands alone on the first step, facing the street, her hands clasped at her stomach, as men, women, and children walk past her. Is she waiting for someone? Or is she simply taking a moment to gaze upon the urban landscape? Either way, it is a striking moment in the film, one that suggests, yet again, that around the fin de siècle women

FIGURE 1.6. This film still shows another example of a woman resisting normative walking practices: as she waits for the tram near the opera house, she strikes an akimbo pose. From *Vienne en Tramway* (Pathé Frères, 1906). Collection Austrian Film Museum, Vienna.

FIGURE 1.7. Gendered conventions also prohibited women from loitering in urban space, as this recalled the streetwalking of prostitutes. And yet, as evidenced by this film still in which a woman stands alone at Praterstern, many women resisted these conventions in everyday life. From *Vienne en Tramway* (Pathé Frères, 1906). Collection Austrian Film Museum, Vienna.

were moving (and not moving) through urban space in a less prescribed fashion.

Although the examples provided above—pedestrian promiscuity, wielding a parasol like a walking stick, posing with arms akimbo, raising the skirt, and loitering—did not constitute flânerie per se, they certainly took cues from it. In other words, years before Magdalene W. and her niece were arrested for what was arguably flânerie, and *before* the First World War, women were already making conscious and unconscious efforts to subvert conventional walking practices by appropriating flânerie for themselves. And like Magdalene W. and her niece, many of these women suffered a similar fate: arrest.

A String of Fin-de-Siècle Arrests: Movement and Countermovement

On 11 March 1901, hundreds of women and girls gathered in the ballroom of the Ronacher Theater in Vienna's Ist District to take a stand against police brutality (*Uebergriffe der Polizei*).[75] It was at the fin de siècle that several incidents occurred in Vienna and its empire in which police mistakenly arrested women not involved in the sex trade—that is to say, "honorable" women whose arrest and forced medical examination shamed and dishonored them.[76] The speakers at the meeting, who included notable leaders of the women's movement, such as the editor-in-chief of the feminist newspaper *Dokumente der Frauen* (*Documents of Women*), Marie Lang, and the social-democratic activist Adelheid Popp, as well as several members of Parliament, drew up a series of demands: more carefully selected police officers and women officers, women police physicians, and monetary compensation for every wronged woman. Ultimately, the goal was to safeguard women's honor and "to protect morality against the overzealous guardians of morality," the police.

But in addition to protecting honor and morality, the other, less explicit goal of the rally was to promote women's flânerie, which the vice police, in their crackdown on clandestine prostitution, were physically hindering. "We modern people do not go veiled and with lowered eyes on the street," declared Lang, "we want to see and hear, we want to have the right to stand and to look around." Indeed, she continued, "a woman can even be more temperamental or love extravagant fashion." If the nascent women's movement (*Frauenbewegung*) in Vienna, in testimony to its very name (*Bewegung* means both movement and *a* movement), was committed to promoting women's movement through city streets, then the police sought to counter this movement.

At the rally, Lang brought up four incidents of police brutality against women—one in 1899, two in 1900, and one in 1901—which differed in remarkable ways. They involved working-class and middle-class women, domestic servants, and ladies of "extraordinary distinction," women wearing extravagant fashions and women wearing unremarkable clothing, Frenchwomen and Bukowinian women. Below, I examine each incident in detail and explore the *apparent* reasons for each woman's arrest, which ranged from wearing a conspicuous red hat to visibly looking like a domestic servant to hunting for an apartment. I then show that what all these women had in common, even in their extraordinary diversity, was the way they walked through urban space. By engaging in historical imagination, I attempt to reconstruct the flânerie that the women may have engaged in as well as to imagine what route they may have taken through the ever-changing Viennese urban space. The point of these small historically imagined anecdotes is to subvert the archival record and its particular epistemology by considering both women and embodied practices that would normally have been overlooked or, at best, glossed over.[77] Ultimately, these anecdotes, when juxtaposed with feminist phenomenology, reveal that, within the context of its time, the practice of flânerie appeared not only unladylike, but subversive and destructive, and thus as warranting arrest. In fact, it was this embodied practice of flânerie, I argue, that served as the more significant—though not necessarily more explicit or conscious—reason for their arrest.

As we shall see, of the four incidents, only one took place entirely on the Ringstrasse, the site par excellence of Viennese flânerie. The other three women were arrested on the peripheries of Vienna, even on the periphery of the empire. Flânerie, evidently, could take place even on non-bourgeois streets beyond the Ring.[78] One reason for this is that Vienna's urban transformation had not been limited to the city center, but extended into the inner suburbs starting in 1850, and after 1890 into the outer suburbs beyond the Linien Wall or Gürtel, as well. Once both inner and outer suburbs became incorporated into the city as districts and underwent significant industrialization and population growth, they began to change.[79] Coupled with the second building ordinance of 23 September 1859, which required streets to be planned in a straight, grid-like pattern—mimicking the horizontal spatial orientation of the Ring—the districts adopted a more modern, urban character. Wolfgang Maderthaner and Lutz Musner have argued that the gloomy, grid-like streets of these districts hampered flânerie, for they recalled the regularity and discipline of factory work. And yet, in the section below, I will historically imagine how these very same urban spaces could also invite flânerie, or at least elements of it. If the *Gigerl* was able to overcome the particular challenges of Viennese urban space—the traffic, the occasional banality of the street, and its increasing rationality—so, too, could the *flâneuse*.

1899: The Red Hat and Other Finery

The first incident took place on an evening in September 1899, when Police Officer Goliczefsky approached an officer's widow and her daughter walking across the Kärntnerring, near the Sirk-Ecke.[80] Having noticed the daughter's conspicuous red hat, the officer accused the mother of being a "procuress" and her daughter of being a "whore." When the daughter called him an "insolent fellow," both mother and daughter were arrested and charged with defaming an officer (*Wachebeleidigung*). Further investigation soon revealed that the police officer had been mistaken, that the two women were not sex workers, and that they were "respectable ladies"—*Damen*—of the middle class whose "feminine honor" had been tarnished.

But, conservative commentators wondered, did women walking on city streets and wearing "obnoxious hats" have any honor to begin with? The young woman's red hat, in particular, became the subject of much discussion, viewed as the *apparent* reason for her arrest. After all, "a ladies' hat trimmed with red silk must have had an extremely titillating effect on Police Officer Goliczefsky," one critic remarked, "[who is] entrusted with maintaining order and also protecting morality."[81] For the moral public in Vienna, including Goliczefsky, "red silk and feminine virtue are incompatible concepts," so a woman wearing red silk was necessarily lacking in virtue. Just why that should have been the case is the question I address in this section. I will explore the cultural and social meaning of this red hat in greater detail before pivoting to what I argue to be another, and arguably more significant, reason for the arrest: flânerie.

Officer Goliczefsky's views were typical for the time. Beginning in the nineteenth century, "finery" came to be a marker of prostitution, which, as Marianne Valverde explains, "meant clothes that were too showy, clothes that looked elegant and striking but were in some unspecified way cheap, if only because the woman wearing them was herself a cheap imitation of upper-class womanhood."[82] Unlike the "honest dress" of proper ladies, finery was, as the writer Stefan Zweig put it, "tawdry elegance which they had gone to great pains to purchase."[83] In this way, sex workers were often accused of engaging in a kind of "moral masquerade"—of trying, but also failing, to pass as "respectable" women by wearing flashy jewelry, plush furs, colorful silks, and conspicuous hats. And while masquerading as someone else was considered morally vicious, what made it even more alarming was its erasure of class difference—for how else could one tell the difference between a working-class woman and a lady than by looking at the style, color, and fabric of the dress? The Viennese writer and artist Emilie Exner expressed this concern already in 1895, observing, "on fine, warm summer evenings there gathered a few years ago in one of the most majestic parks of our metropolis a sizable quantity of shimmering silk, flowers, ribbons, and feathers, whose wearers would have been deeply ashamed had they been able to observe their reflection unguardedly [*un-befangen*]. It had become absolutely impossible to distinguish between good society and the demimonde, and a sense of horror gripped the sober [*kühl*] observer at the sight of this regalia, which had gathered there in the street."[84]

And yet, by most accounts, the color red was actually quite fashionable at the time. Vivid colors became especially popular in the late nineteenth century, thanks to advances made in the dye industry; and, as with most fashion trends, the colors provoked a vast array of responses, ranging from horror to delight.[85] When a colorful room in the Cabaret Fledermaus was unveiled in 1906, for example, some reviewers condemned it as "a colorful chamber of horrors," while others found it breathtaking.[86] Similarly, while some commentators warned that colorful dresses might fatigue or, in the case of Goliczefsky, catch the eyes of male beholders, others celebrated the opportunity to choose, as one 1904 magazine article put it, "the forms and colors that are modern and simultaneously show off all the assets and charms of the wearer."[87] Thus, the "color theory" (*Farbenlehre*) of fashion instructed women on how to choose and pair the colors that would flatter their hair, complexion, and even their "individuality." According to this theory, brunettes with either a "healthy clear complexion" or of the "gypsy type" with a "dark face color" could pull off shades of red best, as well as don shimmering rubies.

The young woman in the red hat may have been a fashion-conscious brunette whose dress was meant to convey her temperament and spunk. What is worth noting is that she chose to wear the hat in public, to show it off and, like a *Gigerl*, make herself into a spectacle. Insofar as flânerie in Vienna consisted of the production and consumption of spectacle, this young woman engaged in it. But to fully engage in flânerie, one must also move through urban space in a certain way. How, then, can we imagine the spectacle produced by her walk along the route she took with her mother that day? Although it is impossible to know, I draw on historical imagination to vividly reconstruct what the walk might have looked and felt like, how the new spaces of the city may have encouraged its manifestation, and how it was perceived as a threat. It is this walk, I argue, that was the less apparent but perhaps more significant reason for the arrest.

On an evening in September 1899, a conspicuously dressed woman and her mother promenaded along the Kärntnerring, a central site of Viennese flânerie.[88] The sun had not yet set, and the women delighted in the late summer air as they strolled and chatted about their recent excursion to "Venice in Vienna," an amusement park built in 1895 in the Prater.[89] Having just finished dining at a nearby restaurant, mother and daughter relished the opportunity to digest their supper, stretch their limbs, and see and be seen by the city's haute monde. As they walked past several dapper gentlemen swinging their walking sticks—*Gigerl*, perhaps—the two women caught sight of the shop windows lining the Ring, their tightly wound parasols giving them license to pause: they admired the fur wares in Josef Krauss's elegant shop and the delicate stationery products on display at Friedl and Baum's (see fig. 1.8). Delighting in the sound of the horses' hooves on the cobblestone streets, they walked by the bellhops flanking the entrance to the Grand Hotel, built in 1871, and made their way toward the spectacle that was the new Opera, which they, along with the rest of Viennese society, derisively called the "sunken treasure chest."

FIGURE 1.8. The Ringstrasse, looking toward the opera house, 1898. Note the woman walking by Josef Krauss's fur shop, and the crowd of pedestrians admiring Friedl & Baum's window display. From Erwin Pendl (photographer), "Wien 1, Kärntnerring," photograph (Vienna, 1898). BAA/ÖNB.

FIGURE 1.9. Had the two women in question walked further down the Ringstrasse, they would have come upon the entrance to the Opera, shown in this 1900 photograph as the large archway on the right. Note the different ways the women in this photograph hold up their skirts: some from the front, some from the side, some with protruding elbows, and some with straight arms. From Martin Gerlach sen. (photographer), "1. Opernring—Allgemein—Blick von Staatsoper gegen Burgring," photograph (Vienna: Gerlach & Wiedling, c. 1900). Wien Museum Inv.-Nr. 229432, CCo.

Quite possibly, it was then that Police Officer Goliczefsky first caught sight of the red hat: it might have stood out in the staidly attired crowd swirling about the Sirck-Ecke (see fig. 1.9). Such an obvious effrontery to good manners required a closer look. As he approached the pair, the policeman might have noticed what he perceived as an equally crass transgression of gender conventions: the women's languid movement. Did he feel morally outraged by such dreadful improprieties? Probably. Who would dare show such brazen insolence? Only prostitutes. Given the mores of the time, Goliczefsky acted logically, even if impulsively, and resolved to counter the women's outrageous physical movement by arresting the women engaging in that movement.

1900: Domestic Servants

The second incident to have sparked controversy was the arrest of a chambermaid, Lina D., in early 1900. In mid-January, one year before the start of the new century, Lina D. was summoned by the police after they received an anonymous letter accusing her of clandestine prostitution. Upon hearing the accusation, the young woman became agitated and protested, demanding to see the letter. The police officer ignored her pleas, took a key from the wall, and ordered her to follow him to an isolated room where he revealed himself as the police physician. He locked the door and demanded that she undress so that he could medically examine her. When she protested, the physician threatened her, sneering, "with me you feel ashamed but with others you do not feel shame."[90] Out of fear, she succumbed to the invasive internal examination. Once it became clear that she was not infected with venereal disease, she was immediately discharged. Lina D. returned home, "crying and trembling," much to the concern of her landlady, Frau Dettelmayer, who promptly put her to bed.

In fact, Frau Dettelmayer was so alarmed by the incident that she decided to take matters into her own hands. She made her way to the police station and found that the very same letter writer who had accused Lina D. of clandestine prostitution had also accused her of sex trafficking. From the handwriting, Frau Dettelmayer immediately guessed the identity of the mysterious letter writer: it was Theodosius Babjuk, her daughter's ex-lover. As revenge for having been left for another man, Babjuk first wrote letters of denunciation against the daughter, then against Frau Dettelmayer, and finally against Lina D.

"How can it happen," demanded a newspaper article, "that a respectable girl is immediately medically examined [on the basis of] an anonymous denunciation? . . . Where will it lead to when an anonymous letter is enough to subject a woman to this unconscionable injury?"[91] Part of this story, then, has to do with the remarkable power that anonymous letters of denunciation held at the time and the fact that "his" word was always favored over "hers." But the other part of this story—and the one more relevant to this chapter—has to do with the question of what made Lina D. such an easy target in the first place: after all, she had nothing to do with the Dettelmayers and their relationship with Babjuk. Consideration of another such false arrest will help us answer that question.

Only a few months after Lina D. had been arrested, a third such incident occurred—this time not in Vienna, but in the city of Czernowitz, located in the eastern crown land of Bukowina.[92] And while the Czernowitz incident seemed far from Vienna, news of it also made its way to the imperial capital, providing fuel for the burgeoning women's movement. "Similar things have also happened in Vienna, and they are still happening," the feminist newspaper *Dokumente der Frauen* reported, "they are happening more inconspicuously, not with the same brutal ruthlessness as in the East of the empire—but they happen here enough so that the blood of our legally-ignorant population should boil."[93] Like the Lina D. incident, the Czernowitz scandal also involved the arrest of domestic servants who had been walking on city streets. The similarities between these two incidents are worth emphasizing, since the vice police in Czernowitz followed the same prostitution regulations as in Vienna.[94]

On the evening of 11 March 1900, Herr Hofrat Ullmann heard frantic sobs coming from the kitchen. Alarmed, he went into the room and saw one of his young servant girls "completely beside herself, confused, and distraught."[95] After several hours of gentle questioning, the fifteen-year-old girl finally revealed what was troubling her. Earlier that day, on her walk home after buying some ham, she was stopped by the police and taken to the city hall, "into a large room, where about fifty women were discarded." The police then led her into another room, in which four men forced her onto a table and medically examined her—a procedure that was so traumatic that she "lost consciousness." After she was declared "untouched"—a virgin—she was released.

Herr Hofrat Ullmann was appalled. He soon learned that his servant girl was not the only young woman arrested that late winter day in Czernowitz. Police apprehended the women employed in the homes of Herr Regierungsrath Klauser and Herr Professor Dr. Rump, as they left Sunday evening church service at seven o'clock. Similarly, as Herr Gemeinderath Professor Bumbacu's servant girl escorted two ladies to their homes, the police immediately apprehended her, while the women screamed in protest. Indeed, the police had raided the entire city and arrested all women they suspected of engaging in clandestine prostitution, forcing them to undergo medical examinations to determine whether they were infected with venereal disease.

Witnesses confirmed that the police had arrested "every girl that looked like a servant girl," including other working women, such as needleworkers, who often returned home late in the evening. Thus, two types of mistaken identity had taken place that evening in Czernowitz: servant girls were mistaken for clandestine prostitutes, and working women were mistaken for servant girls. That the group of women most affected by the police raid in Czernowitz had been working-class women who "looked" the part of domestic servants raises two questions: Why were domestic servants targeted in the first place? And what did it mean to "look" like a servant in fin-de-siècle Cisleithania? In the following section, I will tease out the social and cultural meaning of domestic service at the time. I will then consider what I suggest is the more significant reason for their arrests—namely, flânerie. Using historical imagination, I will conclude this section by imagining how Lina D. and Herr Hofrat Ullmann's servant girl strolled and ambled through urban space, as well as by recreating the routes they may have taken through their respective cities.

Domestic service had much in common with prostitution. It, too, was a heavily gendered profession occupied by mostly young working-class and migrant women.[96] In 1890, for instance, 94 percent of the domestic servants in Vienna were women.[97] In addition, most domestics came from Bohemia and Moravia, Hungary, and Lower and Upper Austria, as well as Galicia and Bukowina; were frequently under the age of thirty; and were often required to remain unmarried.[98] Herr Hofrat Ullmann's servant girl may very well have moved to Vienna after her stint in Czernowitz; likewise, Lina D. may have originally come from outside of Vienna. In addition, like prostitution, domestic service was a precarious type of employment that did not offer a minimum wage, worker protection, health insurance, or old-age and unemployment benefits. It was therefore common for domestics to work around the clock as well as take on additional side jobs to make ends meet. Not surprisingly, during an era that has retrospectively come to be known as the "Age of Questions," next to the "Prostitution Question" (*Prostitutionsfrage*), which tackled sex worker abuse and exploitation, there also existed the "Servant Question" (*Dienstbotenfrage*), which challenged the capitalist system that exploited servants—those "modern-day slaves"—who were forced to cater to the whims of the upper class.[99]

In addition to sharing many similarities with prostitution, domestic service sometimes attracted women who also engaged in sex work.

According to statistics based on a survey from 1906, 44.52 percent of registered sex workers in Vienna were domestic servants.[100] As the historian Ambika Natarajan has observed, as early as 1810 the Vienna Servant Code set a precedent for policing female servants for "'immorality,' 'debauchery,' and 'fornication,'" and the resulting surveillance data were used "to justify extending prostitution regulation to them"—even if these data were not always accurate.[101] A police decree from 21 September 1874, for example, recommended that police pay particular attention to "vagrant servant girls."[102] In their effort to curb unregistered prostitution, police often targeted domestics or women who "looked" like domestics, as these women seemed more likely to be temporary sex workers. And while many of these women, such as Lina D. and Herr Hofrat Ullmann's servant girl, were in fact only servants, many also proved to be sex workers. A woman apprehended on the Praterstrasse in Vienna's IInd District in 1912, for example, was identified as Anna Plaschek, a sixteen-year-old chambermaid working at Herzgasse 43/19 in the Xth District.[103] Likewise, when Marie Tinhoff was apprehended in 1919 near the Hotel Stephanie because she entered it with an "unknown" man, it was revealed that she too worked as a domestic.[104] In many cases, then, domestics and sex workers truly were one and the same: sometimes women engaged in both types of work simultaneously; at other times they moved between domestic service and sex work and would continue to do so for much of their lives.

But even if domestic servants did not turn to sex work in the traditional sense, they sometimes engaged in it in the homes of their employers. As the socialist *Arbeiterinnen-Zeitung* (*Workingwoman's Newspaper*) observed in an article about the "Servant Question" from 1900, "Oftentimes the *Herr* . . . notices the girl's position and gives her the opportunity to improve her situation with the monetary compensation she receives for satisfying his lust. . . ."[105] Thus, even though prostitution typically called to mind working-class women exchanging sex for money in brothels or city streets, the monetary raise an employer gave his servant in exchange for a sexual act—or even, as the anarchist Emma Goldman pointed out, the financial security a husband provided his wife in exchange for sexual monogamy—was also based on a sexual quid pro quo.[106] In this way, the Viennese upper-class home could be viewed as a "hothouse of prostitution," a site of economic transaction and sexual deviance.

Fantasies of sexual encounters between employers and domestics abounded in Viennese popular culture. In one scene in Arthur Schnitzler's controversial play, *Reigen* (*Round-Dance*), published in 1903 and first performed in Vienna in 1921, the Young Man gently orders the Chambermaid to come closer to him so that he may take a look at her blouse. When she hesitates, he tells her, matter-of-factly, "Don't make such a face, Marie . . . I've already seen you in other ways. When I came home last night and got myself water, the door to your room was open . . . so. . . ." Once she comes closer, the Young Man pulls her toward himself, opens her blouse, and observes, "You have beautiful white skin, Marie," and kisses her breasts.[107] Although it is clear that the Chambermaid, by virtue of being the Young Man's employee, has no other option but to comply, for the contemporary theatergoing public it was the maid herself—in other words, her loose blouse, her sweetness, and her sexual availability (she undressed with the door open, after all)—that seduced him first.

Unsurprisingly perhaps, domestic servants occupied a special place in the modern Viennese erotic imagination for many years prior to the fin de siècle.[108] Due to the milder censorship laws that existed during Emperor Joseph II's reign, the late eighteenth century witnessed a proliferation of paperback books that extolled the charms of the city's chambermaids. One such book that appeared in 1781, Johann Rautenstrauch's *Über die Stuben-mädchen in Wien* (*On the Chambermaids in Vienna*), located the source of the chambermaid's "dangerous charms" in her "coquettish" dress and comportment.[109] "She has the most flattering and attractive body; it shows off the shapeliness of her limbs," Rautenstrauch wrote, "in short, she appeals to the eye." The chambermaid was imagined to be so full of sensuality and sentimentality that her gestures seemed to languish, "as if she would melt from so much tenderness and feeling." And soon enough, the chambermaid came to embody the most desirable Viennese woman: on the one hand, she appeared less vulgar and "public" than the streetwalker, and on the other, as a "private" woman she was far more sexually available than the upper-class woman. The chambermaid's sexual desirability was not lost on other Viennese women. Indeed, it was not uncommon for streetwalkers to don their signature "Bohemian bonnets" (*böhmische Haube*) as a way to lure customers, or for upper-class women to pass as chambermaids in order to attend the posh *Stubenmädchen* ball. (The very fact of such a ball shows the degree to which the image of the chambermaid had inserted itself into Vienna's high culture.) As a feminine figure that was imagined to be all body, soft, sensual, and oozing sweetness, the chambermaid became synonymous with sex. It is within this sexual mythology that the conflation of domestic servants with sex workers partly lies.

But what did this imagined chambermaid look like in the first place? And more specific to our inquiry, what did it mean to "look" like a servant girl in fin-de-siècle Vienna and Czernowitz? The chambermaid in Otto Schmidt's 1873 photograph, part of his series "Viennese Types" (*Wiener Typen*), is shown in an elegant interior space, dusting a lamp with a feather-duster and wearing a uniform consisting of a simple, ankle-length dress with a full skirt and long, cuffed sleeves, an apron, and a white bonnet (see fig. 1.10). Although the servant's uniform—along with women's clothing more generally—had changed by 1900, the wearing of uniforms most likely did not, suggesting that one marker of domestic service was a particular form of attire. And even if a servant employed in a bourgeois household was less likely to wear a uniform than was one working for an upper-class family, the former most likely still wore a simple, functional dress and an apron as a visible marker of her status. We may thus assume that both Lina D. and Herr Hofrat Ullmann's servant girl wore something resembling servant uniforms on the days they were arrested: Lina D. may have been wearing a uniform borrowed from her sister's employer; Herr Hofrat Ullmann's servant girl was probably dressed in a uniform suitable enough for employment in the home of a notable civil servant.

Despite serving as a kind of metonym for the chambermaid, the "Bohemian bonnet" may have lost popularity by the nineteenth century's end. When looking at photographs from the period, we notice that many visibly working-class women do not appear to be wearing bonnets or hats; most are seen with their hair exposed or with kerchiefs tied around their heads.[110] And just as domestics were likely to forgo wearing hats altogether, bourgeois women—as we have seen in the previous red hat incident—were hardly seen without them, and often sported large, plumed hats that they firmly secured in their updos with a hat needle. But more than just a fashionable accessory, the hat, according to a contemporary expert, "crowns a woman and completes her image."[111] A working-class woman did not have much of an image to cultivate, nor was she in a position to be crowned. Her bare head thus came to signify her trade and working-class status.

But domestic servants were not the only women who exposed their heads at the fin de siècle. The other women who were known to forgo hats were streetwalkers.[112] When, for example, sixteen-year-old Paula Rubesch went missing on a January evening in Vienna in 1907, witnesses reported that she left home with only her "house dress" and "without a hat or jacket."[113] The implication was that by leaving the trappings of proper femininity behind her—the hat and jacket—Rubesch had also abandoned her sexual propriety. Forgoing a hat, in other words, was seen as the first step on the slippery slope toward venal sex. Part of the reason for this was that women's hair, particularly in its naturally disheveled "nude" state, was viewed as sexually seductive. As an etiquette book put it, "nothing is as disruptive as a disheveled woman's head surrounded by fluttering, wild, and loose strands of hair"—the looseness of the hair presumably indicating a woman's loose sexual mores.[114] In a caricature from 1907, three "Whores

WIENER TYPEN.

13. Stubenmäd'l.

Phot. v. Otto Schmidt. Verlag v. A.F. Czihak Wien

Vervielfältigung vorbeßalten?

FIGURE 1.10. In nineteenth-century Vienna, many sex workers served as domestic servants and vice versa. As such, police often relied on the visual markers of domestics to identify potential prostitutes. These markers often consisted of a uniform and/or simple dress, an apron, and a bonnet, as seen in this photograph from Otto Schmidt's series, "Viennese Types." From Otto Schmidt (photographer), "Wiener Typen, Nr. 13: 'Stubenmäd'l' [Stubenmädchen]," photograph (Vienna: Adolf F. Czihak, 1873–1878). Wien Museum Inv.-Nr. 120735/10, CC0.

Typen aus der Welt der Wiener Prostitution.
Brigittenauer Dirnen und ihre Zuhälter.

FIGURE 1.11. Streetwalking consisted of a leisurely strolling that closely resembled flânerie. According to fin-de-siècle police reports, sex workers would often stroll as a group, keeping a distance of a few steps between them, and with their hair exposed, as seen in this caricature from 1907. From "Typen aus der Welt der Wiener Prostitution. Brigittenauer Dirnen und ihre Zuhälter," *Illustrierte Oesterreichische Kriminal Zeitung*, 2 September 1907, 6. Image taken by author.

from Brigittenau," the working-class XXth District, are depicted walking in profile with their hair exposed (see fig. 1.11).[115] An unruly lock of hair hangs over the face of the woman on the left, while the sex worker entering the frame on the right can barely see because her eyes are partly covered by a thick fringe. In this case, their hair—"fluttering, wild, and loose"—came to represent their sexual promiscuity.

In addition to looking a certain way, many domestic servants also sounded different. They typically came to Vienna and Czernowitz from elsewhere, often from the eastern or rural reaches of the empire, speaking a broken German or a thick dialect. Moreover, their native languages tended to be Slavic, Hungarian, and/or Yiddish—languages that typically sounded loud and vulgar to German ears.[116] The aural quality of these languages thus came to represent the very "backwardness" and "barbarism" of the east.[117] At one point in her 1904 travel memoirs to the Habsburg crown land of Galicia, the Austrian Jewish feminist Bertha Pappenheim (who later achieved notoriety as Anna O. in Sigmund Freud's *Studies on Hysteria*) described local hospital conditions as a *Jammer*, a word that connotes both wailing and wretchedness.[118] The choice of this word is telling because the hospital sounds, consisting of patients wailing in their native non-German tongues, also came to indicate the very wretchedness of the place itself. As a domestic servant in Vienna, Lina D. may very well have been a non-German speaker (her first name could easily be a Slavic diminutive). Likewise, Herr Hofrat Ullmann's servant girl most likely grew up in the Bukowinian countryside speaking Yiddish, Romanian, Ruthenian, and/or Polish, and had come to Czernowitz to find work. Insofar as the official language spoken by the cultural and political elite in both cities was German, these women may have stood out. Not only did they look like domestic servants; they sounded like them, too.

But what made Lina D. and Herr Hofrat Ullmann's servant girl stand out even more was the movement they engaged in: a movement resembling flânerie, through urban spaces that encouraged the practice. Beyond their status and appearance as domestic servants, what served as an even greater though less explicit reason for their arrest was, I argue, the way they moved through urban space. Once again, we can employ historical imagination to understand how both incidents might have unfolded.

On a cold, gloomy January evening in Vienna in 1900, a young domestic servant, Lina D., walked home alone after spending the day laboring at the home of her sister's employer.[119] Tired from a full day of scrubbing, washing, ironing, and sewing, she walked slowly, making her way drowsily from an inner district to the middle-class district of Währing (XVIII), where she was renting a room from Frau Dettelmayer, whose husband was an elderly civil servant.[120] She ambled along the paved Währingerstrasse, which was straightened and extended in 1855, past trams and horse-drawn carriages, and glanced up at the carefree brunette in the large Kalodont toothpaste advertisement on the side of a building (see fig. 1.12). It started to flurry as she walked across the Währingergürtel, the original site of the Linien Wall fortifications that had been razed in 1894, lifting her skirt to increase her mobility and protect her dress from the snowflakes swirling at her ankles. As she caught sight of the cozy Carl Haupt Restaurant on the corner of the Schulgasse—the epitome of Viennese *Gemütlichkeit*—and smelled the smoke, beer, and fat wafting out of the front door, she knew she had finally made it to Währing, a former outer suburb that was known for its more quiet, "rural character," for it had not been incorporated into Vienna until 1892 (see fig. 1.13).[121]

At this hour, very few people were outside, with the exception of a few men standing on the street corner, smoking or loitering with their

FIGURE 1.12. The Währingergürtel, with a view toward Währingerstrasse and the city, 1895. From "Wien 9, Währinger Linie," photograph (Vienna, 1895). BAA/ÖNB.

FIGURE 1.13. Schulgasse, 1905. From "Wien 18, Schulgasse 1ff," photograph (Vienna, 1905). BAA/ÖNB.

hands in their pockets. Unclasping her hands, Lina D. swung her arms as she continued down the Schulgasse until she made a left onto the mostly residential Theresiengasse; it was silent, and all she could hear was the muffled sound of her boots against the snowy cobblestones. Knowing that the servant girl often moved fluently through the streets late in the day—perhaps he had even espied her on several occasions—Theodosius Babjuk, Frau Dettelmayer's daughter's snubbed lover, knew that Lina D. was ideally suited to be misrepresented as part of a prostitution ring run by Frau Dettelmayer: after all, she moved like a streetwalker. Determined to have his revenge on the Dettelmayer mother and daughter, Babjuk included Lina D. in his plot and surreptitiously sent a letter of denunciation to the local police station, effectively alerting the police to what he knew was a way of walking that was socially regarded as suspicious and calling on them to counter her movement with arrest.

Our imagination now shifts to the capital of Bukowina—a city that over the course of the nineteenth century underwent significant urban transformation and whose center came to be known as "Little Vienna." We know that on a Sunday afternoon in March 1900, Herr Hofrat Ullmann's servant girl purchased ham at a market, perhaps the one located on Elisabethplatz, named after the Habsburg empress also known as Sisi. Elisabethplatz would undergo significant renovations a few years later, with the construction of a theater (1904–1905), a palace of justice (1906), and the elegant Café Kaiser.[122] At the market, we can imagine the young girl being acquainted with the vendor, a Ruthenian farmer, who packaged the meat for her while she stood, arms akimbo, exchanging local gossip. The young girl made her way through throngs of kerchiefed women, past the fish vendors, winding toward the city center. Carrying her basket over her arm, she ambled across Gymnasialgasse and toward the Rathaus on Ringplatz, the Habsburg Double Eagle gleaming at the top of the building (see fig. 1.14). From 1897, streetcar tracks divided the Ringplatz into two, with the narrower half being called the "Pardinihöhe" or the "Small Ringplatz." Horse-drawn carriages were parked along the opposite side of the square, and the fifteen-year-old girl stopped and lingered, stroking their soft manes. Her mouth watered as she caught a whiff of the savory Krennwürste being served at Moses Hermann's Delicatessen.[123] As the bells for Sunday evening church service rang in the distance, she wandered past smartly dressed Habsburg officersytjkyu and bourgeois ladies and gentlemen promenading across the Ringplatz, the Pardinihöhe, and up the Herrengasse; oftentimes, they would begin their promenade at the "Kucharcyk" pastry shop in Enzenberg-Haupstrasse.[124] Perhaps the young servant girl also wandered up Herrengasse, the site of flânerie, listening to

FIGURE 1.14. Czernowitz's Ringplatz, 1894. From "Tscherniwzi, Czernowitz," photograph (Czernowitz, 1894). BAA/ÖNB.

the sounds of cues hitting billiard balls at the Café de l'Europe, past elegant boutiques and Jugendstil houses.[125] Alternatively, she may have walked north on Enzenberg-Hauptstrasse, which was likened to Vienna's Maria-hilferstrasse, and toward the imposing Schiffshaus, built in 1902, so called because it resembled a ship's prow.[126] When the local police caught sight of the young servant girl, all too obviously taking pleasure in her stroll, they immediately grew suspicious. Servant girls, they knew, were prone to being prostitutes. Servant girls taking pleasure in their strolls could only be prostitutes. Herr Hofrat Ullmann's servant girl's arrest logically followed, even as it was one of many arrests that day that aimed to counter the movement—the flânerie—of Czernowitz's working-class women.

1901: The Affair of the Frenchwoman

The final incident occurred in late February 1901, when a young French-woman of "extraordinary distinction" named Marie Rose Réaux was arrested while hunting for apartments in the IVth District, Wieden.[127] She was viewing a flat in an elegant building when a doorbell rang and k. u. k. Detective Neuhofer entered, barring her exit. As Réaux backed away, the detective grabbed her by the neck and choked her. She screamed and yelled for help, but Neuhofer only raised his fist menacingly and threatened, "Be quiet or else . . . !" The young lady begged to be released as Neuhofer pulled her by the arm so violently that he tore her dress. He proceeded to drag the panting woman down the stairs, out the door, and across the street, where a crowd of gawking spectators had assembled. Réaux was then taken to the district police station, where she was accused of clandestine prostitution. While there, she was forbidden to sit down, taken to a dirty cell, and examined by a physician. When she pleaded that she was innocent, Neuhofer agreed to escort her back to her dwelling in the Ist District, and when she produced the relevant papers establishing her identity, he responded laconically, "It is fine." "Ever since [the incident]," one newspaper reported, "the lady is suffering and barely capable of moving a limb."[128] In short, she had become immobilized.

Unlike the other women mistakenly arrested in 1899 and 1900, however, "the Frenchwoman in Vienna had in her misfortune the fortune not to be an Austrian woman," commented one article.[129] Indeed, as a French national, Réaux received support from the French ambassador, the Marquis de Reverseaux, who intervened on her behalf.[130] Meanwhile, on 5 March 1901, a member of Parliament, Julius Ofner, brought the incident to the attention of the Austrian Parliament as a way to discuss the larger problem of police brutality, "but especially the brutality against respectable women."[131] The incident was revisited the next day by another member of Parliament, Laurenz Hofer, who called it an example of a "police despotism" that "would continue to threaten the peace, honor, and freedom of even the most virtuous [makellosesten] citizen."[132] "Does the Herr Minister know," Hofer challenged, "that similar sad incidents occur in Vienna with alarming frequency and that so few of them become public only because the women, whose honor was so horribly threatened, remain silent, due partly to helplessness and lack of legal knowledge and partly out of shame about such occurrences?"[133] In an effort also to frame the issue in terms of men's honor, the inquiry ended with a call to "every father and husband" in Vienna who has witnessed his wife and daughter being "sacrificed" to the "villainous police."[134] Finally, on 8 March 1901, yet another member of Parliament, Josef Pommer, requested that the Minister of the Interior further investigate the incident, provide Réaux with compensation, and subject Neuhofer and the Vienna police department to disciplinary measures.[135] The pressure from both the French consulate and various members of Parliament led to the issuance of a formal apology by the police, as well as a payment of 300 crowns to replace Réaux's torn dress.

As the feminist newspaper *Dokumente der Frauen* provocatively asked: "Does a police officer in Vienna have the right to arrest and choke just about anybody without proper evidence?"[136] Even the conservative Christian Social newspaper, *Reichspost,* acknowledged that the Vienna police had crossed a line and insisted on "guidelines that will prevent [police abuse] as much as possible," including "all brutality, all bodily and spiritual torture, even when it involves a guilty woman, a degenerate"—that is, a prostitute.[137] The point is that for many contemporaries, there was no discernible reason for Réaux's arrest. She had not sported finery, nor had she looked working-class. Rather, she was a distinguished, upper-class lady who came to represent "just about anybody." So what led to her arrest? Below, I argue that it had to do with the way she moved through urban space: Réaux dared to practice flânerie.

As the incident gained notoriety among the press and the public, it even became the subject of parody. The Social Democratic *Arbeiter-Zeitung* (*Workers' Newspaper*) lampooned the incident in an imaginary dialogue between an Inspector and a Watchman about a recently arrested woman who was, as luck would have it, neither French nor represented by an ambassador.[138] The dialogue poked fun at the incompetence and ignorance of the Vienna police department as well as the "evidence" it used to make arrests.

INSPECTOR (TO THE WATCHMAN): "What's with the—little lady?"
WATCHMAN: "I arrested her 'cause of conspicuous behavior on the street."
INSPECTOR (SCRATCHING HIMSELF BEHIND THE EARS): "Is she maybe a Frenchwoman?"
WATCHMAN: "Nah, a Bohemian."
INSPECTOR: "If only I knew whether there's a Bohemian ambassador."
WATCHMAN: "Nah, there's none."
INSPECTOR: "Are you sure of it?"
WATCHMAN: "So sure that I can swear to it by my oath of service."
INSPECTOR: "Shut up about the oath of service. What did the broad do anyway?"
WATCHMAN: "She stood there."
INSPECTOR: "Nothin' else?"
WATCHMAN: "Oh yeah. She looked real suspicious."
INSPECTOR: "That's a real mixed-up affair. What else?"
WATCHMAN: "Then she went back and forth."
INSPECTOR: "Oh yeah? It seems to me we've caught ourselves a real piece of fluff."
WATCHMAN: "She also violated public morality."
INSPECTOR: "How'd she do that?"

WATCHMAN: "She raised her skirt above her booties so that I almost saw her stockings."

INSPECTOR: "You wouldn't suspect it at all, she looks so innocent."

WATCHMAN: "Those who look it aren't the problem 'cause we know 'em well anyway. But those innocent-looking ones, with 'em you know nothin,' they need to be examined."

INSPECTOR: "Well. She ain't no Frenchwoman and there ain't no Bohemian ambassador, so go ahead and arrest her for now."

Especially noteworthy is the reason for the woman's arrest—namely, "conspicuous behavior on the street." This included loitering ("she stood there"), walking back and forth, and "raising her skirt"—all elements of flânerie, of which, it seems, Réaux had been guilty, in the mind of the public, the press, and the policeman who arrested her.

Let us now imagine what Madame Réaux's day of her arrest might have looked like. One cloudy morning in March 1901, Marie Rose Réaux

FIGURE 1.15. Michaelerplatz, 1900. This square would undergo significant urban transformation in the years that followed, especially with the erection of the controversial Looshaus, built by the modernist architect Adolf Loos between 1909 and 1911, on the very spot occupied by the Dreilauferhaus, seen here in the center. From "1. Michaelerplatz 3/Kohlmarkt 18/Herrengasse 2—Dreilauferhaus," photograph (Vienna, c. 1900). Wien Museum Inv.-Nr. 106081/43, CC0.

FIGURE 1.16. Wiedner Haupstrasse, a shopping street that extends from the IVth to the Vth District, 1908. From August Stauda (photographer), "4. Wiedner Hauptstraße 10—Freihaus," photograph (Vienna, c. 1908). Wien Museum Inv.-Nr. 33689, CC0.

left her flat in the Schenkenstrasse in the Ist District to go apartment-hunting in Wieden, which was incorporated into the city in 1850.[139] The temperature was milder than usual, so she decided to take a stroll: she walked down the Herrengasse, past the Café Central, where people were enjoying breakfast, and toward the Michaelerplatz, which underwent construction between 1889 and 1893. She put her hands in her pockets, and continued past the Michaelerkirche and toward the Michaelertrakt, the recently completed north facade of the imperial palace, the Hofburg (see fig. 1.15). Holding her skirt with her right hand, she momentarily lingered in front of the "Sea Power" fountain. Réaux continued southward, toward the Opera and the elegant Hotel Sacher, founded in 1876. Her leisurely stroll suddenly turned into a brisk trot as she made her way across the Ringstrasse, swerving around the tramway and winding between horse-drawn carriages and *Gigerl*. As she made her way to the IVth District, she caught sight of the Secession building, "the somewhat bizarre structure" that locals termed the "Cabbage Head" because of its dome of gilded laurel leaves.[140] On the bustling Wiedner Hauptstrasse, lined with handsome Biedermeier and Jugendstil buildings, she walked further south, past eclectic shops selling poultry, home goods, and kitchen appliances, the Paulanerkirche, and Josef Stracker's Delicatessen, where rows of wine bottles lined the shop's windows (see fig. 1.16).

Taking a moment to orient herself, she made her way down a quieter street, and, as she ambled past the front door of a residential building, she caught sight of an advertisement for a flat. It started to drizzle, and after hesitating for a moment, she made her way inside. Having for some time followed the elegantly dressed lady, whose pedestrian promiscuity was suspiciously at odds with her outward propriety and hinted at malign intent and transgressive sexual behavior, k. u. k. Detective Neuhofer was alarmed to see the lady's seemingly aimless wanderings lead her into a strange building. Was she, perhaps, going to work in a secret brothel? Was vice the culmination of her stroll? Acting in accordance with the regnant norms assimilated from his training, he followed her inside, waited a few moments in the corridor as he heard her French accent through the door, and then proceeded to bar her exit by choking her and thereby very effectively—and violently—countering her movement.

Vienna's Flâneuses: Toward a Phenomenology of New Womanhood

Given the logic of the time, it certainly seemed possible that these women—the widow and her fashionable daughter, Lina D., the servants of Czernowitz, Marie Rose Réaux, and over a decade later, Magdalene W. and her niece—were clandestine streetwalkers. Although they were not, of course, these women did have something else in common. Though they might have eschewed the term, they objectively behaved as flâneuses, walking through their cities at a leisurely pace, stopping to look at advertisements and through shop windows, taking spatial ownership of the street. Thus, despite normative walking practices that designated streetwalking as the only version of flânerie available to women at the time and conceded flânerie to the "effeminate" and "Jewish" *Gigerl*, Viennese (and more generally imperial) women from all walks of life started appropriating flânerie for themselves, presumably semi-consciously at first and then, with time, consciously. From this vantage point, something as ordinary as walking could become a radical act that transformed the body into the locus of agency.

But Vienna's flâneuses were not just resisting normative walking practices; they were also—and perhaps more significantly—resisting normative and socialized femininity, again both semi-consciously and consciously. For the feminist theorist Iris Marion Young, socialized feminine movement is related to woman's experience of her body as an object, "a fragile thing, which must be picked up and coaxed into movement, a thing that exists as *looked at and acted upon.*"[141] Because women are often so-cialized to think of themselves as objects enclosed in space "in such a way that the space that belongs to [them] and is available to [their] grasp and manipulation is constricted and the space beyond is not available to [their] movement," they tend to localize movement in one part of the body, rendering the rest of their body immobile. As such, there is a notice-able restraint, a "discontinuous unity" within the body as well as between the body and the space surrounding it.

Normative Viennese femininity—as promoted by etiquette books and conventions—adhered to this modality of discontinuous unity. Insofar as ladies were to maintain a tidy and uniform step, cultivate poise and restraint by localizing movement in their feet, and move with purpose instead of aimlessness, they exhibited a discontinuity within their bodies and with the urban space surrounding them. Similarly, although working-class women were more in sync with their bodies as a result of their man-ual labor, they were also encouraged to maintain a discontinuity within their bodies when walking through urban space, keeping their hands and arms close to their bodies while moving purposefully. And although they were more likely to move swiftly with long strides, they did so as bounded body-objects traversing a treacherous and phenomenologically discon-tinuous urban terrain.

Flânerie, by contrast, was a modality of "continuous unity," and as such it subverted socialized feminine movement. Vienna's flâneuses walked without uniformity, eschewed poise and restraint by moving leisurely and expansively, spreading movement all over their bodies so that they moved as continuous units. Rather than viewing their bodies as objects, these women began locating their subjectivity in their bodies—probably unconsciously at first and then, as the practice took root, with greater consciousness. At the same time, by moving slowly and aimlessly, occa-sionally looking and loitering, and actualizing the city's many spatial and temporal possibilities, they maintained a unity—a trans-corporeality—with the streets around them, extending their subjectivity beyond the boundaries of their skin.[142] In this way, they were, like the streetwalkers and the *Gigerl*, *of* the street, both consumers and producers of urban spec-tacle, both bearers and objects of the gaze, as well as gender deviants. If the *Gigerl*, the Viennese flâneur, was the masculine counterpart to the new woman, then the new woman was the feminine counterpart to the Vien-nese flâneur: the flâneuse.[143] In this way, the modality of continuous unity became part and parcel of the phenomenology of new womanhood. The historian Saidiya Hartman speaks of the "wayward," which encapsulates not only "the unregulated movement of drifting and wandering"—a kind of flânerie—but also the willful agency "to inhabit the world in ways inimical to those deemed proper and respectable," to be deviant and to deviate, and to "create a path elsewhere."[144] Early twentieth-century Viennese new women were indeed wayward: drifters, wanderers, and feminine deviants.

Conclusion: New Cultures of Walking

In a 1901 caricature from the satirical journal *Die Bombe*, a solitary woman walks a little dog on the street as two older women scrutinize her from a window (see fig. 1.17): "How do you find our housekeeper's daughter who walks there?" one woman asks. "I cannot find her at all," the other woman responds, "in fact, she is a lost girl."[145] The joke hinges on the term "lost girl," which referred not only to a woman who was lost and could not be found, but also to a prostitute. What made the joke particularly clever was that the "lost girl" was neither physically lost (she appears front and center in the picture frame) nor a prostitute. She was a different kind of wayward woman.

Published shortly after the infamous Affair of the Frenchwoman, which involved the arrest of the elegant Marie Rose Réaux, the caricature depicts an equally refined young woman doing something equally mundane on the street—namely, walking her dog. The caricature was subversive: it aimed to ridicule the meddlesome onlookers, including the lecherous dandy at the corner, who viewed the woman's expansive and continuous phenomenology on the street as an indication of streetwalking. That the caricature recognized the woman for what she was—not a streetwalker, but a flâneuse and a new woman—is significant because it reveals that, already by the fin de siècle, new womanhood was not only beginning to take shape, but was also being recognized as such. Flânerie, in sum, had become a conscious activity—not because women were reading high-minded intellectual treatises that urged them to do so, but because there were more spaces for it, as well as an established culture of walking.

Women continued to appropriate flânerie for themselves through the first decade of the twentieth century and into the First World War, when Magdalene W. and her niece were apprehended for "walking slowly" on the Mariahilferstrasse in 1916. Even streetwalkers started appropriating flânerie. According to a police report from 1916, the sex workers living in Antonie Brady's tolerated brothel at Bäckerstrasse 16 in the Ist District frequently took daily recreational walks together.[146] By the interwar period, flânerie had become even more widespread, especially with the growing

FIGURE 1.17. The association between prostitution and flânerie is skewered in this 1901 caricature. From "Böse Zungen," *Die Bombe*, 17 March 1901, 8. BAA/ÖNB.

popularity of window-shopping (*Schaufensterbummel*).[147] In fact, one could argue that the shops not only encouraged flânerie, but vice versa— that flânerie inspired the establishment of more shops with colorful windows. Soon enough, Vienna's shop windows were touted for being particularly enticing, luring customers—and flâneuses—from across Europe. "The Danube city jealously guards its distinctiveness, which everyone who

strolls in its streets and alleys comes to love," reported one women's magazine.[148] "Every woman, especially the well-travelled one, will immediately
notice that this distinctiveness comes through especially in the refined,
rather unique taste of Viennese window displays." In a fashion illustration from 1926, two women dressed in street-suits (*Strassenanzüge*) stand
in front of such a window display, featuring a patterned dress with a low
waistline, a blouse, and a coat with skirt-like pleats.[149] They are engaged
in conversation—as evidenced by the gesticulating hand—and comfortably loitering on the street. They would continue on their way, taking
part in a "lively korso" of elegant shoppers along the Kärntnerstrasse and
neighboring streets until they would retreat to a coffeehouse or pastry
shop, the Sacher or Gerstner, for a torte and a mélange.[150] By the interwar
period, it was no longer clear whether the modern city, with its korso and
coffeehouses, continued to inspire walking or whether walking continued
to modernize Vienna, inspiring an even livelier korso and even more coffeehouses. It was, in fact, both.

As a reflection of this growing culture of walking, more flânerie-specific
products flooded the Viennese market.[151] A fashion spread from 1915
featured two head-to-toe outfits "for the street," including a dark green
coat-dress with a brimmed hat worn at a jaunty angle as well as a "street
uniform" made of a striped woolen fabric paired with an umbrella that
could also serve as a walking stick (see fig. 1.18).[152] A similar street outfit—
featuring the same A-line silhouette, dress length, drawstring purse, foot-
wear, and hat—can be seen in a photograph of an anonymous woman
strolling leisurely on the Ring in 1917 as two soldiers look on (see fig. 1.19).

Although the fashion silhouette would change during the 1920s (chapter 2), one element remained the same: namely, a shorter hemline to accommodate greater mobility. By this time, a more specific form of streetwear
took Vienna by storm: the *trotteur* (taken from the French, "a trotter"), a
tailored suit made of woolen fabrics intended to be worn on the street—
"not just [for] leisurely strolling, but also [for] the excited back and forth"
of shopping, for the "quiet stroll in the morning sunshine, the diligent
completion of a lightly athletic, slimming workout, or the aimless splash-
ing through rainy weather."[153] By this point, fashion illustrations not only
included streetwear, but also depicted the women modeling these outfits
on recognizable Viennese streets, such as those near the centrally located
Stephansplatz, or while taking a dog for a walk or even walking to the
office.[154] In one fashion spread from 1928, four women crossing a street
wear long, fur-lined winter coats, as Vienna's Karlskirche looms in the distance and an automobile rolls into the frame.[155] But streetwear was not the
only product both contributing and responding to the growing culture of

FIGURE 1.18. A 1915 fashion illustration of outfits "for the street." From "Für die Strasse," *Das Blatt der Hausfrau*, 22 August 1915, 1. BAA/ÖNB.

walking among women: foot products, such as shoe soles, promised steadiness and elasticity to move freely through urban space, while foot bath powders pledged to relieve pain from navigating cobblestones.[156]

Did the flâneuse replace the *Gigerl*? An art nouveau–inspired 1918 advertisement for Diana face powder featured a woman in a bell-shaped dress, flamboyant checkered scarf, and large, clownish hat walking her little black dog, while a gentleman with a bowler hat and walking stick gets

FIGURE 1.19. A woman walking on the Ring in 1917, wearing what appears to be a "street outfit." From Rudolf Pichler (photographer), "Wien 1, Kärntner Ring," photograph (Vienna, 15 August 1917). BAA/ÖNB.

FIGURE 1.20. In this 1918 advertisement, the woman flâneuse resembles the *Gigerl*, the Viennese flâneur. From "Diana Puder," *Blatt der Hausfrau*, 22 September 1918, 10. ANNO/ÖNB.

entangled in the leash (see fig. 1.20).[157] The woman nonchalantly looks
at him while the man turns his head in bewilderment. "Could it be?" he
seems to wonder. Not only does this flâneuse, this new woman, walk like
a *Gigerl*—she looks like one, too.

✳

This chapter examined flânerie as a practice of new womanhood. It showed
how an ordinary, everyday form of movement—a way of walking leisurely
through urban space—contributed to the transformation of gendered embodiment in early twentieth-century Vienna. In the late nineteenth century, normative Viennese womanhood required a much more restrained
form of movement; those women who dared to wander and stroll through
city streets were typically sex workers—that is, deviant or "fallen" women.
And yet, over time, more and more non-sex workers started walking the
streets of the city, until the practice became more common, though still
deviant, signifying new womanhood. In this way, this chapter revealed
how an everyday embodied practice could generate changes in gender.

Additionally, this chapter identified a dynamic relationship between
urban change and gendered embodiment. As the city of Vienna underwent a series of urban transformations in the late nineteenth century, its
new spaces and boulevards, such as the grand Ring, encouraged flânerie.
While the original practitioner of flânerie was the effeminate Viennese
dandy, the *Gigerl*, soon ordinary women of all backgrounds and classes
started appropriating it too, as evidenced by the series of arrests from 1899
to 1901, as well as the incident in 1916 with which this chapter started. This
trend continued into the interwar period, when a new culture of walking
emerged, which continued to modernize the city even further. Thus, the
modernizing city did not just bring about the new moves of new womanhood; the proliferation of new womanhood inspired the continued mod-
ernization of the city.

As more women walked the streets like a *Gigerl*, some contemporaries
insisted that they assumed his appearance as well. Chapter 2 will consider
what contemporaries perceived as a *Gigerl*-like, "masculine"-looking silhouette. We thus shift our attention from the new moves to the new shapes
of new womanhood.

New Shapes

THE MASCULINE LINE, THE STARVING
BODY, AND THE CULT OF SLIMNESS

On a cool summer evening in early August 1932, two women accused a man of wandering about the IVth District wearing women's clothing and looking to make male acquaintances.[1] Was it a *Gigerl* whose dandyism got the best of him? Was it a male prostitute? As it turned out, it was neither, for the person accused of being a man was actually a woman: a singer named Gisela Piowati.

Piowati pleaded with the police officer, Anton Erasim, that she was not a man. Despite her pleas of innocence, Erasim apprehended Piowati and escorted her to the local station on Rienößlgasse. The next day, the station's cleaning woman, Susanne Donner, physically inspected Piowati, confirming that she was, indeed, female-bodied, which for contemporaries was synonymous with being a woman. Later that month, the police confirmed that there was no evidence to suggest that Piowati was a clandestine sex worker.

As this case study suggests, an associational link existed between cross-dressing, sex work, and male homosexuality in interwar Vienna. Within contemporary sexological discourse, homosexuality was believed to be written on the body, often sartorially.[2] Rumors abounded of bars and coffeehouses catering to homosexual men, where most of the clientele arrived wearing women's clothing.[3] Sensationalist tabloids devoted articles to the Viennese underworld, vividly describing its so-called "lavender lads" (*lila Burschen*), including "Wild Edi," a "small, slender, 'line lad' dressed [in a] hypermodern" style; "Helene," a seventeen-and-a-half-year-old who was referred to with male pronouns in quotation marks; or the "homosexual, 'Adele,'" who roamed the streets of the XIVth District in women's clothing.[4] Given the visibility of cross-dressing homosexuals and sex workers in the Viennese media, the accusations leveled against Piowati may seem less unusual.[5]

But Piowati had been neither a sex worker nor a cross-dresser nor a man. She was, quite simply, a woman wearing women's clothing. What, then, had contributed to this mix-up? Three people had thought Piowati was cross-dressing. While it is possible that the women, Hilda Schuch and Josefine Glinz, may have known Piowati personally and denounced her for their own reasons (although, even if that were so, they obviously must have believed that Piowati looked sufficiently "man"-like for their accusation to be plausible), the police officer, Erasim, continued to think she was a man in women's clothing, despite getting a closer look at her face during the arrest and hearing the sound of her voice as she pleaded her case.[6] Although one reason for this may have been related to her *Gigerl*-like walk through urban space (chapter 1), in this chapter I consider Piowati's misgendering as a result of her *Gigerl*-like silhouette. The shape of Piowati's body appeared masculine to contemporaries precisely because hers was the body of a new woman.

This chapter considers the linear silhouette as a form of gender subversion and, crucially, its maintenance as a practice of new womanhood. Traditionally, Viennese womanhood was imagined to be soft and curvaceous, occupying an hourglass shape. The linear silhouette, by contrast, seemed to conform to a more masculine appearance. And yet it is this silhouette—as we can see from the above-mentioned case—that more and more Viennese women, whether willingly or not, conformed to over the course of the first decades of the twentieth century. Although a body's shape may seem insignificant, the stuff of trivial histories and niche interests, one of the goals of this chapter is to show just how charged and relevant it was at this historical moment, contributing to the very transformation of gender itself. Further, this chapter examines how this new shape and its maintenance emerged within and in tandem with a rapidly modernizing and globalizing Vienna that would come to be devastated by the Great War of 1914–1918 sweeping across the European continent and, eventually, the world.

"Bub oder Mädel?"—"Boy or Girl?"

New women had long been imagined as looking like men physically. "To the first glance of an expert, [emancipated women] reveal some of the anatomical characteristics of the male, some external bodily resemblance to a man," wrote Otto Weininger, author of the controversial book *Geschlecht und Charakter* (*Sex & Character*), in 1903.[7] As he outlined in greater detail, "George Eliot had a broad, massive forehead; her movements, like her expression, were quick and decided, and lacked all womanly grace. The face of Lavinia Fontana was intellectual and decided, very rarely charming; whilst that of Rachel Ruysch was almost wholly masculine. The biography of that original poetess, Anette von Droste-Hülshoff [sic], speaks of her wiry, unwomanly frame, and of her face as being masculine, and recalling that of Dante. The authoress and mathematician, Sonia Kowalevska [sic], like Sappho, had an abnormally scanty growth of hair."[8]

The Viennese media also fixated on the new woman's "manly" appearance, often referring to her as a "man-woman" (Mannweib). In a caricature from 1896, for example, a dapper Gigerl-like "woman of the future" (Zukunftsfrau), dressed in a top hat and bloomers, holding a walking stick under her arm, is preparing to leave for the theater as her daughter and husband look on (see fig. 2.1).[9] Her daughter asks, "Mama, why don't you take Papa and me to the theater?" To which she curtly responds, "The play isn't meant for men and young girls!" By 1908, the New Woman was not only depicted as manly—she was described as "ugly" and "wraithlike."[10] At other times, she was shown having a stockier build with a "coarse [derb]" appearance, wearing "mostly Loden coats and old felt hats, and every once and a while also her husband's boots."[11] By the 1910s and early 1920s, she was imagined as engaging in even more masculine-coded practices, such as rioting, smoking cigarettes, even taking part in drunken brawls.[12] In the 1920s and early 1930s, she was depicted as having "become so slim, so flat-chested that [her] nude [body] hardly differ[ed] from that of a young boy."[13] She had a "sporty boy-body" and she was "particularly garçonne in her manner and taste."[14] When spotting such a woman, contemporaries would wonder, "Bub oder Mädel?"—"boy or girl?"

For Weininger, the new woman looked like a man because she was, in fact, partly male. Weininger, who was widely read by Viennese women, held the view that every human body was made up of a unique composition of male and female cells.[15] "Living beings cannot be described bluntly as of one sex or the other," he insisted. "The real world from the point of view of sex may be regarded as swaying between two points, no actual individual being at either point, but somewhere between the two."[16] As such, "there exist all sorts of intermediate conditions between male and female—sexual transitional forms."[17] A masculine woman, despite being endowed with female genitalia, possessed a greater number of male cells than female cells. Weininger thus looked beyond sexual organs to the very cells of the body to determine sex and by extension gender—because, for Weininger and the majority of his contemporaries, sex and gender expression were one and the same.

Other contemporaries argued that it was modernity that made women's bodies more masculine. According to this neo-Lamarckian evolutionary

Häusliche Sittenpolizei.

— Mama, warum nimmst Du mich
und Papa nicht auch mit ins Theater?
— für Männer und junge Mädchen
ist das kein Stück!

FIGURE 2.1. By the fin de siècle, the Viennese media often depicted the New Woman as manly, as shown in this 1896 caricature. From "Die Zukunfts-Frauen," *Wiener Caricaturen*, 10 May 1896, 4–5. ANNO/ÖNB.

view, which posited that genetic change can be influenced by the environment, although women naturally exhibited feminine bodily characteristics, it was the very particular historical environment—"modernity"—that led to their masculinization. As women started going to school and entering the workforce, this idea became more popular. Education was believed to ruin women's supple bodies and make their hair fall out (the many bald men of letters were supposed to be evidence of this myth).[18] According to the gynecologist Carl Heinrich Stratz, working women's bodies were becoming increasingly "square, their facial expressions sharp and severe, their figure and movement masculinized," so that the "delicate aura of femininity fades."[19] A headline from 1913 provocatively asked whether "women's hands were getting bigger" due to their increased participation in manual labor.[20] Likewise, during the First World War, women's participation in the Auxiliary Labor Force was thought to pose a threat to their nature: their presence in military contexts called into question not only their femininity, but also their future as mothers and homemakers.[21] By 1922, Dr. O. Janetschek announced that "the nervousness of the modern period has blurred woman's natural predispositions."[22] More specifically, it was "the masculine strain of the modern social order [that] has partly de-feminized the female sex."

Although much of this rhetoric was grounded in misogyny and antifeminism, I would like to suggest that it was also partially rooted in material reality. To return to the 1932 case with which this chapter started: we do not know what Piowati's body looked like, but if interwar trends were any indication, there is a good chance that it conformed to what contemporaries referred to as a "masculine" appearance. This chapter considers how, over the course of the early decades of the fin de siècle, many Viennese women's silhouettes and bodies changed—and were imagined to have changed—from full and curvaceous to slender and linear, a change that, given the associations between the linear figure and masculinity, constituted an articulation of female masculinity and (importantly) new womanhood.[23] I argue that while much of this perception of change had to do with the "masculine line" that was popularized by the fashion industry before the First World War, the new figure became more ubiquitous in wartime, when food was scarce and all bodies suffered. In fact, the experience on the Viennese home front played an especially significant role as women felt their emaciated bodies becoming thinner and struggled to survive. The chapter then shifts to the interwar period, to show how fashion and beauty industries continued to emphasize the masculine silhouette, rebranded as the slim line, so that even if a woman wore women's clothing, it may have appeared—at least to some people, such as the police officer

Erasim—as if she were, in fact, cross-dressing as a man. At the heart of this chapter, then, is consumption: the emergence of consumer fashion and beauty industries in modernizing Vienna on the one hand, and consumption (and its attendant struggles) during total war on the other.

As a chapter that considers fashion and beauty trends in conjunction with the physical hardships of war, this text incorporates jarring shifts in tone, from the pleasure of clothing to the pain of hunger to the pleasure-pain of beautification, diet, and exercise. This is unavoidable both because the linear silhouette was ubiquitous in all aspects of society and culture and, thus, in war as much as in fashion, and because women's bodies really did undergo a kind of fragmentation during this transformative time: in fashion, their bodies were reduced to lines; in wartime, they became emaciated and elongated forms; in the interwar period, they became slim and trim. In showing how these fragments—clothing, wartime hunger, dieting, exercise—fit together, I also show that women's physical fragmentation was less a falling apart than a rearranging and putting back together. It was over the course of this period that new women started to lavish their bodies with maintenance and care, because they wanted not to transcend their corporeality, but to come closer to it, and arguably embrace it as the seat of the "self."

Beautiful, Curvaceous Viennese Women

Central European aesthetic norms had long been based on the art of antiquity.[24] Johann Joachim Winckelmann's mid-eighteenth-century writings on the arts of ancient Greece and Rome were especially influential, providing the backdrop to Johann Wolfgang von Goethe's two-year exploratory trip through Italy and the Romantic infatuation with Graeco-Roman statues, temples, and ruins.[25] Over a century later, the Viennese composer Alma Mahler-Werfel (née Schindler) insisted that the question of beauty "can *only* be resolved in Rome, where you see all those exquisite marble figures, the Capitoline Venus and many, many others—then the Apollo of Belvedere, Hermes, and the knife-sharpener."[26]

In 1854, a German professor, Adolf Zeising, even developed a pseudo-scientific doctrine known as the "golden proportion" to evaluate bodily aesthetics, contending that the ideal man's body was linear with narrow hips and wide shoulders, whereas the ideal woman's body was the opposite, rounded, endowed with wide hips and narrow shoulders.[27] Slimness "was then limited solely to the waist," recalled the Austrian women's activist Rosa Mayreder, "while the absence of hips and breasts was considered an unpardonable defect."[28] These physical ideals extended into the twentieth century, although they came to be reframed as representing the "norm." A marriage advice book from 1920, for instance, contained images of the "normal male figure" and the "normal female figure," which directly corresponded to Zeising's ideals.[29] If the male was all muscle, hard and angular, the woman's body was soft, fleshy, and Juno-esque, with thick, curly hair extending to her smooth thighs. The images also revealed opposing gender roles. "Normal man" appeared to be standing on a pedestal—in public—staring intently at his flexed biceps. By contrast, "normal woman" remained indoors, standing modestly with her thighs pressed together, her hips seductively thrust to one side, while she gazed at her reflection in a handheld mirror.

This beauty norm and ideal was especially true of the Viennese woman, who was imagined to be "'mollert'—well-endowed, 'g'stellt'—with a fuller figure, and with a 'süßes G'frieserl'—a pretty little face: above all, she was proud of her large bosom, which had to be displayed in its most advantageous pose."[30] Writing in 1902, Carl Heinrich Stratz mused that what characterized a Viennese woman was her "soft, round, and also well-built body type, beautiful eyelids, dimple in the chin," "straight, long, round legs, narrow knees, round, hearty calves," and "youthful breasts." This was a woman who was "born to be naked" and who shared much in common with "classical statues of goddesses."[31] According to folk songs and tall tales, her round breasts were the most beautiful in the world, and her curves were as round and soft as *Marillenknödel* (apricot dumplings).[32]

Because the ideal Viennese woman's body was curved, "[female] ugliness," according to a 1925 article in a women's magazine, "usually comes from angular and straight lines."[33] Older women were considered to be especially "grotesque," precisely because they developed "sharp lines around the mouth, eyes, and nose."[34] An ugly woman was usually depicted with small and sagging breasts, angular features, narrow hips, wide shoulders, and pronounced muscles—in short, with a masculine figure. As Michael Hau observes, "male proportions in women [were] ugly and degenerate," while "these same proportions represented timeless aesthetic norms for men."[35] The reason for this, he argues, is that many contemporaries regarded beauty as an expression of a "gender-specific telos," so that women's wide hips signaled their capacity to bear children. This idea was widespread; even Mahler-Werfel insisted that "a person is beautiful if every part of their body performs the functions for which it was intended."[36] In other words, not only was a woman with a linear silhouette and narrow hips ugly; she also looked "masculine," which called her "female function" into question.

Proper functioning was a cornerstone of good health, so that beauty also came to signify the mental and physical health of an individual. According to F. König's health guide from 1910, *Ratgeber in gesunden und kranken Tagen* (*Adviser for Healthy and Sick Days*), "In the same way in which beauty bears the stamp of a perfect harmony of all physical, mental, and spiritual functions, ugliness is the expression of all disharmony and of all physical, mental, and spiritual disturbances. Who could doubt," he continued, "that what we call beautiful and ugly can also be termed healthy and sick?"[37] Ugliness referred to more than just aesthetics: it was a sign of poor health, mental illness, and degeneration. The linear and angular female form was thus often viewed as an expression of poor health and a degenerating womanhood.

And yet, as Sabine Wieber explains, this very female form, which she terms the "femme fragile," became the new ideal in naturalist and modernist art at the fin de siècle.[38] Richard Luksch's sculptures for Josef Hoffmann's Purkersdorf Sanatorium (built in 1904–1905), for example, represented this new ideal: the sculptures' "bodies are thin if not emaciated—their shoulder bones stick out, their upper bodies are excessively lean, and their ribs and hip bones protrude through their skin."[39] The secessionist painter Gustav Klimt frequently depicted the femme fragile in his work, whether as the waiflike redhead staring listlessly at the viewer in *Nuda Veritas* (1899), as the slender, angular female figures in his *Beethoven Frieze* (1902), or even as the contorted, red-lipped woman in *The Kiss* (1907–8), whose slight, kneeling body stands straight as a line on a bed of flowers, while her lover engulfs her with a kiss. And the women in Egon Schiele's pre-war canvases are all lines and angles, such as *Seated Female Nude with Raised Right Arm* (1910). For artists such as Luksch, Klimt, and Schiele, the femme fragile represented a new kind of beauty—one that would be further celebrated in the applied arts, specifically in fashion.[40] Just how this new bodily ideal—what came to be known as the "masculine line"—was popularized by the growing Viennese fashion industry is the topic of the next section.

"Straight as a Board in the Front, Straight as a Board in the Back": Fashion's Masculine Line

In 1911, Vienna was overtaken by the "Poiret-Sensation," when the French fashion designer and self-proclaimed liberator of the corset, Paul Poiret, visited the imperial capital.[41] At his showcase, nine slender models, known as his mannequins, glided down the aisle showing off designs in "gold and silver, silk, velvet, lots of velvet, even flowing gauze, mousseline, [and] soft, jeweled brocade," featuring a "splendor of colors," such as deep, saturated shades of red and violet, and graphic textiles inspired by Vienna's decorative arts company, the Wiener Werkstätte, which established a fashion division of its own that same year.[42] The models wore "Oriental" turbans or modern soiree hats. All of this was shocking enough, but perhaps most radical were the designs' looser, vertically oriented, linear silhouettes.

Critics accused Poiret of wanting "to dress women masculine."[43] The *jupe-culotte* of Poiret's spring 1911 collection, a pant-skirt that resembled a harem pantaloon, prompted widespread outrage among contemporaries by seeming to encourage women to cross-dress.[44] In March of that year, local newspapers reported on several incidents in which crowds of people, mostly boys and men, accosted fashionably dressed Viennese ladies for wearing the controversial garment, in a ritual of public humiliation.[45] Although the pant-skirt was often covered by a slitted skirt or appeared skirt-like due to its low crotch, the very idea that women could wear pants was enough to generate outrage.[46] But it was the new silhouette—"'[straight as a] board in the front, [straight as a] board in the back'"—that prompted the most anxiety because it conformed to the very body that other contemporaries viewed as ugly, degenerate, and (significantly) masculine.[47] Even Poiret's mannequins were described as "man-women, a Brunnhilde, a Sieglinde from Wagner."[48]

Poiret's silhouette was a huge departure from the fin-de-siècle S-dress, so called because of the way its straight-front corset pushed up the bust and pushed in the stomach (see fig. 2.2).[49] Its silhouette was hourglass in shape, thereby giving the wearer what contemporaries viewed as a feminine appearance. If the ideal woman's body was meant to be curvaceous, the S-dress sculpted women's bodies into this ideal shape by emphasizing a large bust, a small waist, and full hips. "What strikes our uninhibited gaze today about those costumes, garments so desperately trying to cover every inch of bare skin and hide the natural figure," wrote the Austrian Jewish writer Stefan Zweig years later, "is not their moral propriety but its opposite, the way those fashions, provocative to the point of embarrassment, emphasized the polarity of the sexes." While "the men sported long beards, or at least twirled the ends of a mighty moustache, a clearly recognizable sign of their masculinity," Zweig continued, "a woman's breasts, essentially feminine sexual attributes, were made ostentatiously visible by her corset."[50] Moreover, beneath her tight-laced corset, "countless little hooks," "her petticoats, camisoles, little bodices and jackets," weighed down by jewelry, a plumed hat, and other accessories, "a woman was no longer free," wrote Zweig.[51]

Rosa Mayreder recalled how "the ambition of every young girl was to have the smallest possible waist measurement."[52] "It was a serious beauty flaw that with twelve years I had a waist size of almost sixty centimeters," Mayreder wrote, "while my sister Mitzi, still in her twentieth year, was

FIGURE 2.2. A 1901 fashion illustration of two S-dresses: on the left is a theatre outfit, and on the right a ballgown. From "Mode, Kindergarderobe, Wäsche, Handarbeiten," *Das Blatt der Hausfrau* 12, no. 18 (1901). ANNO/ÖNB.

just forty-eight centimeters around the middle."[53] The ideal waist size at this time was fifty-five centimeters or smaller.[54] To remedy this, Mayreder had to lace in her corset more tightly and more frequently—a practice that made it difficult to do anything, especially eat. She renounced the corset at eighteen, turning instead to the looser garments of the dress reform movement that sought to liberate women's bodies from the frivolous and constraining fashions of the time.

In Vienna, the dress reform movement originated within a medical and feminist discourse that focused on the negative effects of the corset on the body.[55] In 1902, the Clothing Reform Society (*Verein zur Reform der Kleidung*) was established, and in March the feminist journal *Dokumente der Frauen* published an entire issue devoted to the topic. According to an article by Dr. C. Breus, "the breasts and individual organs can be deformed as a result [of wearing a corset], [and] breathing, blood circulation, and digestion suffer."[56] A gynecologist, Friedrich Schauta, explained that a woman's "poor capacity in regard to the physical can be largely traced back to the premature 'armoring' [*Umpanzerung*] of her respiratory and circulatory organs."[57] Going without a corset, contemporaries argued, would allow women to be free. Far from being understood as separate, body and mind were seen as fundamentally interrelated: freedom of the body would lead to freedom of the mind, and vice versa.

The first uncorseted or looser dresses—known as reform dresses— were viewed as primarily functional clothing that was meant to be worn to the spa, during travel, or when engaging in physical activity or labor.[58] Reform dresses did not become fashionable art dresses (*Künstlerkleider*) until a few years later, when members of the Wiener Werkstätte and the Vienna Secession started designing garments meant to reflect modernity— though here too the goal was for form to follow function. Gustav Klimt, for example, had been involved in the production of a variety of reform dresses, modeled by the fashion designer Emilie Flöge, which were documented in a series of photographs taken in summer 1906 in Litzlberg, on the fashionable Attersee near Salzburg.[59] Modeling these loose dresses with long, frilly sleeves outdoors near the lake, Flöge appears relaxed, comfortable, happy. Flöge would go on to sell similar reform garments of her own design in her Schwestern Flöge Salon in the Casa Piccola Haus on Vienna's Mariahilferstrasse. Founded in 1904, the salon catered to a wealthy clientele and offered dresses that promised both freedom and fashion.

By 1907, reform styles began to appear on the pages of Viennese fashion magazines that featured empire waists and looser fits, as well as visual motifs and patterns taken from the Secession or the Wiener Werkstätte, indicating that these dresses were becoming accessible to a wider set of women consumers (see fig. 2.3).[60] When Poiret presented his haute couture dresses during his 1911 visit to Vienna, contemporaries would have observed a similar style and silhouette. Cut along straight lines and constructed of simple rectangles, his dresses featured raised empire waists, longer hemlines, and narrower skirts. Women's fashion magazines

Stilkleider.

Unsere Abendkleidung wird
immer komplizierter. Seitdem ein
Künstler wie Poiret uns neue Ge-
wänder beschert hat, will die elegante
Modedame natürlich ein Poiretkleid
haben. Sie braucht dazu zunächst
eine Combination aus Seide oder
Fil d'écosse, denn ein gewöhnliches
Hemd ist beinahe schon zu voluminös
als Unterkleidung. Ueber diese sehr
anzuratende, weil wärmende Combination ist eine dünne Rockhose mit
angesetzter Untertaille oder ein sehr
kurzer Prinzeßunterrock, stets mit
abknöpfbaren Achseln, zu empfehlen.
Darüber das korsettlose Kleid, in das
ein miederartiger Gürtel eingearbei-
tet ist, unter dem man nur noch
einen Strumpfgürtel oder einen aus
Seidenband geflochtenen Leibhalter
mit Strumpfbändern nötig hat.
Sehr viel Kopfzerbrechen wird das
Knüpfen des Turbans verursachen,
den Poiret zu seinen Kleidern haben
will; er besteht aus einem Tuche,
das dreieckig zusammengelegt, von
vorn nach rückwärts um den Kopf
geknüpft wird, und zwar so, daß die
Enden geschickt versteckt werden.
Neuerdings wird über diesen Sei-
denturban noch ein Goldbandeau
gebunden, das vorn mit einem
Cabochon schließt; oft ragt dahinter
noch ein kleiner beweglicher Glas-
reiher hervor. Schmuck liebt Poiret
nicht, wenigstens keinen modernen;
er läßt nur sehr wenig gelten und be-
vorzugt Perlen- oder Platinketten, an
denen einzelne große Perlen hängen.
Schuhe und Strümpfe sollen wieder
in einer Farbe sein, und zwar gelten Atlasschuhe momentan im
Salon als die elegantesten; auch
schwarze Abendschuhe sind aus
Atlas oder Samt mit Verstickerei
oder mit aparten Schnallen, für
Poiretkleider natürlich im Empire-
geschmack. Sie passen sich den engen
Röcken am besten an. E. H.

Für junge Mädchen.

395. Ballkleid aus hellblauem Voile-Ninon und
gleichfarbigem Libertyatlas. Beschreibung und
Rückansicht in der Rubrik „Reich der Hausfrau".
Schnitt in Größe I u. II erhältlich.

FIGURE 2.3. Uncorseted or looser dresses began to appear in the early 1900s, as
seen in this fashion spread from 1910. From "Stilkleider," *Das Blatt der Hausfrau*,
27 November 1910, 1. ANNO/ÖNB.

reported on the visit, urging readers to copy the new style. Desiring to be fashionable, working-class women sewed the dresses themselves using paper patterns from magazines, while more affluent, bourgeois women went to dressmakers and tailors who copied the styles produced by Poiret or other designers and couturiers, such as Heinrich Grünzweig, S. Ungar, or Schwestern Flöge.[61] With the expansion of mass-produced clothing and a consumer market, some women went straight to the local department store, such as Herzmansky or Gerngross, to buy the ready-made styles known as *Konfektionen* (see fig. 2.4).[62] In this way, Poiret's Parisian styles had the surprising effect of further popularizing a Viennese trend in Vienna.[63]

This new style appealed to such a diverse array of women for several reasons. First, as the latest Parisian-Viennese fashion, the style afforded women pleasure: pleasure derived from the touch of new fabrics between fingers and on bodies; pleasure generated by participating in a community of fashion-conscious consumer women, as friends, neighbors, mothers, sisters, daughters, shop girls, seamstresses, designers, and fashion writers; and pleasure engendered by the fantasy of trying on different identities, in particular the identity of the modern woman.[64] That Mahler-Werfel frequently drew fashion illustrations in her diary is surely evidence of this pleasure, in her case the fantasies that fashionable clothing could evoke.[65]

Second, this loose, linear style promised liberation, an idea that, as the women's movement was gaining ground in Vienna, appealed to women who felt constrained by the burdens of normative womanhood. Although we cannot know if these clothes truly did liberate women—after all, historians should be wary of teleology and skeptical of the narrative of fashion's becoming more liberating over time, a point I also make in the introduction to this book—we do know that many women such as Mayreder did in fact experience the new style as liberating, which is surely significant.[66]

And third, the linear silhouette's appeal was due to its structural simplicity, a necessity for women enduring the hardships of the First World War. The war effectively forced women to abandon their long, ornamental, corseted S-dresses, which they buried deep in closets or reworked into clothing that was shorter, looser, and easier to move in.[67] Insofar as the goal was a "simple elegance" that was, above all, versatile, wartime garments were also referred to as reform dresses.[68] Wartime Viennese fashion did flirt with a bell-shaped silhouette—as a tiered double skirt in which a full overskirt was worn on top of a narrower underskirt, as a pleated or ruffled skirt, and as the "ton-skirt" (*Tonnerock*) whose name reflected its great volume and weight—in an effort to promote a distinctly national aesthetic.[69] But even these flirtations were a radical departure from what

FIGURE 2.4. The department store A. Gerngross opened its doors on Mariahilferstrasse (VIIth District) in 1879. This postcard from 1908 features its extravagant main
hall, with a view of the many display cases on the ground floor. From M. Schulz, "7.
Mariahilfer Straße 42–48—Innenansicht—Lichthalle im Modenhaus A. Gerngross,
Wien," postcard (Vienna: A. Gerngross, 1908). Wien Museum Inv.-Nr. 239075, CC0.

came beforehand, insofar as they featured shorter hemlines, looser waists (which may have been uncorseted), and even, on occasion, pockets. The return to the linear silhouette at the end of the war may therefore be seen as an unsurprising consequence of this shift toward simplicity and versatility.[70] Indeed, "for all the fluctuation of fashion between 1908 and 1928—from the hobble skirt and lampshade tunic through the calf-length 'war crinoline' to the flat-chested, low-waisted Twenties look," writes Valerie Steele, "the dominant trend was away from the full hourglass figure with the narrow waist and toward a vertical line and a relatively unconstructed waist."[71]

Over the next decade, with the further expansion of this culture of consumption and the popularity of Coco Chanel's designs across Europe, the straight and loose "barrel" line would become the dominant form in women's fashion (see fig. 2.5). Chanel adjusted Poiret's style by radically lowering the waistline or by removing it altogether and shortening the hemline to expose a woman's legs in skin-toned silk stockings. Unlike the fin-de-siècle hourglass shape that enhanced the bust and buttocks, and thereby the wearer's femininity, this new silhouette minimized these "feminine" attributes by "remain[ing] slender and straight."[72] While Steele suggests that this new silhouette "was not so much 'boyish' as *youthful*," the fact is that contemporaries often read it as the former.[73] In addition to eschewing the maternal form, the linear silhouette—"straight as a board in front, straight as a board in back"—also conformed to what was imagined to be the "normal" male body. Fashion magazines even referred to the new silhouette as "the masculine line [*die männliche Linie*]," and frequently wondered when this "Garçonne fashion" would become "feminized" (*verweiblicht*) again.[74] Most revealingly, women who subscribed to this new silhouette, donning the popular bob hairstyle, even referred to themselves as *Bubiköpfe*, or pageboys, underscoring the style's masculine connotations.[75] The *Bubikopf*'s message was clear: "Yes, [I] am a boy, am as independent as a boy, am not dependent on a man at all, [but] stand firmly on my female legs."[76] For many contemporaries, the new silhouette constituted the performance of female masculinity.

In order to be effective, however, the new silhouette also required a new body, a slender and boyish body. Although women cast aside their corsets, they soon reached for the girdle, which served to slim down their buttocks, hips, and thighs rather than cinch their waist.[77] The brassiere, too, de-emphasized rather than accentuated the breasts, contributing to the lengthening of the silhouette.[78] Other contouring devices soon flooded the market. The "Diva-Gummi-Fesselformer," for example, promised to "shape the thighs [to appear] slim."[79] Fashion models or mannequins also

FIGURE 2.5. By the 1920s, the "barrel" line increased in popularity, as seen in this fashion illustration of springtime streetwear from 1924. From "Die Strassen-Mode im Frühjahr," *Das Blatt der Hausfrau* 39, no. 9 (1924): 9. ANNO/ÖNB.

underwent a transformation: as the *Neues Wiener Journal* put it, if the "fashion model from the early 20th century" had "pleasant curves," the model from 1925 was, conversely, characterized by "slimness, thinness and angularity"—similar to Poiret's mannequins before the war.[80] Eventually, with the introduction of the helmet-like cloche hat in 1924, which was

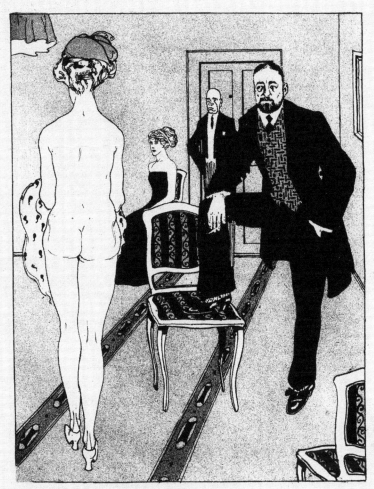

Wienerinnen bei Poiret.

Poiret: Non madame, fir so gut gebautes Frau kann ick nit maken Toilette!

FIGURE 2.6. Given French fashion designer Paul Poiret's penchant for the linear silhouette, some Viennese contemporaries believed his dresses to be unsuitable for Viennese women, whose bodies were imagined to be curvaceous and well-endowed. The apparent incongruence between Poiret's designs and Viennese women's bodies is satirized in this caricature from 1911. From "Wienerinnen bei Poiret," *Der Floh*, 19 November 1911, 5. ANNO/ÖNB.

worn low over the eyebrows and eyes, women were forced to walk with their heads cocked upward to see, thereby giving the impression that they were even taller and slimmer.

Already in 1911, contemporaries noted that Poiret's dresses were meant for a "very particular, slim, preferably tall figure."[81] Indeed, Poiret's fashion heralded what Steele terms a new female body ideal "with smaller breasts, slimmer hips, and long legs."[82] "Poiret creates his designs only for the slim, graceful woman," a newspaper article observed.[83] "The piquant, sylphinidine free spirit [*Rassige*] is his beauty ideal—all more developed and well-nourished women without a pronounced vamp-look [*Dämontypus*] are absolutely not his role models, and these ladies would not feel comfortable in the Poiret designs either!" Commentators seemed to agree that Vienna's plumper women were, "as a rule, far from the Poiret body ideal" and "whoever wants to wear his clothing must first go on a diet."[84] In a caricature depicting "Wienerinnen with Poiret," the French designer stands next to a nude woman, her back turned toward the viewers, and exclaims in broken German, "Non madame, for such strong built woman I cannot dress make!" (see fig. 2.6).[85] If the ideal Viennese woman was curvaceous, then for her to be able to wear a Poiret dress she would have to give up the very thing that made her Viennese in the first place: her curves.

And yet, only a few years later, with the outbreak of war, Viennese women would be forced to do just that.

On the Home Front: Emaciated, Elongated Bodies

Georg Wilhelm Pabst's 1925 film *Die freudlose Gasse* (*The Joyless Street*), based on Hugo Bettauer's serialized novel of the same title, is set in Vienna shortly after the First World War. The film opens with a scene on the fictional Melchiorgasse in the VIIth District, Neubau, as people, mostly women, are seen queuing in front of a butcher shop, falling over from starvation, and ultimately resorting to morally ambivalent behavior to satisfy their need to eat.[86] Indeed, Vienna experienced a mostly homegrown food crisis during and after the war, and it was common to see people queuing in front of market stalls and shops for many hours. While the import of food products to Vienna declined during the war, the population continued to grow, especially with the influx of refugees from the war-ravaged east.[87] Despite war rations, shortages were so acute that Viennese residents often left markets and shops empty-handed. Of the approximately 350,000 people waiting in 1,100 lines on a typical day in 1917, for example, about 47,000 did not get a loaf of bread.[88] Rations also declined over the course of the war: in 1916, a Viennese resident was allotted 17.1 grams

(153.9 calories) of lard per day, whereas, by the end of the war, the lard ration consisted of 5.7 grams (51.3 calories).[89] The people on the home front were starving; some were even dying of starvation.[90]

Maureen Healy argues that over the course of the war, Viennese women followed a trajectory from being willing helpers in the war effort to being soldiers and victims of war. From roughly 1914 to 1916, a spirit of optimism permeated the home front, even in the face of growing food shortages, as women sought to make sacrifices in the name of *Durchhalten* (holding out). By 1917, however, women felt that they were victims of a "starvation war," which they waged by "lining up" (*Anstellen*) for food or rioting, thereby participating in a new sphere of politics. Much of what motivated these practices was the embodied experience of hunger—an aspect of the war I explore in greater detail below.

✳

Building on Healy's groundbreaking work, the following section draws on *Stimmungsberichte*, police reports documenting the mood of the people and the conditions of everyday life during wartime and in the immediate postwar years, juxtaposes the reports with personal letters and diaries, and thereby writes the history of the home front from the perspective of the body—and the stomach. My historiographical intention is mostly additive: if Healy's book was an investigation of everyday life on the Viennese home front, this section adds to this history by considering, primarily, embodied experience. My goal is not to challenge or displace Healy's work, but simply to add some richness, texture, and fleshiness to it—to reframe it as an embodied history. Taking an embodied approach not only allows us, as embodied beings, to better appreciate the motivations and actions of past embodied actors; it also clarifies one of the central points of this book: how the changing city, in this case the war-torn city, remade the body and gendered embodiment. For as Vienna's women starved and their bodies changed, so too did their womanhood. Moreover, as I argue below, self-preservation meant that they increasingly came to identify the body with the "self."

Here again, we are confronted with the limitations of the archive and its epistemology. While *Stimmungsberichte* provide a window into everyday life on the home front, they are mostly opaque when it comes to embodied experience. What they do include is discussions of basic foodstuffs, the state of the markets and shops, and riot activity; occasionally, in passing, they also include direct quotations of comments made by hungry residents. It is these aspects of the archive that I focus on below. Additionally,

I draw on historical imagination, in conjunction with ego documents, to shift the perspective from those in positions of power writing the reports to the embodied subjects on the ground. I focus first on the embodied experience of hunger in people on the home front over the course of the war, and second on how that experience manifested itself in the appearance of the body. As the history of hunger pioneer Alice Weinreb points out, "though experienced as an internal sensation (gnawing in the belly, stomach ache, etc.), hunger also completely remakes the external appearance of the body. Indeed, judgements of the severity of an individual's level of hunger usually rely on changes in the appearance of the body rather than self-reported symptoms."[91] What this means is that "a starving body must look starving to actually be starving—'feeling' like you are starving is not enough. Importantly, there is a general consensus on the appearance of a starving body: skinniness, protruding bones, sunken eyes, etc."[92]

But what did hunger and starvation mean for the Viennese, specifically? In a city that Stefan Zweig described as "epicurean," how did its residents— "gourmets who appreciated good food and good wine, fresh and astringent beer, lavish desserts and tortes"—cope with scarcity?[93] How would the iconic Viennese Sweet Girl (*das süße Mädel*), known for her voracious appetite and sweet tooth, cope (on the Sweet Girl, see chapter 3)?[94] If the ideal Viennese woman was as round and soft as *Marillenknödel*, then what happened to the apricot dumpling once she lost her roundness and softness?[95] In short, if "we are what we eat" (*Der Mensch ist, was er ißt*), to quote Ludwig Feuerbach, then who were the Viennese without their food and drink—without their relaxed air, their *Gemütlichkeit*?

Already by the fall of 1914, bakeries and shops were running out of flour and bread, unable to keep pace with demand.[96] Women shared recipes for *Kriegsbrot* (war bread), which consisted of a mixture of potato, polenta, and rye flours; to make it more palatable, they slipped in a pat of butter and a pinch of sugar, even some pig fat.[97] By 1915, these additions would have been luxuries due to the high price of meat, fruit, and vegetables, as well as a shortage of flour, milk, and sugar.[98] Bread and flour were rationed starting in April of that year.[99] Newly published wartime cookbooks promised to help women make the most of their limited food supplies.[100] One cookbook, *Unsere Kriegskost* (*Our War Fare*), which was tested and approved by the k. u. k. Ministry of Interior, recommended that Viennese residents put aside two "meatless" days a week, reduce their intake of fats and dairy, and make use of different kinds of non-wheat flour, such as potato, rice, corn, oat, and tapioca flour.[101] Using this book, women prepared cabbage soup with oatmeal, yellow beet cake, noodles with potatoes, vegetable schnitzels, "war dumplings" (*Kriegsknödel*), and wheat-free pastries (*Mehlspeisen*) in their kitchens. They would stack pots on top of each other or place them inside a cooking box (*Kochkiste*) to save on fuel.[102] Unsurprisingly, food was often lukewarm and bland.

Gaining access to even the most basic foodstuffs became more difficult over the course of 1915. Some residents living in the XXIst District, Floridsdorf, hunted down stray dogs to eat; they disposed of their carcasses, including heads and limbs, on dark streets.[103] But even bourgeois women faced shortages and were overcome by hunger pangs.[104] Hunger was so acute that some even started contemplating suicide. "Do we and our kids have to starve or can we jump into the Danube?" one woman yelled.[105] But at least there were potatoes. Or so they thought. On the Yppenplatz in the working-class district of Ottakring, women arriving to the market after eight o'clock in the morning eyed the empty potato stalls, "cursing heavily." When a woman was arrested for creating disorder, about thirty other women shouted, "Lock us all up, at least we will get something to eat with our kids."[106]

By 1916, women could feel the "strong undernourishment" in their bodies on a regular basis.[107] Many no longer ate dinner at all and went to bed with their stomachs growling. They would wake up hungry, they would go to work hungry, and they would go to sleep hungry. In feeling this hunger, did they not become more aware of their own embodiment? When soldiers came home on leave, they often shortened their stay because they were better fed at the front and did not want to burden their families.[108] That men preferred to go to the frontlines of war—and risk death—to staying home suggests how dire the situation was. With growing food shortages, the home front was experiencing a war of its own: a starvation war.

Shortages were rarely predictable, nor were they identical in every district. In early 1916, flour was easier to come by in the XXIst District, Floridsdorf, so women from the XXth District, Brigittenau, traveled there for a sack of flour, which they had to haul back home on foot or by tram.[109] It was at this point that the rationing of sugar, milk, coffee, and lard was introduced, and working-class families began living on boiled potatoes and fat-free salted soups.[110] The diet of middle-class families was not much better, consisting of vegetables, coffee substitutes, and occasional wheat-free pastry.[111] In March 1916, the teacher Mathilde (Tilly) Hanzel-Hübner (née Hübner) noted in a letter to her husband, Ottokar, who was stationed on the Italian front, "now it's the 4th week without potatoes."[112] "There is such a fat scarcity," she wrote, "that people are ripping each other's clothes at the butcher's."[113]

Throughout Vienna, hundreds of women and children would stand on long lines that would wind around squares and down streets.[114] People queued, "pressed close together, there for hours," with the stench of unwashed clothing and bodies (due to a soap and clothing shortage) wafting through the crowds.[115] Some women at the Meiselmarkt in the XVth District, Rudolfsheim-Fünfhaus, collapsed from hunger.[116] Other women were "overcome by fainting spells."[117] Mothers exhausted from child care and wage work would wait in front of shops from early morning until noon; sometimes they would "search the district for groceries, often in vain."[118] Some women started queuing even earlier—at midnight; they even brought small stools to sit on.[119] People were so concerned with their survival that they "completely lost interest in the war, there is no trace of enthusiasm left."[120] Even police officers were feeling the effects of hunger, experiencing malnourishment, which sometimes resulted in lung catarrh, even neurasthenia.[121] Many Viennese women experienced similar symptoms, including fatigue, dryness of hair and skin, weight loss, violent irritability, and delirium.[122] Their bodies felt heavy, their muscles hurt, they felt angry and paranoid, they could only think and feel with their stomachs.

Hunger-induced pain, panic, and desperation motivated some women to behave in ways they would never have countenanced in peacetime, so that, as Kathleen Canning notes, "bodily inscription" by the state through food shortages inspired "reinscriptive, embodying responses of citizens and soldiers—through revolution, political violence, and social protest."[123] In May 1916, food riots spread throughout various districts in the city. People yelled, "we are hungry, we have to starve with our children, give us something to eat, down with the profiteers, we want peace."[124] Groups of women and children marched to the Rathaus (city hall), young boys threw rocks at shop windows, and crowds of people upended and plundered food wagons.[125] Another string of riots occurred in September 1916. A gathering of people "scream[ed] and yell[ed]" in front of the Hafner flour company until the police arrived, forcing the crowd to disperse among the viaducts. Meanwhile, on Laxenburgerstrasse, a thirteen-year-old girl holding a white handkerchief in the air urged some six hundred people waiting for potatoes on Eugenplatz to join her in protest. On another day, some five hundred women walked from the XVIth District, Ottakring, to the Rathaus, waving handkerchiefs in a gesture of desperation. Some women were pregnant and in the company of "small children, extremely worn out and undernourished." One woman with two children shouted that she only had one potato left: how was she and her family to survive?[126] In November, shortly after the death of Emperor Franz Joseph, a woman in the XIth District, Simmering, wanted to abandon her eight-month-old on the street because she did not have any way of feeding the child.[127]

By 1917, people no longer just *felt* ravaged by hunger—they looked it, too. Writing to her husband in 1917, Tilly Hanzel-Hübner observed that, "since yesterday, I started to wash my entire body with lukewarm water every morning. I see that I am skinny [*mager*]." She continued, "When I saw Božena yesterday, I found that she lost a lot of weight, but what most shocked me was her tremendous nervousness."[128] Ration cards were introduced for marmalade and for that most critical of foodstuffs, potatoes. Diets relied heavily on turnips: turnip soup, turnip goulash, turnip bread, turnip hash, even turnip pudding.[129] Shrunken women held their emaciated babies in the air and yelled, "one should look at them, they are half starved already."[130] Others pleaded, "don't let us slowly starve, better to shoot us down or lock us up, patience is at its end."[131] Hungry, emaciated women "walked through the market loudly and howled."[132] If, as Elaine Scarry observes, "there is no language for pain," then resorting to non-verbal, guttural sounds—shrieks, howls, and screams—was the only way women could communicate the gnawing aches of hunger.[133] There were "frenzied gatherings" of people queuing for butter, lard, offal, so-called "volk's beef" or "welfare meat" (a mixture of animal bones, skin scraps, and small pieces of meat), sauerkraut, spinach, and dehydrated vegetables.[134] As a newspaper article put it: "Ever more does it move closer to the body [*immer näher rückt es uns an den Leib*], the concern for our daily bread is always growing, the acquisition of necessary foodstuffs is always becoming more difficult, especially for the proletariat."[135] The use of the idiom *ans Leib rücken*, which literally means to "move closer to the body," equated the incessant struggle to acquire food with the embodied experience of hunger.

In 1918, meat rations were introduced.[136] Anna Mahler, Alma Mahler-Werfel's daughter with Gustav Mahler, recalled that "our cook—her name was Agnes—used to prepare a kind of *ersatz* meat for us, a concoction of mushrooms and tree bark, with polenta and potatoes on the side."[137] Other women continued to hunt down stray dogs or consume horse meat.[138] At this point, no residents were allotted dairy products anymore except for the "dairy privileged," such as nursing mothers. "One lives off black noodles [noodles made from coarsely ground wheat-free flour], potatoes, wheat that one grinds in dumpling form, everything prepared with the smallest amount of fat," Rosa Mayreder wrote in her diary in 1918. Mayreder also lost a considerable amount of weight during the war, noting that "I have lost 19 kilos [approx. 41 pounds] in two years."[139] Severe shortages and acute hunger prompted another series of food riots, along with workers' strikes in June 1918. Groups of people overturned bread carts, threw rocks at police officers, hijacked streetcars, and broke into stores to plunder wares.[140] On Neulerchenfelderstrasse, a thousand people tried to hijack a streetcar by shattering its glass windows with rocks and sticks.[141] In the XXth District, about one hundred women raided an Anker bread-factory wagon, violently pelting its driver with stones. Meanwhile in the XVth District, a few women stole ten loaves of bread from a bread wagon parked in front of a grocery store on Hütteldorferstrasse 31.

The feeling of hunger persisted, and bodies continued to wither away. A special correspondent of *The Times* on 4 November described the situation in Vienna in this manner: "There is no trace left of Vienna's famous cheerfulness and of its spirit. It is a mystery to me that the population is even still alive. They are truly starving. You only see people with emaciated, elongated faces."[142] While warfront soldiers returned with mutilated bodies, the bodies of the home front were marked by severe weight loss, protruding bones, sunken eyes and cheeks. According to the educational film *Das Kinderelend in Wien, 1919 (The Misery of Children in Vienna, 1919)*, children were becoming thinner and shorter.[143] The film compared school children in a city elementary school in 1914 to those from 1919 and found that a typical eleven-year-old girl in 1914 weighed 38 kilograms (ca. 84 pounds) and was 132 centimeters tall, whereas the typical eleven-year-old girl in 1919 weighed 23 kilograms (ca. 51 pounds) and was 122 centimeters tall. The food crisis continued even into the interwar period. In November 1919, twenty-one-year-old Christine (Christl) Wastl, the eldest daughter of a Viennese bourgeois *Beamten* family, wrote to her sister, Franziska (Franzi), "For us, it's not going well with food, nor with heat and clothing, which are also limited. . . ."[144]

✳

Writing the history of the home front through the experience of the body has enabled us to attend to the embodied experience of hunger and starvation on the one hand, and to their physical effects on the other. In turn, historical imagination enables us to see how a city ravaged by war shaped the bodies of its residents—specifically, the gendered bodies of its women—in two ways. First, with the sensation of hunger ever present, people on the home front came to experience their bodies (and all the physical hardships associated with starvation) on a permanent basis, thereby coming to see themselves as more embodied and, as a result, rooting their sense of "self" in the omnipresent body. There was, in a word, no escape from the body. Second, their hungering and fragile bodies took on a more elongated and linear shape that deviated from the curvaceous feminine ideal of the fin de siècle. If this new shape was associated with "masculinity" before the war, it took on a new meaning during and after the war. The shape became an expression of a *modern* new womanhood, indicating its greater prevalence and popularity.

Slim and Trim: Modern Bodies in the Interwar Period

In one scene in *Die freudlose Gasse*, the heroine Grete Rumfort, played by Greta Garbo, stands on a queue at the butcher's shop, wearily placing her head against a stone building while she shuts her eyes to get some rest. After eating only vegetable stew for days—which her younger sister, Marianne, complains about in the previous scene—Grete is visibly hungry and fatigued, carrying her body with great discomfort and effort. Even in 1925, when the film was released, this scene must have resonated with many Viennese audiences who had lived through the war. According to one reviewer, the film did not shy away from depicting bleak realities and thereby touched a nerve, reminding audiences of "those days, shortly after the end of war and the outbreak of peace, when middle-class mothers often lacked milk for their little ones while well-nourished cocottes ate *Scheidelkrapfen* (donuts) with whipped cream, when educated men stood in line for bread," and when "so many pre-war well-situated citizens [were turned] into beggars."[145]

But audiences would also have noticed something else: Garbo's slim and trim physique. In addition to wearing 1920s-style clothing—the ubiquitous short tubular dress—she is noticeably slender, her slim arms and small breasts revealed in a pivotal scene toward the end of the film when she considers performing in a racy dress at a nightclub (see fig. 2.7). The mysterious film star was known to be a long-distance runner, who often walked for hours and miles at a time "without a sign of tiring."[146] Her body was far from curved and voluptuous; it was lean and boyish.

Garbo's allure suggests that despite the starvation and resulting weight loss endured so painfully during the First World War, many women still aspired to maintain a slim silhouette after the war. Rather than being viewed exclusively as an expression of subversive female masculinity, this new shape, reinforced by ordinary women and further popularized by the beauty industry, came to be celebrated as a new feminine ideal—a new womanhood. Indeed, by the early to mid-1920s, corpulence was no longer deemed beautiful; rather, it was "a lurking enemy that threatens every woman."[147] An article in a weekly identified 1923 as the start of the cult of slimness, perhaps because the date marked the end of wartime food shortages: "the entire being and striving of ladies . . . is focused on the very slim, narrow, straight line." Hence, "a plump face, voluptuous breasts, a solid tummy,

FIGURE 2.7. Greta Rumfort (played by Greta Garbo) reveals her 1920s linear silhou-
ette, as well as her slim and trim physique, in this pivotal scene from Georg Wilhelm
Pabst's *Die freudlose Gasse* (1925). Note the emotionally expressive look on Garbo's
face, the subject of chapter 3. From *Die freudlose Gasse*, dir. Georg Wilhelm Pabst
(Berlin: Sofar-Film-Produktion, 1925; Munich: Filmmuseum München, 2020). DVD.
Frame capture taken by author.

too wide hips with respectable girth . . . that is the nightmare, equally feared
by the teenage girl [*Backfisch*] as well as the grandmother. . . ."[148] Moreover,
corpulence was, according to a physician, Anne Bernfeld, "unmodern."[149]
For the modern—that is to say, new—woman, achieving and maintaining
a "slim line" was central to her very identity. Through slimness, she could
model the modernity that she represented and embraced. As Ageeth Sluis
puts it, the slim "Deco body" served as "a prime mnemonic device in the
visualization of the modern girl . . . form[ing] the 'bedrock' of her visibility,
identity, and ability to travel the globe."[150] Thus, even the Viennese woman
had to give up her *Marillenknödel*-like curves to be modern; she had to
be slim, her body a "masculine, straight line" that she endowed with her
"eternal feminine" beauty.[151]

   As a result, "all curves are painstakingly monitored [*überwacht*]."[152]
The word *überwachen* is revealing because it gestures toward the modern, self-disciplinary aspect of maintaining a slim silhouette. "Even the

thinnest [woman] is not safe from [the threat of corpulence] and must [take preventive measures]."[153] In fact, it was precisely because slimness required discipline that it was considered more masculine. As Annelie Ramsbrock notes, "since producing a slender figure usually demanded of women a high degree of discipline and motivation, its attainment betokened rational behavior and mental firmness. Corpulence, by contrast, was thought to reveal insufficient rationality and self-control."[154] Insofar as reason has historically been gendered as masculine, the rational disciplining of the body can thus be understood as a masculine act.

Dieting was perhaps the most straightforward disciplinary act to achieve weight loss. Given the mass starvation on the home front during the First World War, many physicians advised women to pursue "healthier" forms of weight loss. "Starvation! That it helps, we learned during the war, but [we] also experienced the terrible results of undernourishment."[155] Thus, a consumer market emerged devoted to "healthy" diets, dietary programs, and weight loss remedies. Experts recommended cutting back on "desserts, baked goods, sweets, fatty meals and so on," and suggested consuming only boiled fruits and vegetables (with only a dollop of melted butter and breadcrumbs), milk diets, or meals consisting of raw carrots.[156] One doctor prescribed "only tea with dry Zwieback, lean, juice-free and fat-free meat, and a bit of boiled vegetables."[157] A number of sanatoria offered weight loss by means of monitored dieting programs (*Abmagerungskuren*) that spanned several weeks.[158] Waldheim's apothecary in the Ist District sold "diet tea" (*Entfettungstee*) that promised a "slim, graceful figure" "without changing of lifestyle."[159] Even so, some women undertook "deadly" diets despite warnings from experts.[160] As the social-democratic-leaning women's newspaper *Die Unzufriedene* (*The Dissatisfied Woman*) pointed out in 1926, the irony was that, "despite there being enough food, shop windows full of the most delightful things that are just waiting to be bought and eaten," women were still starving.[161]

Weight-loss programs also encouraged disciplined body work over a sustained period. This included regular body massages with devices such as the "Diagonal-Doppelroller," which promised to increase blood circulation and reduce fat. Sold at M. E. Mayer's store in the Ist District, the product was promoted in an advertisement featuring three women standing over the logo in high heels and short shorts attentively massaging their thighs, stomach, and buttocks. Resembling a rolling pin, the double roller was particularly easy to use for women who had much experience rolling dough and making cookies in their kitchens. Not only did the product establish a discursive link between cooking and cosmetics; women's skin

FIGURE 2.8. By the interwar period, Viennese women were encouraged to maintain a slim and trim line by engaging in regular physical exercise. From "Fünf Minuten täglich! Gymnastische Übungen zur Erhaltung der Schlankheit," *Das Blatt der Hausfrau* 36, no. 33/34 (August 1921): 3. ANNO/ÖNB.

seemed to become an extension of cookie dough: with enough massaging, the skin could be rolled into something firm, compact, and contained.

If softness was related to the curvaceous body, then firmness corresponded to the "slim line." Hence, gymnastics and physical exercise—both part and parcel of what Erik N. Jensen terms the "somatic revolution"—were touted for having both slimming and firming effects (see fig. 2.8).[162] Through vigorous discipline and athleticism, one could achieve "a leaner, more muscular body composed not of fat but of 'firm healthy flesh.'"[163] Women—even the "most troubled housewife"—were encouraged to spare five minutes per day for gymnastics to maintain "the slim line," including squats, arm circles, planks, and other dynamic, strength-building exercises.[164] According to one female physician, Dr. Zenthner, droopy breasts and hanging bellies in a woman were the result of sitting "crouched over books, needlework, over the drawing board or typewriter, over the piano or the ledger," and could only be overcome with movement.[165] Zenthner thus developed sixteen barre exercises whose purpose was to strengthen and firm the arms, back, breasts, stomach, and legs. After a gymnastics session, she advised women to take showers, get a rubdown with body gel to make the skin firmer and "elastic," and then take a nap.

Exercise was not limited to bourgeois and upper-class women. In Red Vienna, the Social Democratic Workers' Party (SDAP) celebrated this new athletic woman whose "physical appearance was youthful, with a slender-garçon figure [made] supple by sports."[166] The goal, at least in theory, was "easy comradeship" between modern woman and modern man, something that their physical similarities—"both of them tall and slim, both beardless and short-haired"—implied.[167] By 1925, there were around 1,050 sports clubs in Austria, with approximately 80,000 members regularly engaging in gymnastics, fencing, handball, hockey, track and field athletics, and bicycling.[168] Women were especially encouraged to join; in 1925, for example, the Austrian National Association of Body Sports (*Österreichischer Hauptverband für Körpersport*) organized a women's sports festival in which 600 women participated and performed various sporting exercises. The Austrian writer Vicki Baum observed that "muscles are desired on us, [whereas] flab is pityingly laughed at."[169]

Of course, not all women in Vienna subscribed to these regimens, and even if they did, not all of them lost weight. Furthermore, even if they lost weight, their bodies may not have conformed completely to the "slim line"—which was probably more of an elusive beauty ideal than a reality. Similarly, even women wearing the tubular 1920s dress may not have looked slender despite its "slimming" silhouette: because the shape was dependent on the width of one's hips, women with naturally wide hips would have appeared more circular than linear. Nevertheless, given both the pressure and the pleasure many women derived from the consumer-focused fashion and beauty industries—especially those fantasizing about becoming modern women—it is certainly the case that they worked hard to stay slim and trim.

According to Sandra Lee Bartky, the discourse that regulates women's silhouette and form is part of the "fashion beauty complex," an internalized panopticon that produces and maintains the docility of women's bodies.[170] Seen in this light, interwar Vienna's slimness obsession could be interpreted as reflecting this fashion beauty complex, with women engaging in new disciplinary practices—the *überwachen* of the body—ranging from diet to body work to athletics. The shift from the hourglass to the linear figure was, thus, not incontrovertibly liberating; rather, it involved a shift in disciplinary practices.

But why would women want to engage in these practices after the horrors they experienced during the war? While the false consciousness suggested by Bartky is one possible answer, another, arguably more compelling answer looks to women's agency, and specifically to the decision to maintain and care for their bodies. By the mid-1920s, wrote the *Illustriertes Familienblatt* (*The Illustrated Family Paper*), "today more than ever, the maintenance and care of the body occupies the thoughts of [most] people."[171] Another article in that same source insisted that, for modern women in particular, "physical and spiritual health have become a lot more important than for women during the prewar period."[172] As both texts suggest, physical and spiritual health was not just a discourse imposed on women and their bodies, but an active choice they made and practiced. It was precisely because the war years "fatigued the body" and affected the nerves that exercise and other body-shaping practices were seen by women as a means to *revitalize* their bodies after the war—bodies that were increasingly viewed not as separate, but as part and parcel of themselves. "The goal," according to the *Hauptverband für Körpersport*, was to cultivate "the body as a cultural element [*Kulturfaktor*] of high value."[173]

By underscoring women's active choices, the idea of maintenance and care adds nuance to the fashion beauty complex. In contrast to self-discipline, which evokes aggressive asceticism and body mastery, maintenance and care connotes careful attention to and protection of the body. Maintenance and care also appeared during the war years, when women had to find ways to feed themselves despite tremendous food shortages. Even with the gnawing feeling of hunger, the weakness resulting from starvation, and the emaciation it produced, women did their best to stay alive, and to maintain and care for their living and breathing bodies as well as those of their dependents. And they did so consciously. Instead of letting the body fall apart—become fragmented—they cared for it until the formerly fragmented pieces were put back together.

Conclusion: Gisela Piowati's Body

Let us return to Gisela Piowati's arrest in August 1932 and, by drawing on historical imagination, attempt to provide one possible scenario of what may have led to her misgendering. Although a lot of women started aspiring toward the linear silhouette in the 1930s, the shape was still controversial enough to generate anxiety and even, in the case of Piowati, arrest.

One summer evening, forty-nine-year-old Gisela Piowati was dressing in her apartment on the narrow Mühlgasse in the IVth District, Wieden.

She was quite possibly getting ready to sing at the local cabaret, coffee-house, or perhaps the *Tschecherl* (tavern) down the street. Reverently, she pulled out of her wardrobe her most elegant dress, a long red number in a crêpe marocain.[174] Even though she did not have the means to buy the newest styles, we can assume that, as a performer, she wanted to stay fashionable and had reworked one of her old twenties dresses to make this one: she gave this dress a more pronounced waistline, widened the skirt, and attached little billowy sleeves. In the early 1930s, fashion had undergone yet another transformation, when designers such as Elsa Schia-parelli reintroduced the waistline and the bust, giving the silhouette a more "feminine" appearance. This dress did just that. It cut a nice figure, Piowati thought.

She ran her hands through the perfumed fabric, reveling in its heavy texture, and pulled the dress over her long, slender body. As a performer, she was especially self-conscious of her build, and she worked hard to keep herself slim and trim. She had learned to maintain and care for her body during wartime; she had been in her early thirties back then, always hungry, always finding ways to make the most of potatoes and turnips. She still took care of herself, but in different ways: she did calisthenics and enjoyed swimming at the *Gänsehäufel*. Looking at herself in the mirror, Piowati applied makeup, something she started doing after the war when it was no longer considered déclassé. And when she looked up, she was lost in fantasy: she saw herself next to the piano on the stage, looking like a youthful and modern *Bubikopf* despite her middle age—perhaps like Louise Brooks in *Pandora's Box* (1929), whom she carefully emulated (on the emulation of actors, see chapter 3).[175]

She wrapped herself in fur—it was a cool evening, after all—and left her apartment. Suddenly, she was stopped by a police officer. He accused her of being a sex worker, a cross-dresser, and—of all things! Piowati thought—a man.

Standing in the middle of the street and wondering why the police officer had stopped her, Piowati realized how awkwardly her dress fit her long, slim body. She had sewed it herself, and she was not the best seamstress. Moreover, the dress was the newest style—it was feminine, almost too feminine with its two decorative roses on the neckline—and seemed, according to contemporary logic, incongruent with her linear, "masculine"-seeming build. The dress and the fur did not drape over this body; they hung on it. Was that why she had been arrested? Because she had a body that, in 1932, could be mistaken for a man's?[176] Anton Erasim, the police officer who thought he was doing his job by apprehending a thin middle-aged man in frilly women's clothing, would probably have answered with an emphatic *Jawohl*.

＊

In this chapter, I identified the linear silhouette as an embodied expression of new womanhood. As the "masculine line," this new shape deviated from the feminine hourglass ideal, thereby constituting a form of gender subversion and female masculinity. With time, however, as more women's bodies came to conform to this shape, the "masculine line" came to be redefined by its acolytes as the "slim line" and equated with an explicitly *modern* new womanhood. Cultivating this slim line was not necessarily only a form of ascetic self-discipline; it could also be a practice in maintenance and care. This chapter therefore revealed a key point of the book: namely, that the body, including its very morphology, is hardly passive or ahistorical. Rather, it holds great transformative power—for it was because of the body's new shapes that the new woman was, quite literally, formed.

This chapter further explained these new shapes as emerging in tandem with the globalizing and modernizing city, one in which Parisian-Viennese fashion trends and beauty culture came to espouse slimness, on the one hand, and the First World War subjected Viennese residents to starvation, on the other. It was within this space that new womanhood took shape and, as we will explore in chapter 3, expression. Indeed, as we will see in chapter 3, Piowati and women like her did not just aspire toward the slim and trim physique of actors such as Greta Garbo and Louise Brooks—they also aspired toward their emotions.

* 3 *

New Expressions

EMOTION, THE "SELF," AND
THE (KINO)THEATER

On 20 April 1920, the twenty-three-year-old Jewish-Austrian actor Elisabeth Bergner (née Elisabeth Ettel in Drohobycz, Galicia) checked herself
into the Lower Austrian Provincial Institution for the Care and Cure of the
Mentally Ill and for Nervous Disorders "Am Steinhof."[1] For several weeks,
the delicate, brown-eyed brunette had been suffering from nervousness,
insomnia, and malaise (*Verstimmung*) that often led to crying fits, as well
as occasional kleptomania. She cited the hostile environment at the Neue
Wiener Bühne theater as being responsible for her emotional condition.
Bergner decided to stay at the asylum for over a month, where she kept to
herself, wept, and took solitary walks through the extensive gardens and
among the stucco pavilion-villas adorned with secessionist ornamental
bands (see fig. 3.1).[2] In a society that held feminine emotional restraint
in high esteem, Bergner's emotional expressiveness was nothing short of
radical.

Opened in 1907, Steinhof was the largest psychiatric hospital on the
Continent at the time, housing approximately five hundred staff members
and 2,500 patients. Situated in proximity to the Vienna Woods and overlooking the city, the "white city" consisted of sixty buildings and grounds
built in Otto Wagner's new modernist architectural style, which was supposed to reflect the institution's cutting-edge approach to psychiatry.[3]
"The times of cold showers, of chains, of barbaric punishments are past,"
announced a government pamphlet, and indeed, Steinhof's pavilions
were clean and well ventilated, its grounds were unfenced, and the sanatorium's spa (*Kurhaus*) boasted facilities for innovative new treatments,
including warm water therapy, electrotherapy, massage, and sun and air
cures, among others.[4] Whereas Steinhof's asylum was state-funded and
intended for those living with chronic mental illness, its sanatorium was
reserved for paying patients experiencing occasional bouts of nervousness. Sanatorium patients such as Bergner could freely check in and out

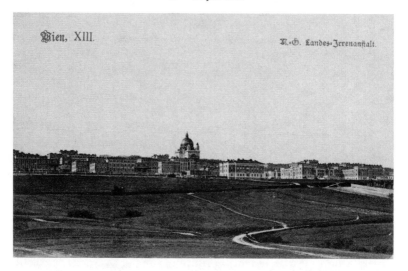

Wien, XIII.   K.-Ö. Landes-Irrenanstalt.

FIGURE 3.1. A postcard of the Lower Austrian Provincial Institution for the Care and Cure of the Mentally Ill and for Nervous Disorders "am Steinhof" from around 1907–1908. From "14. Steinhof—N.-Ö. Landes-Irrenanstalt," postcard (Vienna: Verlag Josef Popper, 1907–1908). Wien Museum Inv.-Nr. 58891/1110, CC0.

and had "complete freedom of movement both within and outside the institution—depending on the doctor's prescription."[5] As Leslie Topp has observed, the sanatorium's explicit orientation toward nervous disease "embodied an attempt to fight the marginalization of the asylum" and cultivate a sense of "permeability, or integration with the outside world."[6]

In fact, nervousness came to be seen as a more socially acceptable form of disorder, and the number of nerve patients and of institutions dealing with nervous illness increased significantly in central Europe around the fin de siècle. Attributed to the overstimulation and fatigue of modern urban life, nervousness—commonly referred to as neurasthenia—was initially constructed as an "invisible, nonlocalizable yet genuinely somatic, illness of the nerves."[7] With its transformation into a mass phenomenon in the 1890s, however, it underwent what Andreas Killen refers to as its psychologization: instead of externally caused by a somatic condition, neurasthenia came to be seen as grounded "more strongly within the self... as an inborn or acquired pathology, one merely *triggered* by external forces."[8] In both cases, however, "neurasthenia was defined by its modernity," so that its cure relied on the patient's removal from modern life—not just physically, but also socially.[9] Citing Thomas Mann's novel *The Magic Mountain*, Killen observes that "being an invalid had its advantages: it meant 'relief from the burden of respectable life,'" as well as "the ambiguous promise of a descent into the body in search of knowledge, new stimuli, pleasures, and refinements."[10] Carroll Smith-Rosenberg makes a similar argument about hysteria, the feminized term for nervousness, suggesting that it functioned for many Victorian middle-class women as a form of resistance or dissent because a woman showing hysteric symptoms, ranging from fits to headaches to depression to loss of hearing, would be relieved of her family and community duties.[11] It was, in other words, a way to subvert the conventions of Victorian middle-class womanhood.

For Bergner, being an invalid also had its advantages. Before coming to Steinhof, she had undergone psychoanalysis with the eminent physician Alfred Adler, a former student of Sigmund Freud. It was during these sessions that Bergner cited kleptomania as an unconscious tactic of resistance, an assertion of agency. Engaging in kleptomania was, in short, a desperate attempt to break her contract with the Neue Wiener Bühne, where she was subjected to relentless harassment by the theater director.[12] Although illness did not release her from her contract, it did give Bergner the impetus to check herself in at Steinhof as a *Nervenkranke*.

In the end, Bergner's nervous disorder was not just a tactic to get out of a contract; it was, I argue, a way to express her emotions in a socially sanctioned and legible way—to express her "self." For the Viennese bourgeoisie, convention dictated that women refrain from expressing their emotions. Thus, while the harassment Bergner endured at the Neue Wiener Bühne most likely filled her with rage and misery, convention dictated that, as a woman, she should refrain from expressing these emotions physically and publicly. Only as a *Nervenkranke* could she indulge in the crying fits and emotional "outbursts" that she so wished to express. Only then could she find relief and descend into her body in search of knowledge, stimuli, pleasures, refinements, and, significantly, feelings. And in the process, she would subvert and reinvent the conventions of normative Viennese womanhood.

※

This chapter identifies the embodied expression of emotion—that is, what contemporaries described as the process of translating "inner" feelings of the "self" into "outer" nonverbal expressions on the body and face—as a practice of new womanhood. It characterizes hysteria as one of several emotional body languages Viennese women learned to draw on to assert them*selves*. But where did they learn these body languages in the first place? As this chapter makes clear, these new expressions became popular within the context of the modern Viennese theater: the first section considers the fin-de-siècle modernist stage, while the second looks to the *Kinotheater* (movie theater). After all, even Bergner blamed the Neue Wiener Bühne theater as the reason for her hysteria. And later, once she became a successful silent-film actor known for her roles as female characters suffering from hysteria, her private emotional outbursts, which had been previously reserved for Steinhof, were made public. Viennese women from the working classes and the bourgeoisie, including the introduction's Hedwig Patzl, chapter 1's Magdalene W., and chapter 2's Gisela Piowati, would sit in theaters and *Kinotheaters* across the city, actively watching and feeling the spectacle of emotions. In this new urban space, women could find relief from bourgeois respectability and descend into their own bodies. Theater and film presented spectators with an emotional body language that went against the conventions and codes of feminine emotional behavior. This chapter therefore points to a central theme in the book: that the modern city developed in tandem with new embodied possibilities, including new gender expressions.

Toward a History of Emotional Expression

The Viennese socialite and composer Alma Mahler-Werfel (née Schindler) "hate[d] all outward show of sentiment."[13] And on All Souls' Day in 1900, when she accompanied her mother to the Central Cemetery to visit her father's grave, she "couldn't bring [her]self to stimulate emotion [*mich gewaltsam in ein Gefühl hinein puffen*]." According to William M. Reddy, although emotion is a biologically grounded universal experience, emotional expression—or the "outward show of sentiment"—varies individually and culturally.[14] That is to say, *whether* we express a feeling and *how* we express it—what emotional vocabulary and gestures we draw on—are contingent on the structures of power and social norms within a historical time and space, so that even our most "authentic" emotional expressions must be understood as historically situated. In fact, according to this logic, authenticity does not exist; as Reddy insists, "virtually all social roles are associated with emotional norms, and every human being constantly engages in a kind of emotional self-shaping."[15] Furthermore, emotional expression is contingent on what Barbara Rosenwein has termed "emotional communities," social communities such as families, milieus, and institutions that govern systems of feelings, including "the modes of emotional expression that they expect, encourage, tolerate, and deplore."[16] Thus, even within a historical time and space, there is a varied landscape of feeling.

A foundational text in the history of emotions canon, the German sociologist Norbert Elias's *The Civilizing Process*, explained civilization and modernity in terms of emotional restraint and control.[17] Elias's relevance to the fin-de-siècle culture of the Viennese bourgeoisie is self-evident, as emotional self-control—or the severing of emotional experience from expression—was deemed by that culture to be absolutely central to everyday life and to the upbringing that prepared people for it. Thus, a fundamental aspect of a lady's *Erziehung* (upbringing) involved the separation of an "internal" or "private" emotional life from the dispassionate "outside" and "public" world of interaction. No matter what a woman may have experienced internally, she had to refrain from showing it on her face or body.

The Viennese bourgeoisie maintained a Cartesian worldview, in which the "inner" rational mind—and, by extension, the soul—was considered separate from and superior to the "external" body, which was base and in need of manipulation.[18] "Why has God locked our spirit, the soul, in this worthless prison?" Tilly Hanzel-Hübner asked in 1902.[19] For her, the body was a burden that she had to "haul" through life. By contrast, consciousness was the soul, "something that differs from the body [*etwas vom körperlichen Verschiedenes*]." Insofar as it involved the translation, or transgression, of the interior feelings of the soul into bodily expression, the physical or nonverbal expression of emotion undermined this dualist logic.

Malvine von Steinau's etiquette book, *Der gute Ton für Damen* (*Good Tone for Ladies*), placed particular emphasis on self-control and restraint and devoted an entire section to "Facial Expression and Gaze," which were to remain cool and dispassionate. A proper *Dame* avoided grand emotions and expressions and yet still managed to avoid coming off as affected and contrived. She had to have her body, the vehicle through which she could express her emotions, "under her control [*Herrschaft*]" and "in her power [*Gewalt*]." Even if she experienced deep emotion, a *Dame* was "not allowed to make expressive folds on the forehead or furrow eyebrows over the nose. . . . [She was] not allowed to press the lips together, especially one over the other. . . ."[20] According to Edward Ross Dickinson, a German etiquette book from the same period similarly instructed women to "avoid strong facial expressions, grimacing, squinting, and the like; and 'one should master one's glance, as one masters one's passion.' Frowning, nervous ticks, looking around too often, or staring were 'evil habits.' 'Sad thoughts' should be 'mastered' as well, so that one did not present a 'dark, ill-humored aspect.' . . . For men 'a robust, hearty laugh is permissible'—but not for women."[21] Ideally, a woman's face was like a "mask . . . behind which thoughts worthy of concealment and flickers of wicked emotion hide."[22]

This dualism began to change during the fin de siècle, which witnessed the emergence of a new emotional community that understood the embodied expression of emotion as a form of "self"-expression and a vital aspect of new womanhood. This chapter partakes of the trend in the history of emotions that challenges Elias's thesis, calling into question both his teleological approach to modernity and his conception of civilization.[23] It argues that despite the Viennese bourgeoisie's valorization of emotional restraint, by the fin de siècle women increasingly found ways to subvert it. The first section of this chapter, "Hysteria and *Temperament* at the Theater," considers two such ways. The first, as Bergner illustrates, was through the idiom of hysteria—nervousness, kleptomania, and madness. With the consolidation of psychiatry as a profession, a visual iconography of hysteria spread across the continent that was reproduced as a body language on the stage. Ultimately, women's exposure to that iconography shaped their experience and expression of emotionality.

The second way Viennese women subverted the gendered conventions of emotionality was through the idiom of *Temperament*. In the early fin de siècle, Temperament belonged to a mythical Viennese folk figure, the Sweet Girl, who existed in the plays of Arthur Schnitzler and the operettas of Oscar Straus. Referring to liveliness and exuberance, Temperament was conveyed through music and dance and in particular through the revolutionary Viennese waltz: it was dizzying, infectious, life-affirming. Modern dance reimagined the waltz in an even more expressive way, producing a body language of Temperament consisting of clearly defined mimetic actions, gestures, and movements. The early women's movement celebrated Temperament; it sought to turn this mythical quality into something universal for all Viennese new women.

The first section concludes by tracing the origins of both body languages—of hysteria and Temperament—to the modern Viennese theater, and specifically to its use of modern dance. It was in the early fin de siècle that Viennese modernists became particularly skeptical of language; as a result, they turned to extralinguistic modes of expression to convey emotion. With its insistence on bypassing the verbal altogether, modern dance came to be viewed as a vehicle particularly well suited to the physical expression of emotion and, by extension, the "self." Even further, the kinetic and affectual qualities of modern dance made it particularly captivating to watch, offering a descent into the body, so that emotions were transferred from the performer/dancer to the audience.

With the emergence of silent film, many modern dancers became film actors. And indeed, film became the natural successor to modern dance. The second section, "Emotional Expression at the *Kinotheater*," thus examines the emotionally charged body language of silent-film acting and the "intoxicating" effect it had on its women spectators. But film, this chapter explains, also ushered in two major changes. First, it exposed women to an embodied emotional vocabulary that went far beyond hysteria and Temperament, including a whole range of emotions. Second, film was part of an elaborate industry that was keen on promoting its film stars, building a fan base, and establishing a celebrity culture that encouraged aspiration and, crucially, emulation. This chapter concludes by considering how this culture inspired audience members, especially women, to emulate actors *and* their emotionality, leading to the emergence of a new emotional community of new women.

Susan A. Glenn argues that women theater actors and comics may be regarded as the very first "new" women; it was through their dynamic, emotive, and spectacular performances that they "demonstrated and encouraged new ways of acting female" and "acting out."[24] In fact, actors "helped make unorthodox female behavior more attractive and enjoyable than the nineteenth-century political radicals had been able to do and, as a consequence, helped give new views of women wider acceptance."[25] This chapter extends Glenn's argument to other performers, including modern dancers and film actors, to suggest that their emotionally expressive body language can be read as a challenge to bourgeois respectability and a performance of new womanhood. The women watching these performances, feeling and living through them and later even emulating them, would be the new women of Vienna.

In the following pages, we will travel back in time to the prewar period, when these new emotional body languages were beginning to emerge in defiance of bourgeois conventions of gendered emotionality. But before we can understand these languages, we must consider the conventions in greater detail.

Hysteria and Temperament *at the Theater*

PRIVATE EMOTION AT THE FIN DE SIÈCLE AND TILLY HÜBNER'S DIARIES

For many bourgeois women at the fin de siècle, a carefully cultivated and restrained outer physicality was key to being ladylike. The resulting dualism separated the world of public interaction from the inner and private world of emotion. The diary functioned as a manifestation of this inner world and was therefore an important part of a bourgeois woman's everyday life. (For this reason, many women's diaries were adorned with functioning locks and keys that further emphasized the separation between public and private selves.) The diaries of Tilly Hanzel-Hübner, which I examine in greater detail below, provide us with a window onto this inner world.

Born into a middle-class Viennese family in 1884, Hanzel-Hübner devoted her life to education and the Austrian women's movement until her death in 1970.[26] Since Hanzel-Hübner was keenly attuned to the emotional community in which she was raised, her diaries provide insight into the fin-de-siècle Viennese bourgeoisie's oftentimes contradictory systems of feeling and modes of expression.[27] As Rosenwein has observed, "people move (and moved) continually from one such community to another," suggesting that "not only does every society call forth, shape, constrain, and express emotions differently, but even within the same society contradictory values and models, not to mention deviant individuals, find their place."[28] This is also the case with Hanzel-Hübner's diaries: on the one hand, there is resistance and subversion in the form of emotional outbursts (what she flippantly but revealingly referred to as "hysteria"); on the other hand, there is a notable urge and desire to conform to the emotional norms of her community through *Erziehung*.

Between 1901 and 1910, Hanzel-Hübner graduated from the women's teachers' college, worked as a teacher, and met and married Ottokar Hanzel. It was at this time that she filled her diaries with declarations of physical and existential pain (*Schmerz*), writing in verse form: "Where is there space for my tears? / Where is there room for my pain? / When will my terrible yearning be put out? / Unloved, hot heart?"[29] Her diary was the only legitimate space for her "emotional outbursts" (*Gefühlsausgüsse*).[30] There she could experience her emotions deeply and fully, so that the world "would not know of [her] sorrow in its full glory."[31] When she felt particularly emotional, Hanzel-Hübner's handwriting would shift from Latin script to *Kurrentschrift*, a German-language cursive, becoming messier, looser, and less legible, almost as if her body lost some of its restraint in the process of writing. In one such loosely written *Kurrent* passage she wrote, "I cannot describe how sad I am sometimes. . . . And also, it seems to me as if, from time to time, something inside me slowly lets its petals wilt and die."[32] But even this private space of emotion could become too overwhelming: Hanzel-Hübner would sometimes write herself into such a frenzy that she would be forced to stop. On 22 May 1907, she wrote, "I want to throw myself to the ground and scream. . . . I can't do it any other way, I am becoming hysterical [*hysterisch*]. . . . My infuriation has reached its peak; I am not capable of writing anymore."[33]

Just as the diary functioned as a subversive space for emotion, it simultaneously served to fuel the disciplinary project of *Damenerziehung* in an emotional community that valued emotional restraint. On the pages of her diary, a woman either willfully acknowledged the community's *erzieherisch* purposes or coaxed and coerced herself back into *Erziehung* so that she could return to the outside world of respectability. Reflecting in 1903 on the year just past, Hanzel-Hübner remarked, "the year passed by in worry [*Ärger*], attempts at improvement, small successes; I set myself a nice goal."[34] By observing that her failures and ambitions contributed "to [her] self-*Erziehung* [*Selbsterziehung*]," Hanzel-Hübner recognized that she was her own disciplinarian, her own personal *Erzieherin*. Likewise, on Easter Monday in 1904, she observed, "I have the feeling that I am truly changing. But it's for the better. I think that in the last days and years I have become more mature."[35] Expressions of wanting to "improve" and become "more mature" abound and appear to be tied to an impetus toward self-discipline. This was particularly crucial, given that she felt her "self" to be "a changeable, just qualitatively consistent I," an "I" that needed to be consolidated and made consistent for the outside world.[36] The goal of diary-writing, then, was not only to express emotion, but ultimately to *overcome* it. "I want to be good or, at the very least, always have the will power to do so."[37]

By the same token, when Hanzel-Hübner fell short of self-discipline, when her emotions got the better of her, she berated herself, writing, "I can barely conceive of how I am so unable to control myself; I am so profoundly ashamed of this weakness. . . ."[38] In 1908, she chastised herself for being weak: "Oh shame, you weak woman, how can you cultivate such pity in yourself?"[39] Insofar as she was "still too uneducated [*unerzogen*]," her diary also served to further discipline her, to "push back" (*zurückdrängen*) the uncouth, so that she could become mistress of her emotions and desires.[40] "I need to gather up my strength . . . succeed or rapidly sink," she wrote to herself.[41] In sum, diary-writing served the dual and somewhat contradictory functions of subverting ladylike composure via emotion on the one hand, and cultivating it on the other. In other words, only by acting out and "becoming hysterical" on the page could a writer "push back" and conform to *Dame*-like restraint.

EMOTION AS THEATER

For Hanzel-Hübner and other women in her emotional community, the expression of emotion was not only a weakness, but also a form of theatricality. In a diary entry from 1900, Alma Mahler-Werfel disparagingly compared the expression of emotion with "strik[ing] theatrical poses."[42] Here she referred to the German idiom "to make a theater (*ein Theater machen*)," which can be roughly translated as making a spectacle in front of others. By likening the expression of emotion to theatricality, Mahler-Werfel also implied that it was somehow inauthentic, a mere performance to be witnessed by an audience (*den Leuten vormachen*). For Mahler-Werfel and women in her milieu, "making a theater" belonged exclusively to actors.

That Mahler-Werfel used a theater metaphor is noteworthy. According to Alys X. George, in the early twentieth century the Viennese stage was undergoing a transformation as theater actors began to deploy a theatricality that was more embodied in its technique. While nineteenth-century acting was characterized by a "mimetic, declamatory" style that prioritized words, by 1900 it began to privilege "gestural forms of performance" that privileged the actors' physical presence.[43] The German theater director Georg Fuchs even compared this new physical theater to dance, observing that "the means of expression in dance"—in other words, the parts of the body—"are also the natural means for the actor."[44] For many contemporaries, the Italian actress Eleanora Duse's (1858–1924) acting technique best captured the turn to physical theater. In her guest performance in Vienna as the blind Anna in Gabriele D'Annunzio's play "The Dead City" (1896), Duse was praised for the way "her tone and hands had to speak for the eyes" and for how she engaged her entire body to render Anna's soul visible.[45] In fact, Duse herself saw her embodied acting as a new kind of language—a body language—that might replace the language of words.[46] By prying off the mask of bourgeois respectability and rendering a greater spectrum of human emotion, her deeply emotive and embodied performance was deemed a "masterpiece."

George has argued that, by the fin de siècle, Viennese modernists had lost faith in the power of language and in words' expressive capacity. In the wake of this crisis of language—or *Sprachkrise*—the body was "increasingly viewed in utopian terms as a medium for rendering visible and material the innermost stirrings of the subject in a way that words could not."[47] This position challenged the dualism of the Viennese bourgeoisie: mind and body were not separate but interrelated entities, so that the inner working of the mind could be seamlessly translated into the material body and vice versa. Moreover, in contrast to contemporaries such as Mahler-Werfel, this view assumed that the physical expression of emotion was not only authentic, but also a form of "self"-expression precisely because the self *was* embodied. As a result, many contemporaries looked for "extralinguistic modes of expression" that aimed to expand the definition of language to the nonverbal, so that the body would be not just a vehicle for language, but also a language unto itself. Modernists thus produced their own emotional community, one that viewed the physical expression of emotion as rife with meaning.

Inspired by the "gestural expressivity" of Duse's acting technique, the Austrian writer Hugo von Hofmannsthal turned to prolific experiments with pantomimic form. In his 1911 essay "On Pantomime," Hofmannsthal described the expressive possibilities of the genre and explained that, as opposed to the language of words, "which in reality is generic," the language of the body "is in reality highly personal. The body does not talk to the body," he continued, "but rather the human whole to the whole."[48] Indeed, for Hofmannsthal, gestures "are words" that "are translated into a better material [Materie]."[49] Between 1909 and 1911, Hofmannsthal collaborated with the Viennese modern dancer Grete Wiesenthal on two pantomimes, Amor und Psyche (Cupid and Psyche) and Das fremde Mädchen (The Foreign Girl).[50] Writing to Wiesenthal, Hofmannsthal insisted that pantomime would allow for "endless possibilities to unfold your inner self, create from our inner an outer with an endless variety."[51] If the bourgeois code of etiquette insisted on the separation of the inner from the outer, the modernist projects of physical theater and pantomime sought to transcend it.

But Wiesenthal had her own vision: modern dance. Originally trained in classical ballet, Wiesenthal came to experience the highly technical dance as stifling and inhibiting. "When I joined the ballet school as a student, it was a period when ballet and all of dance in general was in decline," wrote Wiesenthal in her 1919 memoir, Der Aufstieg (The Ascent). "The audience also had no reason to be interested in ballet because there was no leading spirit at the time, no ballet directors who could bring ballet and dance back to life. [There were] no dancers inspired by the will to express themselves. . . ."[52] In short, ballet had lost its expressive capacity and was, much like language more generally, in a state of crisis. When she left her position at the Imperial Royal Court Opera Theater in 1907 to begin her career in Ausdruckstanz (expressive dance), Wiesenthal did so in pursuit of self-expression.

That same year, the modern dance pioneers Mata Hari, Maud Allan, and Isadora Duncan all performed in Vienna, signaling growing interest in the new genre.[53] Although many of these performances appealed to niche audiences, their influence on Viennese cultural life was palpable, so that even less adventurous Viennese spectators may have come into contact with this body language without quite knowing it. In the following pages, I consider two popular fin-de-siècle theater performances—Richard

Strauss's *Salome* and Oscar Straus's *A Waltz Dream* (*Ein Walzertraum*)—
that intersected with modern dance in surprising ways and examine how
this intersection contributed to what I identify as two body languages of
emotion: hysteria and Temperament. The American dancer Isadora Duncan's technique would play an especially important role in this process.

Although my argument is indebted to Alys X. George's work on Viennese modernism, it deviates from it in two significant ways. First, I shift
the focus from the modernists above to the women spectators and consumers below to creatively bring the latter's experiences to life. With the
help of primary sources such as reviews, ego documents, musical scores,
libretti, films, and film fan magazines, in conjunction with theories of spectatorship, I historically imagine what the experience of spectatorship may
have been like for Viennese women, how it changed from the fin de siècle
to the interwar period, and how this experience contributed to a greater
emotional expressiveness. Second, unlike George's work, this chapter is,
first and foremost, a gender history: it considers how the modern theater
not only reconceptualized the body, but also created possibilities for a
new gendered body—the emotionally expressive body of the new woman.

THE BODY LANGUAGE OF HYSTERIA: *SALOME* (1907)

Tilly Hanzel-Hübner's use of the word "hysterical" in her diary entry
from 22 May 1907 is significant. On the one hand, it suggests that Hanzel-
Hübner, a highly educated and middle-class woman in her early twenties,
was dimly aware of Freud's psychoanalytic revolution in Vienna at the
time. For Freud, hysteria was the conversion of psychical conflict, such as
repressed sexual trauma, into physical disability, therefore constituting a
breach of the mind/body dualism so central to bourgeois conceptions of
civilization.[54] Unlike the French neurologist Jean-Martin Charcot, who
insisted that hysteria was a dysfunction of the central nervous system,
Freud argued that hysteria did not have an organic cause, but a mental one.
His talking cure, which he developed during the publication of *Studies on
Hysteria* (1895) with Josef Breuer, guided a hysteric patient in a process of
free association and analysis to uncover past sexual traumas and desires
that had been locked away in the unconscious. Seen from this vantage
point, diary-writing could be viewed as a kind of confessional talk therapy
leading to catharsis.

On the other hand, even if Hanzel-Hübner was unaware of Freud's theories, "hysterical" could also have served as shorthand for the extravagant
physical expression of emotion, as popularized by the iconography of hysteria.[55] The photographic images of female hysterics from the *Iconographie*

photographique de la Sâlpetrière (IPS), published in three volumes in 1876–1880 under the direction of the chief physician of La Sâlpetrière hospital in Paris, Charcot, reinvented hysteria by making it a more coherent and easily identifiable disorder. The IPS journals were widely disseminated across Europe to eager readers who were both shocked and titillated by the images of female patients in states of hysterical attack, ranging from *"grands mouvements"* (known as *"clownisme"*) to *"attitudes passionelles"* to states of sobbing delirium. Moreover, these images informed not only medical practice, but also—and significantly—politics, the visual arts, even the performing arts.[56] In fact, Nathan Timpano argues that "there was a clear vogue for hystero-theatrical gestures among both physicians and playwrights in *fin-de-siècle* Central Europe, the latter of whom adapted these clinical movements to the theatrical stage."[57] Thus, while Hanzel-Hübner may not have come across an IPS journal, she very well may have come across the iconography of hysteria in another forum.[58]

Indeed, the same month that Hanzel-Hübner alluded to hysteria in her diary, a guest performance of Richard Strauss's modernist opera *Salome*, based on Oscar Wilde's "perverted" play, was first staged in Vienna.[59] Originally banned by censors, the opera premiered in Vienna as a guest performance at the less imposing Volkstheater by the provincial Vereinigte Theater of Breslau, generating both controversy and acclaim. Critics noted Strauss's "captivating" score, which occasionally lapsed into "screaming, bellowing, or screeching," in conjunction with its "hideous" libretto.[60] Perhaps most controversial, however, was Princess Salome's theatrical descent into hysteria, when, after being rejected by John the Baptist, she demands his beheading so that she may kiss him on the mouth. As Sander Gilman observes, "in a German reading of 1905, *Salome* would have been a study on hysteria. The symptom, the sadism of Salome as represented by her desire to possess a fetish, the severed head of a man who has rejected her, had its origin in the trauma of her attempted seduction by her stepfather Herod. . . ."[61] Indeed, according to the contemporary music critic Julius Korngold, it was precisely for these reasons that Salome "became very au courant in our time of neurasthenia, of the hysterical disposition, of sexual problems."[62]

Gilman argues that *Salome* "is more than an opera about perverted sexuality, it is a play about Jewish sexuality and criminal incest."[63] At a time when Jews were believed to be more susceptible and predisposed to neurasthenia and hysteria due to their alleged otherness and imagined sexual selectivity, while Jewish women were "conflated with hysterical women in general," Salome-the-hysteric was not only coded as Jewish, but also read as such by contemporary audiences.[64] Thus, in Strauss's opera, "what dominates the representation of the women is their femininity but always with the racial quality of the 'seductive Jewess' present"—a Jewish femininity that constituted an emotional threat to gentile, bourgeois decorum and, ultimately, civilization.[65]

Salome's hysteria comes through in the music, specifically in "the slippery chromatic deviations from normative diatonicism."[66] At the very end of the opera, while holding her beloved's head, Salome sings in a hushed, manic voice, "Ah! I have kissed thy mouth, Jochanaan" (*Ah! Ich habe deinen Mund geküsst Jochanaan*). The musical texture becomes unsteady through a dissonant chord and the wavering and sinister trills of the winds. Salome's vocal line—"I have kissed thy mouth, there was a bitter, bitter taste, on thy red lips. Was it the taste of blood? Nay! But perchance this is the taste of love"—gradually grows in intensity and emotion toward the opera's climax, when she sings in a high, piercing voice, "I have now kissed thy mouth" (*Ich habe ihn geküsst, deinen Mund*). Immediately following this last exclamation of the phrase, the music seems to end with a resolving chord, but is suddenly interrupted by an extremely dissonant chord, which signifies her Jewish otherness and madness—and perhaps also her eventual execution.[67] To be sure, as Susan McClary has observed, "the triumphant, C#-major conclusion of Salome's 'Liebestod' is greeted by Herod's command that his guards crush her to death beneath their C-minor shields . . . bring[ing] the piece to an abrupt halt. The monstrosity of Salome's sexual and chromatic transgressions is such that extreme violence seems justified—even demanded—for the sake of social and tonal [and gentile] order."[68]

If the opera's music was one indicator of Salome's emotional state, then the "Dance of the Seven Veils" was the other.[69] At the beginning of act II, Salome agrees to perform an erotic dance for her father, King Herod, in return for the severed head of John the Baptist.[70] Wilde's stage directions for the dance were famously brief, while Strauss insisted on "the simplest and most restrained of gestures" that mimicked the "decorum with which women [in the Orient] behave."[71] The result was that each opera production had its own version of the dance. In the Vienna premiere, it would be neither restrained nor overtly erotic, but something else entirely: a work of modern dance. This dance, I suggest, would play an important role in translating the iconography of hysteria into a distinct body language, making it accessible to a wider audience.

Vienna's Salome was played by the curly-haired Franchette Verhunk, whose exotic appearance, "glowing black slit eyes and tan complexion," made her particularly suitable for the role (see fig. 3.2).[72] Unlike most singers before her, who relied on a professional dancer to play Salome,

FIGURE 3.2. In 1907, the soprano Franchette Verhunk played the role of Salome in a guest performance of Richard Strauss's opera in Vienna by the Vereinigte Theater of Breslau (present-day Wrocław). In this postcard from the production, Verhunck kneels tenderly in front of John the Baptist's severed head. From Marie Müller (photographer), "Portrait of Franchette Verhunk in the role of Salome," postcard (Breslau: Verlag Breslau, ca. 1910). Wikimedia Commons.

Verhunk insisted on performing the "Dance of the Seven Veils" herself. More unusual still, Verhunk had been inspired by the American modern dance pioneer Isadora Duncan's "free dance" technique, which sought to liberate the inner feelings of the soul into "natural" bodily expression. Although we do not know what Verhunk's dance looked like, we can imagine it as highly emotive and expressive. "The whole body heats up and soars," Verhunk explained. "A particularly tender vocal section immediately follows the dance. I have to claw my palm with my fingers [*die Finger in die Hand einkrallen*] to overcome the excitement." So captivating was Verhunk as Salome that a Budapest journalist allegedly asked her whether she was just as "hysterical" off stage as on. Although a profile of the actress in *Die Zeit* confirmed that "she is absolutely everything but hysterical," it is worth noting that for many operagoers at the fin de siècle Verhunk's musical and bodily performances of Salome were so striking, so "natural" and authentic, that the dance of hysteria and the symptoms of hysteria seemed to be one and the same.

The most iconic version of the Salome dance was developed and performed by the North American modern dancer Maud Allan, plunging Europe into a "Salomania" so great that, by the time Verhunk performed in Vienna, the body language of hysteria had been drawn on, added to, and reimagined.[73] In her sensational "Vision of Salome," performed first at the Carl-Theater in Leopoldstadt in late December 1906 and early January 1907 and then at the Apollotheater in the VIth District in February 1907, an "almost naked" Allan danced with graceful, rounded movements, her face full of expression: "she strides slowly across the stage, while her hands are constantly in motion," like "snakes that twist and turn" until she "sinks down exhausted next to the severed head of Johann [the Baptist], grabs it, and kisses it passionately."[74] Like Duncan, Allan sought through her technique to liberate the inner workings of the soul, and she was regularly lauded for her ability to translate feeling into movement. What contemporary audience members experienced, according to Judith Walkowitz, would have been a "solitary, autonomous, unfettered, mobile, weighted, and scantily clad female body whose movements delineated emotional interiority, shifting states of consciousness, and autoeroticism."[75]

Although it is unlikely that a proper middle-class woman such as Tilly Hanzel-Hübner would have seen Allan's "Vision of Salome" or Verhunk's Duncan-inspired dance that spring, it is quite possible that, given Salomania and the scandals it provoked, she became aware of it through the media or conversation. (After all, it stands to reason that some of her friends or acquaintances would have seen both productions.) Through these publicized modern dances, hysteria became shorthand not only for a medical condition, but also for the physical expression of emotion. To return to her diary entry from May 1907, then, as the gentile Hanzel-Hübner became acutely aware of her escalating infuriation and her inability to restrain it, she began to feel "hysterical." She wanted to express and perform this emotion through grand gestures and weighted movement by "throw[ing] [her]self on the ground and scream[ing]." She wanted to showcase her unrestrained, unfettered, and raw emotions like Salome and "make a theater."

Ironically, in October of that same year, Steinhof opened its doors.

THE BODY LANGUAGE OF TEMPERAMENT:
EIN WALZERTRAUM (A WALTZ DREAM, 1907)

At the anti-police brutality gathering on 11 March 1901 that was discussed in chapter 1, the Viennese women's rights activist Marie Lang described some of the qualities of modern womanhood. "We modern people do not go veiled and with lowered eyes on the street," she declared, "we want to see and hear, we want to have the right to stand and to look around." In fact, continued Lang, "a woman can even be full of *Temperament* or love extravagant fashion."[76] In chapter 1, I discussed the first part of this statement, relating it to walking practices and movement through urban space. In this section, I consider its second part, that "a woman can even be full of *Temperament*." Originally referring to a person's disposition or behavior, Temperament became, by the fin de siècle, a synonym for an emotionally expressive disposition or behavior, encompassing such characteristics as liveliness, fieriness, and great excitability. For Lang and other women, Temperament became shorthand for new womanhood's emotional expressiveness. No longer were emotions to be hidden beneath the mask of bourgeois respectability; rather, they were to be physically expressed through the body. If hysteria was one way in which fin-de-siècle women dared to express their emotions physically, the other, distinctly Viennese way was Temperament. In contrast to hysteria, which was derogatorily classified as both mad and Jewish, Temperament, while also posing a threat to bourgeois respectability and decorum, was deemed more benign and gentile.

Temperament was a quality most often associated with the mythical Viennese folk figure, the working-class *süßes Mädel* or Sweet Girl.[77] Popularized by the plays of Arthur Schnitzler, the Sweet Girl was not a serious love interest, but a good-time girl with charm and personality whose main purpose was to amuse her gentlemen admirers. Schnitzler's 1895 play *Liebelei*, for example, centered on the flirtatious dalliances—*Liebeleien*—between two Sweet Girls, Mizi and Christine, and two upper-class gentlemen, Theodor and Fritz. To help his friend forget his doomed love affair with a married woman, Theodor introduces Fritz to Christine. As a Sweet Girl, she is "a very sweet little lady, with whom one can thoroughly amuse oneself, as with all young and pretty women who have a little *Temperament*."[78] And yet, it is precisely her Temperament that turns the pleasant flirtation into a tragic love story when Christine falls in love with Fritz, who ends up killed in a duel.

If Christine represented one iconic Sweet Girl, Franzi, who was popularized in Oscar Straus's operetta *Ein Walzertraum* (*A Waltz Dream*), was another.[79] The operetta premiered in Vienna's Carl-Theater the same month that Maud Allan performed her "Vision of Salome" and received glowing reviews. Critics called it "a sensation for musical connoisseurs" (*Feinschmecker*), "with charming melodies that sound endlessly enticing to the ear."[80] By early May tickets were sold out, and by October, once the operetta reached its two-hundredth performance, it came to be the most performed piece in the early history of the Carl-Theater.[81]

The operetta's plot follows the Habsburg lieutenant Niki as he marries the cool German Princess Helene and is forced to leave his cherished Vienna for the dreary German principality of Flausenthurn. One night, upon hearing the enchanting melodies of a Viennese waltz playing at a distance, Niki surreptitiously leaves the palace and wanders to a nearby music pavilion in the park. There, he meets Sweet Girl Franzi, the charming and emotive leader of a Viennese women's music ensemble. The contrast between Franzi and Helene—between Vienna and Flausenthurn, Temperament and respectability—is what drives the plot forward, culminating in Helene's transformation. Worried about Niki, blue-blooded Helene seeks the help of Franzi to school her in the ways of Viennese charms. At the end of the operetta, Helene's transformation is complete: Niki finds her singing a waltz, accompanied by Franzi on the violin. Helene has become a Sweet Girl.

At the Vienna premiere, the soubrette role of Franzi was played by "the jolly Diva of the Carl-Theater," Mizzi Zwerenz, who was lauded for her "amazing naturalness, tragic primal force, [and] earthy delicious humor" (see fig. 3.3).[82] In Vienna theater circles, the curly-haired and grinning Zwerenz was known for being "attractive, authentic [*urwüchsig*], and always merry," an actor-singer whose performances promised to be "full of *Temperament*."[83] Indeed, local critics considered Zwerenz to be the Sweet Girl of the Viennese stage and, as such, "naturally" suited to play the role of Franzi. Although other actors would go on to play Franzi, it was Zwerenz's performance and her "Viennese *Temperament*" that would be best remembered. In fact, when she passed away in 1947, obituaries described her as the embodiment of "Viennese musicality, Viennese character, and the best Viennese operettic art."[84]

FIGURE 3.3. The soprano Mizzi Zwerenz played the role of Sweet Girl Franzi Steingruber in the Vienna premier of Oscar Straus's operetta, *Ein Walzertraum* (*A Waltz
Dream*), in 1907. This postcard shows Zwerenz in her role as Franzi, exuding her
iconic Viennese Temperament. This emotionally expressive disposition can best
be described by the handwritten line below Zwerenz's portrait—"zest for life and
lightheartedness"—taken from the operetta's song, "G'stellte Mädeln" (the accompanying music appears below the text). From "Portrait of Mizzi Zwerenz in the role of
Franzi Steingruber," postcard (Vienna, 1907). Wikimedia Commons.

A trio in act II (*"Das Geheimnis sollst du verraten"*—"You should be-
tray the secret") describes Temperament as the "secret" characteristic that
makes Viennese women particularly alluring. To the rhythm of an upbeat,
brisk polka, Franzi sings, "Temp'rament, Temp'rament, and the guy burns
with excitement." The qualities of Temperament are further elaborated in
"G'stellte Mädeln," when Franzi sings: "Even when someone is cranky,
pulls a face, I take my violin and suddenly there's light! Zest for life and
light-heartedness, laughing humor. And last but not least, there's love, for
which I only live, for which I only live!" The music breaks into a waltz
when she sings, echoed by the chorus, "It crawls and creeps, I dunno what
to do, and without knowing it, a waltz bursts forth!" And it is here that it
becomes clear that Franzi signals her Temperament through the dizzying,
rhythmic exuberance of the Viennese waltz, which, like an emotion waiting to be expressed, must "burst forth." With the fullness of the orchestra

playing in three-four time, her soprano soaring over the chorus in a playful coloratura, Sweet Girl Franzi not only expresses life-affirming emotions, but also conjures them up in her audience of captivated listeners.

That the Viennese waltz came to stand for Temperament has much to do with its dynamic, unrestrained style of dance. Originally a peasant dance or *Ländler*, the waltz surpassed the minuet as the dominant ballroom dance by 1800. While the orderly minuet required its dancers to follow complex rules and configurations that mirrored courtly social conduct, the waltz's disavowal of classical choreography posed a challenge to it by eschewing restraint in favor of dynamism and expression. Not only did the waltz combine classical dance positions in unorthodox ways (its whirling step, the *Pas zum Drehen*, for example, consisted of a combination of three different positions); it also encouraged greater intimacy and touch between dance partners.[85] And as a dance that was based on revolutions—revolving couples revolving around the central axis of a ballroom—the waltz not only produced sensations of exuberance and dizziness in its dancers, but also became a symbol for societal and emotional revolution writ large.

Given its expressive connotation and revolutionary history, the Viennese waltz became a common motif in fin-de-siècle modern dance.[86] Grete Wiesenthal performed to a waltz in her 1908 debut at the colorful Cabaret Fledermaus on the Kärntnerstrasse in the Ist District. Wiesenthal, who was originally trained in classical ballet, developed a technique referred to as "spherical dance" (*sphärischer Tanz*) that drew on the revolutionary movement of the waltz (see fig. 3.4). While she arched her upper body and threw her head back, her torso would form a wide arc and, with her arms and legs extended, she would rotate in this position in order to achieve, as Wiesenthal put it, "the greatest possible reach and swinging of the body into all sides."[87] Spherical dance was Wiesenthal's attempt to turn the Viennese waltz into a "work of dance art" (*Tanzkunstwerk*).[88] Writing in 1934, she reflected that "I lived with the music of the great musical composers. . . . I danced an allegretto by Beethoven and I worked on my first waltz, the 'Blue Danube' by Johann Strauß, as if it had been something sacred, finding the right form here straightaway for the first time. This form was both firm and elastic . . . it was not just primitive, buoyant joie de vivre that these musical creations represented but also Dionysian ecstasy and heavenly lightheartedness."[89] Even though Wiesenthal's interpretation of the dance differed from the traditional Viennese waltz performed in ballrooms across the empire, it nevertheless captured a similar quality of Temperament.

Wiesenthal's spherical dance was most likely inspired by Isadora Dun-

FIGURE 3.4. Grete Wiesenthal performing her exuberant "spherical dance" (*sphärischer Tanz*) to Johann Strauss's "Donauwalzer." From Arnold Genthe (photographer), Rudolf Jobst (photographer), "Grete Wiesenthal (Donauwalzer)," photograph (Vienna, ca. 1907). Library of Congress, Prints & Photographs Division, Arnold Genthe Collection [LC-G4085- 0019 [P&P]].

can, who danced to Johann Strauss II's *The Blue Danube* (1866) during her 1904 performance at the Carl-Theater—the same venue where *Ein Walzertraum* would later be performed.[90] Reviewers described Duncan as "gripped by a waltz frenzy" (*Walzerrausch*), with eyes "glow[ing] [with] a zest for life" and "flash[ing] [with] a happiness at being here." Her waltz erupted with emotion, feeling, and freedom, with all the exuberant qualities characterized by Friedrich Nietzsche's Dionysus. "As she whirls around and the light, transparent robes flutter around her," the reviewer continued, "she seems to have returned to the present from the cold, faraway past [*Altertum*] with all her suffering and all her joy. Not a Viennese waltz perhaps, but a more general one, a human, a womanly [one]. . . ."[91] Duncan's waltz physically conveyed suffering and joy—in short, emotion—establishing a more recognizable iconography of Temperament. Moreover, rendered as a modern dance, Temperament was translated into a body language, a series of physically expressive forms, gestures, movements, and mimed actions.

The linkages between Temperament and the waltz were not lost on Marie Lang. When she saw Duncan perform in Vienna, she likened the experience to a "revelation."[92] "She came in with shy steps, almost timid," observed Lang, "she moves slowly and, encouraged by the rhythm of her own limbs, she frolics by herself in a sweet game of delight."[93] Duncan's modern dance seemed best to express the possibilities of Temperament; it was emotion expressed through the body and conveyed to the audience. After the performance, a young woman artist in the foyer complained to Lang that the performance had given her a hangover. "How is that possible?" Lang wondered. "Don't the wings of our soul expand at the sight of beauty, does such an hour of great joy not give us the strength to go through the trials and tribulations of daily life?" Watching Duncan dance, Lang felt inspired by the liberating, "self"-actualizing possibilities of emotional expression.

ISADORA DUNCAN: THE DANCER/WOMAN
OF THE FUTURE/THE NEW WOMAN

Twenty-five years old, with a childlike expression on her face, Duncan was "a slim figure that looks more secession-like than she actually is," perhaps because, unlike the secessionists' *"femmes fragiles,"* she was full of vitality and vigor, which endowed her with more earthbound movement.[94] Of Duncan's 1902 performance at the Vienna Secession, the journalist Ludwig Hevesi observed, "they are not actually danced dances. More like mimed actions, series of gestures that glide into one another and where visual memories come to mind." After performing a string of pieces that took inspiration from classic themes, Duncan attempted to dance her entire life, expressing and miming every feeling and event linearly. Particularly captivating was her treatment of pain and grief (*Schmerz*), which she "abstracted . . . in a curve that she laid out and shaped to completion."[95] In this way, remarked another observer, "her entire being becomes pain."[96]

According to Edward Ross Dickinson, "an essential starting point for the theory of modern dance, in fact, was the idea of feeling, of emotion. Modern dance, its advocates argued, was simply the richness and the power of human feeling expressed in movement."[97] Duncan believed her modern dance to be induced by "the profound rhythm of inner emotion."[98] According to one Viennese reviewer, Duncan's movements were "guided by the heart" so that they appeared "at one with the emotions from which they emerged"; her "arms and hands" seemed to "express a moving language of the soul," as well as her very being.[99] Because modern dance was believed to involve the unmediated expression of emotion free of technical training, it was viewed as more "natural" than other forms of dance, such as ballet, which Duncan criticized as "a false and preposterous art, in fact outside the pale of all art . . . an enemy to Nature and to Art."[100]

Equally significant was Duncan's prioritization of "kinesthetic empathy," the belief in the communicative and contagious power of dance that, "if you had before you a dancer inspired with this feeling, it would be contagious. You would forget the dancer himself. You would only feel, as he feels, the chord of Dionysiac ecstasy."[101] This means, according to Kimerer LaMothe, that "dancing communicates not only because spectators see bodies moving, but because they themselves are also bodies moving, if less vigorously, during the moment of performance."[102] Spectators identify with the dancer on both visual and visceral levels, and in the process, they "catch" their "own recreation of the emotion that the dancer's kinetic images (recreated impulse-response) appear to express to [them]."[103] Through dance, an emotion would not only be made physical, it would also become contagious—and we can imagine that it would be felt throughout the bodies of the audience. Watching Duncan, spectators, many of whom were women, would feel what she felt.[104] While watching Duncan dance her grief, Lang felt overcome by sadness, so that "tears were running continuously."[105] Presumably other women spectators felt the same way.

In Duncan's 1903 manifesto, "The Dance of the Future," which was originally delivered as a speech to the Berlin Press Club, she elucidated her theory of modern dance. Opening her speech with a meditation on the free "movement of waves, of winds, of the earth," she insisted on equally free movement in dance. "The movement of the free animals and birds remains always in correspondence to their nature," she wrote. "It is only when you put free animals under false restrictions that they lose the power of moving in harmony with nature, and adopt a movement expressive of the restrictions placed about them." Classical ballet represented these false restrictions, which modern dance sought to counter in its espousal of natural rhythm and movement. But dance, according to Duncan, was not just about dance; rather, it represented a particular way of being in the world. Ballet stood for the respectable, civilized, Apollonian element, which led to "degeneration" and "living death."[106] It was a state of discord and paralysis. Modern dance, by contrast, embodied the spirit of Dionysus, freedom, regeneration, and life. Duncan's modern dance, then, was more than just a new dance aesthetic, for it represented the very freedom of humanity itself. Thus, like Nietzsche, who sought to liberate the Dionysian element within Apollonian civilization, Duncan sought to free civilized humanity through dance, through "limbs rejoic[ing] in dithyrambic, Dionysian sweet joy."[107] Nietzsche looked to the *Übermensch* for salvation, while Duncan looked to the dancer of the future. "Let us prepare the place for her. I would build for her a temple to await her," wrote Duncan reverently.[108]

Although Duncan's manifesto referred to humanity (or "man") writ large, modern dance was especially relevant to women. If classical ballet had led to the "deformation" of women's bodies and souls, then modern dance sought to strengthen and rebuild them. Thus, the dancer of the future "will dance not in the form of nymph, nor fairy, nor coquette, but in the form of woman in her greatest and purest expression. She will realize the mission of woman's body and the holiness of all its parts." Ultimately, "she shall dance the freedom of woman." Duncan's dancer of the future was not only a woman, but a *new* woman. "O, she is coming, the dancer of the future: the free spirit, who will inhabit the body of new women."[109] In this way, modern dance was not just a tool to express emotion, but also, and precisely because of this, the means to renew women.

＊

The following section will shift the focus from the modern Viennese theater—the site of modern dance—to the *Kinotheater*. Specifically, I will examine how the emotional body languages of the stage, Temperament and hysteria, were translated onto the silver screen by considering the 1925 film adaptation of *Ein Walzertraum* (*A Waltz Dream*) and the 1924 Elisabeth Bergner film *Einmal kommt der Tag* (*Husbands or Lovers*), respectively. In both cases, I will show that silent-film acting encompassed a greater range of emotions, exposing its spectators to a more varied landscape of expression. I will then direct our attention to the spectators themselves, and using the 1926 film *Varieté* (*Variety*) as a reference point along with the method of historical imagination, I will argue that the women sitting in Vienna's *Kinos* felt intoxicated by the film actors' emotions, actively experiencing them by living through the actors. With the help of a vibrant interwar celebrity culture, which peddled popular print media such as magazines and film-acting guides to fans everywhere, women spectators learned to emulate actors, including their transgressive emotional expressiveness. In so doing, they would subvert the conventions of normative feminine emotionality, modeling a new expression of womanhood in the process.

Emotional Expression at the Kinotheater

EMOTION AS *KINOTHEATER*: TEMPERAMENT IN

EIN WALZERTRAUM (A WALTZ DREAM) (1925)

In 1925, *Ein Walzertraum* (*A Waltz Dream*) was released as a silent film, directed by Ludwig Berger.[110] In this version, the princess of Flausenthurn, Alix, does not transform into a Sweet Girl: she becomes a new woman. With the help of Franzi, she bobs her hair, shortens her hemline, and learns to play the waltz—much to Niki's delight. And while haircuts and clothing are fundamental to this transformation, even more important is her Temperament.

If Franzi originally conveyed her Temperament musically as a waltz, then how did she convey it in a silent film, with neither music nor sound at her disposal? Despite the film's lack of audio, reviewers noted that she nevertheless "embodies the three-four time, the gracefulness of the Viennese waltz in her *movements*."[111] Unlike the more stoic and timid princess, the cinematic Franzi, played by the Kyiv-born film star Xenia Desni, was effusive and expressive in gesture and movement (see fig.3.5). As one critic

FIGURE 3.5. In the 1925 film version of *Ein Walzertraum*, Franzi Steingruber, played by Xenia Desni, conveyed her Temperament through movements—specifically, by dancing the Viennese waltz. In this photograph, Franzi waltzes with Habsburg lieutenant Niki, played by Willy Fritsch. From *Ein Walzertraum*, dir. Ludwig Berger (Berlin: Universum Film, 1925). Photograph courtesy of Collection Austrian Film Museum, Vienna.

put it, the film "is basically not an operetta film. It can exist without the 'Walzertraum' music. Yes, completely without any accompanying music. Because it holds its music within itself, in harmonious restraint and in signs of a Viennese 'note' [*der wienerischen 'Note'*]"—all conveyed, as previous reviewers pointed out, through body language.[112] It would be this body language, this Temperament, that the princess, played by Mady Christians, would learn to emulate.

Although silent film has traditionally been thought of as a language of images, it can also be likened to a body language.[113] Mary Ann Doane observes that "the absence of voice re-emerges in gestures and the contortions of the face—it is spread over the body of the actor."[114] And indeed, according to the contemporary American silent-film actor Lillian Gish, the goal of silent-film acting was "tell[ing] the story without saying a word" and "mak[ing] the plot apparent."[115] For this reason, the silent-film actor had to use her entire body to develop her character, convey feeling and meaning, and move the plot forward. The body's movements and gestures also changed depending on the actor's proximity to the camera. A full shot required Gish "to be almost gymnastic"—one could even say dancerly—"in my technique, my actions." Everything became exaggerated, "the lips are drawn down to what would be a ludicrous degree if you could see a closeup of them. My eyelids go far beyond what they would in real life if I were really fatigued; and my whole body droops and contracts at least an inch. . . ." By contrast, a close-up entailed more animated facial expressions, but with greater subtlety, with "my head replac[ing] the pictured fatigue of my whole body by moving a fraction of an inch to one side and then being jerked back to motionlessness, while the eyes pile up the drama of utter weariness." In the words of Alma Mahler-Werfel, Gish "made a theater"—or more appropriately, a *Kinotheater*.

Silent film can therefore be seen as a form of extralinguistic expression, an iteration of modern dance.[116] In fact, many of the silent film industry's first actors had originally worked in the theater as mimes and dancers. Grete Wiesenthal, for example, would go on to star in the 1913 film *Das fremde Mädchen*, directed by Mauritz Stiller in Stockholm and based on Hugo von Hofmannsthal's pantomime of the same name. At one point in the film, as its protagonist dances before a mesmerized male onlooker, "it dawns on her that this man is the first who sees her in her own self, her longing and her pain, the gleaming and dark sadness in her soul."[117] Her body language expresses her emotions, making them legible to the man within the film as well as to those watching it. Viennese film critics praised the work for its emotive and expressive acting style, attributing its success to the fact that pantomime and modern dance were "the closest art form[s] to film-dramas."[118]

By the mid-1920s, silent film exposed Viennese women to yet another body language of emotion. And like the cultural modes of production that came before, it too was kinetic and affectual, moving spectators to feel with its actors. To return to the film *Ein Walzertraum*, the princess was not the only woman who underwent a transformation. In addition to telling a story of romance and transformation, the film contained a pedagogical element that schooled its women spectators in the ways of modern Viennese charms. For the ordinary women sitting in Vienna's *Kinos*, watching the princess transform into an exuberant new woman, Franzi's lessons in Temperament were directly applicable, providing a blueprint for new womanhood.

ELISABETH BERGNER AS FILM ACTOR:
HYSTERIA IN *EINMAL KOMMT DER TAG* (1924)

Let us return to where this chapter started. On 30 May 1920, Elisabeth Bergner checked out of Steinhof. Shortly thereafter she made her film debut; in 1924, Bergner gave a captivating performance as the dissatisfied housewife, Nju, in the popular film *Einmal kommt der Tag* (*Husbands or Lovers*).[119] Unhappy in her marriage, Nju abandons her doting husband, played by Emil Jannings (later to play the authoritarian professor seduced by Marlene Dietrich in the 1930 talkie *The Blue Angel*), and daughter, as well as the comforts of her bourgeois home for the thrill and adventure of true love. Her lover, a lanky and effeminate poet played by Conrad Veidt, ultimately abandons her, and the film ends with Nju jumping to her death off a ledge overlooking Warsaw. Nju embodies the new woman of the 1920s, a fiercely independent being who looked beyond the confines of the home to find true happiness and who pursued romance at all costs. But even more importantly, Nju conspicuously conveys emotion through a distinct body language, culminating in a highly theatrical suicide in the center of the city.

Reviewers of the film made note of this body language and Bergner's mastery of it. One critic insisted that her "perfect art of gesture" (*vollendete Gebärdenkunst*) had "predestined" her for film.[120] As Nju, Bergner "expresses all the nuanced feelings of a woman's soul. There is not a moment in the film that remains empty of soulful expression or that lacks transition. . . ." Specifically, it was her body that served as the vehicle of this soul or "self"-expression. "Elizabeth Bergner's boyish, delicate, supple body is as eloquent as her fine vibrating hands, as her gaze." To be sure, her eyes "were capable of expressing the meaning of the imaginary, unspoken word," glowing when expressing joy and dim when conveying sadness. According to one critic, Bergner managed to disrupt the alienation effect so central to Brechtian theater by pulling her audience into the drama—and into her feelings—so completely. He used the same word to describe Bergner's performance that Marie Lang had used in her review of Isadora Duncan: it was a "revelation."

Bergner's body language comes through most explicitly toward the end of the film, when she engages in a lengthy gestural soliloquy which serves to communicate the emotional arc of her character.[121] The scene begins with Bergner facing the camera, her head sullenly bent down. In the next shot, we see her shuffling slowly and aimlessly to the door and then through the entire room, around its perimeter, and then toward a small table, where she picks up a photograph of her lover and presses the frame against her chest in a gesture that conveys intimacy and love. Again, she limps around the room, pausing to look at the photograph, until she places it on the ground and sits down before it. In the next shot, we see her lying at the foot of the bed, her eyes peering listlessly, while her head nods ever so slightly. She is in despair. Suddenly, as if she has finally found a remedy for her grief, she moves her body upright and looks upward. She stands up, but the room begins to spin, and, as we see her stumbling from side to side and in different directions, the audience also experiences the gyration through her eyes, so that we too feel nauseated. Finally, she collapses to the ground, her body limp, lifeless, and, as she makes one last effort to pick herself up, she collapses again, anticipating her eventual suicide at the end of the film. Bergner's facial expression and body serve as the vehicles through which she expresses Nju's emotions: first, the sadness of being left alone; second, the love she feels toward her lover; third, the despair of losing him; fourth, her determination to win him back; and finally, her abandonment of hope and the will to live.

Ofer Ashkenazi observes that *Einmal kommt der Tag* can be read as a Jewish text; director Paul Czinner's "focus on the outsiders of middle-class society and their quest for a more 'authentic' life within the bourgeoisie associates his works with key aspects of modern Jewish experience in Central Europe."[122] Specifically, Nju "experiences an unjust (and outmoded) social order that assigns her a 'Jewish'-like position of the 'other from within.'"[123] Ashkenazi makes a good point, but it is, I suggest, even more significant that this bourgeois social order represents an emotional community that prioritizes emotional restraint. Nju's quest for an "authentic life," then, is also about her embodied self-expression, calling to mind the disruptive "Jewish hysteria" of Salome. Like Salome, Nju subverts gentile respectability through her supple body, vibrating hands, and shining eyes, which she masterfully wields in her dancerly technique and gestural soliloquies. Could Bergner (who was herself Jewish) trace her own performance to the "Dance of the Seven Veils"? It is certainly a possibility, given that the official Viennese premiere of Richard Strauss's opera was in 1918, when Bergner, who had just returned to Vienna from a two-year stay in Zürich, was twenty-one years old. Then again, why would Bergner need to take inspiration from a performance of hysteria when she had engaged in it herself at Steinhof a few years earlier?

In both above cases, we examined how Temperament and hysteria were respectively translated onto the silver screen, thereby contributing to the emergence of a richer and more nuanced body language of emotion that further subverted the conventions of normative feminine emotionality. Like the modern theater, the *Kinotheater* also moved audiences to feel with its actors. But, as we will explore below, the *Kino* also had the ability to thrust women spectators into a state of intoxication and all-encompassing fantasy.

FEMALE FANTASIES: *VARIETÉ* (1926)

Between 1911 and 1914, Vienna experienced a veritable cinema boom, with permanent theaters opening even in the outer districts of the city, especially Ottakring and Neulerchenfeld.[124] This explosion continued into the First World War, and even with the ban on international—with the exception of German—films in 1917, the Viennese public continued to attend film screenings regularly.[125] A Viennese household journal from 1918 confirms this, citing that "Film" and "Kino" were among the well-situated Kling family's most common monthly household expenses.[126] Moreover, the accessibility (by 1926, there were cinemas in every Viennese district), cheap ticket prices, and informality of the venue made it possible for anyone in Vienna to enjoy this new form of entertainment, which thereby became the popular theater of its time.[127]

Women made up one of the largest demographics of early cinemagoers; a 1914 sociological study concluded that bourgeois women went to the cinema even more frequently than working-class women.[128] This was also the case in Vienna. According to Monika Bernold, "since its emergence at the beginning of the 20th century, the cinema . . . was a phenomenon largely supported by women. Women were present on the screen and in the theaters as pictures and consumers of pictures."[129] As women started to go outside and walk expansively through Viennese streets (chapter 1),

FIGURE 3.6. A woman spectator fixing her gaze on a male member of the trapeze act. From *Varieté*, dir. E. A. Dupont (Berlin: Universum Film, 1925; Wiesbaden: Friedrich-Wilhelm-Murnau-Stiftung, 2015). DVD. Frame capture taken by author.

they would find their way into the dark, intimate rooms of the *Kinotheater*. At the cinema, they would sit for long stretches of time, rubbing elbows with men and women from different classes and social groups, gawking at the silver screen shimmering before them. Here they would watch as Franzi played the violin, smile as Alix transformed into a new woman, and sigh as Nju fell to her death.

Women's spectatorship is a central motif in the film *Varieté* (*Variety*), directed by E. A. Dupont, which was screened at a number of different cinemas in Vienna in 1926, in both inner and outer working-class and bourgeois districts.[130] The film follows the tragic tale of a husband-and-wife trapeze act, played by Emil Jannings and the Vojčice/Vécse-born Lya de Putti, respectively. During a trapeze scene toward the beginning of the film, the camera pans across the faces of members of the audience, which includes men and women and young and old, as they look up with expressions of excitement, fear, and exhilaration. One woman in the audience stares up at the trapeze artists while she stuffs her mouth full of sausages, while another woman readjusts her opera glasses with an expression of pleasure and delight (see fig. 3.6). But it is not until the camera focuses on a woman lustfully fixing her gaze on someone who, in the next shot, turns out to be a male member of the trapeze act that the subversive quality of women's spectatorship—that despite being embedded in a patriarchal structure, it can nevertheless contain pleasure—becomes apparent.[131] Soon the entire frame is covered in a sea of peering eyes, so that the spectators in the audience are reduced to the body part doing the looking. As viewers watching the film, we too become aware of our subjectivity.

But women spectators did not only experience pleasure when watching film. An article in a film magazine put it this way: "When one watches a film, you become the hero or heroine. You laugh and cry when they laugh and cry. You suffer the torment of despair the way they do. When, in the end, a battle triumph crowns the hero, you feel the triumph, too."[132] Lya de Putti insisted that "every person who has once seen me on the screen will recognize me in a new role. [The spectator] will—at least I hope—live through the character that I play, will laugh and cry with me and will feel my face under the makeup and behind the role."[133] Film spectatorship, then, was not just passive and voyeuristic, but also deeply active and affective, with audience members "living through the characters," feeling and even physically *expressing*—in the form of a smile, frown, or tears—the characters' (and by extension the actors') emotions. The parallels with modern dance's quality of "kinesthetic empathy" are worth emphasizing here.

Writing in response to Mary Ann Doane, whose "female spectator-consumer" solely engages in a passive process of self-commodification, Lori Landay suggests that women's spectatorship, while consumerist, could *also* be "embodied and productive."[134] "There is a ludic embodiment of femininity that transcends the limited subjectivity of self-commodification," she argues, "and encourages the flapper spectator to imagine and emulate a playful subjectivity that is not simply enslaved to commodity culture."[135] As I showed above, it was precisely because silent-film acting was based on an emotionally expressive body language that films moved female spectators to identify with the characters shimmering before them. Spectatorship involved not just passive desire and consumption, but also active identification and embodiment. In the words of John Crary, it encompassed a "corporeality of vision."[136] Instead of thinking of mass culture as mere entertainment, I argue along with Mary Louise Roberts that it must be reconceived as profoundly radical, as something that subverted rather than only diverted.[137]

We can therefore historically imagine that the experience of watching a film was very similar to what film critics accused it of being, namely, intoxicating—insofar as the state of intoxication refers to a kind of emotional and physical exhilaration.[138] Film fans everywhere felt this intoxication and even referred to themselves as *Filmschwärmerinnen*, with the word *Schwärmerei* referring to a highly emotional state of passion and rapture. In a short story by the Viennese Jewish writer Else Feldmann, a woman at the cinema is described in similar terms, as gazing with "half-closed eyes," as if she were "hypnotized."[139] Likewise, a newspaper serial described the experience of watching a film as producing noticeable physiological effects of "slightly opened lips, hungry eyes, and quick deep breaths."[140] There was an almost erotic quality to the experience of watching film, with some women, like the "little seamstress," "shiver[ing] sensually at the sight of dangers. . . ."[141] Another *Filmschwärmerin* "felt her soul gripped by the artistic force and depth of this masterpiece and carried away, like a thunderous surge. . . . [I]t was intoxicating [*wie ein Rausch*]."[142] The experience of emotional and physical exhilaration was so strong, in fact, that this very woman ended up writing a letter to the film director, Fritz Lang, expressing her "burning desire to take part in such an impressive artwork," taking her affective identification with the film character/actor to the logical conclusion by offering to *become* her. This woman, the article reported, was Brigitte Helm, the actor who would go on to play Maria in Lang's famous science fiction masterpiece, *Metropolis* (1927). Thus, in addition to being intoxicating, films also fueled feelings of desire and aspiration—in short, of all-consuming fantasy—in women spectators. No longer could subject be separated from object, spectator from film, outside from inside. As Vivian Sobchack puts it, "there are always two embodied acts of vision at work in the theater, two embodied views constituting the intelligibility and significance of the film experience. The film's vision and my own . . . meet in the sharing of a world and constitute an experience that is not only intrasubjectively dialectical, but also intersubjectively dialogical."[143]

The sensual space of the *Kinotheater* also played an important role in shaping the cinematic experience and furthering spectators' all-consuming fantasy. As one contemporary commented as early as 1911,

Even the external furnishings of the *Kinematographentheater* have considerably improved in the last years. In some ways, [the theater] has almost become luxurious. The entryway is watched over by a self-important doorman, who comes close to possessing the [same] detached dignity of a doorman in a grand hotel. The lobby and theater hall in the bigger *Kinematographentheaters* are mostly . . . white and gold. . . . [And] one sits on soft cushions, almost like in the orchestra of a fashionable theater. All of this contributes to a sense of comfort and luxury . . . and partly explains the remarkable attraction the *Kinematographentheater* has on both young and old, rich and poor.[144]

In addition, unlike most public spaces, the cinema was completely dark, with the exception of the bright screen flickering at the front of the room. We can historically imagine this new urban space. In its darkness, reminiscent of a bedroom at night, a member of the audience could not

FIGURE 3.7. When Bertha-Marie (played by Lya de Putti) sees Boss wash blood from his hands, she succumbs to an emotionally palpable state of shock and despair. From *Varieté*, dir. E. A. Dupont (Berlin: Universum Film, 1925; Wiesbaden: Friedrich-Wilhelm-Murnau-Stiftung, 2015). DVD. Frame capture taken by author.

easily discern who was sitting to her left and right, as well as in front or behind her, and it was this sense of mystery that allowed for the further intoxication (*Rausch*) of the cinematic experience. The only thing an audience member could discern was the gentle tapping of her neighbor's foot, the sleek pageboy of the figure in front of her, and the perfumed scent of the person behind her. Who they were she did not know. Furthermore, the music accompanying silent-film screenings—at first produced by a gramophone or piano and, by the interwar period, by an orchestra or organ—included an aural component in the experience.[145] And given the emotive valences of music, the cinematic fantasy became even more intoxicating for the audience. Sitting in comfortable plush seats in a luxurious setting, surrounded by darkness, resonant music, and the vibrations and scents of strangers, film spectators engaged in a titillating multisensory experience.[146]

To return to *Varieté*, when Emil Jannings's character, Boss, kills his wife's lover and walks away from her, the reaction of Lya de Putti's Bertha-Marie becomes so emotionally palpable to the viewer that it is difficult not to experience her pain and shattering despair. After she hunches over, paralyzed with shock, Bertha-Marie stumbles after Boss down a hallway and stairs. Her eyes bulge and she pulls her hair, and when he ignores her, she stops in her tracks and, in a truly gut-wrenching shot, gives a silent howl (see fig. 3.7). She throws herself at him, clinging to his body as he slowly moves forward until her entire body is dragged across the floor and she tumbles, head-first, down the stairs. As the Viennese audience, sitting in the dark and crowded *Kinotheater*, watched Bertha-Marie howl and cry to the deep sounds of an organ, they might very well have felt intoxicated by her emotions, actively experiencing them by living through her.

EMOTIONAL LITERACY AND
SELF-EXPRESSION: FILM-ACTING GUIDES

In 1926, the Viennese film fan magazine *Mein Film* announced a competition for "aspiring film actresses."[147] The magazine urged its readers to consider which "film star type" they most closely resembled. Did readers look like the "adorable film teenager," Mary Pickford? Or "the hot-blooded and coquettish woman in film," Lya de Putti? Or, perhaps, "the beautiful film actress with the lively 'Viennese face' [*Wiener G'sichtel*]," Liane Haid?

Celebrity look-alike contests were popular in the 1920s and contributed to the emergence of a celebrity fan culture that took hold of Europe and Vienna alike, providing "innumerable reference points and role models for recognition, belonging and emulation."[148] While Viennese spectators had most likely fawned over stage actors and dancers before the 1920s, it was the film industry's celebrity culture that moved women spectators from merely feeling and empathizing with performers to emulating them outside of the theater as well, in an effort to—paradoxically—express "themselves."

By the mid-1920s, women's newspapers and film magazines began publishing film-acting guides for fans. In one such guide from 1926, the American film actress Lillian Rich provided a lesson in "the language of hands" to convey anger, shock, contemplation, indifference, alarm, anticipation, suspicion, horror, and irritation (see fig. 3.8). "It is fundamental to the film actress to use her hands in a skillful way in order to convey meaningful expressions [*Ausdrucksmöglichkeiten*]," Rich insisted. "I first concentrate my thoughts on the feeling that I need to express. Already as I think about the feeling, my hand begins to find its most expressive movement."[149] A similar acting guide appeared on the pages of *Bettauers Wochenschrift* (*Bettauer's Weekly*) a year later: "Become an Actor in 8 Lessons," this time with a mustachioed man demonstrating anticipation, shame, passion, disappointment, embarrassment, joy, worry, and rage using only his face, hands, and hat, while the rest of his body remained concealed.[150] The implication was that facial expressions—which relied on the eyes, mouth, and head position—and hand gestures were fundamental to the silent actor's (and, by extension, the film fan's) tool kit. Not surprisingly, the gossip-filled pages of *Mein Film* often emphasized that film actors did not necessarily

FIGURE 3.8. In this film acting guide from 1926, the American film actress Lillian Rich models different emotions using hands, body, and face. From "Die Sprache der Hände," *Mein Film* 12 (1926): 13. ANNO/ÖNB.

have to be "beautiful." What mattered most were an actor's "interesting features" and her "soulful gaze and delicately expressed movements of the body and limbs."[151]

The pedagogical function of these film-acting guides is worth emphasizing. We can imagine hundreds of fans using the guides as referents as they attempted to imitate facial expressions in front of bathroom and bedroom mirrors. One 1922 film-acting guide, *Mimik im Film (Mimic in Film)*, described mirror use as a "fundamental condition" (*Grundbedingung*) in the training process, as it allowed fans—or "acting students"—to watch themselves as they performed exercises in which they manipulated their eyes, eyebrows, forehead, mouth, nose, and tongue into different expressions. The purpose of this was to train "individual muscle functions, to clearly define each, and to expand the expressive richness [*Ausdrucksreichtum*] of the face." For example, the section on the eyes contained seven exercises on how to widen, narrow, roll, and close them, making specific reference to the irises, eyelids, and outer eye corners.[152] Done in conjunction with the eyebrows, these exercises would teach students how to become fluent in the very subtle and powerful "language of the eyes" (*Augensprache*), which allowed for a more extensive body language. After imitating these expressions at home and on the street, film fans learned how to become more emotionally literate and expressive of their "selves" in everyday life. A new emotional community was being forged.

It is important to underscore the vast array of emotions presented in these pedagogical texts, ranging from the life-affirming to the more painful and disruptive. Curiously, neither hysteria nor Temperament appear. That may be because each served as an umbrella term for a subcategory of deeper, more nuanced emotions, which the guides assiduously put on display. Hysteria, for example, could refer to anger, shock, alarm, horror, worry, and rage, while Temperament could denote anticipation, passion, and joy. Moreover, the guide that featured Lillian Rich, a woman actor, mostly focused on the former emotions, suggesting that Viennese new womanhood was based not just on Temperament, as Marie Lang had originally anticipated, but on a full spectrum of emotions. An angry woman no longer had to go to Steinhof. She could simply stand erect, ball her hands into fists, flare her nostrils, and give a look of disdain.

Conclusion: The Smiling Lieutenant (*1931*)

In 1931, *Ein Walzertraum* was remade into *The Smiling Lieutenant*, a Hollywood talkie directed by Ernst Lubitsch and starring Claudette Colbert and Maurice Chevalier.[153] Unlike the 1925 version, Lieutenant Niki meets Franzi at the very beginning of the film, before his marriage to the princess of Flausenthurn. Only after Niki smiles and winks at Franzi during an imperial parade does he meet the princess, who believes his smile and wink to have been directed at her. During their tense meeting, the naive princess asks Niki, "when you smiled at me, you also did something else . . . something with your eyes. . . . What does it mean?" And Niki responds, "When we like somebody, we smile but when we want to do something about it, we wink." At that, the princess leaves the room and, as she opens the door, she turns around, looks at Niki, and winks at him. I read this scene as a meta-moment that exposes the very mechanics of film spectatorship: just as the princess learns to express desire through the physical act of winking, so too does the film's audience become more emotionally literate and expressive. It is this very wink—the closing of the eyelid over the eye—that serves as the first step toward "self"-expression, and crucially, new womanhood.

As in the operetta version, music plays an important role in the film. In fact, it is Niki and Franzi's mutual love of music-making—she on the violin and he on the piano—that first ignites their passion. The film's music, however, is different from Oscar Straus's original score: it is jazz and ragtime, rather than the Viennese waltz, that now signify Temperament. Thus, when Franzi makes over the princess into a new woman, she does so by transforming her wardrobe, but also, most importantly, by encouraging her to "choose snappy music." After looking through the princess's piano music—"Etude for Five Fingers, Cloister Bells, Maiden's Prayer"— Franzi demands that she show her underwear. After the audience gets a shot of the princess's billowy bloomers, Franzi observers that they look like "cloister bells." She then pulls up her own skirt, exposing her lacey slip, and coyly remarks, "That's the kind of music you should play." At the piano, Franzi begins to sing, "Jazz up your lingerie, just like a melody! Be happy! Choose snappy music to wear!" Music becomes a metaphor for lingerie, emotion, and, importantly, new womanhood.

With its use of improvisation, syncopation, and polyrhythms, jazz is arguably more emotionally expressive than the more predictable and rhythmic Viennese waltz. This can be extended, also, to jazz dance. As a 1927 advertisement for Odol mouthwash put it, while the waltz was "an anachronism," surrounded by the "scent of lavender from grandmother's youth," jazz was "a return to the primitive, rousing, ecstatic"—both in music and dance.[154] When the princess finally adopts new womanhood, she abandons her conventional piano music and takes to vigorously playing ragtime on the piano while nonchalantly smoking a cigarette out of the corner of her mouth. She is buoyant in her playing, her face expressive and shimmering. The very particular emotional expressiveness of Viennese new womanhood was thus rendered more universal, becoming accessible to an international audience of intoxicated women spectators.

This chapter identified the embodied expression of emotion as a practice of new womanhood that subverted bourgeois conventions of feminine emotionality. If the feminine ideal was emotional self-control and restraint, then the embodied expression of emotion defied this ideal. Thus, to return to this chapter's opening microhistory, Elisabeth Bergner's "hysteria" was an act of defiance against reigning Viennese emotional norms and the definition and performance of conventional womanhood. By acting "hysterical" and checking herself in at Steinhof, Bergner practiced new womanhood. This confirms a central point in this book: namely, that everyday embodied practices hold great power to generate change and transform discursive and cultural conceptions of gender.

It would take a new emotional community, one that conceived of the embodied expression of emotion as a form of "self"-expression, to make these practices more widespread. Naturally, the emotional landscape in Vienna would continue to be diverse and multifaceted, but the mere fact that, by the early twentieth century, an emotional community had emerged that not only celebrated emotional expression, but also viewed the body instead of language as the more authentic communicator of emotion is significant, posing a challenge to Norbert Elias's thesis that civilization and modernity meant greater emotional restraint and control. It was within the new urban space of Vienna's modern theater and *Kinotheater*, this chapter argued, that this community would emerge. Thus, beginning as early as the fin de siècle, ordinary Viennese women attending the theater would come face to face with woman performers like Bergner who, in the words of Susan A. Glenn, "acted out"—whether by physically expressing hysteria, Temperament, a combination of both, or something else entirely. This chapter historically imagined how spectators would have marveled at the performance's kinetic and affectual qualities, experienced emotions through the performers, and descended into their bodies. With time, they would learn to physically express these emotions in their own everyday lives as forms of "self"-expression—and as assertions of new womanhood. Chapter 4 will consider another form of "self"-expression: sensual desire.

New Sensuality

A SEXUAL EDUCATION IN DESIRE
AND PLEASURE

"As a 24-year-old married woman, I still long madly for the romantic hero of my girlish dreams," Hilde R. wrote in her letter to the advice column in *Bettauers Wochenschrift* (*Bettauer's Weekly*), a sex reform newspaper, in 1926.[1] "Our marriage is so cold," she continued, "that when I look more closely, [I notice] that my heart is frozen. No tenderness, no passion!" Hilde R. turned to romance novels to find solace. "I devour Courths-Mahler novels, imagine myself to be the heroine."

Hilde R. was not the only woman devouring novels by the hugely popular author Hedwig Courths-Mahler. According to an article from 1922, Courths-Mahler's readership consisted of around five million German speakers.[2] A library in Vienna reported having sixty copies of every one of her novels—and she published over two hundred—making her one of the most widely read authors in Vienna at the time.[3] Known for her sweetly sentimental prose, the reading of which the contemporary journalist and writer Hugo Bettauer likened to spooning up a bowl of sugary condensed milk, Courths-Mahler was beloved by her mostly female readership and reviled by sex reformers and the avant-garde intelligentsia.[4]

Indeed, Courths-Mahler's novels have often been characterized as conservative, *völkisch*, and backward-looking, glorifying the "bourgeois morality" against which reformers such as Bettauer fought.[5] According to Bettauer, "one basically has the feeling that [her work] has to do with crotchless protagonists."[6] Likewise, the cabaret artist Hans Reimann described her protagonists as "crotchless Nippes figurines."[7] The romance of Courths-Mahler's novels, critics argued, was sexually repressed and repressive: virginal, prudish, and sexless.

Reimann parodied Courths-Mahler's prudishness in a book from 1922, which consisted of short chapters devoted to mocking both the flowery language and the formulaic narrative structure for which her novels were known.[8] Sexually explicit and crude illustrations by the New Objectivity pioneer George Grosz appeared alongside excerpts of Courths-Mahler's highly sentimental prose. In a chapter devoted to her 1920 novel *Liane Reinold*, one of Grosz's illustrations depicts "poor Liane" partially nude, smoking a cigarette and sitting on a sofa with her legs barely crossed (see fig. 4.1).[9] Insofar as Courths-Mahler's protagonists were criticized for being crotchless, the rendering of the fresh-eyed, sweet Liane as having both a crotch and a sex added to the chapter's satirical effect.

While her heroines were depicted as having crotches, Courths-Mahler herself was shown as having lost hers. The first chapter, in which Reimann includes a biographical sketch of Courths-Mahler and parodies her desire (*Drang*) to express herself through the written word, includes a picture of the young "Courthsmahlerin" as she walks toward her future wearing nothing but a bow, a hat, and stockings (see fig. 4.2).[10] By the end of the book, above the caption *"Auf Wiedersehen!"* the very same Courths-Mahler, this time elderly and heavy-set, is depicted with her breasts and crotch erased (see fig. 4.3).[11] All trace of desire has disappeared, and she is rendered sexless.[12]

The reader first encounters the sexless, deformed Courths-Mahler at the beginning of Reimann's book, shuffling around her bedroom in slippers. The implication seems to be that the bedroom, and not the office, was—and should be—the site of her creative process. Indeed, part of what made Courths-Mahler's novels so insidious, according to Reimann, was that they were so "banal": they were art without a purpose, art without fulfillment—in short, they were bad books. This banality is also conveyed on the book's jacket, which depicts two women, a crone and a matron, at home. Sitting at a table set with a coffeepot, cups, a bread roll, and what appears to be a flyswatter, the women are engaged in trite conversation and gossip. These women represent what Reimann imagined to be Courths-Mahler's readership: sexually repressed, "narrow-minded," "petty-bourgeois women" who spend their days at kitchen tables, shuffling around in bedrooms, and engaging in the banalities of everyday life.[13]

Courths-Mahler's readership, however, was far more diverse than Reimann imagined it to be. Not only older women enjoyed her novels; young women did, too. Her readership also straddled the class divide, consisting of bourgeois and working-class women. Bettauer acknowledged that, for the "immense army of working, tired, depressed women," Courths-Mahler's books fulfilled their "yearning for light and happiness." And it was not only ordinary women who read her work; even the popular Swedish actor Vera von Schmiterlöw insisted that Courths-Mahler, whose

Arme Liane ı

FIGURE 4.1. George Grosz poked fun at Hedwig Courths-Mahler's sentimental novels by portraying the protagonist from *Liane Reinold* (1920) as nude and vulgar. From George Grosz, "Arme Liane," in Hans Reimann, *Hedwig Courths-Mahler: Schlichte Geschichten fürs traute Heim* (Leipzig: Paul Steegemann Verlag, 1922), 101. Image courtesy of HathiTrust Digital Library/Google Digitized. © 2022 Estate of George Grosz/Licensed by VAGA at Artists Rights Society (ARS), NY.

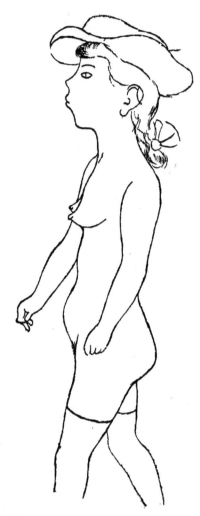

Eine Courthsmahlerin, in welcher der Drang mächtig wird — analog zu Seite 11. Oder: Der Weg in die Öffentlichkeit.

FIGURE 4.2. In this illustration, George Grosz skewers the romance novelist Hedwig Courths-Mahler by portraying her as a sexualized young woman, wearing nothing but a hat and stockings. From George Grosz, "Eine Courthsmahlerin, in welcher der Drang mächtig wird—analog zu Seite 11. Oder: Der Weg in die Öffentlichkeit," in Hans Reimann, *Hedwig Courths-Mahler: Schlichte Geschichten fürs traute Heim* (Leipzig: Paul Steegemann Verlag, 1922), 9. Image courtesy of HathiTrust Digital Library/Google Digitized. © 2022 Estate of George Grosz/Licensed by VAGA at Artists Rights Society (ARS), NY.

Auf Wiedersehn!

FIGURE 4.3. George Grosz's illustration of an older Hedwig Courths-Mahler with certain body parts erased. From George Grosz, "Auf Wiedersehn!" in Hans Reimann, *Hedwig Courths-Mahler: Schlichte Geschichten fürs traute Heim* (Leipzig: Paul Steegemann Verlag, 1922), 149. Image courtesy of HathiTrust Digital Library/Google Digitized. © 2022 Estate of George Grosz/Licensed by VAGA at Artists Rights Society (ARS), NY.

novels she read "with real enthusiasm," was responsible for her joy and success.[14] This suggests that Courths-Mahler's books were hardly as sexually repressed or repressive as many sex reformers insisted, but rather quite open-minded. In this way, far from perpetuating bourgeois morality, her books actually subverted it.

This chapter argues that Courths-Mahler's novels were part of a larger body of "bad books" that were consumed by women at the fin de siècle, constituting an early form of sexual education and knowledge, and that the roots of the interwar sex reform movement, spearheaded by figures such as Bettauer, can be found in this literature. Further, it traces how this new print culture, arguably one of the most important facets of urban modernity, inspired a new practice of womanhood: namely, the recognition, experience, and occasional pursuit and fulfillment of sensual desire. One of the more theoretical arguments this chapter makes is that Viennese women at the fin de siècle and into the interwar period came to understand sensual desire in a temporal sense, with a beginning (the recognition), middle (the experience), and end (the pursuit and fulfillment), and that these components were not always felt as equally significant. In this way, this chapter seeks to call the naturalness of desire into question by historicizing it, as well as to highlight the intersection of new womanhood and (hetero)sexuality.

This chapter begins with an overview of fin-de-siècle bourgeois morality, which cast sensual desire as opposite and inferior to holy love. It also considers how women transgressing bourgeois morality would justify it by describing sensual desire as spiritual. The first section, "Learning from Bad Books," proceeds to analyze "bad books," so-called tasteless or immoral books that women surreptitiously read for pleasure. I will provide close readings of three such bad books—an erotic text, a romance novel, and an emancipation novel—and historically imagine how they shaped women's recognition and experience of sensual desire, which came to be seen and felt as related to love instead of opposed to it. The second section, "An Interwar Sexual Education," explores how the interwar sex reform movement, spearheaded by figures such as Bettauer, drew on some on these ideas about women's desire while simultaneously emphasizing something else—namely, its pursuit and fulfillment in the form of sexual intercourse. As I trace these continuities and discontinuities, I examine how sensual desire and pleasure became an aspect of new womanhood and how, to reiterate a central point of this book, this sensuality contributed to the transformation of what it meant to be a woman. In fact, toward the end of this chapter, I show how, for many Viennese women by the late 1920s and early 1930s, a cold marriage was grounds for separation or divorce.

Bourgeois Morality: Pure Love/Impure Desire

For many bourgeois women at the fin de siècle, love was idealized as something holy and pure, emanating from God and standing in opposition to sensual desire. In a revealing love letter to her beau from 1904, thirty-year-old Marie Fröhnert (née Landa) explained that "what has come to pass is not just passion. . . . [I]t is a heartfelt and indelible affection based on the greatest respect, which the good Lord alone gives to people."[15] Not only did she emphasize that her feelings were rooted in deep respect (*Hochachtung*); she provided evidence of her love's purity by connecting it to God's grace. "The good Virgin Mary alone was responsible for putting you in my path. . . . [She] wanted it this way." Fröhnert maintained that "I no longer want to be ashamed of my feeling, which is not even a sin!" Because her love was God's will—as opposed to her own desire—it did not warrant any shame. In fact, it was an indication that Marie and Alfred Fröhnert were meant to marry, which they did in 1906.

The association between love and holiness was echoed by the teacher Mathilde (Tilde) Halarevici-Mell (née Mell) in a 1904 letter to her friend, Tilly Hanzel-Hübner, as part of the weekly epistolary correspondence the two engaged in from 1903 to 1913. Halarevici-Mell described love as "a feeling" that is "wonderfully beautiful" and "unquestionably holy," the purpose of which was to bring two people together, "so that they gift themselves to each other for their entire lives."[16] Notably absent from this description is any mention of sensuality. At a time when the Viennese bourgeoisie subscribed to a Cartesian mind-body dualism in which the mind and spirit were considered superior to the body, sensual desire, insofar as it constituted a physical drive, was lesser than "holy" love. This logic was also promoted by religion. Within Catholicism, lust was one of the seven deadly sins that could cut one off from God's grace.[17] Love, by contrast, was the very embodiment of God's grace and thus had to be protected from anything that might tarnish it. So pure and holy was love, in fact, that it was synonymous with marriage itself, which, as a Catholic publication from 1906 put it, functioned "as a protective dam against the flood of passion, as a faithful guardian of conjugal love and fidelity."[18]

The Viennese bourgeoisie viewed purity as one of the most important feminine virtues, so that the proper enactment and embodiment of womanhood required the assertion of pure love and the disavowal of desire.[19] Writing years later, the novelist Stefan Zweig ironically recalled, "A young girl of good family was not allowed to have any idea of how the male body was formed, she must not know how children came into the world, for since she was an angel she was not just to remain physically untouched, she must also enter marriage entirely 'pure' in mind."[20] Once a young girl was of proper courtship age, she was advised, according to an etiquette book, to exercise great "caution and restraint ... in the company of men," as well as to maintain strict social and physical boundaries.[21] Cross-gender courtship was limited to eye gazing and careful hand touching. In her diary, Alma Mahler-Werfel (née Schindler) recounted a moment of touch with her love interest, which elicited a sense of propriety and then of despair. She described how "he took both my hands in his and squeezed them hard. I offered no resistance—let it happen—on the contrary, I gave him my hands—just had to." And yet, she revealed, "it made me despondent, and that he noticed. Then Mama returned, and he gave me his hand again—formally."[22]

Why had Mahler-Werfel felt despondent? If purity was a feminine virtue, then sensual desire—as embodied by an erotically charged touch of the hands—was a vice that belonged to women whose femininity was in jeopardy, that is, to "fallen" or "degenerate" women such as sex workers. Reflecting in 1904 on her recently ended relationship, Hanzel-Hübner observed that "today it became clear to me that I sold my love with the first friendly kiss that I allowed him."[23] Because she had granted her former beau permission to kiss her, Hanzel-Hübner reprimanded herself for having "sold her love" like a prostitute. "I consider those people morally degenerate who are unable to repress their sexual drive," she wrote, "and who do not want to have offspring."[24] Indeed, desire, insofar as its end was pleasure, was believed to lack the "higher purpose" of reproduction. "Ideally," Hanzel-Hübner wrote, "I would be the wife of a man who understands me as much as possible and who is committed to having children."[25] This point is worth emphasizing: the only acceptable form of sex was reproductive and within marriage. As a marriage advice book put it, "sexual intercourse as an end in itself ... is an error and abuse. ..."[26]

In addition to being associated with "fallen" womanhood or prostitution, arguably the most widespread form of illicit sex, desire was also considered a masculine quality. Hanzel-Hübner observed in a diary entry from January 1904: "A man has 10 times as much sensuality as a woman. But instead of elevating themselves to humans, they . . . become animals."[27] And yet, a month later, once she realized that she was "10 times more passionate than [her beau]," Hanzel-Hübner feared that "now I am too masculine, full of passion, full of egoism, and hedonism."[28] Rather than reassess her conceptions of male and female sexualities, she convinced herself that her desire was evidence of her abnormal and manly nature, calling her femininity into question. Proper bourgeois femininity seemed so delicate that it needed to be constantly monitored, as well as performed over and over again, lest it "fall" and degenerate.

Because desire was viewed as an innate masculine quality and as distinct from love, men's philandering and brothel visits were silently condoned. Although the Catholic Church was committed to the abolition of prostitution and called for a return to chastity, many people, even Catholics, disregarded this admonition in practice.[29] In fact, for the bourgeoisie, men's desire made prostitution a necessary evil which could be regulated through hygienic measures and compulsory medical examinations.[30] The regulation of prostitution in Vienna, which was introduced in 1873, was the result of this belief (chapter 1). Given that lust was understood as sullying marriage, the existence of prostitution allowed husbands to take their sensual desire elsewhere, lest they taint the marriage bed. "A man can do whatever he wants," observed the Viennese socialist and women's rights activist Adelheid Popp. "If in addition to his wife, he has other women on the side, as many as he wants, and exchanges one woman for the next from day to day, a woman must tolerate it because she is a woman [Weib], because she is weaker, viewed as the one without rights, because a girl has already been raised to obey her husband." Marital fidelity therefore meant something quite different for bourgeois couples at this time: it was about preserving the holiness of the marriage union by eschewing desire within it completely. In this case, love was not only *separate* from desire, it was *opposed* to it. The contemporary writer Arthur Schnitzler, who was known for his insatiable sexual appetite, alluded to this in his controversial play, *Reigen* (*Round-Dance*). First performed in Vienna in 1921, the play was set in the 1890s and consisted of a string of sexual encounters between a variety of characters, two of whom—a young wife and husband who had been married for five years—reveal that they had had sex only ten to twelve times.[31] "One only loves where there is purity and truth," states the husband, who regularly visits a prostitute. A marriage advice book from 1907 even provided strategies on how to minimize physical intimacy within marriage, which included avoiding soft, enticing-looking beds and suggestive literature—to the latter of which we will return later in this chapter.[32]

"WHEREVER MY BODY TOUCHES YOURS, IT GLOWS": SENSUAL DESIRE AS SPIRITUAL

And yet, bourgeois women at the fin de siècle *did* sometimes succumb to desire—though not without feeling shame. A month after kissing her beau, Hanzel-Hübner exclaimed, "I am ashamed of myself and him!"[33]

This feeling of shame was loud ("screeching") and all-encompassing. "Yes, you wretched woman, have you no pride?" Hanzel-Hübner asked herself. "You lose your pride and your entire being trembles for him. —And then your . . . brain becomes small." In a bourgeois universe that privileged mind-body dualism, an increase in desire corresponded to a decrease in virtue. "And he who has a small brain and a lot of body," Hanzel-Hübner anxiously wrote, "becomes half-animal."[34] It was her sensuality, she feared, that would turn her into something grotesque and barbaric, stripping her of femininity and, worse, humanity.

To counteract feelings of shame, bourgeois women who partook in sensual transgressions often framed their desire as spiritual. Shortly after engaging in a romance with her piano teacher, the Austrian composer and conductor Alexander von Zemlinsky, Mahler-Werfel wondered how "anyone [could] find [sex] offensive?"[35] "The flow of one into the other—I find it beautiful, *wondrously* beautiful. I long for it." She ended her diary entry with an almost Catholic invocation: "Alex, my Alex, let me be your font. Fill me with your holy fluid." By referring to sensual love as "*wondrously* beautiful" and "holy," as a means to achieve unity ("the flow of one into the other"), Mahler-Werfel found justification for her desire: far from being *opposed* to spirit, it was its extension. In an act reminiscent of worship at a religious service, she imagined "kneel[ing] before him," experiencing "a pure, holy sensation."[36]

Similarly, writing only a year after she agonized over her manly sexuality, Hanzel-Hübner filled her diary with rich descriptions of her desire, which she likened to a spiritual fire (*Glut*) "so hot, so strong, so unspeakably blissful."[37] Addressing her private tutor, lover, and future husband, Ottokar Hanzel, she wrote, "desire rises higher and higher, the yearning becomes ever wilder, and the languor always sweeter. I want to tear myself from you just so that I can press myself against you anew." No longer was Hanzel-Hübner concerned about propriety; no longer was she maintaining the strict separation of physical boundaries that a lady of her stature was required to maintain; and no longer was she eschewing Hanzel's touch. "You should want me as hotly as I desire you," she demanded of him. "Wherever my body touches yours, it glows." And indeed, she described how "[his] breath blends with [hers]," how her heart beats so loudly in his presence that he, too, can hear it, and how their eyes shine and "blind one another."[38] In the winter of 1905, Hanzel-Hübner observed in the letter diary she shared with Ottokar, "but I no longer have a 'myself'; I am 'with you.'" Sensuality, in other words, was the highest expression of their glowing love, "the melting and unity of bodies."[39] Even Ottokar Hanzel, writing to Tilly Hanzel-Hübner, compared love to prayer: "Give me your body [*Leib*] for caresses, for worship"; "Love is my belief [and] caresses are my prayers."[40]

These descriptions of desire and sensuality have a devotional and notably Catholic tone, recalling the holiness traditionally ascribed to true love. In all these ways, a woman could justify her sensuality as serving a higher purpose: every caress was a means to spiritual unity, a prayer at the altar of love. But despite the devotional tone, the language was decidedly sensual. Where, then, did it come from? While aspects of this language surely originated in the highly tactile and earthly Viennese culture of Catholicism—the consumption of the body and blood of Christ during communion; the sitting, standing, kneeling during church service; prayer with rosary beads; pilgrimages; Corpus Christi processions; the Emperor Franz Joseph's Holy Thursday foot-washing ceremonies—it could also be found in the very suggestive literature the marriage advice book warned against: bad books.[41]

Learning from Bad Books

Young Alma Mahler-Werfel often went out on her own. During these promenades through Vienna, she would occasionally visit a secondhand bookshop, where she would exchange her old children's books for other books, such as modern literature or philosophy. On her way home she would discreetly carry them under a wide cape, for she knew that such books were considered unsuitable reading material for young women.[42]

Mahler-Werfel was only one of many women secretly reading esoteric literature and bad books. In her 1905 feminist work *Zur Kritik der Weiblichkeit* (*Towards a Critique of Femininity*), Rosa Mayreder noted the widespread "rumor that many sheltered girls do not play by the rules, but rather secretly help themselves to worldly knowledge through prohibited reading material."[43] They helped themselves in bookshops or in the collections of family members or friends. The Austrian Jewish social democrat Käthe Leichter, for example, recalled in her memoirs how, as a young girl attending the Vienna School for the Daughters of Civil Servants, she read books by Oscar Wilde, Arthur Schnitzler, and Hermann Sudermann because "Jewish girls experience puberty and maturity earlier."[44] Meanwhile, Ida Bauer, who achieved notoriety as "Dora" in Sigmund Freud's case study of hysteria, was said to have read Paolo Mantegazza's *Physiology of Love* and "books of that sort" with her neighbor, Mrs. K.—away from the discerning eyes of her parents.[45] Finally, some women checked out bad books from lending libraries. In a scene in a serialized novel from around 1900, an eighteen-year-old girl is caught with a book by Marcel Prévost, who came to be known as "the portrayer of piquant secrets of the bedchamber," which she took out of the library under the pretense of wanting to improve her French.[46] As the novel's protagonist notes, however, "this was decidedly not quite honest, for why would she otherwise flinch and blush?"[47]

From the 1870s onward, with the aid of new technologies, widespread literacy, innovative marketing strategies, and the relaxation of censorship laws, print media in central Europe expanded rapidly, the number of periodicals and (importantly) books increasing steadily (see fig. 4.4). By the fin de siècle, a "reading mania" flourished across classes in Vienna.[48] "One positively devours interesting books," reported the *Wiener Hausfrau* (*Viennese Housewife*) magazine in 1906. With so many interesting books flooding the market, the Viennese became especially concerned with regulating women's access to them. Zweig recalled how "every book they read was checked, and above all young girls were kept constantly occupied in case they indulged in any dangerous ideas."[49] Mothers were also called upon to inspect their daughters' books, specifically their light reading material (*Unterhaltungslektüre*).[50] And when governesses and mothers were unavailable to continue this project of *Erziehung* (upbringing), print media published articles that warned Viennese women against penny dreadfuls that seemed to "shoot up so quickly and in large numbers like . . . poisonous plants."[51] Even the working-class *Arbeiterinnen-Zeitung* (*Workingwoman's Newspaper*) instructed its readers to avoid reading "something bad or stupid" because it "can injure [the] brain and spirit far more often than whoever reads nothing."[52] And sometimes readers would write to newspapers asking for advice from other readers on the appropriateness of certain reading material for *Backfische* or teenage girls.[53]

Bad books eventually came under the scrutiny of the anti-vice movement, which viewed them as a threat not only to proper *Erziehung*, but also to society. Ernst Schultze's 1909 study *Die Schundliteratur: Ihr Vordringen, ihre Folgen, ihre Bekämpfung* (*Trash Literature: Its Advance, Its Consequences, Its Curtailment*), announced that "in the last years, interest in the fight against *Schundliteratur* has fortunately increased."[54] And in 1911, the *Warte gegen Schund, Schmutz und Unsittlichkeit* (*Guard-Post against Smut, Trash, and Immorality*) was established, while a newspaper devoted solely to the issue, *Österreichs Reichswehr* (*Austria's Reich Defense*), was founded two years later. Led by state-run associations, school groups, educational clubs (*Deutsch-Österreichische Volksbildungsvereine*), youth welfare organizations (*Jugendfürsorge*), and Christian charities, the anti-vice movement found support from a large and diverse group of people engaged in a vociferous crusade to reform morality well into the interwar period.[55]

FIGURE 4.4. With the expansion of print media in the second half of the nineteenth century, more bookstores opened their doors to the Viennese public. In this image from 1911, a group of people stand looking at the books displayed in the windows of Huber & Lahme, located on Herrengasse in the Ist District. Note that most of the people are men, not women. From August Stauda (photographer), "1. Herrengasse 6–8—Liechtensteinpalais—Blick Richtung Freyung," photograph (Vienna, ca. 1911). Wien Museum Inv.-Nr. 41996/1, CC0.

According to Schultze, bad books could be divided into two types. The first consisted of those that were morally innocuous but that "confuse and spoil [the reader's] taste and thereby make his enjoyment of artistically valuable books impossible."[56] These were books that challenged bourgeois aesthetic taste (*Geschmack*) and artistic sensibilities, such as the realist work of Fyodor Dostoevsky, avidly read by Hanzel-Hübner, and the naturalist novels of Émile Zola, whose work Mahler-Werfel collected in her secret library.[57] The second type was far more dangerous, comprising "literarily worthless but also morally dangerous books that not only distort taste, but also confuse the moral judgment of the reader and ravage his fantasy."[58] Within this second type were two subtypes: books that made readers immoral and books that heightened readers' fantasies. For contemporaries such as Schultze, books were believed to have tremendous power over their impressionable female readers—so much so that, if they depicted something wicked in a romantic light, the women's moral judgment would be negatively influenced.[59] Reading about prostitution, the logic went, could very well turn readers into prostitutes. Immoral books included lowbrow penny dreadfuls with lurid plots involving sex, violence, and crime, as well as the modernist and reformist writings of Henrik Ibsen, Franz Wedekind, Arthur Schnitzler, Grete Meisel-Hess, and others. Alternatively, sentimental works of fiction such as sappy romance novels with happy endings were believed to awaken and thereby "ravage" readers' fantasies, giving them a false picture of reality.

The French philosopher and feminist Simone de Beauvoir recalled in her memoirs how, as a child, "every time I found myself alone in the house, I dipped quite freely into all the books in the bookcase. I spent wonderful hours curled up in the leather armchair, devouring the collection of paper-backed novels which had enchanted my father's youth: Bourget, Alphonse Daudet, Marcel Prévost, Maupassant, and the Goncourts. They completed, in a very inconsequential way, my sexual education."[60] Bad books, I suggest, had a similar function for many Viennese women at the fin de siècle. In fact, perhaps the simplest definition of a bad book was that it was a text from which a reader might learn about sensuality.

Britta McEwen has argued that fin-de-siècle sexual knowledge production consisted mostly of scientific texts and the occasional sex-education work aimed at preparing young men for manhood.[61] It was not until after the First World War, McEwen writes, that this changed, with "authors and directors of this new information cho[osing] to frame medical and scientific subjects within testimonial confessions, melodramatic themes, and short stories. In this way, narratives of sexual science and reform, leavened with emotion, were repackaged for female audiences."[62] This chapter argues that woman-focused sexual knowledge production already existed *before* the war in the form of bad books. Although most of these books were *not intended* as works of sexual knowledge—most were fiction, after all—many were unintentionally (and on occasion intentionally) read this way by women readers. As Franz X. Eder rightly observes, "fiction was also influential in the construction of sexual knowledge" in the German-speaking world.[63]

In the following sections, I provide close readings of three books that contributed to bourgeois women's sexual education: Paolo Mantegazza's "erotic" text, *Physiology of Love* (1874); E. Marlitt's romance novel, *Goldelse* (1866); and Grete Meisel-Hess's emancipation novel, *Fanny Roth* (1902). Not only were these books popular among women at the fin de siècle; they also generated controversy as bad books. It is therefore highly likely that their readers were well aware of their status as bad books and read them precisely because they were bad books. As we do not and cannot know for sure, the following discussion serves also as an exercise in historical imagination that aims to conjure up how Viennese women readers might have read and responded to these texts. By filling in the gaps between facts with a plausible interpretive narrative, historical imagination allows the historian to come closer to teasing out the relationship between bad books on the one hand, and the embodied practice of sensual desire on the other.

TRANSCENDING THE LOVE/DESIRE BINARY: VOLUPTUOUSNESS IN PAOLO MANTEGAZZA'S *PHYSIOLOGY OF LOVE* (1873)

Sigmund Freud's *A Case of Hysteria (Dora)* described the three-month treatment in 1900 of eighteen-year-old Ida Bauer, known as "Dora," who had suffered from a disparate set of hysterical symptoms, including the loss of voice, migraines, and suicidal thoughts. Throughout the case study, Freud employed talk therapy and dream interpretation to reveal a drama between the Bauers and the meddlesome K. family, in which the young girl was at the very center. According to Ida Bauer, Herr K. had made sexual advances on her, while her father was involved in an adulterous relationship with Frau K. Rather than take this story at face value, however, Freud dismissed it as pure sexual fantasy. Most important was Freud's insistence that "[Dora's] mind has become overheated by her reading."[64] A bad book, it seems, had fanned the fiery flames of desire.

The book in question was Paolo Mantegazza's *Physiology of Love*. A physician by training, the Italian author was known for his eclecticism, making a name for himself in science, anthropology, and literature. With his widely popular *Physiology of Love*, which would be reprinted twelve times and translated into several European languages, including German, between 1877 and 1899, he established himself as a forerunner in the science of sex—sexology—influencing figures such as the University of Vienna professor of psychiatry Richard von Krafft-Ebing, whose *Psychopathia Sexualis* (1886) provided an elaborate taxonomy, with illustrations, of sexual abnormalities and pathologies, including masochism, bestiality, masturbation/onanism, and sodomy, and would go on to become a best-seller read by experts and laypeople alike.[65] By the fin de siècle, Vienna had established itself as one of the great European capitals of sexology.[66]

Unsurprisingly, women were no strangers to sexological texts. Ida Bauer had been able to access Mantegazza's *Physiology of Love* through Frau K., and similar "books on sexual life" from yet another woman, her governess.[67] An article from the *Neues Wiener Journal* in 1922 examined women's reading trends and noted the popularity of Freud's works, which were read "less for instruction than for erotic diversion."[68] And precisely because these books could be read by non-experts in such unintended ways, contemporaries such as Ernst Schultze attacked them for undermining the moral order. In Germany, for instance, illustrated, low-priced editions of Mantegazza's books were banned on the grounds that they attracted readers who would read them in unintended, erotic ways.[69] Meanwhile, Krafft-Ebing's work was attacked for disseminating "homosexual propaganda," while Freud shocked contemporaries with his frank discussion of sexuality with his patients.[70] In fact, in the foreword to the eighth edition of *Psychopathia Sexualis*, Krafft-Ebing wrote that "its unexpected commercial success is the best proof that large numbers of unfortunate people look for and find in the book enlightenment and comfort with respect to enigmatic manifestations of their vita sexualis."[71] Thus, when Mahler-Werfel noted in her diary that "whenever I read anything erotic, I always think of Alex," it is highly likely that by "erotic," she meant the books of Mantegazza, Krafft-Ebing, or Freud.[72]

Hannah Decker observes that Ida Bauer may have "been swept away by Mantegazza's romantic rhapsodies and titillated by his anthropological revelations," that she read the book as an erotic text and not to find out "facts about the body."[73] Decker's argument is persuasive. After all, given its flamboyant writing style and vivid language of sensual desire, Mantegazza's book appealed to a general audience, including women.[74] In the traditionally overwrought style of some erotic texts, *Physiology of Love* described love as "religion," in which "all becomes an object of worship."[75] Waxing poetic, Mantegazza wrote, "for love, everything is holy that has been touched by the hand, eye, and thought of the beloved, everything is holy in which the dear image has been reflected."[76] The person who "feels, desires, and loves very much" always "erects an altar with whatever he has of beauty or riches, and there on his knees he prays and adores."[77] Not only are these meditations on love striking; they are also reminiscent of the language of worship that bourgeois women drew on in their defense of desire. Like them, Mantegazza also frequently employed fire imagery. "From the moment in which a man and a woman have pronounced together these sweet words, *I love you*, they unconsciously become the priests of a temple in which they must guard the sacred fire of desire."[78] And once the fire has been kindled, it "must [be kept] burning."[79] Krafft-Ebing was also quick to describe love as "an unbridled passion . . . like a fire that burns and consumes everything."[80]

As Nicoletta Pireddu observes, it is significant that this religion of love was replete with sensual desire.[81] In fact, as the above allusion to touch, sight, and feeling makes clear, Mantegazza was deeply committed to love's "voluptuousness," which referred to "the greatest pleasure of the senses."[82] The term, insofar as it connotes an excess of body on the one hand, and an excess of pleasure on the other, is especially appropriate because it underscored his belief in "the excessive and not simply utilitarian quality of love." Love could never be economical or restrained; instead, it was an "unconditional, sumptuous expenditure," a "sublime lavishness"—in short, voluptuous. Furthermore, love was neither solely emotional nor solely cerebral; it was emotional, cerebral, *and* physical, so that "two creatures in love with each other are two bodies excessively electrified."[83] "There is no love without voluptuousness," Mantegazza declared, "but voluptuousness of itself alone is not love [it is lust], neither is that which is ridiculously termed *platonic*."[84] Indeed, voluptuousness was not the same as lust; it was the wondrous alchemy of love that turned lust into voluptuousness and something divine. "What are the Angels, Archangels, Cherubim, Thrones, and Dominations of the Christian paradise in comparison with all those living creatures who, at every throb of our pulses, unite on earth in the embrace of voluptuousness?" Writing with the passion of an erotic poet, Mantegazza announced that "wherever a man and a woman find themselves together and can desire each other, voluptuousness weaves its garlands and says to the man and the woman, 'Be gods for an instant!'"[85] By describing voluptuousness, or sensual desire, as godlike and spiritual, Mantegazza breached the mind-body divide and made sensuality respectable.

Although we do not know for certain whether Alma Mahler-Werfel, Tilde Halarevici-Mell, or Tilly Hanzel-Hübner read Mantegazza, the fact that Ida Bauer—a woman from a similar bourgeois milieu—did makes it highly likely that they did as well.[86] (And it seems equally likely that they, like many other bourgeois women, would have read Krafft-Ebing, who like Mantegazza argued that "[love's] strongest root is still sensuality."[87]) We can imagine women reading these bad books, feeling titillated by their imagery of love's voluptuousness. Indeed, in 1907, three years after describing love as "holy," Halarevici-Mell wrote to Hanzel-Hübner that love was the union of spiritual *and* sensual intimacy. But, Halarevici-Mell lamented, the latter was considered "indecent" (*unanständig*) because of women's upbringing, or *Erziehung*.[88] "Our senses are cultivated in such a way that every sexual stimulus seems like a sin. . . . On my part, I definitely do not want to put sensual love in first place, but it irritates me when I notice how much . . . we don't see, and then how . . . we are left with disgust." Had Halarevici-Mell read Mantegazza? We can certainly and quite plausibly imagine that she did.

And yet, Mantegazza's conception of female sexuality was far from radical. Not only did he understand it solely in relation to male sexuality, and thus solely within a heterosexual paradigm; he also viewed female sexuality as defensive and passive. While "the human male has been allotted the aggressive mission," he wrote, "to the female [has been allotted] the difficult task of defending herself."[89] Only men actively desired, while women had to work hard to be desired by being beautiful and withholding themselves. Describing woman as "the ancient teacher of sacrifice," Mantegazza declared that "she must never say *yes* before having said at least one *no*."[90] Although Mantegazza sought to teach women how to say "yes" eventually, he nevertheless insisted that they partake in voluptuousness sparingly.

Mantegazza's conception of feminine desire was not unique to him. Within the new medical discourse of sex, women were generally believed to be less sexual, even frigid. In fact, starting in the eighteenth century, many physicians and scientists insisted that the only desire women could speak of was that for love, a *Liebestrieb*, as opposed to a desire for sensuality or lust (*Wollust*).[91] Krafft-Ebing drew on these ideas: "Undoubtedly man has a much more intense sexual appetite than woman," whose "sexual desire is small."[92] Similarly, he argued that women's minimal desire could only exist in relation to another individual of the opposite sex with whom sexual intercourse was possible.[93] While sexologists like Mantegazza and even Krafft-Ebing radically reframed sensual desire as part and parcel of love, they also managed to reinforce a vision of women's sexuality remarkably similar to the one found within bourgeois morality.

The women writing the love letters and diary entries, however, were quick to identify their sensual desire. They were neither asexual nor sexually passive. After all, it was Hanzel-Hübner who wrote to Ottokar Hanzel, "you should want me as hotly as I desire you." Even Mahler-Werfel observed, "I'm a lustful person, indeed very much so."[94] Notwithstanding the sexologists, women were learning how to recognize their sensuality in a different kind of bad book: the romance novel.

RECOGNIZING DESIRE IN E. MARLITT'S
GOLDELSE (1866/1890)

Writing to Hanzel-Hübner in November 1907, Halarevici-Mell reflected that "it appears as if I am about to get entangled in a romance novel again. . . ."[95] For Halarevici-Mell, life occasionally seemed to resemble romantic fiction, with its drama, conventionality, and heavy sentimentality. Like Hilde R., the enthusiastic Courths-Mahler reader with whom this chapter opened, women across Vienna were already devouring romance novels at the fin de siècle, viewing their lives as an extension of the romantic drama unfolding between the pages.

German romance novels were part of what Todd Curtis Kontje more broadly terms "domestic fiction."[96] Beginning in the late eighteenth century, a growing number of women began writing novels about women for women, focusing on themes of romance, marriage, and the family—although, as Kontje points out, not without considering public issues as well.[97] One of the most popular romantic fiction authors of the late nineteenth century was the realist writer E. Marlitt, the pseudonym used by Eugenie John (1825–1887), who achieved fame through her serialized novels in the widely circulated *Gartenlaube* (*Garden Arbor*) magazine from 1866 onward.[98] Her avid readership consisted of mostly women from the middle classes and numbered in the hundreds of thousands.[99] Her novels were eventually published in their entirety as beautifully designed, illustrated editions to be purchased at bookstores or borrowed from libraries, thereby ensuring Marlitt's popularity into the twentieth century, years after her death.[100] "If you present one of these young girls, for example, a modern Nordic novel and a book from Marlitt or Heimburg to choose from, she will most likely greedily reach for the latter," commented an article in the *Wiener Hausfrauen-Zeitung* (*Viennese Housewives' Newspaper*) in 1893.[101] "'Goldelse' on the one hand or 'Das Eulenhaus,' 'Herzenskrisen' and 'Kloster Wendhusen'! How these will be devoured, read, and reread until one almost knows the most beautiful parts by heart! How much one loves and suffers with the heroine and almost more with the hero!" Even the Jewish anarchist Emma Goldman recalled reading Marlitt novels with her teacher at the Realschule in Königsberg as a young girl. "She loved Marlitt more than the others," Goldman wrote, "so I, too, loved Marlitt."[102] Marlitt's popularity was so great that many women writers would imitate her style, including Wilhelmine Heimburg (pseudonym of Bertha Behrens [1848–1912], who even completed Marlitt's posthumous novel, *Das Eulenhaus*) and Courths-Mahler.[103] In 1925, in honor of what would have been Marlitt's one-hundredth birthday, Courths-Mahler published a tribute to her beloved predecessor.[104] Women and girls loved Marlitt's books, she wrote, because they were comforting and pleasurable. "For women and girls, the fragrance and spirit of Christmas are lacking if a Marlitt [novel] cannot be read under the crackling [candle-bedecked] Christmas tree," observed Courths-Mahler.

Written in a florid, sentimental style, Marlitt's novels tended to follow a predictable Cinderella narrative that involved a young woman overcoming various challenges and limitations to achieve a victory that often ended in marriage to a hero of higher social status. It was precisely because of their formulaic narrative structure and saccharine style that many commentaries, especially by the 1880s, considered them bad books.[105] Ernst Schultze dismissed romance novels as offensive to taste, as well as ravaging readers' fantasies. A how-to manual aimed at the proper *Erziehung* of young bourgeois girls from 1912 argued that such "sweet, sentimental fare . . . confuses and clouds the hearts and minds of our daughters . . . [and] brings about an unhealthy romance, on the one hand, and hysteria and unrealistic passion [*Schwärmerei*], on the other."[106] Comparing these books to sugar or bonbons, an article in a women's magazine advised mothers and caretakers to make sure "the dear youngsters [don't] spoil their stomach with that sweet stuff."[107] Meanwhile, feminists such as Rosa Mayreder denounced Marlitt's novels for being kitsch, as well as for peddling a regressive and conservative agenda that viewed "the wedding day [a]s the pinnacle of [woman's] life and the happy ending to all worries and disappointments."[108] More generally, insofar as they catered to women's tastes, Marlitt's novels were often considered to be second-rate, banal, and "trivial" literature (*Trivialliteratur*). They continued to be remembered as such until the 1970s and 1980s.

Goldelse, Marlitt's first novel and the one that launched her career, would eventually be published in its entirety in 1890, which means that many of the young women discussed in this chapter may very well have come across it. The plot is structured around the kindhearted and independent Elisabeth Ferber, the "golden Else" of the book's title, who, together with her poor middle-class family, moves to a run-down Thuringian castle inherited by her mother. Although the novel deals with many themes ranging from class conflict to family secrets, perhaps the most important one concerns women's desire.[109] As the Ferber family settles into their new home, Elisabeth's desire is gradually kindled when she meets the cold and melancholy Herr von Walde, who also harbors feelings for her.[110] As Lynne Tatlock has observed, it is during Elisabeth's informal piano recital toward the beginning of the novel, at which von Walde is present, that her sensuality and desire are awakened. As she begins playing, she realizes that "to-day there was something blended with the tones that she could not herself comprehend; she could not possibly pursue and analyze it, for it breathed almost imperceptibly across the waves of sounds. It seemed as though joy and woe no longer moved side by side, but melted together into one." Watching Elisabeth, Herr von Walde is visibly moved: his "features were as calm as ever, only a slight flush coloured his brow; the cigar had dropped from his fingers and lay upon the ground."[111]

Elisabeth does not immediately recognize this desire. But since, according to Kristen Belgum, the ultimate purpose of all of Marlitt's novels—as well as their resolution—is for the heroine to understand and accept her desire for her hero, by the end Elisabeth does just that: she "burst into tears and threw her arms around the neck of her lover, who clasped her to his heart."[112] Marlitt withholds further descriptions of physical intimacy because desire's fulfillment is less important than its recognition.

Readers learn of this desire well before Elisabeth does. Marlitt provides subtle cues, often through descriptions of body language or inner monologues to convey "every wild throb of [Elisabeth's] heart." We are told, for example, of Herr von Walde's smile, "which had lately possessed such a peculiar charm for Elisabeth," or of the flirtatious "smile [that] played around Elisabeth's mouth" when he asked for a birthday greeting from her.[113] In fact, as Belgum says, one "component that must have attracted [Marlitt] to readers again and again was the opportunity [her novels] provided to live out the experience of desire."[114] Thus, we can historically imagine readers accompanying Elisabeth on her path to understanding and accepting her desire for Herr von Walde and willy-nilly learning how to identify and experience desire themselves, thereby effectively realizing that women in general can also desire. Although the intention behind these books was to entertain a female readership, the unintended consequence was a lesson in desire. It would take another kind of bad book to give women the courage to experience this desire in their bodies as well as to understand it as a form of agency: the emancipation novel.

SENSUAL DESIRE AS AGENCY IN
GRETE MEISEL-HESS'S *FANNY ROTH* (1902)

In March 1905, Hanzel-Hübner went to see the influential Swedish feminist philosopher Ellen Key speak.[115] "A lasting impression," wrote Hanzel-Hübner—though "I don't want to be Ell. Key, after all." One reason for Key's notoriety was her insistence on women's sexual emancipation. She argued that women needed to experience sensual desire not only to have richer, more satisfying love, but also to realize their personhood and sense of "self" (on "self"-expression, see chapter 3). Indeed, "'to be fully human' does not mean . . . that the spirit suppresses sex, or sex the spirit," but that spirit and sex should be in unity and harmony.[116] Edward Ross Dickinson observes that, at its core, the pre-war sex reform movement of which Key was a part "held that sexuality was an integral element in the human personality, and thus that the authentic subject was a sexual subject."[117] "Sexuality, and specifically women's sexuality, therefore had to be acknowledged as a legitimate and positive force in individual and social life." And to get this message across, Key and other like-minded individuals gave talks and wrote books, occasionally even penning what came to be known as *Emanzipationsromane* (emancipation novels).[118]

In 1902, the Jewish sex reformer Grete Meisel-Hess published the groundbreaking novella *Fanny Roth*, which would go on to become a bestseller, reaching thirty editions by 1913.[119] According to one reviewer, the novella was evidence "that many other souls feel this way and an even greater number stand in the background and darkly and vaguely perceive the same with their instincts."[120] Bourgeois women sympathetic to the women's or sex reform movements may very well have read this or other emancipation novels of the time, such as works by Helene Böhlau (1859–1940), Ilse Frapan (1848–1908), Else Jerusalem (1876–1943), Rosa Mayreder (1858–1938), Gabriele Reuter (1851–1841), and Irma von Troll-Borostryáni (1847–1912), as well as the scandalous, anonymously published fictional diaries *Eine für Viele* (*One for Many*, 1902) and *Tagebuch einer Verlorenen* (*Diary of a Lost Girl*, 1905), which was made into a German silent film, directed by G. W. Pabst, in 1929.[121] But even women who were indifferent or unsympathetic to these movements may very well have come across these books due to the scandal they caused. Insofar as they talked about sexuality so openly, were they not, some commentators wondered, immoral? Ernst Schultze dismissed avant-garde and reformist literature as confusing readers' moral judgment. His contemporary, Hermann Hölzke, described emancipation novels as "modern accusatory literature" lacking in objectivity and quality—in short, as bad books.[122]

Another contemporary derided *Fanny Roth* for its brutality, describing the book's eponymous protagonist as a "woman who, born to be a whore, becomes a young girl 'from a good family' thanks only to favorable external circumstances."[123]

Set in Vienna, *Fanny Roth* tells the story of the eponymous composer and violinist, an "emancipated" twenty-year-old woman who had always been driven by the "Apollonian" forces of intellect and creativity.[124] Her life undergoes a transformation once she meets the handsome Josef Fellner, plunging her into a world of sensual desire. They embark on a biking excursion on the outskirts of Vienna that culminates in an erotically charged scene in which they drunkenly kiss and he promises to return the next day to ask for her hand in marriage. Shortly thereafter, they marry. But the union does not last, for he demands that she give herself up—her music and compositions, her *personality*—and be his alone. "You can only be mine—only mine," Josef says. Although he had awakened her "blissful, trembling desire," Fanny soon realizes that "he held her back." Indeed, sex was not enough because "the best was missing—personality." "This man she married was not bad and not evil. But he was empty—terrifyingly empty—on the inside, and hard and rough on the outside." By the same token, he loved her only "as the object that appealed to him most at the moment" and not for "her self." The novella ends with Fanny leaving her husband; "full of renewed fervor," she packs her bags, takes her violin, and walks into the spacious outdoors. "Far behind her lay the sufferings of a young girl. As a redeemed person, as free as a bird, she held her fate in her own hand."[125]

Although Fanny relishes her new freedom, it is noteworthy that she never regrets marrying Josef Fellner. "He, with his ravishing eroticism—yes, he was the right person to redeem a girl from the suffering of virginity, to take the pain of blood from her." As a young virgin committed solely to her music and art, Fanny had led an unbalanced existence, which manifested itself in persistent "nervous conditions," most likely an allusion to hysteria (chapter 3).[126] Her relationship and eventual marriage to Josef culminates in Fanny's sexual awakening, producing an erotic drive that serves as a counterbalance to her creative drive. As a Nietzsche-inspired Viennese *Emanzipationsroman*, the novel thus centers on Fanny's emancipation, her maturation from a girl possessed by Apollonian intellect to a young lover overtaken by Dionysian sensuality and, finally, to a distinctly Viennese new woman committed to balance, harmony, and unity.[127] Josef's presence was crucial to Fanny's development; although she ends up outgrowing him, his "ravishing eroticism" brought her one step closer to adulthood.

Indeed, for Meisel-Hess, women could only be emancipated once they liberated their sexuality, an idea she would further develop in her most important nonfictional work, *Die sexuelle Krise* (*The Sexual Crisis*), in 1909.[128] Society was in a state of sexual crisis, insofar as it was governed by the double standard of bourgeois morality that required women to refrain from sexual exploration, forcing them into celibacy on the one hand, while encouraging men to engage in sexual adventures, upholding the institution of prostitution on the other. "According to the duplex code, sexual need exists only for the male, and the woman who satisfies this need must be plunged into disgrace and misery," wrote Meisel-Hess.[129] As a result, a marriage could rarely be fulfilling for a woman, because, unlike the man, she entered into it without any sexual experience whatsoever. In *Fanny Roth*, the protagonist epitomizes the predicament of the bourgeois everywoman, having blindly entered into a marriage with neither experience nor forethought. Fanny is brutally shaken out of her romantic reverie on her wedding night, when "a wild, terrible struggle" ensued and she felt as though "a beast . . . had torn her to shreds."[130] Meisel-Hess's inclusion of a violent marital rape scene was intentional, an attempt to cast light on the moral double standard that rendered women frail and childish, and men brutal and monstrous. The implication is clear: had Fanny—and women like her—been given the chance to explore her sexuality prior to marriage, this wild struggle might not have occurred.

At first glance, Fanny's and Josef's respective sexualities appear to conform to the sexual paradigm promoted by the likes of Mantegazza and Krafft-Ebing, for whom woman's sensual desire was weaker and more passive—verging on frigid—than man's. But as Agatha Schwartz points out, "against all expectations, despite the traumatic experience of the wedding night, Fanny does not become a 'frigid' woman; instead, she feels relief the following morning."[131] In fact, "Meisel-Hess lets Fanny's sexual desire unfold and eventually manifest itself very strongly and satisfactorily in her marriage." In fact, it is this same desire that allows Fanny to unfold her*self* and ultimately leave her loveless marriage behind to become free. Meisel-Hess thereby does something especially radical, suggesting that all sexual experiences can aid in a woman's development and allow her to become an independent, liberated human being.

Sexuality was believed to be linked to the unfolding of the self because, for Meisel-Hess and many other sex reformers at the time, body and mind (and spirit) were inextricably linked—an idea that was rooted in the monism of the zoologist and philosopher Ernst Haeckel.[132] Monism recognized the unity of all things, thereby challenging the dualism that governed much European thought. Abstaining from sexuality—and the body—was therefore a rejection of who we are, "the attempt to renounce the implications of that matter out of which [we] [are] compounded," and a "sin against the laws of [our] being."[133] Our being was made up of body, mind, and spirit, so that the rejection of any one of these was a rejection of the whole.

Consistent with this view, Meisel-Hess uses the language of the body and the senses to describe Fanny's transformation from naive girl to mature woman. Throughout the novella, Fanny glances at herself in the mirror, each time becoming more aware of her physicality—something women readers would surely have noticed. After she and Josef plan their first outing together, Fanny sees her reflection, which appeared changed and seemed to be "glowing pink." She then "closed her eyes and spread out her arms as if in a dream, and the white teeth shimmered moist between the burning lips." Later on, Fanny looks at herself again, and this time "the lines [on her face] no longer seemed to her blurred and wandering, the features set firmer and more deeply, the colors richer and the complexion fresher." "So this is what a demi-vierge looks like," Fanny remarks, referring presumably to Marcel Prévost's bad book, Les Demi-Vierges (The Half-Virgins, 1894). After they marry and move to a villa on the outskirts of Vienna, Fanny notices her reflection yet again and soon thereafter feels her new embodiedness, marveling that "her body was healthier from her marriage, the nerves were calmed, the hot-blooded turbulent demands were satisfied."[134] If Viennese readers of Marlitt had learned to recognize desire, readers of Meisel-Hess, who most likely felt especially close to Fanny for also being Viennese, would have known to locate it in their bodies. We can historically imagine readers feeling the glowing, shimmering, burning, and hot-bloodedness of embodied desire.

Indeed, for Meisel-Hess, new women such as Fanny—"those exceptionally active specimens of womanhood filled with the joy of life, who blossom among us in ever-increasing number"—were women who actively desired with their bodies. "We know that women's sexual need is as great as and even greater than that of men," she wrote. Thus, women's "enfranchisement" needed to be "erotic," "restor[ing] to [them] the independence and self-respect [they] ha[d] lost."[135] Desire, according to Kathleen Canning, is a "very interesting kind of agency"—indeed, Audre Lorde describes the erotic as a kind of power, "a measure between the beginnings of our sense of self and the chaos of our strongest feelings."[136] Meisel-Hess's conception of sensual desire can be similarly viewed as a vehicle for (new) women's self-actualization.[137]

The notable German sex reformer Helene Stöcker, who would go on to establish the League for the Protection of Mothers and Sexual Reform

(*Bund für Mutterschutz und Sexualreform*) in the German Reich in 1904 and in Austria in 1907, praised *Fanny Roth* for both its literary artistry and its philosophical insight. Women were raised to "underestimat[e] the physical ground on which [they] stand," and books such as *Fanny Roth* encouraged them to "take in the senses . . . and meld them with [their] idealistic daydreaming" and thoughts.[138] Citing Mantegazza's books, Stöcker insisted that the "modern woman," the new woman, was a sensual and desiring woman, "born to love with all the fires of her nature—with all her soul, heart, and senses."[139]

In sum, I argue that a crucial practice of new womanhood was the recognition and experience of sensual desire, and that books such as Mantegazza's, Marlitt's, and Meisel-Hess's contributed to this shift. We can historically imagine how a young Viennese woman who stumbled upon Mantegazza's impassioned writings on voluptuousness would have found his exaltations of sensual desire surprising and shocking—radically different from the dualistic bourgeois morality governing Viennese society. Reading Marlitt's *Goldelse*, in which the novel's heroine, Elisabeth, comes to realize her desire for Herr von Walde, she would have learned how to recognize this desire in herself. And finally, leafing through *Fanny Roth*, we can imagine her coming to experience this desire as an embodied form of agency, an expression of a distinctly Viennese new womanhood. These bad books, which largely constituted her sexual education, may have even given this bourgeois reader the courage to utter those transgressive words: *I desire you.*

✳

While the historiography of Viennese sexual knowledge has traditionally placed emphasis on the interwar period, this chapter has shown that woman-centered sexual knowledge already existed prior to this period in the form of bad books. It is precisely because these books were never officially part of the reform literature that they have been overlooked by scholars. The purpose of the above section was to bring this literature to light and to imagine, via close readings, how it may have been read by young women embarking on journeys of sensual "self"-discovery. By juxtaposing ego documents with three types of bad books, I have tried to extrapolate the latter's lessons in sensuality.

The next section shifts the focus to the interwar sex reform movement. My purpose is not to give a comprehensive overview of this movement— for that, readers would be advised to turn to the work of scholars such as Maria Mesner and Britta McEwen—but rather, to tease out first how social-democratic and more radical literature drew on and deviated from the sexual knowledge of bad books, especially the three books discussed above, and second, how these texts continued to shape the practices of new womanhood.[140] Most importantly, I am interested in this literature's conceptions of sensual desire—the focus of this chapter—and its espousal of the recognition and experience of desire as well as the pursuit and fulfillment of desire with another body. I argue that sensual desire came to be understood in a temporal sense, with a beginning (the recognition), middle (the experience), and end (the pursuit and fulfillment), and that while bad books emphasized the beginning and the middle, sex reform literature prioritized the end. Ultimately, this chapter will reveal that given the interwar reform movement's fixation with the end (the pursuit and fulfillment of desire), as well as its insistence that this end be shared with another body, its conception of sensuality was, ironically, more rigid than that which came before it.

An Interwar Sexual Education

In 1926, at the age of thirty-two, the recently divorced Viennese Jewish writer Lilli Wehle-Weber (née Weber) became infatuated with a man, filling her small diary with sensual poems devoted to him. Her desire was hot and physical and her nights were restless: "At night, hot and wild / where my body rears alone / where my head burrows feverishly into the pillows / and alone my blood foams."[141] Once her love was reciprocated, Wehle-Weber felt her body come alive: "Didn't think about my body for a long time / I was like a child, quiet and cold / Only through you have wishes in me been awakened / After a wildly hot, blissful night."[142] In another poem, she expressed her desire to "want nothing but to know love / [to know] wild, hot sensual pleasure."[143] For Wehle-Weber, love was synonymous with sensual desire and pleasure.

By the interwar period, more Viennese women were, like Wehle-Weber, able to recognize and experience sensual desire. According to the sex reformer Johann Ferch, the experience of the First World War contributed to women's sensual and sexual awakening.[144] "Contact with foreign elements, the absence of loved ones, the example of friends who lost their lovers or . . . gave themselves to strangers, created enough temptations to undermine popular morality," Ferch wrote.[145] He continued that, as more women became nurses tasked with treating and touching "naked male bodies," even "particular organs," they became less prudish.[146] Ferch credited "the wartime hospital" as having "brought about the . . . liberation of [women] from forced blindness."[147] And "once the spell of sexual shame was lifted, sensuality suppressed every moral thought," and women could finally feel their desire more fully.[148]

But another reason for women's sexual "liberation," to use Ferch's term, was related to the emergence of a visible, full-fledged sex reform movement that drew on the sexual knowledge of the fin de siècle and re-packaged it in an intentionally pedagogical and pragmatic way via advice manuals, popular *Sittenromane* (novels of manners), pamphlets, advice columns, exhibitions, films, and public clinics. This sexual *Aufklärung* (enlightenment), as Britta McEwen calls it, was produced by physicians and reformers across political and party lines—ranging from members of the Social Democratic Workers' Party (SDAP), which was in politi-cal control of Vienna, to the Catholic, antisemitic Christian Social Party (CSP), to radicals, such as Hugo Bettauer, who did not subscribe to either party—with the shared goal of regenerating society in postwar Vienna.[149] Despite their multifaceted and varied nature, these media had two things in common: first, they were mostly focused on "normal" as opposed to pathological sexuality, and second, they explicitly targeted women.[150]

This multivocal movement, especially its social democratic and radical parts (the focus of this section), exhibited continuities as well as discon-tinuities with the pre-war sexual education trends already discussed. Like their pre-war predecessors, many sex reformers emphasized the unity of love and sensual desire. They also continued to view women as desiring subjects, urging them to recognize and experience sensual desire in the body. According to the SDAP feminist Therese Schlesinger's "On the Evo-lution of the Erotic," Viennese women were finally evolving erotically.[151] And yet, it was not enough to just feel sensual desire; it had to be actively shared with another body of the opposite sex—preferably the body of your spouse. One key discontinuity was thus the emphasis on sensuality's hetero-sexual fulfillment, its consummation within marriage in the form of sexual intercourse. As Atina Grossmann put it, "the Sex Reform leagues recog-nized and encouraged female sexuality, but on male heterosexual terms—in defense of the family."[152] In this sense, Ferch's characterization of this pe-riod as defined by women's sexual liberation is somewhat misleading.

Unsurprisingly, the interwar sex and marriage reform movements were closely aligned. Their shared goal was to transform "normal" heterosexual unions into strong, companionate marriages by encouraging couples to explore sensual desire instead of repressing it, as had been the case under nineteenth-century bourgeois morality. While most reform media from the period provided information on basic anatomy, sexual hygiene, vene-real disease, and contraception, they also aimed to instruct ordinary mar-ried couples on the mechanics of mutually satisfying sex. As the author of one such book asserted, "marriage should have long taken prostitution's place" as the site for sensual desire and fulfillment.[153] The very definition of marital fidelity thereby changed: if, traditionally, bourgeois marriage condoned husbands' philandering, within the modern, social democratic marriage it would no longer be allowed. Instead, marriages were to become even more exclusive than before.

As a result, Viennese women continued to learn to recognize and experience their desire, but also to occasionally try to pursue and fulfill it with another body. They turned to marriage advice books, visited clinics, even wrote to newspapers. We can imagine how Viennese women drew on the sexual knowledge derived from these interwar sources, integrating it into their relationships with their husbands, and sometimes even with their beaux. As a result, the pursuit of desire—and its fulfillment in the form of "wild, hot sensual pleasure," in the words of Wehle-Weber—came to be a practice of new womanhood.

Below, I consider the continuities between pre-war and interwar sexual knowledge, highlighting how certain ideas from bad books, including Mantegazza's *Physiology of Love*, Marlitt's *Goldelse*, and Meisel-Hess's *Fanny Roth*, found their way into interwar literature. I then consider the discontinuities between these two bodies of knowledge by examining two marriage advice books: Bernhard Bauer's *Wie bist du, Weib?* (*How Are You, Woman?* 1923) and Theodoor Hendrik van de Velde's *Die vollkommene Ehe* (*The Perfect Marriage*, German edition, 1928). Finally, I conclude this section with an analysis of separation and divorce proceedings from the late 1920s and early 1930s, to understand how these radical new ideas may have shaped the practices of new womanhood on the ground.

CONTINUITIES AND DISCONTINUITIES

As I have argued, there was great continuity between the interwar sex reform movement and its pre-war predecessors—though it bears mentioning that the former hardly considered the latter its predecessor. Thus, the language of interwar sex reform closely mirrored the idea of voluptuousness articulated by Mantegazza decades earlier: instead of being opposed to love, desire and (significantly) the sex act itself came to be seen as its most spiritual and sublime expression. A 1925 article in the sex reform newspaper *Wir beide* (*Both of Us*), for example, urged its readers to "leave your bashfulness and all old-fashioned prudery behind."[154] Non-reproductive sex, the article maintained, is hardly shameful, but the highest expression of true love. "Lovemaking (*Liebesakt*) is the apex of spiritual and bodily tenderness, the conclusion of a natural, steadily intensifying passion.

Everything else is immoral." The article thus found a way to repackage sex-for-the-sake-of-sex as something moral: despite its non-reproductive end, it was different from other "immoral" sex acts insofar as it was the most supreme expression of love. Rather than "mere bodily expression," sex, according to an article in the newspaper *Sexual-Reform*, "builds on spiritual experience."[155]

Sensuality, which bourgeois morality had associated with the body, was thereby shown to be connected to the spirit. If love was a tree, its "roots," wrote the Viennese gynecologist Rudolf Glaessner in his 1921 guide for young women, "are the sensuality which organically spring from the sexual organs," while its "crown of leaves and flowers is the spiritual in love."[156] Despite being rooted in the material world, sex was nevertheless connected to the spiritual "crown" of love. Not only did this new conception of sex breach the mind-body dualism pervasive in earlier bourgeois morality and culture; it also remade the profane into something sacred. Indeed, if love was "holy" and "pure," then how could the physical union of lovers be profane? "Every sex act that is spiritually and bodily aligned towards the goal of intimate union and the full blossoming of the lover," the sex reformer Joseph Carl Schlegel insisted in his marriage advice manual, "is humane-moral!"[157] Instead of being viewed as tarnishing the purity of love, sex became its extension, so that "sexual intercourse" (*Geschlechts-verkehr*) came to be known more euphemistically as "lovemaking" (*Liebe-sakt*). If love was the feeling, then lovemaking was its noblest expression.

By the same token, if sex was spiritual, then love was sensual and voluptuous. According to the 1923 guide for women, *Wie bist du, Weib?* "true love shows us that what is commonly called love is not a unified concept, but a summation of many and varied feelings. . . . [A]ll of it, however, is built on the great foundation of sexuality!"[158] Echoing Mantegazza, it declared, "there is no such thing as platonic love!" If love was sexual in nature, then platonic love was an oxymoron. When an article in *Wir beide* asked readers whether love had to be sensual, Emma S. wrote, "Yes, absolutely!"[159] She elaborated: "After a certain longer and shorter period of time, even platonic love will become sensual or it will perish."

That Emma S.—an anonymous woman—recognized the sensuality of love is revealing, suggesting that she and Viennese women like her were also attuned to their own desire for it. "I have a hot desire for love, for happiness, for everything elegant, noble," wrote a certain Lissy in a letter published in *Bettauers Wochenschrift*'s advice column.[160] Another woman wondered what she should do with the "hot blood flow[ing] through my veins" if her beau's "caresses leave me cold."[161] Was a relationship without mutual desire unsuitable? she wondered. Meanwhile, another "very passionate" reader, Helly, felt consumed by her desire for her beau. "Like a man, I know very much," she wrote, "and we torment each other every time we meet because we don't have the thing that all of our thinking is focused on."[162] This language of desire echoes Marlitt's *Goldelse* and Meisel-Hess's *Fanny Roth*. There is the recognition of "hav[ing] a hot desire" and of "lik[ing] a man very much," as well as the experience of this desire in the body, of "hot blood flow[ing] through my veins."

In addition to transcending the love/lust binary, the interwar sex and marriage reform movement was also committed to continuing to help women recognize and experience their sensual desire. The Socialist Society for Sexual Advice and Research, for example, viewed bourgeois morality as responsible for women's frigidity and sexual neurosis—a point also made by Meisel-Hess.[163] Founded in 1928 by the psychoanalyst Wilhelm Reich and his colleague, Marie Frischauf, its seven clinics in Vienna aimed at counteracting the negative, repressive, and neurotic effects of bourgeois morality by providing visitors with frank information about sex, as well as by encouraging all heterosexual, pleasure-oriented sexual activity. Indeed, in contrast to Freud's view that sexual sublimation was necessary for civilization, Reich made a case for sexual expression and release—which would ultimately lead to proletarian revolution.[164] Reich's ideas were quite popular among the Viennese: in 1928–1929, about seven thousand people attended the Society's public lectures.[165]

Since Reich believed that seventy percent of all women had been raised to be sexually frigid, many members of the Society were particularly committed to women's social and, by extension, sexual liberation.[166] As a result, women from all social classes visited the clinics.[167] "They come with some kind of worry related to their marital or love life, which they have viewed as unalterable and no longer tolerable. They learn to recognize that trained psychological insight, combined with a lot of practical experience, will give them solutions."[168] And once women learned to work through their sexual neuroses, they could use techniques to recognize and experience their desire, which would, in turn, lead to their liberation—the unfolding of their selves. They could be like Fanny Roth: their desire would serve as a form of self-actualization and agency.

And yet, it was not enough to just help women identify and experience their desire in themselves. As noted above, one of the most important goals of the reform movement was the pursuit and fulfillment of these desires in the form of mutually pleasurable sex within marriage. The Viennese sex reformer Johann Ferch and his wife, Betty, founded the League Against Forced Motherhood (*Bund gegen den Mutterschaftswang*) in 1919, with the goal of improving Viennese marriages with "sexual education and enlightenment."[169] There is a "deliciousness [*Köstlichkeit*] and richness in a marriage," an article in the league's newspaper, *Sexual-Reform*, stated, "that is built on a carefree sexuality."[170] Although reproductive sex was still held in high esteem, especially with the rise of pro-natalism in the 1920s, the league's Lamarckian belief that the environment could affect hereditary characteristics implied that good, carefree non-reproductive sex was also necessary to enhance the quality of a baby.[171]

Because of its eugenic stance, the league was also committed to providing women with access to birth control methods and devices, as well as repealing Austria's strict anti-abortion laws, §§ 144 to 148.[172] In contrast to the SDAP's more conservative Marriage Advice Centers, which emphasized the reproductive goals of marriage, the league's Women's Advice Centers provided "every woman (and girl) without means" a referral to a physician "who will provide her with an examination and a pessary fitting free of charge."[173] By 1930, the league opened a total of seven Women's Advice Centers in different districts in Vienna—and twenty-two in Austria as a whole—that received some 250 visitors per week.[174] In addition to providing access to pessaries, the centers advised women on how to use chemical contraceptives, such as Semori. The league believed chemicals to be "the ideal protective device of the future because they have the inestimable advantage of rendering women independent of doctors," so that they could someday make their own sexual and reproductive choices (on reproduction, see chapter 5).[175]

Once anxiety-free non-reproductive sex became more accessible to married couples, they had to learn how to make it fulfilling and pleasurable.[176] "Oftentimes a man puts a woman in a position in which she goes through sex without experiencing any pleasure," Glaessner observed. "In order to also provide the woman with full pleasure, the man will, as far as possible, not proceed hastily through the sex act." This meant a significant amount of time devoted to foreplay, a "slow sequence of events," as well as "deep, soulful penetration." Furthermore, because a woman's "sexual feelings are much more spread out over her entire being [*Wesen*]," it was necessary for sex to involve a greater range of acts over a greater range of body parts.[177] It was also necessary, we shall see, to involve the five senses.

PLEASURE IN THEODOOR HENDRIK VAN DE VELDE'S
DIE VOLLKOMMENE EHE (1928) AND BERNHARD
BAUER'S *WIE BIST DU, WEIB?* (1923)

The Dutch physician Theodoor Hendrik van de Velde's *Die vollkommene Ehe* was one of the first books to provide direct strategies in the art of lovemaking that called on the use of the entire body and all five senses. First published in German in 1928 to great press attention and acclaim, it became, according to the Viennese sex reformer Sofie Lazarsfeld, the most widely read sex and marriage advice book in 1930.[178] In Vienna, the gynecologist Bernhard Bauer devoted dozens of pages to the art of love-making in his 1923 book, *Wie bist du, Weib?*, but instead of exploring the senses of sex, he looked instead to the senses of seduction.[179] Both these books continued what bad books such as *The Physiology of Love*, *Goldelse*, and *Fanny Roth* had started: if Mantegazza taught readers to think of love in sensual terms, and Marlitt and Meisel-Hess helped them recognize and experience desire in the body and self, interwar reform literature taught readers how to fulfill this desire and feel pleasure with the body and senses of one's spouse.

According to van de Velde, foreplay (*Vorspiel*) involved the first three senses: sight, sound, and smell. Sight was important because it produced "the first impressions between the sexes," the initial attraction. People first notice superficial characteristics, van de Velde observed: a "man will be attracted to a woman's well-formed breasts," while a woman will be attracted to "a man's strong body build."[180] To this Bauer added fashion, fabric, and color, as well as body comportment and movement.[181] But sound, van de Velde insisted, played just as important a role in generating feelings of attraction during foreplay, which he described in musical terms as "sempre crescendo."[182] In addition to discussing the sensual aspects of music (of Richard Wagner's opera, *Tristan and Isolde*, he wrote that "no person can experience the orchestral torrent of the [opera's] second act without being overcome with sexual feelings"—a point also made by Bauer) as well as the "primordial" power of rhythm, he emphasized how the particular "timbre" of a person's voice could work wonders in producing sexual arousal.[183] Was he, perhaps, urging his readers to seduce each other with words, whispers, moans, and groans? Indeed, van de Velde wrote that "the most important instrument of foreplay . . . is conversation. Its most important topic is—love."[184]

With regard to smell, van de Velde encouraged his readers "to be attentive to it, so that you can become aware of the pleasure that your body's tender fragrances can produce."[185] People were to maintain proper hygiene—regularly clean their body, change underwear and clothing, avoid pungent foods such as garlic, and wear perfumes—as well as become more sensitive to their lover's natural scents. Bauer noted the erotic effect the smell of tobacco—the "pleasant tickling scent of a smoked cigarette"— had on women.[186] The smell of genitals, van de Velde observed, could be particularly arousing. Even semen, he argued, could produce sexual

feelings—though only in women and not in men, reinforcing the heterosexuality of these sex acts.[187] Meanwhile, the smell of a menstruating
woman, wrote Bauer, had an especially adverse effect on men.[188]

Touch and taste, van de Velde wrote, were related to the next stage in
sex: the "loveplay" (*Liebesspiel*). He urged his readers to consider the taste
of their lover's saliva, which "can often have a stimulating effect." The "love
kiss" (*Liebeskuß*) was of utmost importance in this regard, the "tongue kiss
[being] the most important variation of the kiss," with taste playing a key
role. "The kiss's taste also becomes very personal because . . . a little saliva
goes from one mouth into the other." He continued that "some, if not all
lovers, even prefer to purposefully produce more [saliva]. . . . Poets who
sing: 'I want to drink your kisses as often as I used to' are not fantasizing,
at least not with regard to the technique of love; because love kisses are
[to be] imbibed."[189]

It is worth noting that, writing some twenty years earlier, Tilly Hanzel-
Hübner also described kisses in these terms. "If I were to translate his
kisses into words," she wrote of her beau, "they say: give me love, I am
thirsty."[190] The thirst metaphor appeared again a couple of years later,
when she mused, "love is just a shallow stream that runs beside the street
of life, not everyone can stoop down and be refreshed, he does not have
time. Out of thirst, some do not get any farther. . . ."[191] She viewed herself
as "a dehydrated woman" (*eine Erdurstende*), and it was through kisses that
she finally could quench her thirst.

Van de Velde believed that touch was "the most important of all senses
in producing sexual feelings during the loveplay"—a point made also by
Bauer, who argued that for women, touch was the most erotic sense—and
he made note of the body's different erogenous zones, including earlobes,
inner thighs, breasts, and nipples.[192] "Light pinching and kneading of the
whole breast with the entire hand moves a woman into the beginnings
of sexual arousal," he wrote. During the sex act, "all forms of touch, in all
gradations, from the quiet tickle to the gentle stroking with finger tips"
are stimulating, he argued, although the softest touches tend to be "most
effective."[193]

After the loveplay came coitus, or *Vergattung*, a neologism that drew
on *Vermählung* (marriage) and *Begattung* (copulation). This stage involved
the penis entering the vagina and the attainment of orgasm—the highest form of pleasure—for both partners. Here the sense of touch reigned
supreme, and van de Velde argued that even a rough touch, such as a firm
grip leading to bruising, could be part and parcel of this stage. He even
encouraged lovers to tap into "a certain rawness and severity," as this was
related to humans' "primitive" instinct to reproduce.[194] By this stage, the

mind-body and human-animal dualisms that had been so central to the bourgeois worldview were clearly undone.

Once the penis exited the vagina, wrote van de Velde, the lovers found themselves in the final stage of sex, known as the "afterplay" (*Nachspiel*), "the most delicate and tender part of the entire sex symphony."[195] Here, exhilarated lovers would experience a heightening of the senses: "The eye is more sensitive to light that usual," "the sense of smell is sharper," "even hearing is more refined." But it is ultimately the sense of touch, he argued, that becomes most sensitive. For this reason, he recommended that the couple indulge in a long embrace, relishing their physical and sensual unity as their bodies have finally become one.

SENSUAL MARRIAGES/COLD MARRIAGES

As van de Velde and Bauer touted the benefits of a sensual marriage, Viennese women came to notice when their marriages lacked sensuality and grew cold. Recall Lilli Wehle-Weber's love poems above. In one of them, she thought back to an earlier time: "Didn't think about my body for a long time / I was like a child, quiet and cold." Was this, perhaps, a reference to her marriage, which ended in divorce in 1925? Below, I draw on separation and divorce proceedings from the late 1920s to the early 1930s to investigate how ordinary Viennese women like Wehle-Weber came to understand the role of sensuality in their marriages. Although this analysis is hardly comprehensive, it does reveal that for many Viennese women a cold marriage was no longer sustainable.[196]

The First Republic's marriage and divorce laws were a remnant of the imperial General Civil Code of 1811 (the *Allgemeines Bürgerliches Gesetzbuch* or ABGB), which made the solubility of a marriage contingent on the religious denominations of the married parties. Catholic couples looking to dissolve their marriage were limited to "perpetual separation" from bed and board (*a thoro et mensa*), which, according to Ulrike Harmat, "nullified their 'life partnership' without affecting their 'marriage bonds.'"[197] Because the Catholic Church viewed marriage as a sacrament that could not be broken until death, separation did not allow parties to remarry.[198] In order for a Catholic couple to be granted a separation, one party had to petition for a separation and accuse the other party of one or more of the following infractions (§109): adultery, conviction for a crime, wicked desertion, disorderly conduct, physical abuse, repeated insults, and infection with venereal disease. Non-Catholics, meanwhile, had a much easier time obtaining separation and divorce. If both parties professed a non-Catholic Christian religion at the time of the marriage, they could obtain a divorce by mutual consent in case of "insurmountable aversion" (*unüberwindliche Abneigung*—§115), or if one party accused the other for reasons similar to those applied to Catholics. (Interestingly, §115 did not include disorderly conduct, repeated insults, or infection with venereal disease as reasons for divorce.) Likewise, if both parties were Jewish, divorce was permitted (§§133–37) either by mutual consent or if the husband accused the wife of adultery.[199] In cases of mutual consent, Jews did not have to assert insurmountable aversion like non-Catholic Christians did, which made it significantly easier for them to obtain a divorce. Finally, a couple could apply to have their marriage declared invalid—a practice that became common immediately following the collapse of the Habsburg Empire, when provincial governments started granting (re)marriages by dispensation.[200]

In Vienna, the number of separations and divorces began to increase dramatically by the fin de siècle, with most petitioners being women.[201] According to Evan Burr Bukey, this was due to economic changes that gave women more financial independence and a "disillusionment with the prevailing notion of romantic love."[202] This latter point is significant. It indicates that petitioners, mostly women, wanted separation or divorce because romantic love—that is, a voluptuous love grounded in sensual desire—came to be seen as necessary to sustain a marriage and its parties. Indeed, as I show below, sensual desire was often referred to in separation and divorce cases in the late 1920s and early 1930s, at the peak of the sex reform movement in Vienna, thereby demonstrating that women did not shy away from discussing it even in the "public" setting of the court.[203] Sexual matters would come up in different ways, whether framed as or subsumed under a legitimate reason for separation and divorce, or simply as further evidence to strengthen a case. Moreover, sex seemed to be on the minds of women across classes and religions, indicating that a cold marriage was universally reviled in interwar Vienna.

Of all the legitimate reasons for separation and divorce, adultery was most obviously related to a lack of sexual intimacy between parties. In 1927, the seamstress Anna Winz accused her husband, Alois Winz, of infidelity.[204] Alois was known to write personal ads in newspapers to meet women—a pastime he described as "a joke." He also infected Anna with venereal disease, which confirmed his promiscuity. While adultery and VD infections were legitimate reasons for separation *a thoro et mensa*, they also implied a lack of sensual desire between married parties. That Anna dared to accuse her husband publicly and petition for a separation clearly suggests that she believed that her cold marriage was no longer sustainable and that her desire for romance was legitimate.

Adultery also came up in the divorce proceedings between Bianka Kopetzky, a company employee, and Franz Kopetzky, a businessman.[205] Bianka explained that when it came to sexual matters, her husband was "violent and insatiable" and often resorted to harassing their sixteen-year-old nanny, Yvonne Bringolf. In fact, the nanny testified against Franz, confirming that he sexually assaulted her three times during her employment at the Kopetzky residence. As discussed in chapter 1, it was not uncommon for male employers to sexually harass and rape domestic servants. The court first pushed back against the nanny's testimony, asking whether it was based on malicious intent, "youthful fantasies" (perhaps she had read too many bad books?), or a lack of understanding of what constituted a sexual assault to begin with. Then, somewhat surprisingly, the court sided with both the nanny and the wife, stating that Franz "had sexual intercourse [with Yvonne Bringolf] despite her resistance and thus committed adultery." In November 1930, Franz Kopetzky was found guilty, and divorce was granted.

Besides adultery, physical abuse was also a legitimate reason for separation and divorce that could be framed in sexual terms. For example, Karoline Ludwig accused her husband, Oskar Ludwig, of sexual abuse.[206] In her testimony, she claimed that her husband, a sewer worker, "abus[ed] me sexually over the course of our living together in that he [had sex with me] without consideration of my health, often several times a day." "He beat me constantly, he often brutally abused me," Karoline continued, "and from the very beginning, this treatment was the order of the day." As a result, she had become "an utterly sick woman." Sexual abuse also came up in the 1929 divorce proceedings between Marie Margarete Weingarten and her husband, David Moriz Weingarten.[207] In addition to committing adultery repeatedly, David was beholden to so-called "sadistic" inclinations that manifested themselves in the bedroom. He was, Marie insisted, "perverted in the highest degree," often hitting her or throwing things at her when they engaged in sexual intimacy, as well as demanding that she engage in practices she did not want to do. As a result, Marie left Vienna and moved to Leipzig to protect herself from her abusive husband. In both cases, the marriages had turned not only cold, but icy.

In addition to adultery and sexual abuse, wicked desertion was also a common accusation that had clear sexual implications, as we can see from the case of the embroidery shop owner Klara Wimmer, who accused her husband, Josef Wimmer, a municipal servant, of deserting her.[208] After living together "like husband and wife" and "having sexual intercourse," their marriage grew cold once Josef began spending all his income on building a small house in Vienna's XIIIth District, which became his primary residence in 1925. He thereafter abandoned Klara, including their marital bed, and shared his new home with three different women. In another case, Helene Klotz accused her husband, Viktor Klotz, of deserting her financially, emotionally, and physically.[209] She described him as being susceptible to "egoism and coldness of heart [*Herzenskälte*]," focusing only on the "satisfaction of his own inclinations and whims." Meanwhile, her needs and desires, most likely also her sensual desires, were never considered or fulfilled.

But wives also deserted their husbands. After marrying in 1919, Rudolf Wilhelm and Margarethe Wilhelm moved to Munich and lived there until 1926, when Rudolf lost his job and returned to Vienna to work for Schidloff & Co.[210] Margarethe refused to follow him back to Vienna because she felt that their marriage was "a huge mistake." In fact, she was completely uninterested in her husband sexually. Beginning in 1923, the couple ceased having sexual relations with each other after Margarethe was apparently diagnosed with a mysterious medical condition that prevented her from engaging in sexual intercourse unless she had surgery. She admitted that she was "not suited to be a wife, it is not her nature," and that "she will never have an operation to enable sexual intercourse." Whether she did not sexually desire men (the reference to her "nature" may have been an allusion to homosexuality) or was simply uninterested in sexual relations altogether, the point is that Margarethe did not desire Rudolf. She wanted a separation so that she could pursue, experience, and fulfill her own desires, whatever they might be.

Some couples were more explicit about sexual matters—even if they had to be subsumed under a more legitimate reason for divorce. This was the case with Hedwig Wesely and her officer husband, Alois Josef Wesely.[211] Hedwig accused Alois Josef of failing to fulfill his coital duty due to impotence or an inclination "towards perversion [*pervers veranlagt*]." According to Hedwig's testimony, she and her husband had only been sexually intimate three times in the seven years of their cold marriage. Although her husband countered that his wife was "emotionally cold" and hysterical, suffering from occasional fainting spells, the court ruled that it was Alois Josef's "complete sexual neglect of his wife" and the physical abuse he subjected her to (the legitimate reason for separation) that contributed to her frigidity in the first place. The court even noted that far from being emotionally cold, Hedwig was actually a "temperamental and affectionate woman"—a *desiring* woman—who was forced into a state of hysteria due to Alois Josef's neglect (on Temperament and hysteria as emotional expressions, see chapter 3). That the court ultimately sided with Hedwig shows that sex reform ideas were even penetrating the legal apparatus and bureaucracy.

Non-Catholics often cited "insurmountable aversion" in terms of sexual incompatibility or sexual estrangement as the reason for their divorce. Hermine Wieder and Karl Wieder, for example, claimed such an aversion in February 1927. Separated *a thoro et mensa* in 1922, they decided to fully dissolve their marriage several years later, given that they "no longer had any marital dealings with each other" or engaged in sexual intimacy. In fact, they wanted to divorce precisely because the "marriage had never been sexually normal," given that they had only been intimate three times throughout the duration of the marriage.[212] One reason for this was that Hermine had only been eighteen when they married, with little to no understanding of sensual desire. Meanwhile, Karl's libido was beholden to a "strange weakness," which the court speculated was due to either "the clumsiness of the first sexual encounter with his wife, to early masturbatory excesses, to a lack of ambition, or to all factors combined." Karl's inability to fulfill his marital coital duty was therefore the reason for Hermine's "constant and insurmountable aversion," and divorce was granted. Although we do not have direct access to Hermine's thoughts, we can imagine that, at a time when sex reform resources were becoming more available across the city and women's frigidity was coming to be reevaluated as a product of upbringing and circumstance, these ideas may have influenced her understanding of her marriage.

The absence of a "normal" sex life also came up in the divorce proceedings of Johann Gubin and Rosalia Gubin.[213] Two physicians served as witnesses, confirming that Johann "could not have normal sexual intercourse" with his wife because of her anxiety and nervousness—in short, her frigidity. Another physician confirmed that Rosalia was often suffering from pain during intercourse; for this reason, he subjected her to a medical examination, but was unable to find the source of this pain. But perhaps Rosalia simply did not desire Thomas? After all, she apparently did not marry him out of love or affection (*Zuneigung*)—or sensual desire, for that matter—but rather, to secure a stable future. Despite the plausibility of this interpretation, the court concluded that the Gubins' insurmountable aversion was not related to sex at all, but to "origin, religion, and race." While Johann was born and raised in a middle-class Christian family in Vienna, Rosalia was an eastern European Jew whose father was a cattle-dealer in Bukowina. Antisemitic logic would have dictated that this relationship was doomed from the start.

But women were not the only ones who described sexual intimacy as painful. In 1928, another non-Catholic couple, Gustav and Marie Leist, claimed insurmountable aversion because "for the past 2 years a cooling gradually set in between them, which, over time, developed into a complete estrangement."[214] According to Marie, her husband ceased having sex with her because he "no longer feels anything for her, he is interested in other women." Her husband confirmed this, stating that whenever he tried to be intimate, he would be overcome by "pain in his soul" (*seelische Schmerzen*). He believed that his wife's or his own vital fluids had changed, which affected their attraction to each other—a possible reference to the popular science of mesmerism, which posited the existence of a magnetic force or "vital fluid" in all animal and human bodies. Although Marie had hoped that Gustav's feelings might change, she ultimately acknowledged that separation was necessary, for a cold marriage was not a sustainable one.

Some women looked outside their marriages for sexual fulfillment. Irma Wessely, the wife of a businessman, described feeling "completely neglected" by her husband, who "went out alone every night, came home late at night, and even spent time without her at the coffeehouse on Sundays and holidays."[215] Likewise, Margarethe Weinmann accused her husband, Joseph Adolf Alexander Weinmann, a bank employee, of only being interested in his profession and music, and, when she invited him to take part in "harmless entertainments," he was "completely unsympathetic."[216] (Indeed, Joseph believed his wife to have an addiction to pleasure and fashion.) Both women ended up engaging in extramarital relationships. Irma started dating Josef Singer, and Margarethe expressed a desire to leave her husband for a cobbler that the court described as "significantly younger than her."

As this section has argued, separation and divorce cases from the late 1920s and early 1930s, at the peak of the sex and marriage reform movement, enable us to understand how Viennese women came to understand the role of sensuality within marriage. The pursuit and fulfillment of desire in the form of mutually satisfying sex had become a necessity for many women, who rejected a cold marriage as being unsustainable. That ordinary women would go to such lengths to dissolve their marriages, subjecting themselves to the public spectacle of the court while describing in detail their intimate lives and desires, is remarkable. It indicates that Viennese women were beginning to engage in womanhood differently by no longer ignoring or feeling ashamed about their sensual desire, but rather, identifying, experiencing, and pursuing it fully. As Helene Stöcker insisted, the new woman was "born to love with all the fires of her nature—with all her soul, heart, and senses."[217]

Conclusion: Reading for Pleasure in Hedwig Courths-Mahler's
Eine ungeliebte Frau (1918)

We return to where we started, to Hilde R. Let us imagine her sitting in her rocking chair in the late evening, reading a Courths-Mahler novel, while her husband snores in the bedroom. It is 1926, and despite all the sex and marriage reform resources available, she finds solace in a romance novel, a book looked down on by reformers for being prudish and sexually repressive. If Hilde R. wants tenderness and passion, why not turn to van de Velde or Bauer? Arthur Schnitzler remained popular among Viennese women; his 1921 play *Reigen* was especially beloved, given women's "addiction" to "eroticism," according to one contemporary.[218] Meanwhile, Freud displaced Mantegazza as the erotic writer of choice.[219] Instead of reading these luminaries and despite writing a letter to Hugo Bettauer's advice column, Hilde R. continues reading bad books. In fact, these books seem to satisfy her more than anything else—precisely because, as Atina Grossmann puts it, within the sex reform movement "women were never given the chance to define, envision, and experience their own sexuality."[220] In contrast to the highbrow literature, bad books gave Hilde R. that chance. Hilde R. was not alone. Despite the many pamphlets, advice books, lectures, and other resources of the sex reform movement, bad books had not fallen out of favor in the interwar period.

Let us imagine that Hilde R. is reading Courths-Mahler's 1918 novel, *Eine ungeliebte Frau* (*An Unloved Woman*), which takes place in the mythological past, sometime in the nineteenth century. The plot centers on the eighteen-year-old orphan Maria (Ria) Rottmann, who is taken in and cared for by the Matern family. The timid Ria ends up falling in love with the family's son, Heinz, who sees in her a sister and not a lover. It is Heinz's inability to both feel and detect desire that serves as the main obstacle in the story. He was a man who "did not ask for great passion. . . ."[221] Heinz is an unusual, even subversive romantic male hero, the opposite of *Fanny Roth*'s Josef Fellner: a hero for whom sensual desire does not come naturally.

Heinz initially views his relationship with Ria as that between two siblings. He "brought Ria sweets, teased her about her bad habit[s] . . . and asked her if she still played with dolls." Even when he asks for her hand in marriage—out of obligation to her and to fulfill his dead father's wish—he frames it in terms of fraternal love. He says to her, "stay with me, Ria. I love you like a sister and I see you as my father's prized legacy. Because people will talk, we cannot live together as brother and sister. . . . Do you want to be my wife, Ria?" Because Heinz believes that "a marriage that is based on mutual esteem has more potential than one that is based on the intoxication (*Rausch*) of passion," he feels that his proposal is persuasive. It is at this moment that the book's title makes its first appearance: Ria accepts the proposal but believes that she will forever remain "an unloved woman."[222]

Instead of simply living together as brother and sister, they marry as brother and sister. In a subversive twist, the story follows how these pseudo-siblings come to be lovers. Indeed, over time Heinz's fraternal affection for Ria metamorphoses into desire. At an important turning point in the plot, Heinz has a revelation: he "saw [Ria] the way a man looks at a woman"—that is, with sensual desire. "He desired to kiss her red mouth and to softly open her tightly pressed lips." With marriage, his desire grows. "Since Ria became his bride, he detected new charms about her almost every day." He noticed her "delicate little ears that always blushed when she was excited, her beautiful, slim hands with their narrow, rosy fingernails and the soft, elegant neckline. . . ."[223] If Heinz had disregarded Ria's body at the beginning of the book, toward the end he becomes obsessed with it, even spending time in her bedroom while she is away to take in her scent.

By contrast, in an interesting reversal of the gendering of sensual desire, Ria is naturally inclined toward it. In this way, she is very different from both Goldelse and Fanny Roth, who had to learn to recognize and experience desire. When Ria first meets Heinz, "a feeling came over her, as if something miraculous had happened to her, as if the world shone in a new light." Heinz—without doing much of anything at all—"conquered her young, untouched heart," and she felt "that something in her had completely changed, that something new had seized her soul—and everything that had existed until now stood in the shadow." In addition to recognizing desire as illumination, Ria also experiences it in her body: the rush of her "blood puls[ing] wildly into her heart" and a dizzying sensation "as if the floor would give way beneath her feet."[224]

And yet, Ria does not act on her desire—quite the contrary: she does everything possible to conceal her true feelings from Heinz. It is precisely because she does not pursue and fulfill the desire with Heinz that contemporary sex reformers such as Hugo Bettauer viewed this book and others by Courths-Mahler as sexually repressed. For reformers, desire was only the prelude to the main event—sexual fulfillment—and not the event itself. Pleasure did not seem to exist outside the confines of heterosexual intercourse.

Darüber hinaus.

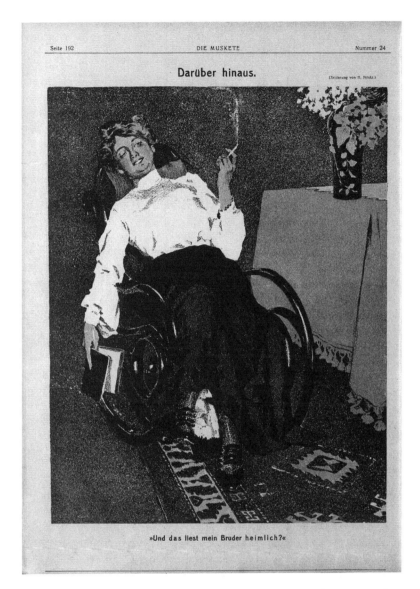

»Und das liest mein Bruder heimlich?«

FIGURE 4.5. This caricature from 1906 depicts an intimate scene of a woman reading a bad book—a book that "my brother reads in secret." From "Darüber hinaus," *Die Muskete*, 15 March 1906, 192. ANNO/ÖNB.

But not pursuing desire is not the same as extinguishing it. A desire that is not pursued is still a desire recognized and experienced in the body. It becomes a desire turned in on itself: not only is it sustained, but it also turns burning hot, becoming a source of power and, crucially, pleasure. In a caricature from 1906, a young woman is shown leaning back in a rocking chair, her legs crossed, as she loosely holds an open book in one hand and a cigarette in the other (see fig. 4.5). As she grins, she thinks to herself, "and this is what my brother reads in secret?" Although we do not know what the book is, we do know that it must be a bad book. We also know that she finds sensual pleasure in reading it: her eyes are half closed, her cheeks are rosy, and her body is limp with delight. Reading Courths-Mahler's novel, the new woman Hilde R. not only learned *recognition* and *experience* of her own desire in her body; she also attained *fulfillment* in that same body. She was reading for pleasure, after all—and she found it: within herself.

※

This chapter identified sensual desire—that is, the experience of desire through the body and senses—as an aspect of new womanhood. It traced how, despite bourgeois morality, which equated womanhood with purity, Viennese women from different class and religious backgrounds started flouting moral conventions by seeking a sexual education that introduced them to the practices of sensual desire. In this way, they became desiring women, expressing their agency and sense of "self" through their sensuality. And insofar as gender constitutes a series of embodied practices, the practice of desiring both generated and, ultimately, constituted a new kind of woman.

It was the city's booming publishing industry that laid the groundwork for sexual education and knowledge in the form of, first, bad books and, second, sex reform literature. Bad books were not intended to be educational, yet these so-called tasteless and immoral texts taught Viennese women to recognize, experience, and—as the above close reading of Courths-Mahler's *Eine ungeliebte Frau* makes clear—fulfill sensual desire in their own bodies. To stress one of the main points of this book, if the gendered body is interconnected with its urban environment, then urban modernity, in this case the publishing industry, emerged in tandem with the practices of new womanhood.

Like bad books, interwar sex reform literature had a similarly pedagogical effect on women, but with one slight difference: it claimed that desire should be pursued and fulfilled with the body of a heterosexual partner, preferably within marriage. While many Viennese women still read Courths-Mahler novels and followed their more nuanced advice, others derived their education from the reform movement's heteronormative and marriage-centric literature. In fact, marriage became *the* site of sensual desire, so much so that a cold marriage became grounds for separation or divorce.

Insofar as bad books often de-emphasized the pursuit and fulfillment of sensuality with another body, they came to be viewed as sexually repressive and regressive. And yet, the sex reform literature that came after it was arguably much more rigid, given its uncompromising emphasis on the triad of heterosexuality, marriage, and sensual fulfillment. As I argued in the introduction, the history of gender and sexuality does not follow a teleological path toward progressive liberation; instead, it is "syncopated" and replete with contradictions.[225] Unsurprisingly, the practices of new womanhood were similarly replete with ambivalence. Both contradiction and ambivalence will figure prominently in chapter 5, which considers how Viennese women started internalizing the medical gaze and directing it at their own bodies and selves.

* 5 *

New Visions

REPRODUCTIVE EMBODIMENT
AND THE MEDICAL GAZE

In May 1927, a young housemaid by the name of Julianne Schneeberger was convicted of abortion under §144 of the Austrian Criminal Code.[1] The seventeen-year-old pleaded guilty and, in her testimony, recalled that in October 1926 her menses had failed to appear and "I thought to myself that I am pregnant." She paid a visit to a local physician, Dr. Muska, who confirmed her pregnancy.[2] Not knowing who the father was—it may have been her abusive boyfriend at the time, Anton Zöhling, or someone else, "because I also had sex with other men"—she contacted a midwife (*Hebamme*), most likely forty-three-year-old Elisabeth Steffl.[3] Schneeberger recalled that a "woman unknown to me came over and put something inside of me down there." That "something" was "a little tube" that "remained inside for a half hour." Afterward, the midwife "took it out again and left and in the evening I started bleeding again." Schneeberger observed closely and deliberately as the midwife inserted and removed the catheter from her vagina—a procedure that she knew would terminate her pregnancy. By observing closely and deliberately, by wielding the medical gaze, Schneeberger engaged in a practice of new womanhood.

The Austrian Criminal Code of 1852 criminalized all instances of abortion, with one notable exception: if it transpired in circumstances involving a mother's ignorance.[4] The anti-abortion legislation was divided into two parts: the first part, §§144 to 146, targeted mothers and fathers; the second part, §§147 to 148, targeted abortion providers. Article §144 criminalized women who "deliberately" (*absichtlich*)—that is to say, without ignorance—underwent abortions, while §§145 and 146 articulated the details of their punishment. If a woman deliberately attempted to abort her fetus, but failed, she could be sentenced to hard labor (*schwerem Kerker*) for six months to one year. If she succeeded in aborting her fetus, she could be sentenced to one to five years. Article §147 criminalized those who attempted to provide or succeeded in providing abortions "against the knowledge and consent of the mother." In other words, the abortion provider was guilty if the mother was ignorant of the procedure and, according to §148, could be sentenced to one to five years of hard labor and, in case the mother was harmed (*Gefahr am Leben oder Nachteil an der Gesundheit*), to five to ten years.

By pleading guilty, Schneeberger admitted to having deliberately undergone an abortion. But not all women who terminated their pregnancies acted as Schneeberger did. Some Viennese women pleaded ignorance—not only of the abortion, but also and more significantly even of the pregnancy.

Elisabeth Töpfel was one such woman. A shopgirl living in the working-class XVth District, Fünfhaus, Töpfel was convicted of abortion in December 1899. According to her police testimony, Töpfel had intercourse with her brother-in-law, Wilhelm Bauernfeind, in October of that year, and after her menses failed to appear for two months, Bauernfeind advised her to see a midwife whose advertisement he found in a newspaper.[5] According to Töpfel, the midwife, Hermine Rambousek, examined her, "yet could not give any definite information about my pregnancy." After inserting something into her vagina, she reportedly showed Töpfel blood on her finger and said, "you see, blood is already flowing, it is nothing." For Töpfel, the blood was evidence of her never having been pregnant in the first place; it was, she believed, not the blood from an abortion, but from the two missed menses. The underlying assumption was that the body could withhold menstrual blood without being pregnant, and that a midwife could coax it to be released. By the end of the trial, Töpfel's charges were dropped.

Although the anti-abortion legislation did not change in the period under investigation, women's stories did.[6] For years, Viennese women like Töpfel pleaded ignorance. By the 1920s, however, more women were likely to follow Schneeberger's lead. By wielding the medical gaze, they saw themselves as pregnant and willingly chose to undergo abortions. Some women invoked eugenics to argue that their commitment to the health of the social body led them to seek abortions. Others drew on modern medical knowledge to self-induce an abortion, identify a natural miscarriage, or evaluate whether a sensation was painful or not. These latter women engaged in a form of medical literacy that allowed them to make calculated decisions about their bodies. At the root of this medical literacy was a new vision of woman's body as primarily reproductive.

This chapter uses archival abortion trial records from 1899 to 1931 to examine how women living in and around Vienna experienced their reproductive bodies over time. Because many of the women accused of abortion belonged to the working class, the primary focus of this chapter will, with some exceptions, be working-class women. The first section considers late nineteenth- and early twentieth-century folk medicine, which was rooted in a Hippocratic medical tradition and its conception of bodies as fluid, fickle, and porous. Within this paradigm, women's ideal state was during menstruation, which signified fertility and promoted bodily flow. The second section teases out the relationship between city and body and traces how, with the emergence of a modern medical paradigm, the displacement of lay midwives by professional medicine, and the proliferation of a bourgeois language and culture of hygiene in nineteenth- and early twentieth-century Vienna, women came to see bodily flow as something abject and shameful, in need of cleansing and containment. Pregnancy— the condition in which women's menstrual flow temporarily ceased—thus became women's ideal state, so that the female body came to be defined by its reproductive capacity. The third section returns to the issue of abortion. Given the new vision of the reproductive body, what many women formerly experienced as a procedure to unblock blood came to be understood as an abortion. In this manner, women—in yet another facet of new womanhood—drew on contemporary medical knowledge (as largely practiced by men), as well as on its shame-less—as in being exercised without shame—medical gaze (as largely engaged in by men), to advocate for themselves and their reproductive bodies. Wielding this medical gaze vis-à-vis one's own body thus became an act of new womanhood, an everyday practice that, over time, contributed to the transformation of what it meant to be a woman in Vienna.

The Fluid, Fickle Body: Redefining Ignorance

In 1902, three years after Elisabeth Töpfel pleaded ignorance, Marie Kratochwil, a young woman who migrated to Vienna from Galicia—the crown land just north of Bukowina—employed a similar defense.[7] Like Töpfel, Kratochwil claimed ignorance of the abortion, stating, "I had no idea that what the midwife was doing with me was punishable." According to her, she "had done all of this because she thought that, as a result, the period would return," thereby suggesting that the visit to the midwife was related to her menstrual cycle and not to pregnancy. Although the court pronounced Kratochwil guilty, she was only sentenced to two months of hard labor.

It is quite probable that both Töpfel and Kratochwil had knowingly undergone abortions but feigned bodily ignorance.[8] After all, as I discussed in chapter 4, most fin-de-siècle intellectuals understood ideal womanhood to be primarily asexual. The sexologist Richard von Krafft-Ebing, for example, insisted that women were sexually passive, lacking desire, and naturally inclined to chastity and monogamy.[9] How, then, could women be expected to know anything about their sexual bodies? Claiming ignorance may have been a useful strategy for maintaining innocence.

And yet, as Leslie Reagan argues, "blocked menses cannot be dismissed as an excuse made by women who knew they were pregnant."[10] Indeed, it is equally probable that they truly were ignorant—not of their own bodies, but of the body imagined by the medical profession, or what I call the modern female reproductive body. Most Viennese women were somatically in tune with their physical bodies, sensitive to their menstrual cycles, and committed to their cycle's consistency, so that their experience of bodily processes differed from modern physicians' understanding of it. As Cornelie Usborne has observed, "according to medical teaching a foetus in the womb was viable from conception but this had little resonance with many women" who "recognized only what they could actually see and feel: the lack of blood stains."[11] Thus, if physicians understood missed menses as a sign of pregnancy, many women saw and felt it as a lack of blood; what physicians understood to be an abortion, many women saw and felt as a procedure to restore blood. Lay women's knowledge about their reproductive bodies was thus rooted in that which they could perceive with their senses: what they saw, felt, smelled, heard, and tasted.[12] Theirs was an epistemology grounded in the senses.

Historians have often "tried to interpret the observations of the past within the logic of contemporary medical 'theory.'" This, writes Barbara Duden, is problematic because it "presupposes the rationality of a constituted, modern body."[13] I therefore take the Viennese women's testimonies at face value while bracketing my own medical assumptions and bodily experiences—the point being to understand what they felt as real. As I show below, ordinary Viennese women at the fin de siècle were only just beginning to become familiar with the medicalized reproductive body. In fact, many women, whose medical knowledge was mostly derived from medical lay culture traditions passed down from generation to generation, occasionally experienced and sensorily perceived their bodies in ways similar to those described in Duden's study of women patients in eighteenth-century Eisenach, a town in what is now the German state of Thuringia. Although some 150 years separate the early modern patients from the Viennese women in this chapter, striking parallels exist, especially in matters concerning menstruation, suggesting the resilience of early modern ideas in the face of growing medical professionalization in the nineteenth century.

MAINTAINING (MENSTRUAL) FLOW

Referred to as "the rule" (*die Regel*), "the period" (*die Periode*), or "being unwell" (*unwohl sein*), menstruation was a deeply holistic experience that most Viennese women—bourgeois or working-class—not only learned to live with, but also anticipated. The feminist phenomenologist Iris Marion Young describes menstruation as giving "a unique temporal shape to a woman's life."[14] "The monthly bleeding punctuates [women's] lives, marking significant events, and it is also routine"—so routine that German speakers refer to it as "the rule."[15] Furthermore, Young notes that it "mundanely organizes [women's] everyday adult memory" and "orients [women's] self-narrative"—including the narrative of womanhood.[16] Although bourgeois women rarely wrote at length about menstruation in their diaries or personal letters, they occasionally made note of "being unwell" precisely because of its routineness. After strolling around Munich, for example, the Viennese socialite and composer Alma Mahler-Werfel (née Schindler) "realized that I'd been unwell—and hadn't even noticed. The pain comes so often," she continued, "I hadn't even given it a thought."[17] Often accompanying menstruation, pain also became routinized so that it could occasionally, but certainly not always, be ignored or at least remain unarticulated.

If menstruation added a temporal shape to women's lives, then missing a period became a noticeable, even anxiety-inducing event—though less so for working-class women, who often missed their periods due to inadequate nourishment, frequent pregnancies, and other circumstances. After the factory worker Katharina Wyzliba noticed that "her monthly 'rule' failed to appear" for sixteen weeks, she immediately consulted with a midwife.[18] She reiterated that her period had always been "regular" (*regelmässig*) and "normal," indicating that she expected it to appear on a monthly basis. Another factory worker, Marie Wesely, observed that, "because in the past I was always unwell on a regular basis, I noticed immediately this time [when] . . . I was not unwell for five weeks."[19]

At the fin de siècle, many bourgeois and working-class women did not see menstruation as the pathology that the medical profession would eventually deem it to be, but as a healthy and cleansing process. Within the Hippocratic tradition, which was developed and popularized by the ancient Greek physician and philosopher Galen, menstruation was believed to be the shedding of an excess of blood, a plethora.[20] According to this tradition, the body was composed of four humors, including blood, that needed to be kept in a state of balance and flow; menstruation signified a body whose humors were in this state, and which therefore was fertile.[21] These ideas continued to be popular in the early modern period, with contemporaries likening menstruation to a self-healing process, a discharge of a plethora inside the body that maintained bodily flow.[22] But even at the fin de siècle, these ideas persisted, so that despite its association with "being unwell," menstruation continued to be experienced as the very opposite or, as Cornelie Usborne puts it, "an essential ingredient of [women's] well-being."[23] That this view was shared across classes is not surprising: bourgeois women were often raised by working-class nannies who would expose them to folk medical wisdom, thereby shaping their understanding of their bodies.

If menstruation referred to the healthy flow and discharge of blood, then missed menses could be equated with misdirected blood or what Duden describes as "matter [that] let itself be lured away" from being discharged. By the same token, "the inner flow, if not drained off, engendered a hardening, a petrification; it was actually viscous and clogging," leading to decay and, eventually, death.[24] Because the womb was likened to a basin collecting blood, it posed a threat to the healthy flow of blood; thus, the menstrual process was replete with competing forces: one that led to plethora, petrification, and stagnation and one that led to flow and discharge. The threat of stagnation was therefore always present. Even an early pregnancy could be a form of stagnation, a growth of excess matter that needed to be expelled.[25] Only at quickening did the stagnation come to be viewed as a fetus in need of preservation.[26] This last point is worth emphasizing because it highlights the instability of the category and experience of pregnancy.[27] According to Duden, "the true thing hidden behind a big belly came to light only with birth."[28] Only once women could sensorily perceive the baby—whether by feeling movement in the belly or by giving birth—could pregnancy be confirmed.

Because good health involved the flow and discharge of excess blood, some early modern contemporaries believed that men could menstruate as well.[29] Within the plethora model, the body was viewed holistically, its interior likened to what Duden describes as "unstructured osmotic space," so that all blood, including menstrual blood, was one and the same.[30] Furthermore, excess blood could exit the body via many different pathways through the process of "vicarious menstruation." A man could experience menstrual bleeding when he had a nosebleed or hemorrhoids. A woman could still menstruate, even if she bled from some place other than her vagina. What defined womanhood was not the act of menstruation per se, but its regularity and rhythm—a definition that would undergo a drastic shift within the new medical paradigm.[31]

Although many of these ideas were popular in the early eighteenth century, they continued to inform both working-class and bourgeois women's perceptions of their bodies into the twentieth century in the form of folk medicine.[32] Precisely because menstruation was regarded as a cleansing, fin-de-siècle women often avoided changing their underwear or washing their genitals so as not to interfere with the process. A body was more "open" and vulnerable during menstruation, so exposing it to the environment was a risk to be avoided.[33] As the Viennese sexologist Rudolf Glaessner observed, for many years "changing underwear during the period, the washing of external genitalia, or even bathing [were] often viewed as a dangerous experiment and the reason for many women's illnesses."[34] Some women would even forgo wearing pads, the logic being that these could block blood from being discharged properly, as one late nineteenth-century physician explained: "and so it happens that in addition to underwear, also the genitals, the abdomen, and the thighs are more or less stiff with dried blood."[35]

A similar logic of not wanting to interfere with the process dictated bourgeois women's practice of taking to their beds when menstruating—something that working-class women would not have been able to do. In a letter from 1911, the teacher Tilde Halarevici-Mell (née Mell) wrote to her friend, Tilly Hanzel-Hübner (née Hübner), that "I had a really bad Easter because ever since my last period of being unwell, I have been suffering from a vaginal infection that requires daily medical attention and is very painful."[36] She spent days in bed, avoiding all forms of movement. Hanzel-Hübner noted that due to being unwell she did not go to school for three days straight.[37] Resting in the privacy of their bedrooms protected women from the forces that might interfere with the flow, leading to stagnation.

In the early modern period, anger and fear, a cold wind and sudden rain shower, an injury, or other "shocks to the system" were frequently cited as causing stagnation.[38] The body was believed to be covered in orifices; it was permeable, so that the inside of the body was, to some extent, always in touch with the outside world. Fin-de-siècle women similarly viewed their bodies in relation to the environment, so that strong emotions, bad weather, or a tight corset could be sources of stagnation, commonly referred to as "blood blockage" (*gestocktes Blut*).[39] Ida Haudek, for instance, believed that her menses were late due to "agitation" (*Aufregung*), which in turn blocked her menstrual blood from flowing. She went to see a midwife who conducted a procedure during which she felt that "something firm was discharged, I think it was dried blood."[40] Haudek insisted that this was the very blood that her body had initially blocked—that it was a petrified, clogged plethora. Elisabeth Töpfel and Marie Kratochwil, the women discussed at the beginning of this chapter, felt their blood to be similarly blocked and in need of discharge. Kratochwil's mother even explained her daughter's blockage as a result of a cold: "because she went out in bad weather."[41] Many testimonies contain similar references to clumps of blood.[42] If those accused of having abortions, like Töpfel and Kratochwil, referred to the discharged blood as "dried blood" or a "bloody clump," they were effectively denying that they had been pregnant and that an abortion had taken place. Instead, they had suffered from a blood blockage—stagnation—and the blood clump was just that, a clump of excess blood that had been "lured away" from its normal trajectory toward discharge.

There is a somatic quality to women's descriptions of blood blockages, which conjure up physical sensations and images of blood accumulating in the body, decaying, and then being released as a dried-up mass. The images are bloody, based on sensory perception, and stand in stark contrast to the overly sanitized narratives of the medical profession, which neatly explained missing periods as a symptom of pregnancy.[43] Blood blockage is also a messy explanation because it characterizes menstruation—and the female body more generally—as tentative, a product of whim instead of scientific regularity. Julia Kristeva identifies menstrual blood as societally "abject" for drawing attention to the permeability of the body's borders.[44] There is, she argues, nothing inherently dirty about these fluids; rather, a fluid becomes dirty as it exits the body and enters a space in which it does not "belong," thereby disrupting order. Menstrual blood, in particular, acquires its status as abject because it cannot be contained; despite efforts to conceal and monitor it, the blood leaks and spills unexpectedly.

Pace Kristeva, for many women living in and around Vienna at the fin de siècle menstrual blood was not, as I have shown above, necessarily abject. While the accumulation of it was dangerous, the blood itself was considered to be nutritious and healthy.[45] Blood blockages, bloody clumps, and fickle periods were simply several aspects of the much messier and more fluid worldview—what Luce Irigaray might describe as a feminine-centered metaphysics of fluidity and tactility—that celebrated, rather than contested, the permeability of the body.[46] What did it matter if genitals, abdomen, and thighs were covered in dried blood, if fluids were moving and flowing regularly?

Ordinary women would frequently discuss their menses, share stories, and exchange advice with one another, including recipes for emmenagogues, substances that stimulated menstrual flow.[47] One reason so many women visited midwives to "unblock" their blood in the first place was because friends and family members urged them to do so. Kratochwil admitted that while she initially believed her missed menses to be an indication of pregnancy, after discussing the issue with her mother and aunt she became convinced that she was suffering from a blood blockage. This episode hints at a significant change taking place at this time: while mother and aunt (women most likely born in the mid-nineteenth century) still held on to folk wisdom, Kratochwil (born in 1882) was beginning to view matters—and matter—differently, including her sense of womanhood.

The Modern Reproductive Female Body: Viennese Physicians and the Medical Gaze

Despite the successful unblocking of blood, most of the women in the trial records were forced to go to the hospital due to severe, sometimes fatal cases of blood poisoning. It was there that police would arrest the women. Once in the hands of the authorities, women would undergo invasive medical examinations by court physicians that resulted in detailed descriptions of their body parts and reproductive organs as well as their medical histories. Physicians would squeeze, touch, press, and insert hands and objects into the accused's body. In the case of Barbara Müller in 1916, for example, Prof. Dr. Haberdas and Dr. Max Wimmer engaged in an intrusive physical examination and made the following observations: she is of "average height, has middle-sized flaccid breasts, which, when squeezed, produce a yellow drop . . . the vulva is loose. . . . Both vaginal walls are somewhat collapsed, the vagina is short, the womb is bigger, coarse, anteflexed."[48] In their examination of Müller, Haberdas and Wimmer deployed what Michel Foucault has referred to as the medical gaze, "a perceptual act sustained by a logic of operations" in which the patient's body comes to be known, via the techniques of observation, palpation, percussion, and auscultation, and diagnosed as a medical object.[49] Foucault argues that this penetrating gaze was the same one deployed by physicians during autopsies—which, in Vienna after the 1850s, were a fundamental aspect of world-renowned clinical education. As a gaze that peered into the innermost recesses of the body, it was shame-less through and through. In this way, the medical gaze must be understood as a mode of power, for those who wielded it came to know the body-object, even its most vulnerable parts.

What sort of knowledge were physicians looking for in the first place? They focused primarily on determining whether the accused women had been pregnant, inspecting breast size, nipple pigment, abdominal marks, vaginal discharge, labia color and length, uterus size, and cervix texture.

Lactating breasts, stretch marks on the abdomen and "a stretched out" uterus, for example, indicated that the accused had in fact been pregnant. And if she had been pregnant, physicians argued, then she may have undergone an abortion. Unlike lay medical culture, which described pregnancy as unstable and occurring only at quickening, modern physicians understood pregnancy as starting at conception and as soon as menstrual blood ceased to flow. "If pregnancy occurs, then there is the well-known symptom of no period," concluded Wilhelm Hahn in 1905.[50] For Julianne Schneeberger—the woman who pleaded guilty at the beginning of this chapter—her missed menses were quite simply a symptom of pregnancy.

Perhaps most significantly, while lay culture viewed menstruation as women's ideal state of health, professional medicine believed pregnancy to be that ideal state. Indeed, physicians increasingly came to view menstruation as a pathology, a deviation from health, and a "failed production."[51] By the same token, the menstruating uterus was imagined as pathological, an "open wound" that required the utmost cleanliness and care.[52] Menstrual blood was, accordingly, contaminating, dirty, and abject—and, significantly, a source of shame—so that even sex workers had to stay celibate during their periods, lest they "contaminate" their clients with their blood.[53] But menstruation was also tied to deviance. Bouts of "menstrual madness," such as hysteria (chapter 3), were believed to be common among young women and girls. For example, physicians at the Lower Austrian Provincial Institution for the Care and Cure of the Mentally Ill and for Nervous Disorders "Am Steinhof," noted that the psychiatric patient Rosa Jahn regularly suffered from "states of agitation" when menstruating, while another, Vinzencia Kacafirek, was prone to suicidal thoughts during her cycle (she was found trying to jump into the Danube in the late summer of 1921).[54] Similarly, physicians claimed that menstruation set in earlier among girls of deviant "racial groups" (including those living in warmer and southern climates), brunettes, and urban dwellers.[55]

One reason for the new conception of menstruation-as-pathology was a paradigm shift in medicine. By the late eighteenth century, a new Western medical paradigm began taking hold which came to see the body no longer holistically but as composed of discrete organs with specific faculties and secretions.[56] This paradigm became more widespread once autopsies became a fundamental aspect of diagnostic medicine, which dissected a body to render its different parts visible. Starting in the mid-nineteenth century, Vienna established itself as a leading center in the fields of pathology and anatomy, known for its widespread use of autopsy in medical research.[57] While one reason for the popularity of autopsy was

Vienna's intellectual commitment to scientific materialism—the idea that the observable natural body could be the greatest source of knowledge— another reason was, according to Tatjana Buiklijas, related to the city's cult around death, rooted in a Roman Catholicism characterized by ornate Baroque churches, *memento mori*, relics, All Souls Day celebrations, elaborate rituals of mourning, and funeral marches.[58] Even Vienna's Habsburg rulers were embalmed and buried in monumental caskets in the city's *Kapuzinergruft*, which can be visited to this day. For the Viennese, death was the fulfillment of life, and "it was the ambition of every true Viennese to end up as 'a handsome corpse' [*schöne Leich'*] with a fine funeral procession and many companions escorting him on his last journey," recalled the Austrian Jewish writer Stefan Zweig.[59] It was precisely this "exaggerated reverence for the dead that encouraged indifference to the living," observed William M. Johnston, so that "Vienna's physicians seemed to prize the results of postmortem autopsies more highly than saving a patient."[60]

Once on the autopsy table, a body could be opened up, its insides rendered visible, its organs and parts laid bare to the piercing medical gaze. And if the body was no longer viewed as fluid and holistic, but as constitutive of solid parts, then it was not the whole body that produced menstrual blood, but a specific body part—namely, the uterus. By locating the site of menstruation (a "pathology") in the female genitalia, such phenomena as male menstruation and vicarious menstruation came to be considered improbable, if not impossible, and were therefore dismissed. In fact, menstruation, as well as its "cure," pregnancy, were what came to define womanhood and distinguish it from the other sex.[61] As Duden observes, "the new 'body' was defined through the process of isolating the female organs from the traditional undefined body: not only the 'mother' (womb) and the woman who carried it were defined, but male and female bodies."[62] The modern reproductive female body was born.

In the eyes of the Viennese court physicians who examined the women accused of abortion and whose reference point was always pregnancy, the blood clump was always an aborted fetus. After Barbara Müller admitted to having had an abortion and noted experiencing "strong bleeding" after the procedure, the physicians explained that the blood clump had been a fetus (*Leibesfrucht* or *Frucht*). Beholden to the medical gaze that was sustained by diagnostic logic, the clump was no longer just a clump. Unsurprisingly, over time, many women's testimonies reflected this change: if knowledge about their reproductive bodies had previously been rooted in what they could access via proprioception and perceive with their senses, soon that source of knowledge came to be replaced by the diagnostic gaze of professional medicine. In Anna Koller's testimony to the police from 1924, she recalled going to the toilet and observing the *Frucht* come out.[63] "Everything came together. The *Frucht* was in the sack. She showed the length of the fruit to be around 15 cm." After the physician, Dr. Axelrod, arrived, he insisted that the fetus be given a proper burial. Another woman, Aloisia Geringer, instantly started "wailing" (*jammern*) once she aborted the fetus and "recognized it clearly as a human."[64] In all these accounts, the clump was no longer blocked menstrual blood but a tiny human in need of mourning, a proper burial, maybe even a funeral march. By the same token, as professional medicine and its medical gaze became more pervasive, women themselves began to view their own bodies in a completely new light. One practice of new womanhood, I argue, was the adoption of this medical gaze vis-à-vis one's own body. In the following two sections, I explore how this shift came about by examining first the fight against "quackery" or lay midwifery, and second the proliferation of modern hygiene initiatives in late nineteenth- and early twentieth-century Vienna. As the city was remade into a center of modern medicine and hygiene, the body changed along with it.

DISCREDITING FOLK MEDICINE:
THE FIGHT AGAINST QUACKERY

The shift to a new medical paradigm went hand in hand with the emergence of a physician-dominated medical establishment, which institutionalized obstetrics within the university setting and absorbed midwifery into the professional fold. For years, midwives had been lay practitioners whose knowledge was derived from years of experience and folk medicine. With the founding of the first school of midwifery in Vienna in 1752, the practice changed as more midwives received formal medical training.[65] In 1808, the *Midwives' Instruction* (*Hebammen-Instruktion*) formalized the rules of the new licensed profession, outlining midwives' responsibilities, including their availability, religious duties, even their moral demeanor.[66] The Midwives' Instruction was revised in 1874 and 1881, subjecting midwifery to further regulation. Licensed midwives were henceforth required to take antiseptic measures, including the use of carbolic acid. The process of professionalizing midwifery—and the field of obstetrics—effectively placed what had traditionally been the domain of lay women under the control of the male-dominated medical establishment.[67] Within the hierarchy of professional medicine, the physician stood above the licensed midwife, his knowledge and practice always being superior to hers.

As a result, midwives without formal training were marginalized and treated as frauds. "The quacks are giving me much grief," wrote one licensed midwife in 1906. "The quack does not need to practice antisepsis at all; she does not ask for clean clothes the way they are prescribed for the midwife; apparently, she does everything herself, even [procedures] that require a doctor's presence. . . ."[68] Publications reporting on quackery (*das Pfuscherinnenwesen*) listed the lay midwife's many infractions: she forgot to wash her hands, thereby infecting her patients; she did operations without proper knowledge or training, often resulting in death; she was not credible, relying on unenlightened medical practices akin to sorcery or witchcraft; and finally, as someone who stood outside the establishment, she performed illegal abortions under the "guise" of unblocking blood.[69] And in the process of equating lay midwifery with quackery, folk medicine—and its practices of unblocking blood—came to be discredited as well.[70]

The fin-de-siècle movement against quackery extended into the interwar period, especially within debates concerning abortion reform.[71] "For a large sum of money, wealthy women can get an abortion at a sanatorium unscathed," observed the socialist activist Adelheid Popp in 1921, "while poor women are threatened by the harshest punishments, if not also forced to put their lives into the hands of quacks."[72] Over the course of the 1920s, the abortion reforms proposed by the Austrian Social Democratic Workers' Party (SDAP) became more physician-centered and dismissive of lay midwives. The SDAP first proposed the *Fristenmodell*, which gave a woman the right to terminate her pregnancy for whatever reason in the first three months prior to quickening; but by the early 1920s, the Party abandoned it in favor of the *Indikationsmodell*, which would make abortion contingent on the approval of physicians.[73] At the Physicians' Conference in May 1924, the Viennese City Councilor for Welfare, Dr. Julius Tandler, expressed his concerns about the practical aspects of the *Fristenmodell*, which relied on women's "dubious" body knowledge.[74] He thus insisted that a panel of medical and legal experts decide whether an abortion was appropriate on a case-by-case basis. If there were medical grounds, or *Indikationen*, for an abortion, the mother would consult with three physicians: a specialist, a gynecologist, and a physician who would serve as the "mandator of society and representative of the authorities."[75] A mother seeking abortion for eugenic *Indikationen* would follow the same procedure, with the addition of consultation with two experts. Finally, if she sought an abortion for social *Indikationen*, a commission consisting of a judge, a physician, a woman, a lawyer "of the embryo," and a chosen representative of society would come to a decision after considering the mother's "social milieu" and "living conditions."[76] In all instances, the intention was the same: to strip lay midwives of their medical authority and to subsume licensed midwives under the authority of the physician.

Despite the movement against quackery, many working-class women continued to view lay midwives as more trustworthy than both their licensed counterparts and physicians. After all, both Schneeberger and Töpfel sought out a midwife. There were several reasons for this. First, lay practitioners often came from the same class as their patients; some of them were a known fixture of their community, district, street, or apartment complex. Second, many lay midwives were old enough to be mothers themselves, and it was their embodied experience of pregnancy, birth, and motherhood that made them more knowledgeable in the eyes of ordinary women.[77] Third, because licensed midwives had to call on a physician in cases of emergency, their services were often costlier than those provided by lay midwives. Traditionally, midwifery was believed to be done out of benevolence for the community, without monetary compensation. Finally, ordinary people were both attached to folk medicine (as evidenced in the above discussion of menstrual flow) and suspicious of professional medicine, which came to be associated with a Jewish, cosmopolitan elite.[78] Perhaps because it was transmitted orally and prioritized the patient's self-diagnosis, folk medicine remained especially popular among women. It would take further "enlightenment," in the form of citywide modern hygiene initiatives, to discredit folk medicine even further and teach ordinary women how to engage in a new embodied practice: wielding the medical gaze.

HYGIENE AS ENLIGHTENMENT: EMBODYING THE MEDICAL GAZE

The Viennese General Hygienic Exhibition (*Allgemeine Hygienische Ausstellung*) opened its doors on 12 May 1906 in the Prater's Rotunde, the large circular construction from the 1873 World's Fair (see fig. 5.1).[79] For about two months, thousands of working-class and bourgeois people from across the Habsburg monarchy and beyond visited the exhibition, for "the great public has a vibrant interest, or let us say a preliminary curiosity, in everything that has to do with healing arts [*Heilkunde*]," reported the *Wiener Sonn- und Montags-Zeitung (Vienna's Sunday and Monday Newspaper).*[80] Visitors were invited to walk through the imposing Rotunde and marvel at displays of model kitchens, bathrooms, and bedrooms, dioramas of local sanatoria and spas, models of trash-collecting apparatuses and "hygienic automobile street cleaners" (*hygienische Automobil-Straßenkehrwagons*), new technologies in dentistry, a collection of strollers and mattresses, reform clothing, and bottles of "healing" liquors and herbal spirits, among many other expositions.[81]

Souvenir
der Allgemeinen hygienischen Ausstellung
Wien – Rotunde 1906.

FIGURE 5.1. A souvenir postcard from the Viennese General Hygienic Exhibition of 1906, featuring the Prater Rotunda. It was inside this circular building that various exhibitors set up interactive displays and dioramas intended to educate the public about personal health and hygiene. This postcard also doubled as an advertisement; on its side, it says in Kurrentschrift: "Unikum Margarine is truly superb." From "2. Prater—Rotunde—Souvenir der Allgemeinen hygienischen Ausstellung Wien," post-card (Vienna: 1906). Wien Museum Inv.-Nr. 238068, CC0.

One of the central goals of the exhibition was to "enlighten" ordinary Viennese people—such as Elisabeth Töpfel, who may very well have visited the exhibition—who still held on to "old, entrenched beliefs" and other "suspicions." The exhibition was believed to "chase away stupidity and darkness," as well as "gradually wipe out superstition," "destroy the conceit of half-knowledge and show the people the true light." Around 1,200 exhibitors took part in this self-styled enlightenment project, engaging visitors and introducing them to the most up-to-date innovations and technologies, including concrete strategies on how to lead a healthier life. This last point is worth emphasizing. Given the exhibition's emphasis on accessibility, exhibitors strove to "translate" the "fruitful thoughts" of science and medicine into the "trivial everyday," to turn an "ingenious thought into useful action."[82]

The science of "useful action" was centered on prophylaxis—that is, preventive medicine. Instead of curing illness and disease, hygienic practices were aimed at preventing them and as such were a huge departure from the more popular tendency, especially among the working classes, to seek medical help only in case of emergency.[83] Hygiene encouraged ordinary people to take responsibility for their own health, ensuring that their homes were well-maintained and that they bathed regularly and washed their clothes. As Alys George has observed, "the goal of hygiene exhibitions was to show people how their bodies could be—that is to create a kind of static exhibition of body techniques that modeled how to achieve aspirational physical ideals."[84] One of the most important body techniques, I argue, involved the embodiment of the medical gaze: the visual, shame-less, and tactile diagnostic examination of one's body in the manner of a physician. Significantly, by embodying this medical gaze, individuals came to view the body as theirs—that is, as part of them*selves*.[85] In fact, this gaze was part of what Jonathan Crary has described as "subjective vision," in which subjectivity "became synonymous with the act of seeing, dissolving the Cartesian ideal of an observer completely focused on an object."[86] Wielding the medical gaze meant becoming aware of a sense of "self" that was embodied: *video ergo sum* (I see, therefore I am). With the institutionalization of hygiene over the course of the nineteenth and early twentieth centuries, individuals learned to deploy this medical gaze themselves vis-à-vis them*selves*, their bodies, as well as the social body or *Volkskörper*.[87] The city's municipal hygiene initiatives created the conditions for this new embodied practice, just as its deployment reinforced the city's initiatives.

Hygiene first became a state concern in the second half of the eighteenth century, in the context of Josephinian reforms and the consolidation of the Austrian Empire into a unified state in 1804. Like other enlightened monarchs, Joseph II believed that the state's well-being depended on its citizens, on "their wealth, their strength, and their capacity to be useful."[88] Strong, healthy citizens meant a stronger, healthier state. And because "only a healthy population is desirable to a state," a "medical policy" (*medicinische Polizey*) was established that was tasked with upholding the hygienic standards and health of the citizenry.[89]

Prophylaxis became a particularly significant concern with the outbreak of two epidemics—cholera between 1831 and 1873, and tuberculosis, known as *"morbus Viennensis"* (the Viennese illness), between 1867 and 1900.[90] Across Europe, physicians and state officials implemented various strategies, such as social distancing and isolation, to maintain public health and prevent the spread of disease. Miasma theory, which explained disease transmission as produced by noxious smells, was particularly widespread during the cholera years. In Vienna, the medical profession was especially drawn to this theory, insisting that individual hygienic conduct was key to disease prevention.[91] A similar emphasis on hygienic conduct informed the discourse around tuberculosis later in the century. A 1911 poster, for example, recommended that Viennese residents engage in the following body techniques: "strict cleanliness of the apartment, clothing, and food, concern for fresh air also in the winter, concern for the bodily thriving of adults and children."[92]

With the growth of the bourgeoisie in nineteenth-century Europe, hygiene became a marker of class status.[93] Cleanliness and purity came to represent refinement and bourgeois civilization—in short, enlightenment—while filth and disease were associated with backwardness and the poor.[94] Bourgeois hygienic norms dictated that not only clothing, but even the body wearing the clothes had to be cleaned, preferably immersed in water and scrubbed with soap.[95] A Viennese etiquette book directed at ladies, published in 1878, insisted that "without cleanliness there is no health, without health there is no true beauty and . . . whoever neglects one's body loses one's right to nature, to oneself, and to one's environment."[96] The bourgeoisie would eventually impose their hygienic norms on others, especially the lower strata of society, framing this imposition as a civilizing mission to make bodies healthier, more beautiful, and more virtuous.[97] And in the process of their implementation the body came to be seen as a closed system: contained, separate, and private.

The liberal bourgeoisie's accession to power in the 1860s ushered in a new era of public health and hygiene in the Habsburg lands. In 1864, the Vienna Municipal Health Office (*Stadtphysikat*) was established, tasked with collecting information and analyzing statistics about the health of the

Volkskörper, as well as documenting cases of pollution and disease.[98] The Sanitation Law (*Reichssanitätsgesetz*) of 1870 placed sanitation workers, physicians, pharmacists, the sanitation police, medical institutions, and hospitals under the control of the urban administration (*Staatsverwaltung*), thereby centralizing a system of sanitation and hygiene. Meanwhile, Josef Nowak became the first professor of hygiene in Vienna in 1875; his *Lehrbuch der Hygiene* (*Hygiene Textbook*, 1881) was the first modern textbook on the subject published in Austria.[99] To ensure that this knowledge could be made accessible to ordinary people, the Austrian Society for Hygiene (*Österreichische Gesellschaft für Gesundheitspflege*) was launched. Exhibitions became an increasingly popular means to "enlighten" people beyond the bourgeoisie, as evidenced by the International Congress for Hygiene in 1887 and the Viennese General Hygiene Exhibition in 1906. Hygiene exhibitions also cropped up across Europe, notably in London in 1884 and Dresden in 1911.

The concern with hygiene was also a function of urban growth, modernity, and science and technology. Over the course of the late nineteenth century, many European cities underwent rapid expansion. Between 1850 and 1910, the imperial capital ballooned in size and population, increasing from about 431,000 to 2 million inhabitants, so that maintaining public health became an important municipal concern.[100] To house Vienna's many new residents, the number of residential buildings mushroomed, and overcrowding, along with all its attendant ills, became commonplace. New industries and factories cropped up on the city's peripheries, such as the Ottakringer Brewery in 1890, the Anker Bread Factory in 1891, and the Meinl Coffee Factory in 1912. Public transportation expanded to include streetcars (first steam-powered, then electric) and a city railroad. And by this time, city streets were no longer occupied only by horse-drawn carriages, but also by newfangled automobiles emitting clouds of exhaust. Increased urbanization and industrialization forced the municipality to implement numerous sanitary measures, including a sewage system, a system of trash collection, paved streets, clean drinking water and public baths, and parks and green space.[101] Although the system of public sanitation broke down during the First World War, the city continued to make efforts to revitalize it after the war.[102]

The emphasis on sanitation and hygiene was reinforced by the European panic over the spread of venereal diseases such as gonorrhea and syphilis. Contemporaries believed that the best strategy to control the spread of disease was through a system of regulation that subjected sex workers to invasive medical inspections. In the Habsburg monarchy, the regulation of prostitution was introduced in 1873 (chapter 1): it required sex workers to carry health books (*Gesundheitsbücher*) containing their medical histories. Although sex workers did not write in their health books themselves—this was done by a physician during their routine examinations—the existence of such a document was further evidence of the new awareness of personal health and hygiene. In fact, sex workers were instructed to engage in a range of body techniques, especially before and after sexual intercourse, including cleaning outer and inner genitals.[103] Moreover, they were to inspect their genitalia, especially the urethra and labia, to make sure there was no discharge, redness, signs of abrasion, sores, or roughness. Finally, sex workers were asked to identify sensations of pain (*Schmerzen*) or burning (*Brennen*)—a theme I return to below—as these were indicators of disease. If they felt any of these, they were urged to check themselves into a hospital.

Unlike the state, the Austrian Society for the Fight Against Venereal Diseases (*Gesellschaft zur Bekämpfung der Geschlechtskrankheiten*) was committed to fighting VD through the "enlightenment" (*Aufklärung*) of the entire population, not just sex workers.[104] At the International Hygiene Exhibition in Dresden in 1911, the Society had an exhibit that displayed colorful wax renderings of sores, ulcers, and growths, as well as other deformities related to syphilis and gonorrhea.[105] The purpose of these "horrifying" and "disgusting" sculptures was to educate the public, because "it is good to clearly see the bad and the worst of life . . . [so that] one will be able to protect oneself better than before." The Society made a point of emphasizing that its work was part and parcel of the larger fight against "ignorance" and "false shame": "[We] cannot rely on hygiene alone; only with the harmonious cooperation of hygienic, educational, and social measures can there be success." Insofar as personal hygiene practices relied on becoming acquainted with and inspecting "shameful parts" of the body, the Society's second mission, to combat ignorance and shame, was an important one. Instead of experiencing the body intuitively or somatically, personal hygiene required an individual to know one's body and to embody the medical gaze. Seen in this light, ignorance could refer both to a *lack* of knowledge and to incommensurate knowledge that did not fit within the paradigm of professional medicine.

During the First World War, venereal disease became an especially important issue for the military.[106] Concerned that an increase of VD infection rates among Austro-Hungarian soldiers would weaken their ability to fight, Habsburg authorities broadened their gaze to include military men. Soldiers received pedagogical-prophylactic literature to encourage proper health and hygiene before, during, and after intercourse. The military also established field brothels and clinics for VD sufferers, and subjected soldiers to medical examinations. No longer were sex workers the only ones believed to be responsible for infection; soldiers were, too.

With the National Decree of 21 November 1918, the Austrian government required anyone infected with venereal disease to take personal responsibility for examination and treatment, as well as to inform others of the illness. Women not engaged in sex work were required to become informed, because they "have too long been in the dark about these things."[107] Unsurprisingly, the interwar period witnessed a marked increase of sex advice manuals aimed at enlightening women in particular. For example, an entire section in the book *Reif zur Liebe!* (*Ripe for Love!*) was devoted to women's sexual organs, which "are not only considered reproductive organs, but also as the main carriers of infection of venereal disease." According to the book, it was necessary for "a young woman ready to have sex" to have "knowledge of how easy and yet also how difficult it can be to identify [whether these] organs [are infected with] venereal disease."[108] The sex advice book *Unter vier Augen* (*Among Four Eyes*) included colorful illustrations of venereal disease, so that a woman could read the detailed descriptions in order to deploy the medical gaze while examining herself in the mirror.[109]

After the war, the municipality established a new public health and welfare office under the leadership of Julius Tandler, the central aim of which was to strengthen and regenerate the city's weakened *Volkskörper* through a program of sexual hygiene.[110] As a distinguished anatomist with years of dissection experience under his belt, Tandler was well equipped to deploy the medical gaze and to aid Vienna's citizens in doing so, too. During his tenure, he created a Marriage Advice Center, VD testing and treatment clinics, mothers' clinics, and family support services. He also employed physicians as public servants, so that their numbers increased from 326 in 1920 to 544 in 1930.[111] This period also witnessed the proliferation of other urban exhibitions about the body and hygiene, such as the popular 1925 Viennese Hygiene Exhibition at the Messepalast, which further sought to bring the techniques of the body, and the medical gaze, to ordinary people—including, as I explore below, menstruating women.[112]

MENSTRUATION HYGIENE:
CONTAINING/CLOSETING THE SHAMEFUL BODY

A woman flipping through the pages of a 1913 issue of *Häuslicher Ratgeber für Österreichs Frauen* (*The Home Advisor for Austrian Women*) would have come across two advertisements for menstrual products on the same page (see fig. 5.2).[113] Just below a serialized novella, she would have noticed, on

FIGURE 5.2. In this 1913 issue of a women's magazine, there are two advertisements for menstrual products on the same page. On the left there is an ad for a "Venus Belt," and on the right (under "Damen") there is an ad for menstruation drops. From *Illustriertes Familienblatt, Häuslicher Ratgeber für Österreichs Frauen* 28, no. 24 (1913/14): 244. ANNO/ÖNB.

the left side, an advertisement for a "Venus Belt" (*Venus-Gürtel*), a harness worn during menstruation that included cotton inserts and could be purchased at J. Appel on Josefstädterstrasse no. 48 in the VIIIth District. To the right of this, under "Ladies!" she would have spotted an advertisement for "painless, reliable, harmless drops" that were to be taken in the absence of menstruation and could be discreetly procured, presumably via post, from the Greenfod Laboratorium in Berlin. That two such advertisements would find their way onto the same page of a print magazine is significant; what is even more significant, however, is that, despite their shared interest in menstruation, these advertisements represented two very different medical paradigms. The Venus-Gürtel was a modern product, one meant to help women maintain a sense of hygiene during their cycles; the advertisement tactfully made no mention of the bloody process. The drops, by contrast, were a more traditional product, an emmenagogue, that helped women maintain their "flow" in the face of "stagnation." The advertisement did not equate missed menses with pregnancy, but with something else entirely. It also made a point of using the word "menstruation," high-lighting it in bold, as if it were something to call attention to instead of to hide. As I have argued, the transition from one medical paradigm to the other was a slow, piecemeal process; in 1913, both paradigms still appeared to coexist, even though a program of "menstruation hygiene" was actively being disseminated by the medical profession to replace the folk wisdom or "fairytales" once and for all.[114] "Unfortunately, [in matters concerning menstrual hygiene], old foolish prejudice and superstition hold a lot of sway in this area," observed Rudolf Glaessner in 1921.[115]

Physicians were in the forefront of a campaign to "enlighten" ordinary women in matters concerning their bodies and proper hygiene. "Regarding the hygiene of menstruation," wrote Werner Fischer-Defoy in 1927, "it [is important], first, to avoid excessive bodily exertion during this time and, second, to keep oneself meticulously clean."[116] "It is not right to behave in such a way as if the whole event were not here at all, to deny it." Unlike the plethora model, which viewed menstruation as a routine part of a woman's everyday life, it now became an "event," a significant occurrence with its own beginning, middle, and end, which required preparation, even a way of being. A woman during her menses was to avoid certain physical activities, such as horseback riding, biking (physicians would have disapproved of Alma Mahler-Werfel when she insisted on riding her bicycle despite being "unwell"), dancing, ice skating, or simply bending over, while menstruating schoolgirls were to refrain from participating in gymnastics at school. "Either they let their mother write a note or they say, 'Ma'am knows why,'" observed the Viennese socialist Margarete Rada in her 1931 study *Das reifende Proletariermädchen* (*The Maturing Proletarian Girl*), published as a series of articles by the Institute for Pedagogical Psychology. "Others, meanwhile, let a knowing friend report it to the teacher; [they] also feign a headache. But once the teacher knows, [their periods] will often be discussed without shame."[117] The socialist physician Karl Kautsky even recommended the adoption of a law that would provide women time off from work during their monthly bleeding.[118] Though a form of protection, this law also emphasized women's bodily frailty compared to men.

And yet, just because menstruation required a break from physical activities, it was, as Fischer-Defoy wrote, "wrong to ascribe to it exaggerated importance and to view oneself at this time as a critically ill patient."[119] To be sure, physicians insisted that bed rest—popular among bourgeois women, in particular—was a "bad habit" (*üble Angewohnheit*) that not only prevented blood from flowing properly, but also exacerbated menstrual pain, even leading to serious illness.[120] Bourgeois women's practice of taking to their rooms when they were on their cycle was considered outdated, a product of superstition. Although physicians recommended rest, they also instructed women to avoid the "horizontal position" at all costs and to rest in a more active way, preferably outdoors in the fresh air.

In addition to avoiding excessive bodily exertion, menstruation hygiene involved regular douching, bathing in warm water, and regularly changing underwear and pads. Young girls in particular were encouraged to "wash themselves especially often and meticulously" during their period.[121] Douching, which involved the repeated application of a disinfecting liquid into the vagina via a (preferably) glass syringe, was believed to rinse out "old blood that is withheld there and rots." Not only would this rotting blood lead to disease, physicians argued, but it also produced an offensive stench. "A woman must quite literally emanate the scent of purity," wrote a physician in 1913. "No perfume can conceal the smells that an unclean body gives off." As a result, even those parts of the body "concealed by clothing should, already out of health considerations, be carefully tended to."[122] Thus, physicians advised women to regularly bathe their entire bodies, including their genitalia (here the use of a bidet was encouraged), using a terry sponge with mild soap, once or twice a week.

Equally important to cleanliness was the need for effective materials to absorb menstrual blood. Working-class women often constructed pads out of canvas or cotton rags from old bed sheets and hand towels, which they would wrap in a T-shape around their hips and between their thighs, covering the genitals.[123] Women who could afford to purchase disposable pads often utilized bandages of wood-wool or pulp, which were known for their absorbency.[124] By the fin de siècle, physicians recommended that women primarily use thick strips of cotton instead, believed to be more hygienic than old rags and more comfortable than wood-wool. Women attached these cotton pads in their underwear or on a menstruation harness that could be buckled around the waist.[125] Likewise, "the wearing of pads is just as much an absolute requirement of cleanliness as the changing of dirty laundry."

Beholden to the diagnostic and shame-less medical gaze, women practicing menstruation hygiene came to view their own blood as dirty and abject and in need of proper cleanliness. Unlike the folk medical paradigm, which framed menstruation as healthy for its promotion of flow, the new scientific medical paradigm viewed it as a shameful pathology, a deviation from the "healthy" state of pregnancy. As one twelve-year-old working-class girl stated in 1931, "my mother told me I shouldn't even talk about [menstruation] with my best girlfriend, and I really don't do it."[126]

Menstruating women were thereby relegated to what Iris Marion Young refers to as the "menstrual closet," the experience of knowing oneself as "shameful, as an abject existence that is messy and disgusting," and thus in need of concealment.[127] The modern women of interwar Vienna strove to conceal and contain their bodies via menstrual pads and Venus belts lest they erupt with abject fluid. That said, for all its utility the image of a closet is also misleading: as more menstruating women came to be "closeted," menstruation itself entered the public realm and became an important issue for politicians, physicians, and women alike. Indeed, women's shame around menstruation was accompanied by a shame-lessness generated by their deployment of the medical gaze vis-à-vis their own bodies. As I suggest below, wittingly or not, women also pushed back—especially when it came to pregnancy. The new women of Vienna became their own lay medical practitioners.

Revisiting Abortion:
The New Lay Medical Observers and Practitioners

While women accused of violating the anti-abortion legislation §§144–46 often pleaded ignorance of their bodies in the early fin de siècle, arguing instead for a fluid metaphysics of blood blockages, blood clumps, and fickle periods, over time their testimonies changed, reflecting a more modern medical understanding of their bodies and reproduction. For these mostly working-class women, their missed menses meant one thing: that they were pregnant. Despite this paradigm shift, however, they were hardly the passive objects of a disciplinary medical gaze. In fact, they appropriated this medical gaze for them*selves*; as active medical observers and practitioners, they employed medical knowledge about the body—the *Volkskörper* and their own reproductive bodies—to formulate diagnoses and treatments. Whether they cited eugenic reasons, participated in their own abortions, provided convincing accounts of natural miscarriages, or recounted pain narratives effectively, Viennese women became adept at asserting their agency—an embodied sense of "self"—within the paradigm of professional medicine.

PROTECTING THE *VOLKSKÖRPER*

By the early twentieth century, eugenics—the attempt to improve the quality and not just the quantity of a population—became especially popular across Europe, including the Habsburg lands.[128] While positive eugenics encouraged the "fit" members of society to reproduce (the logic being that fit people would give birth to fit children), negative eugenics was focused on discouraging and preventing the "unfit" from doing so.

Although controversial today, given its racist, ableist, and ageist assumptions as well as its association with the Holocaust, eugenics was a popular social strategy that aimed to maintain and strengthen the health of the social body, thus appealing to reactionaries and radicals alike. After the First World War, faced with the task of regenerating their broken populations, many European states adopted eugenics as a top-down policy. In the Austrian capital of Vienna, it was Julius Tandler who implemented a series of welfare and sexual hygiene measures that were grounded in eugenic logic and beliefs.

Not surprisingly, some women accused of abortion cited eugenic reasons for having undergone the procedure in the first place. According to the domestic servant Aloisia Witzer's testimony from 1914, "I am very well aware that [abortion] is forbidden, but I didn't see another way out."[129] Her thirteen-month-old child was in the care of relatives, for which she "pays 18 *Kronen* for its lodging out of [her] 24 *Kronen* wage" every month. "My complete inability to afford a second child and the knowledge that I would see it raised by strangers . . . forced me to make the decision, not to bear the child" (*dass Kind nicht zur Welt kommen zu lassen*). Likewise, Theresia Horvath was struggling to raise her children and dealing with a physically abusive lover.[130] A factory worker, Horvath explained that she lived in a "crisis situation" (*Notlage*): "I have not been able to find any work for six weeks, my lover spends everything on booze [*versauft alles*], and when I speak to him of marriage, he gets rough."[131]

At the root of these declarations was women's conviction that their bodies and circumstances were not strong enough to carry, bear, and raise healthy children. Choosing to have an abortion was thus implicitly framed as being for the good of the health of the *Völkskörper*. An illustration accompanying an abortion reform article from 1924 depicted a woman crawling on the ground, looking helpless, her foot attached to the ball and chain of "forced motherhood."[132] Although this woman was a stand-in for every working-class woman in Vienna, she was also a representation of the city itself, whose body was falling apart due to postwar poverty and hunger. As I discussed in chapter 2, Vienna's population starved during much of the First World War, their bodies becoming severely undernourished and emaciated. How, women wondered, could they give birth to productive and fit members of society if they were barely fit themselves? For them, abortion was a form of negative eugenics, even if articulated indirectly.

Women aligned with the Austrian Social Democratic Workers Party (SDAP) placed explicit emphasis on eugenics to argue for abortion reform. In 1924, Adelheid Popp wrote in the SDAP women's newspaper *Die Unzufriedene* (*The Dissatisfied Woman*): "The sick, war-torn, crippled father, the exhausted mother collapsing under the weight of her responsibilities [*unter ihrer Last schwer zusammenbrechende*], the children screaming for bread: where should she find the courage to bring another child into the world—one that was most likely infected [with venereal disease] before birth?"[133] The hope was that with abortion reform, women would no longer be forced to bear sick and unfit children; instead, they would give birth only to offspring that would grow up to be *neue Menschen,* or new people, in a social-democratic utopia. Hence, SDAP women emphasized quality over quantity, insisting that, if "we want to conduct a healthy population politics, the precondition is that youth is healthy, that girls are healthy, so that they can become efficient women and healthy mothers"—and, not incidentally, new women.[134]

TUBES AND FALLS

Many working-class women included detailed descriptions of the abortion procedure in their testimonies and thereby proved themselves to be very keen medical observers. The domestic servant Ida Münster observed that the midwife "inserted a tube into the genitals [*Geschlechtsteil*]," which she removed several days later.[135] "On Monday," Münster reported, "the fetus [*Leibesfrucht*] was gone." Likewise, in her testimony from 1914, Aloisia Witzer described the catheter as a roughly twenty-centimeter-long "tube" attached to strings "that served the function that when I feel pain and start bleeding, I can pull [it] out."[136] This "tube" was a syringe-tipped catheter, which a midwife would insert into a woman's cervix, after having dilated it with a gauze tampon or with her hand.[137] Once inside, the catheter would either inject the uterus with a Lysol solution or simply irritate the cervix, thereby inducing labor.[138] The midwife sometimes advised the patient to wait several hours until the catheter "turned red" with blood before removing it.[139] In other instances, however, the midwife removed the catheter from the cervix shortly after insertion. This was the case in 1927 with Julianne Schneeberger, with whom I opened this chapter.[140]

Schneeberger learned about the midwife through friends she met at a tavern, indicating that working-class women passed medical knowledge along informal networks of friends, family members, and neighbors.[141] Even bourgeois women occasionally engaged in similar networks. The Austrian women's rights activist and philosopher Rosa Mayreder insisted that the "women in my surroundings" were "more keen observers than the doctors."[142] While some women used these networks to obtain and share names of trustworthy (and often lay) midwives, others used them to gain medical knowledge so that they could induce an abortion themselves, often with fatal consequences. In her testimony from 1915, for example, the factory worker Julie Wobĕrek admitted that she "succeeded in making the blood come."[143] After consulting with Frau Aloise Schaffhauser about logistics, she traveled to Vienna to purchase "a rubber tube with a wire"—presumably, a syringe-tipped catheter—which she later, after locating the "little dimple" (*Grüberl*) that was her cervix, succeeded in inserting into her vagina.[144] That a woman became comfortable enough to inspect her own genitalia and insert a catheter was at least partially due to the new hygienic practices that encouraged the shame-less inspection of the body as a medical object.

The line separating a self-induced abortion from a natural miscarriage was often ambiguous; it was thus a point of contention in most abortion trials. Many working-class women were aware of what the medical establishment believed to be the causes of natural miscarriage (*Fehlgeburt*), and frequently alluded to them in their testimonies. According to many physicians at the time, there appeared to be a direct connection between heavy labor and miscarriage. The Viennese gynecologist Friedrich Schauta observed in his medical textbook that "traumatic situations, such as a fall, blow, kick, especially in the lower abdomen," often lead to miscarriage, and court physicians acknowledged this in their reports.[145] Thus, the factory worker Julia Baumgarten stressed that the very nature of her work—which often involved the moving (and inevitable dropping) of heavy machinery—put her at risk. According to her testimony from August 1915, after lifting a heavy sewing machine, she "suddenly . . . started bleeding heavily." Another factory worker, Agnes Waleczka, slipped and fell on the "newly washed cement floor" and, after experiencing nausea, went home and apparently miscarried.[146] Whether these were self-induced abortions or natural miscarriages remains unclear; what matters is that working-class women became fluent enough in medical discourse to become keen medical observers and practitioners.

PAIN NARRATIVES

Physicians claimed that the abortion procedure used by lay midwives was particularly dangerous and painful. In the trial against the midwife Anna Holzer in 1916, for example, court physicians repeatedly alluded to her dangerous methods: "The catheter-based method of abortion is very effective, but puts the pregnant woman at risk [*gefährdet aber die Schwangere*] because the instrument remains inside and increases the possibility of an infection in the womb."[147] Furthermore, Holzer was accused of repeatedly endangering women (*noch mehr gefährdet*), having inserted catheters in Frau Müller and Frau Gamauf more than once. Physicians eschewed the catheter method, using the standard medical approach instead. Known as dilation and curettage or "D and C," the procedure involved the dilation of the cervix using metal dilators or gauze tampons and then the scraping of fetal and placental tissue out of the uterus with the help of a small, sharp tool known as a curette. Unlike the catheter method, D and C was almost always performed with an anesthetic.[148]

In most of the above-mentioned testimonies, women made strategic references to physical pain, or *Schmerzen*. Within the medical paradigm, pain was considered to be a direct sensation caused by a dangerous event or a pathological condition.[149] Insofar as a midwife's catheter method was considered dangerous and usually performed without an anesthetic, medical logic dictated that it would produce a painful sensation. Similarly, because catheter-induced abortions often led to blood poisoning (arguably a pathological condition), physicians believed a patient would also feel pain post-procedure. By the same token, the absence of pain would indicate the absence of an event or condition.

Joanna Bourke argues that pain "is not an intrinsic quality or raw sensation; it is a way of perceiving an experience." As such, "the body is more than merely a sensory indicator. It does not simply *register* a throbbing sensation, for instance, but simultaneously *evaluates* it as unpleasant."[150] At the fin de siècle, working-class women may not have been as likely to evaluate a painful sensation as something out of the ordinary and thus worth mentioning. Given women's routinized experience of bodily pain— produced by menstrual cramps, childbirth, constricting fashion, and so on—they would, according to Bourke's logic, have first had to learn to perceive—and "see," via the medical gaze—it as something notable and worth expressing before regarding it as exceptionally and unusually painful. As Alma Mahler-Werfel observed, women and pain were virtually synonymous: "Do men even have the slightest notion of pain and suffering? Women already grow accustomed to physical pain during childhood."[151] But, as Bourke suggests, there is a difference between the ordinariness of everyday pain, which requires no articulation to be felt as something routine, and its recontextualization within a pain narrative that ascribes to it out-of-the-ordinary importance.

And indeed, prior to the mid-1910s, many accused women either denied feeling pain during the abortion procedure or claimed to forget it. In 1899, Rosa König cavalierly reported that once the midwife "inserted an instrument into the vagina, [it] did not hurt me at all."[152] (Note that König spoke of the vagina, and not my vagina, testimony to her having appropriated the medical gaze.) In her 1902 statement to the police, Marie Kratochwil first described feeling "great burning" during the procedure, but then later recalled that, "the entire time, I no longer felt any pain."[153] Other women denied feeling any sensation at all. Antonie Neswadba, a cobbler's wife, noted that "of the procedure, I felt nothing," and that the only reason she knew something had been inserted into her was because the midwife had "told her."[154] "It all went so quickly," she observed, "I just let everything happen to me." In fact, she felt so little that she "could pursue [her] regular activities" later that day; she "even bathed."

With the proliferation of hygiene initiatives in the first decades of the twentieth century, the Viennese public was encouraged to identify and express pain for the sake of health. But just as accused women employed medical terminology and the medical gaze for their own ends, they also made reference to pain depending on how they pleaded. Women who acknowledged that an abortion or miscarriage had taken place usually made reference to pain: it was their way of linking the abortion or miscarriage to health and of suggesting that the termination of their pregnancy was a heavy price to pay. After Julie Wobĕrek admitted to having undergone a self-induced abortion, she emphasized that "I had great pains. I also noticed that large pieces of me fell away."[155] In 1924, twenty-eight-year-old Ann Koller testified that she had naturally miscarried when four months pregnant.[156] A working-class woman, Koller described feeling "a pulling sensation [ziehen] in the navel region," after she had hauled bags of coal and her child in a stroller up several flights of stairs. Two nights later, "she was in pain and had to urinate frequently [Harndrang]," until, finally, she miscarried. Other women made strategic references to pain as a way of accusing midwives of providing them with poorly executed services. For example, in 1915, Amalia Belada observed, "since that time [when I had an abortion] . . . I no longer feel healthy. Every now and then, I have pain in my stomach." Belada also highlighted the causality between the procedure and the painful sensation by stating that "the effects of the abortion are terribly painful."[157] Finally, those women who pleaded innocent often denied feeling pain or sensation altogether. In 1931, Leopoldine Heinz denied having an abortion, arguing that she naturally miscarried after consulting with a midwife. Suspicious about the sequence of events, the lawyer asked her what the midwife had done to her during the examination. Leopoldine stated that "she did nothing to me."[158] She continued, "I did not allow anything to be aborted. I never saw anything, nor did I hear or feel [anything]." By emphasizing that she never felt pain, Leopoldine made a convincing case for herself. Since she did not express pain, it seemed unlikely that she had had an abortion.

Conclusion: The Displacement of Feelings with Vision

Women in fin-de-siècle Vienna relied on their senses to access knowledge about their bodies. A woman who "felt herself to be unwell," for example, knew she was menstruating. Womanhood involved being somatically in tune with the body, which was felt to be porous and bloody, and committed to its flow.

Years later, this body feeling dissipated and was replaced by a different kind of body knowledge based on the discerning medical gaze. Fluidity came to be seen as shameful and threatening the body's borders, as well as its primary function, reproduction. Women stopped recording the subtle physical changes of embodiment; rather, they began drawing on medical logic and "expert" advice—derived from the city's many hygiene exhibitions, VD prevention pamphlets, and sex advice manuals, among other things—to "see" their female reproductive bodies for the first time as *theirs* and treat them as such. On the one hand, these new ways of seeing were imposed on women by the evolving medical profession and its gaze. On the other, women adapted these new ways of seeing to their own bodies and their own needs, thereby developing a deeper and more embodied sense of self. In fact, they even learned to use the language of professional medicine in ways that its practitioners might have disputed.

Let us draw on historical imagination to understand Julianne Schnee-berger's new vision. The seventeen-year-old housemaid lived near the Schmelz, a heathland named after a foundry (*Schmelz*) built on the site in the early nineteenth century, then used for military exercises and parades from 1864 to 1918, and finally developed into working-class housing that became notorious for its poverty and crime. She shared a small apartment, most likely a room, with her boyfriend, Anton Zöhling, and her young brother, on the busy Hütteldorfstrasse. As a poor young woman living on the periphery of Vienna, Schneeberger did not read the *Medizinische Wochenschrift* (*Medical Weekly*) or attend highbrow lectures on public health. But she became medically literate in other ways: through physicians, such as the local Dr. Muska, popular hygiene exhibitions, including the 1925 Exhibition at the Messepalast, visually enticing advertisements for hygienic products featured in print media or apothecary shop windows, and word of mouth. Let us assume that she was a practitioner of some menstruation hygiene (she tried not to let the blood spill down her thighs) and would occasionally wash herself after sexual intercourse to prevent venereal disease (after all, she had many sexual partners starting at the age of thirteen). She was used to closely observing her body and tending to it. When her menses failed to appear, she noticed immediately. Subjecting her body to the detached medical gaze, Schneeberger diagnosed herself as pregnant.

Even though people said children were a gift from God and that women's primary function was to reproduce, Schneeberger chose to do something radical: terminate the pregnancy. She talked to women at a local tavern and learned about a lay midwife who performed abortions. This woman came to her home one day and inserted a catheter into her for half an hour. Schneeberger was stretched out on a bed, and with her head cocked downward, watched the medical procedure. After the midwife left, she noticed a swelling and a steady discharge of blood—too much blood. If blood had traditionally been viewed as healthy and a sign of proper flow, now the blood was a warning sign. She instructed Zöhling to seek out another midwife, who came to her bedside with tea and warm compresses, which she wrapped around Schneeberger's abdomen. The bleeding eventually stopped.

We know that Schneeberger was found guilty of deliberately terminating her pregnancy. But as a medical observer and practitioner, she did not dispute the charge. She acknowledged it, for this new vision was a fundamental aspect of new womanhood.

※

This chapter traced the emergence of yet another practice of new womanhood: the medical gaze. I used abortion trial records to trace how women's changing testimonies about their reproductive bodies reflected and resisted a shift from a somatically based epistemology to one based on the diagnostic gaze of bourgeois medicine. Although it privileged sight, the gaze was a mode of perception that was sustained by a diagnostic logic grounded in scientific medicine. If women's body knowledge had previously been based on sensory perception, on what one could see, taste, touch, smell, and feel, by the fin de siècle it was slowly being replaced by the knowing, penetrating gaze. Beholden to the gaze, the porous, fluid body transformed, phenomenologically, into a more solid, contained body that could be divided into distinct parts with particular functions. A missed period was no longer seen as a lack of blood, but rather as a symptom of pregnancy and, crucially, as a distinctly *female* reproductive process.

And yet, as I tried to show above, the practice of wielding the medical gaze also provided women access to a medical language and culture that had been previously denied to them. As active medical observers and practitioners, they formulated diagnoses and treatments for their own pregnant bodies, which sometimes meant inducing an abortion, as was the case with Schneeberger. Armed with a new sense of self, they felt responsibility for a body that they perceived and understood to be theirs. Thus, by wielding the medical gaze, many Viennese women found ways to express agency, an embodied subjectivity.

As I have argued throughout this book, this everyday practice had its roots in the modernizing city of Vienna, and specifically its municipal health arrangements. If, according to Elizabeth Grosz, "the form, structure, and norms of the city seep into and affect all the other elements that go into the constitution of corporeality," then Vienna's form, structure, and norms—in this case, the professionalization of modern medicine, the fight against quackery, and the establishment of a modern hygiene apparatus—shaped the contours and constitution of the embodiment of womanhood.[159] With the shift from a Hippocratic medical paradigm to a modern scientific one, the medical gaze emerged as a practice that was deployed not only by physicians, but even by ordinary people. New womanhood involved the deployment of this medical gaze; new women gazed at their own bodies, other bodies, and of course, the city-as-body. Within a more spectacularized, ocular-centric world, the gaze became a modern embodied practice in a modern time.

Epilogue

We return to the coffeehouse.

In 1927, Walter G. traveled from Germany to Vienna, to admire the city's women and coffee culture. What he found there was shocking. Viennese women "are horribly lazy," he fumed in a letter to *Bettauers Wochenschrift* (*Bettauer's Weekly*), for they spend most of their time sitting in coffeehouses.[1] "The girls and women are on average prettier here than in our Germany," he wrote, but they "would be one hundred percent nicer if they were somewhat more agile." In another letter to the editor, Wilma P. furiously responded that Viennese women were perfectly agile; they hiked through the Vienna Woods, did gymnastics, swam in local pools, and labored at jobs.[2] But they also liked to relax—sometimes "in the coffeehouse with music" and sometimes "to snack or read the newspaper just like a man does." In a city characterized by its culture of corporeality, what better way to practice new womanhood than through the sensual experience of relaxation: listening to music, savoring a piece of layered cake, leafing through the crinkly pages of a newspaper, and taking in the sights of one's surroundings?

This book has reframed the history of the New Woman in terms of new womanhood-as-embodied-practices. In five embodied histories, it traced the emergence of different practices of new womanhood, including the "new moves" of *flânerie* (chapter 1), the "new shapes" of women's more linear silhouettes (chapter 2), the "new expressions" of emotion (chapter 3), the "new sensuality" of desire (chapter 4), and the "new visions" of modern medicine (chapter 5). Each chapter followed the same chronology of continuity, locating the roots of these practices in the fin de siècle and tracing how they became more pervasive during the First World War and the interwar period. For contemporaries, these practices were especially controversial because of their perceived unwomanliness—that is, their tactical subversion of normative, hegemonic femininity. But in subverting normative femininity, they also managed to offer new ways of acting and being a woman, of transforming womanhood for years to come. Changes in gender and sexuality, I showed, occurred not only from the bottom up, but from the *body* up.

One of the subtler arguments of this book has been that new womanhood brought with it a growing sense of the self that was embodied, breaching the mind-body dualism so pervasive in nineteenth-century culture and thought. Much of this had to do with the transformation of Vienna into a modern, global metropolis, a change that occurred in tandem with ordinary people coming to understand the body as *theirs* and using it in new ways. And only in a city with an established culture of corporeality—its *Gemütlichkeit* and epicureanism, music and theater, sensuous rituals of Catholicism and empire, and eerie cult around death—could this new sense of embodiment become a source of so much meaning and controversy.

Chapter 1 traced how urban renewal projects and the practice of flânerie made Vienna's streets pedestrian-friendly, inspiring women to engage in a phenomenology of "continuous movement" that located their subjectivity in their bodies interacting with their environments. Meanwhile, as shown in chapter 2, the growth of fashion and beauty industries popularized a new linear silhouette, which became more pervasive during the "starvation war" on the Viennese home front. This new shape brought with it a greater sense of embodiment: survival and self-preservation during the war, and the maintenance and care of a "healthy" slim and trim body during the interwar period. Chapter 3 considered how the emergence of Viennese popular culture, specifically the performances and spaces of modern theater and cinema, inspired women spectators to express their emotions through the body, which increasingly came to be associated with *self*-expression. Chapter 4 traced how the growth of print media—salacious literature, romance novels, and advice literature—taught women readers to actively desire with their body and senses. Thus, the sensual act of desiring (and its fulfillment in the form of pleasure) can be understood as a kind of agency, an assertion of subjectivity through the body. Finally, chapter 5 traced how modern medicine and urban hygiene initiatives in Vienna encouraged women to wield the diagnostic medical gaze, a "subjective vision" that viewed the body as the extension of the self.

Over time, the practices of new womanhood crossed and converged, producing new subjectivities, or what we now, retrospectively, call new women. In fact, by the late 1920s and 1930s, it seemed that many women in Vienna were new women—not because they identified as such, but because they drew on most, if not all, of the practices of new womanhood.

FIGURE E.1. We can historically imagine Wilma P. sitting alone at a Viennese coffeehouse, reading a newspaper. Perhaps she is the quietly assertive woman at the
bottom left of this watercolor painting. From Robert Fuchs (artist), "Wr. Kaffeehaus
Heinrichshof," watercolor on paper (Vienna, ca. 1925). Wien Museum Inv.-Nr. 57250,
CC BY 4.0.

And yet, just because these practices became more common and, as we
saw, sometimes commercialized does not mean that they were considered
less deviant by some contemporaries. After all, Hedwig Patzl, with whom
this book opened, was arrested for standing as late as 1934. Similarly, what
Wilma P. described as relaxation was disparagingly referred to as laziness
by Walter G. Thus, even as the practices of new womanhood became more
common, they continued to spark controversy, even backlash.

What if Wilma P. was one of those Viennese women whom Walter G.
criticized? We can historically imagine the following scenario. After sitting
down at a table in a coffeehouse and ordering a mélange, she may have
picked up a local newspaper and flipped to the very back, to the classifieds,
her favorite section (see fig. E.1). There she would have found columns of

personal ads—mostly men seeking women and women seeking men—under innocuous headings such as "Correspondences" or "Wedding Mail." Skimming through the ads, either to find love or simply as a form of relaxation, Wilma P. would have noticed references to a new kind of woman—the *Wiener Mädel* or "Viennese gal"—a woman who appeared to be quite unlike herself.

In one man-seeking-woman advertisement, a "24-year-old federal officer" expressed his wish to make "the honorable acquaintance with a pretty [and] respectable *Wiener Mädchen*."[3] Another man, a "27-year-old civil servant, graduate, 1.75 [meters] tall, attractive," described his ideal mate as a "respectable, chic, merry *Wiener Mädel*," who had to be, he insisted, an "Aryan."[4] A twenty-nine-year-old man searching for love was even more specific in his ad: he wanted a "beautiful blonde [of] medium height," "a *Wienerin*"—but absolutely "not a *Bubikopf*."[5] After all, a *Bubikopf* was not respectable. She was lazy.

Viennese women writing personal ads in the interwar period were also more likely to identify as *Wiener Mädels* than before. Writing in 1928, a "pretty 25-year-old *Wiener Mädl*" wrote that she hoped to make "an honorable acquaintance" with a special someone, possibly for marriage.[6] Meanwhile, an "attractive, merry 20-year-old" wishing to meet a "well-situated man" specified that she was not only a *Wiener Mädel*, but also "not a *Bubikopf*."[7] In another advertisement, a "19-year-old, pretty blonde *Wienerin*" looking for a "gentleman" warned that "only Aryans" need respond.[8] What becomes clear from these advertisements is that the designation of *Wiener Mädel* was code for a newer woman, the antithesis of the lolling *Bubikopf*—and of Wilma P.

Who was the *Wiener Mädel*, and what kind of womanhood did she practice? Despite being a newer woman, she was imagined to be an old-fashioned girl plucked from Vienna's mythologized imperial past, an interwar incarnation of Arthur Schnitzler's *süßes Mädel* or "Sweet Girl" with an Aryanized twist. Unlike the androgynous *Bubikopf*, she was imagined as a "complete woman" with soft curves and a full figure, who was devoted not to feeling sensual desire, but to fulfilling her "natural" role by one day becoming a mother.[9] Her hair was long (not a *Bubikopf!*), and she preferred to dance a Ländler at the Heurigen wine garden instead of the Charleston at the café. And despite being from the city of Vienna, the *Wiener Mädel* was neither urban nor modern nor cosmopolitan. She represented a pre-industrialized Vienna, one untouched by urban modernity and globalization. For Wilma P., this newer woman seemed to represent one thing: backlash.

It is unsurprising that the *Wiener Mädel* emerged around the same time that Viennese politics shifted toward the right. As the Social Democratic Workers' Party (SDAP) lost control of municipal politics and Austro-Fascism was on the rise, womanhood was to become more *völkisch* and traditional, heterosexual and reproductive. And once Austria was annexed by the Third Reich in 1938, this womanhood would become further actualized—indeed, the *Wiener Mädel* even found her way into Reich films, such as the popular hits *Schrammeln* (*Schrammel Music*, 1944) and *Wiener Mädeln* (*Viennese Girls*, completed in 1945 but not released until 1949), both of which were set in an imagined imperial past.[10]

But here is a paradox. A central argument in this book has been that new womanhood emerged in tandem with urban modernity. Despite positioning herself as neither urban nor modern nor cosmopolitan, the *Wiener Mädel* emerged, in part, within the pages of personal ads, or what Tyler Carrington has described as modern, "emerging technologies of love."[11] With the print media boom at the end of the nineteenth century, personal ads became a more popular and acceptable way to find love. For two schillings, a person writing in 1928 could send a fifteen-word ad to the *Illustrierte Wochenpost*, with each additional word or number costing eight groschen. And yet, between the eye-catching title, the list of one's basic attributes—including approximate age, profession, financial status ("well-situated"), and physical and personality traits—and, finally, a description of one's ideal mate, most ads ran over fifteen words, increasing an already frivolous-seeming expense. To encourage potential writers, newspapers sometimes included vouchers for the first personal ad, knowing, of course, that most ads would have to reappear (and would need to be paid for) in later issues. Indeed, personal ads were hardly an efficient technology of love; they were, rather, aspirational, encouraging a distinctly modern fantasy of romance that was rarely found in real life. Thus, even though the *Wiener Mädel* was "not a *Bubikopf*," she was hardly as unmodern or retrograde as she made herself out to be. As it took a very particular kind of new woman—and new womanhood—to write an ad in the first place, the *Wiener Mädel* was not so much a repudiation of the new woman as her transcendence.

This leads to a second paradox: that new and newer womanhoods—despite being "new"—are not necessarily more liberated or emancipated versions of womanhood. What *Embodied Histories* has shown is that the history of gender and sexuality does not follow a teleological path, that it swerves and meanders, moves back and forth—perhaps even goes in circles. While new and newer womanhood could sometimes feel more liberating to contemporaries—the removal of the corset, for example, seemed to free women's bodies from constraint—this does not mean that it was necessarily, incontrovertibly so. Is it a surprise, then, that the seemingly retrograde and reactionary *Wiener Mädel* would emerge shortly after—or out of—the *Bubikopf*?

But there is a final paradox, one that was articulated by Simone de Beauvoir in 1949, when she published *The Second Sex*.[12] Writing after the Second World War, at a time when gender and sexuality were undergoing a palpable transformation, de Beauvoir asked: What is femininity? Is it "secreted by the ovaries? Is it enshrined in a Platonic heaven? Is a frilly petticoat enough to bring it down to earth?"[13] For "although some women zealously strive to embody it, the model has never been patented." And if it has not been patented, then womanhood must always be changing. But if womanhood is always changing and being displaced by a new womanhood and a newer womanhood, then, to quote de Beauvoir: "Are there even women?"

Drawing on historical imagination, we may picture an undercover police officer watching Wilma P. turn the pages and, as befitted a new woman, continue to relax. What was the world coming to? The flabbergasted official may have scratched his head and wondered, "Are there even women *left*?"

Acknowledgments

Writing a book about embodiment during a time when the body and its vulnerabilities are most palpable is a curious thing. In the winter of 2020, as the world shut down due to the COVID-19 pandemic, I became uniquely aware of my mortality and my embodiment. This awareness accompanied me as I wrote this book, which, while a history of new womanhood in early twentieth-century Vienna, is also an appeal to scholars to take seriously the body and embodied experience.

It's also an appeal to readers to take their own bodies into account, to feel with their bodies, to engage in proprioception. I certainly had to do this in the process of writing this book, which was not just an intellectual endeavor, but also, crucially, an embodied practice. My labor was uniquely physical, something I realized when I was diagnosed with carpal tunnel syndrome in my right arm midway through writing this book, and then struggled with a nasty bout of COVID-19 that left me bedridden for weeks. Shortly before the book went into production, I also learned that I was pregnant, which forced me to come to terms with my reproductive embodiment in ways I had never experienced before. Soon, I came to see how much my body mattered in every aspect of life, even in the so-called "life of the mind."

Despite a global pandemic, this book miraculously made its way to publication—a feat I would not have been able to accomplish without the support of many far and wide, past and present. I would not have had the courage to embark on this path had it not been for Deborah R. Coen, whose brilliance and mentorship continue to sustain me. At the University of Chicago, I benefited from the generosity and guidance of faculty and colleagues. I am particularly grateful to Tara Zahra for being such a generous adviser, intellectual interlocutor, and friend. I am also indebted to Leora Auslander for her feedback, wisdom, and creativity; she inspired me to think theoretically and pursue new historical methodologies. She helped me realize that things and bodies matter. Additionally, I thank John Boyer, Michael Geyer, Eleonory Gilburd, Jan Goldstein (her "Paris–Chicago" seminar initially sparked my interest in gender and urban space), Faith Hillis, and Fredrik Albritton Jonsson for their generosity and support.

Graduate school is not for the faint of heart, and it was the intellectual companionship and camaraderie of friends and colleagues at the University of Chicago that sustained me. I thank my fellow modern Europeanists in the Department of History, as well as my colleagues and friends at the Center for the Study of Gender and Sexuality, which provided me with office space (and countless bánh mì) for two years in a row. I especially thank Michaela Appeltová, Robin Bates, Amanda Blair, Chris Dunlap, Abigail Fine, Emily Lord Fransee, Phillip Henry, Britta Ingebretson, Deirdre Lyons, Emily Marker, Lisa Scott, Caroline Séquin, Jake Smith, Madeline Smith, Lauren Stokes, Greg Valdespino, and Michael Williams for friendship and solidarity. I thank Lauren, Lisa, and Robin in particular for regular Zoom dates during the pandemic. Your friendship has buoyed me during some very difficult times.

This book is the product of over a decade of research, writing, and editing, including countless trips to Vienna, which were made thanks to the generous support of the Department of History at the University of Chicago; the Center for the Study of Gender and Sexuality at the University of Chicago; the Austrian Fulbright Commission; the Austrian Cultural Forum New York; and the Temple University College of Liberal Arts. In Vienna, I benefited from the wisdom and guidance of many librarians and archivists—in particular Li Gerhalter at the Sammlung Frauennachlässe, and Michael Winter from the Archiv Bundespolizeidirektion Wien. At the Österreichische Nationalbibliothek, I particularly thank the sparkly-eyed mustachioed man working at the circulation desk for learning my name because according to him, I was "amtsbekannt." No one was probably ordering as many sex-related titles as I.

My year in Vienna was a transformative one. I thank Matti Bunzl for a stimulating meeting at the Wien Museum, and Margarete Grandner and Gabriella Hauch for their support. I also thank friends and fellow researchers, including Betsy Akins, Roman Birke, Michelle Duncan, Veronika Helfert, Michaela Hintermayr, and Amy Nelson. Special thanks to Hugh Schmidt for his continued research assistance even after I left Vienna, and to Phil Pierick for many late-night conversations over glasses of Zweigelt at Liebling. Vienna continues to inspire and stimulate me to this day, and there is nothing more gratifying to me than walking its many little streets.

I was privileged enough to spend a year on a Max Weber Postdoctoral Fellowship at the European University Institute in Italy. It was there, under the generous tutelage of Pieter Judson, that I came to think about the global dimensions of my project, as well as to develop a love for all things Italian. I also benefited from the mentorship of Laura Lee Downs, whose long conversations about feminism, gender history, and cats over big bowls of pasta were one of the highlights of my time there. At the EUI, I met some very dear friends and fellow world-travelers—in particular, Matthew Canfield, Ioanna Hadjiyianni, Pavel Khazanov and Gabi Kattan Khazanov, Cynthia Malakasis, Aris Trantidis, and Anna Wallerman Ghavanini. Special thanks to my fellow Quindis, Christopher Baum and Aydin Yildirim.

During the time when I was rewriting this manuscript, I was lucky enough to be employed as an assistant professor in the Department of History at Temple University. I am grateful to my colleagues who have helped me navigate my first years as a professor. An especially big thanks to my colleague and mentor, Eileen Ryan, whom I am proud to call a dear friend. Thanks also to my department chair, Petra Goedde, and fellow central Europeanist, Rita Krueger, for their guidance in navigating the Temple academe. I also thank the undergraduate and graduate students for entrusting their education to me; it is an honor.

All the chapters of this book benefited from thoughtful critique and feedback from participants of the University of Chicago's Transnational Approaches to Modern Europe Workshop and the Gender and Sexuality Working Group; the Midwest Historians of East Central Europe Workshop; and countless panels and seminars at the German Studies Association Annual Conference and the Association for Slavic, Eastern European, and Eurasian Studies Convention. I especially thank panel chairs and commentators Kathleen Canning, Winson Chu, Edward Ross Dickinson, Maureen Healy, Katrin Paehler, Keely Stauter-Halsted, Nancy Wingfield, and Nathaniel Wood. I am especially grateful to Nancy for her mentorship; she has gone out of her way to make me feel welcome in a community of Habsburg historians. I also thank fellow panelists, colleagues, and friends in the field: Michael Burri, Kate Densford, Jennifer Evans, Alys X. George, Cathleen Giustino, Ke-Chin Hsia, Anita Kurimay, Richard Lambert, Britta McEwen, Ambika Natarajan, and Alison Orton, and my partner-in-crime, Michał Wilczewski.

In recent years, I was lucky to take part in two seminars at the German Studies Association that have radically altered my approach to history. Both seminars were sponsored by the Body Studies Network, of which I am now a co-coordinator. The 2022 seminar, "Vulnerability and Embodied

Subjectivity," was especially significant in helping me consider the role of my own body in my work. I especially thank my co-coordinators, Paul Dobryden, Heikki Lempa, and Caroline Weist, for welcoming me into this community. I would also like to thank former network coordinator Kristen Ehrenberger for her help with the history of medicine aspects of this project.

I am humbled that the University of Chicago Press has decided to publish this manuscript. I am grateful to my two editors for believing in this project: Mary Al-Sayed shepherded the manuscript through the first stages of the process, while Dylan Montanari has seen to its completion. Thank you to the two anonymous referees for extremely constructive reader reports. Thanks also to the staff at the University of Chicago Press, especially Fabiola Enriquez Flores, for their help with navigating the publishing process. Parts of the introduction and chapter 1 appeared in "Re-Embodying History's 'Lady': Women's History, Materiality and Public Space in Early Twentieth-Century Vienna," *Gender & History* 33, no. 1 (March 2021): 169–91. I appreciate having the permission to use them in my manuscript.

This book would not have made it into production had it not been for generosity of the Center for Austrian Studies at the University of Minnesota and the Department of History at Temple University. In particular, I thank Howard Louthan, the director of CAS, for his mentorship and assistance.

Last but certainly not least, I want to thank my friends and family. Thank you to Kelli Gardner and Aaron Hollander, Pierce and Lindsey Gradone, and Katharina Gratz for your love and support. Cory Dahn, Emma Greenstein, and Tyler Pearson: I am thrilled to call you family. Thank you to my friends in and from Philadelphia. Thank you to Amy and Bill Dahn, as well as the Dahn and Greenstein families, for welcoming me with open arms. I always dreamed of being part of a bigger family, and now I am. I also thank my extended family, in particular my aunt and uncle, Mary Motyl and Joseph Laraia, as well as my Viennese cousins, Genija Mudretzkyj and Sophie Rosenmayer. Thank you to my feline assistants, Lila and Lenu, for making the process of writing an endeavor both challenging and cuddly. My parents, Irene Motyl-Mudretzkyj and Alexander Motyl, I thank for their unconditional love and endless encouragement. My mother was the first *Wienerin* I came to know, and I thank her for sharing Vienna with me. I also thank her for introducing me to yoga and mindfulness, two embodiment practices that have shaped not only my academic project, but the code I live by. Additionally, I am endlessly grateful to my father for his faith in me as an academic. He read countless drafts of this manuscript, providing me with detailed feedback. His enthusiasm for this project sometimes surpassed my own, and I am thankful to him for encouraging me every step of the way—even when our minds and hearts were with Ukraine.

This book would not have been possible without the loving support of Ryan Dahn, my exceedingly smart and kind husband. Although it took a while for us to find each other, the wait was well worth it. Thank you for indulging me when I get on my soapbox, for listening to me talk theory even though you are more of an empiricist, and for trying to follow my train of thought as I explain to you a detailed, verging on conspiratorial, chapter outline over an entire dinner at a local restaurant. Thank you for being my COVID-19 quarantine companion, and for encouraging me to take breaks even when I was "locked in." Ryan, thank you for loving and believing in me, and for seeing me as the strong, resilient, and ambitious woman I have always aspired to be.

Notes

Introduction

1. ABpdW, P/M, 1930–1936, Sittenpolizeiliche Agenden (hereafter SA), Patzl Hedwig, Vienna, 21 January 1934.

2. "Das Wetter," *IKZ*, 20 January 1934, 2.

3. Charlotte Ashby, "Introduction," in *The Viennese Café and Fin-de-Siècle Culture*, ed. Charlotte Ashby, Tag Gronberg, and Simon Shaw-Miller (New York: Berghahn Books, 2013), 3.

4. "Die Zukunfts-Frauen," *WC*, 10 May 1896, 4–6.

5. "All' Heil," *Der Floh*, 8 July 1894, 5; *Der Floh*, 15 April 1894, 5; "Sport," *Der Floh*, 18 March 1894, 5.

6. Sarah Grand, "The New Aspect of the Woman Question," *North American Review* 158 (March 1894): 270; Ouida, "The New Woman," *North American Review* 158 (May 1894): 611.

7. Patricia Marks, *Bicycles, Bangs, and Bloomers: The New Woman in the Popular Press* (Lexington: University of Kentucky Press, 1990), 2.

8. Mary Louise Roberts, *Disruptive Acts: The New Woman of Fin-de-Siècle France* (Chicago: University of Chicago Press, 2002), 26.

9. "The Modern Girl as Heuristic Device: Collaboration, Connective Comparison, Multidirectional Citation," in *The Modern Girl around the World: Consumption, Modernity, and Globalization*, ed. Alys Eve Weinbaum, Lynn M. Thomas, Priti Ramamurthy, Uta G. Poiger, Madeleine Yue Dong, and Tani E. Barlow (Durham, NC: Duke University Press, 2008), 2.

10. "The Modern Girl as Heuristic Device," 9.

11. Grete Meisel-Hess, *Fanny Roth: Eine Jungfrauengeschichte* (1902; Berlin: Hermann Seemann Nachfolger Verlagsgesellschaft, 1910), 18.

12. Meisel-Hess, *Fanny Roth*, 6–7, 32, 9.

13. See, for example, "In der Radfahrschule," *Der Floh*, 11 July 1897, 5; "Ja, ja, Fräulein Mizzerl . . ." *Der Floh*, 18 July 1897, 5.

14. See, for example, "Wiener Humoresken," *WC*, 13 June 1897, 1.

15. "Ihre Frage," *WC*, 14 July 1907, 1.

16. Otto Weininger, *Sex & Character*, 6th ed. (1903; New York: G. P. Putnam's Sons, 1906), 64.

17. See, for example, "Steinstoßen," *Die Muskete*, 6 June 1912, 3.

18. "Imperial-Feigen-Kaffee," *IFHR* 28, no. 1 (1913): 14.

19. On degeneration, see Daniel Pick, *Faces of Degeneration: A European Disorder, c. 1848–c. 1918* (New York: Cambridge University Press, 1996). On sexual crisis in Vienna, see

Nike Wagner, *Karl Kraus und die Erotik der Wiener Moderne* (Frankfurt: Suhrkamp, 1982); Chandak Sengoopta, *Otto Weininger: Sex, Science, and Self in Imperial Vienna* (Chicago: University of Chicago Press, 2000); David S. Luft, *Eros and Inwardness in Vienna: Weininger, Musil, Doderer* (Chicago: University of Chicago Press, 2003); Scott Spector, *Violent Sensations: Sex, Crime, and Utopia in Vienna and Berlin, 1860–1914* (Chicago: University of Chicago Press, 2016).

20. See, for example, Schani Adabei, "Schuld ist nur der Bubikopf!" *Kikeriki*, 23 May 1926, 2.

21. See, for example, "Was ist die moderne Frau?" *Die Dame*, November 1925.

22. See, for example, A. O. Weber, "Die moderne Frau," *Der Floh*, 3 February 1918, 3

23. "Was ist die moderne Frau?"

24. "Ein modernes Weib," *WC*, 1 May 1924, 8.

25. "Gnädige Frau!" *DmF* 1, no. 1 (mid-May 1926): 2.

26. M. H. F., "Die neue Kammerzofe," *MW* 7, no. 21 (1926): 27.

27. "Korrespondenzen," *BW* 3, no. 16 (1926): 20–21; "Korrespondenzen," *BW* 3, no. 51 (1926): 21.

28. Helmut Gruber, *Red Vienna: Experiment in Working-Class Culture, 1919–1934* (New York: Oxford University Press, 1991), 147.

29. Gruber, *Red Vienna*, 148.

30. Gruber, 150.

31. For some examples of work that primarily considers the image of the New Woman, see Debora L. Silverman, *Art Nouveau in Fin-de-Siècle France: Politics, Psychology, and Style* (Berkeley: University of California Press, 1989): 63–74; Patricia Marks, *Bicycles, Bangs, and Bloomers*; Mary Louise Roberts, *Civilization Without Sexes: Reconstructing Gender in Postwar France, 1917–1927* (Chicago: University of Chicago Press, 1994); Tina O'Toole, *The Irish New Woman* (London: Palgrave Macmillan, 2013); Patricia Murphy, *The New Woman Gothic: Reconfiguration of Distress* (Columbia: University of Missouri Press, 2016).

32. Silverman, *Art Nouveau*, 63.

33. Roberts, *Civilization Without Sexes*, 10.

34. Carroll Smith-Rosenberg, *Disorderly Conduct: Visions of Gender in Victorian America* (New York: Knopf, 1985), 247.

35. Talia Schaffer, "'Nothing but Foolscap and Ink': Inventing the New Woman," in *The New Woman in Fiction and in Fact: Fin-de-Siècle Feminisms*, ed. Angelique Richardson and Chris Willis (New York: Palgrave, 2001), 49.

36. Gruber, *Red Vienna*, 154.

37. "The Modern Girl as Heuristic Device," 1–24.

38. See, for example, Gillian Sutherland, *In Search of the New Woman: Middle-Class Women and Work in Britain, 1870–1914* (New York: Cambridge University Press, 2015).

39. On new women as actors, performers, and journalists, see Susan A. Glenn, *Female Spectacle: The Theatrical Roots of Modern Feminism* (Cambridge, MA: Harvard University Press, 2000); Roberts, *Disruptive Acts*; Ageeth Sluis, *Deco Body, Deco City: Female Spectacle & Modernity in Mexico City, 1900–1939* (Lincoln: University of Nebraska Press, 2016). On new women as sex workers, see Jill Suzanne Smith, *Berlin Coquette: Prostitution and the New German Woman, 1890–1933* (Ithaca, NY: Cornell University Press, 2013); Judith Walkowitz, *City of Dreadful Delight: Narratives of Sexual Danger in Late-Victorian London* (Chicago: University of Chicago Press, 2013). On new women as consumers, see Kathy Peiss, *Cheap Amusements: Working Women and Leisure in Turn-of-the-Century New York* (Philadelphia:

Temple University Press, 1986); Barbara Sato, *The New Japanese Woman: Modernity, Media, and Women in Interwar Japan* (Durham, NC: Duke University Press, 2003).

40. On Austrian feminism, see Harriet Anderson, *Utopian Feminism: Women's Movements in Fin-de-Siècle Vienna* (New Haven, CT: Yale University Press, 1992); Margarete Grandner and Edith Saurer, eds., *Geschlecht, Religion und Engagement: Die jüdischen Frauenbewegungen im deutschsprachigen Raum* (Vienna: Böhlau Verlag, 2005); Agatha Schwartz, *Shifting Voices: Feminist Thought and Women's Writing in Fin-de-Siècle Austria and Hungary* (Montreal: McGill-Queen's University Press, 2008); Gabriella Hauch, *Frauen bewegen Politik: Österreich 1848–1938* (Innsbruck: StudienVerlag, 2009).

41. The *Bund für Mutterschutz*, led by Helene Stöcker, Lily Braun, and Adele Schreiber, was founded in Germany in 1905. The Viennese branch was established two years later. See Tracie Matysik, *Reforming the Moral Subject: Ethics and Sexuality in Central Europe, 1890–1930* (Ithaca, NY: Cornell University Press, 2008); Britta McEwen, *Sexual Knowledge: Feeling, Fact, and Social Reform in Vienna, 1900–1934* (New York: Berghahn Books, 2012).

42. On Jewish women in Austria, see Harriet Pass Freidenreich, *Female, Jewish, and Educated: The Lives of Central European University Women* (Bloomington: Indiana University Press, 2002); Alison Rose, *Jewish Women in Fin de Siècle Vienna* (Austin: University of Texas Press, 2008).

43. See Julie M. Johnson, *The Memory Factory: The Forgotten Women Artists of Vienna 1900* (West Lafayette, IN: Purdue University Press, 2012); Megan Brandow-Faller, *The Female Secession: Art and the Decorative at the Viennese Women's Academy* (University Park: Pennsylvania State University Press, 2020).

44. Nancy M. Wingfield, *The World of Prostitution in Late Imperial Austria* (New York: Oxford University Press, 2017). For wartime work, see Sigrid Augeneder, *Arbeiterinnen im Ersten Weltkrieg: Lebens- und Arbeitsbedingungen proletarischer Frauen in Österreich* (Vienna: Europaverlag, 1987); Erna Appelt, "The Gendering of the Service Sector in Austria at the End of the Nineteenth Century," in *Austrian Women in the Nineteenth and Twentieth Centuries: Cross-Disciplinary Perspectives*, ed. David F. Good, Margarete Grandner, and Mary Jo Maynes (Providence, RI: Berghahn Books, 1996), 115–32; Gudrun Biffl, "Women and Their Work in the Labor Market and in the Household," in Good, Grandner, and Maynes, *Austrian Women in the Nineteenth and Twentieth Centuries*, 133–56.

45. See Maureen Healy, *Vienna and the Fall of the Habsburg Empire: Total War and Everyday Life in World War I* (New York: Cambridge University Press, 2004), 31–86, 122–59; Christa Ehrmann-Hämmerle, *Heimat/Front: Geschlechtergeschichte/n des Ersten Weltkriegs in Österreich-Ungarn* (Vienna: Böhlau Verlag, 2014).

46. See, for example, Gabriella Hauch, *Vom Frauenstandpunkt aus: Frauen im Parlament, 1919–1933* (Vienna: Verlag für Gesellschaftskritik, 1995); Birgitta Bader-Zaar, "Women in Austrian Politics, 1890–1934: Goals and Visions," in Good, Gardner, and Maynes, *Austrian Women in the Nineteenth and Twentieth Centuries*, 59–90; Gerda Neyer, "Women in the Austrian Parliament: Opportunities and Barriers," in Good, Gardner, and Maynes, *Austrian Women in the Nineteenth and Twentieth Centuries*, 91–114; Veronika Helfert, *Frauen, wacht auf! Eine Frauen- und Geschlechtergeschichte von Revolution und Rätebewegung in Österreich, 1917–1924* (Göttingen: Vandenhoeck & Ruprecht, 2021).

47. Roberts, *Disruptive Acts*, 104.

48. Liz Conor, *The Spectacular Modern Woman: Feminine Visibility in the 1920s* (Bloomington: Indiana University Press, 2004); "The Modern Girl as Heuristic Device," 12.

49. Lena Wånggren, *Gender, Technology and the New Woman* (Edinburgh: University of Edinburgh Press, 2017), 24.

50. "Jugend und Alter in der heutigen Zeit," *IFHR* 31, no. 4 (1925): 2.

51. Judith Butler, *Gender Trouble: Feminism and the Subversion of Identity* (New York: Routledge, 1990); Judith Butler, *Bodies That Matter: On the Discursive Limits of "Sex"* (New York: Routledge, 1993).

52. I draw on the phenomenology of Maurice Merleau-Ponty, who argues that our being-in-the-world constitutes us as "body-subjects."

53. By "material turn" in history, I mean the growing interest in histories that focus on the interplay between discourse and materiality. This includes environmental history, the history of the senses, the history of emotions, the history of food, the history of material culture, and disability history, as well as the history of medicine.

54. Simone de Beauvoir, *The Second Sex*, trans. Constance Borde and Sheila Malovany-Chevallier (New York: Vintage, 2011), 308.

55. Iris Marion Young, *On Female Body Experience: "Throwing Like a Girl" and Other Essays* (New York: Oxford University Press, 1990); Susan Bordo, *Unbearable Weight: Feminism, Western Culture, and the Body* (Berkeley: University of California Press, 1995).

56. I draw on R. W. Connell's study of masculinities to argue that there are multiple femininities, with some considered more legitimate or "hegemonic" than others. See R. W. Connell, *Masculinities* (Berkeley: University of California Press, 2005).

57. I use the terms "womanhood" and "femininity" interchangeably.

58. I draw on Pierre Bourdieu's concept of habitus, which refers to socially ingrained practices and dispositions that are done neither mechanically nor willfully, but nevertheless contain within themselves the capacity for "regulated improvisation," and as such, change. See Pierre Bourdieu, *Outline of a Theory of Practice*, trans. Richard Nice (1977; Cambridge: Cambridge University Press, 2002).

59. Michel de Certeau, *The Practice of Everyday Life*, trans. Steven F. Rendall (1984; Berkeley: University of California Press, 2011), 29–42.

60. As a genealogist, I "disaggregate those [practices of new womanhood] by tracing their separate histories as well as the process of their interrelations, their crossings, and eventually, their unstable convergence." See David M. Halperin, *How to Do the History of Homosexuality* (Chicago: University of Chicago Press, 2004), 106–7.

61. Jack Halberstam makes a similar point about female masculinity. See Jack Halberstam, *Female Masculinity* (Durham, NC: Duke University Press, 1998).

62. Dagmar Herzog, "Syncopated Sex: Transforming European Sexual Cultures," *American Historical Review* 114, no. 5 (2009): 1287–1308.

63. Elizabeth Grosz, "Bodies-Cities," in *Space, Time, and Perversion: Essays on the Politics of Bodies* (New York: Routledge, 1995), 108.

64. Grosz, "Bodies-Cities," 108–9.

65. To get at the heart of this dynamic, I eschew the language of causality and emphasize, instead, how urban and embodied changes occurred *in tandem*. When I do use words that seem to indicate causality—for example, the city "inspired" or "invited" certain practices—I am not denying the existence of an interrelatedness, but simply highlighting one aspect of it in a way that is linguistically intelligible to the reader.

66. See, for example, Nathaniel D. Wood, *Becoming Metropolitan: Urban Selfhood and the Making of Modern Cracow* (DeKalb: Northern Illinois University Press, 2010), 13.

67. On urban habits, see Peter Fritzsche, *Reading Berlin 1900* (Cambridge, MA: Harvard University Press, 1996). On urban "routinized rituals," Elizabeth Wilson, *The Sphinx in the*

City: Urban Life, the Control of Disorder, and Women (Berkeley: University of California Press, 1992), 7. On the new "culture of time and space," see Stephen Kern, *The Culture of Time and Space: 1880–1918* (Cambridge, MA: Harvard University Press, 1983). On urban sensory experiences, see Vanessa R. Schwartz, *Spectacular Realities: Early Mass Culture in Fin-de-Siècle Paris* (Berkeley: University of California Press, 1998).

68. See, for example, Jonathan Crary, *Techniques of the Observer: On Vision and Modernity in the Nineteenth Century* (Cambridge, MA: MIT Press, 1990).

69. See, for example, George Chauncey, *Gay New York: Gender, Urban Culture, and the Making of the Gay Male World, 1890–1940* (New York: Basic Books, 1994); Katharina von Ankum, ed., *Women in the Metropolis: Gender and Modernity in Weimar Culture* (Berkeley, CA: University of California Press, 1997).

70. Wilson, *The Sphinx in the City*, 7.

71. Allan Janik and Stephen Toulmin, *Wittgenstein's Vienna* (1973; Chicago: Elephant Paperbacks, 1996), 42.

72. Carl Schorske, *Fin-de-Siècle Vienna: Politics and Culture* (New York: Vintage Books, 1981), 24–115; Peter Payer, "The Age of Noise: Early Reactions in Vienna, 1870–1914," *Journal of Urban History* 33, no. 5 (July 2007): 775.

73. J. Robert Wegs, *Growing Up Working Class: Continuity and Change Among Viennese Youth, 1890–1938* (University Park: Pennsylvania State University Press, 1989), 12–13. See also David F. Good, *The Economic Rise of the Habsburg Empire, 1750–1914* (Berkeley: University of California Press, 1984); Wegs, *Growing Up Working Class*, 100.

74. See Marsha L. Rozenblit, *The Jews of Vienna: 1867–1914: Assimilation and Identity* (Albany: State University of New York Press, 1983); Monika Glettler, "Minority Culture in a Capital City: The Czechs in Vienna at the Turn of the Century," in *Decadence and Innovation: Austro-Hungarian Life and Art at the Turn of the Century*, ed. Robert B. Pynsent (London: Weidenfeld and Nicolson, 1989), 49–60.

75. Between 1850 and 1910, Vienna's physical footprint expanded from 55.4 to 275.9 square kilometers and its population increased from 431,000 to around 2 million. Payer, "The Age of Noise," 775.

76. Although Lueger won the election in 1895, the emperor refused to confirm him until 1897. On the Christian Social Movement and Karl Lueger, see John W. Boyer, *Political Radicalism in Late Imperial Vienna: Origins of the Christian Social Movement, 1848–1897* (Chicago: University of Chicago Press, 1981); John W. Boyer, *Culture and Political Crisis in Vienna: Christian Socialism in Power, 1897–1918* (Chicago: University of Chicago Press, 1995); John W. Boyer, *Karl Lueger (1844–1910): Christlichsoziale Politik als Beruf* (Vienna: Böhlau, 2010).

77. The number of shops almost tripled between 1870 and 1902. See Elisabeth Lichtenberger, *Vienna: Bridge Between Cultures*, trans. Dietline Mühlgassner and Craig Reisser (New York: Belhaven Press, 1993), 52. On mass culture in Vienna, see Wolfgang Maderthaner and Lutz Musner, *Unruly Masses: The Other Side of Fin-de-Siècle Vienna* (New York: Berghahn Books, 2008), 77–94, here 89.

78. David Rechter, "Galicia in Vienna: Jewish Refugees in the First World War," *Austrian History Yearbook* 28 (1997): 113–30.

79. Stefan Zweig, *The World of Yesterday*, trans. Anthea Bell (1942; Lincoln: University of Nebraska Press, 2013), 305.

80. Eve Blau, *The Architecture of Red Vienna 1919–1934* (Cambridge, MA: MIT Press, 1999); Alfred Georg Frei, *Rotes Wien: Austromarxismus und Arbeiterkultur: Sozialdemokratische Wohnungs- und Kommunalpolitik, 1919–1934* (Berlin: DVK Verlag, 1984); Gruber, *Red Vienna*.

81. Janek Wasserman, *Black Vienna: The Radical Right in the Red City, 1918–1938* (Ithaca, NY: Cornell University Press, 2014).

82. Anson Rabinbach, *The Crisis of Austrian Socialism: From Red Vienna to Civil War, 1927–1934* (Chicago: University of Chicago Press, 1983).

83. Julie Thorpe, *Pan-Germanism and the Austrofascist State, 1933–38* (Manchester: Manchester University Press, 2011); Emmerich Tálos and Wolfgang Neugebauer, eds., *Austrofaschismus: Politik—Ökonomie—Kultur 1933–1938*, 5th ed. (Vienna: Lit Verlag, 2005); Florian Wenninger and Lucile Dreidemy, eds., *Das Dollfuß/Schuschnigg-Regime 1933–1938: Vermessung eines Forschungsfeldes* (Vienna: Böhlau Verlag, 2013); Lucile Dreidemy, *Der Dollfuß-Mythos: Eine Biographie des Posthumen* (Vienna: Böhlau Verlag, 2014).

84. Zweig, *The World of Yesterday*, 34–36, 39–40, 45.

85. Schorske, *Fin-de-Siècle Vienna*.

86. For a reconsideration of liberal crisis, see Boyer, *Political Radicalism in Late Imperial Vienna*; Boyer, *Culture and Political Crisis in Vienna*; Pieter Judson, *Exclusive Revolutionaries: Liberal Politics, Social Experience, and National Identity in the Austrian Empire, 1848–1914* (Ann Arbor: University of Michigan Press, 1996). For a reassessment of the nature of Austrian liberal rationalism, see Deborah R. Coen, *Vienna in the Age of Uncertainty: Science, Liberalism, and Private Life* (Chicago: University of Chicago Press, 2007). For a reconsideration of Viennese modernism, see Janik and Toulmin, *Wittgenstein's Vienna*; Steven Beller, *Vienna and the Jews, 1867–1938: A Cultural History* (New York: Cambridge University Press, 1989).

87. Nathan J. Timpano, *Constructing the Viennese Modern Body: Art, Hysteria, and the Puppet* (New York: Routledge, 2017).

88. Alys X. George, *The Naked Truth: Viennese Modernism and the Body* (Chicago: University of Chicago Press, 2020), here 13.

89. Maderthaner and Musner, *Unruly Masses*; Peter Payer, *Der Gestank von Wien: Über Kanalgase, Totendünste und andere üble Geruchskulissen* (Vienna: Döcker Verlag, 1997); Payer, "The Age of Noise"; Spector, *Violent Sensations*; Wingfield, *The World of Prostitution in Late Imperial Austria*; Healy, *Vienna and the Fall of the Habsburg Empire*; Lisa Silverman, *Becoming Austrians: Jews and Culture between the World Wars* (New York: Oxford University Press, 2012); McEwen, *Sexual Knowledge*; Michaela Hintermayr, *Suizid und Geschlecht in der Moderne: Wissenschaft, Medien und Individuum (Österreich 1870–1970)* (Boston: De Gruyer Oldenbourg, 2021).

90. On embodied acts as transmitters of knowledge, see Diana Taylor, *The Archive and the Repertoire: Performing Cultural Memory in the Americas* (Durham, NC: Duke University Press, 2003).

91. Carolyn Steedman, *Labours Lost: Domestic Service and the Making of Modern England* (Cambridge: Cambridge University Press, 2009), 351.

92. On the gendered history of the discipline of history, see Bonnie Smith, *The Gender of History: Men, Women, and Historical Practice* (Cambridge, MA: Harvard University Press, 1998).

93. Caroline Bynum, "In Praise of Fragments: History in the Comic Mode," in *Fragmentation and Redemption: Essays on Gender and the Human Body in Medieval Religion* (New York: Zone Books, 1991), 25.

94. I also found inspiration in Saidiya Hartman's method of "critical fabulation." See Saidiya Hartman, "Venus in Two Acts," *Small Axe* 12, no. 2 (June 2008): 1–14.

95. Hugo von Hofmannsthal, "Über die Pantomime," in *Gesammelte Werke, Bd. 8: Reden und Aufsätze I, 1891–1913*, ed. Bernd Schoeller and Rudolf Hirsch (Frankfurt am Main: Fischer Verlag, 1979), 502–5.

Chapter One

1. ABpdW, P/M, 1917, Vienna, 22 December 1918.

2. See, for example, Judith Walkowitz, *City of Dreadful Delight: Narratives of Sexual Danger in Late-Victorian London* (Chicago: University of Chicago Press, 1992).

3. Elizabeth Grosz, "Bodies-Cities," in *Space, Time, and Perversion: Essays on the Politics of Bodies* (New York: Routledge, 1995), 108.

4. Nancy M. Wingfield, *The World of Prostitution in Late Imperial Austria* (New York: Oxford University Press, 2017), 61–62.

5. ABpdW, P/M, 1907/2, "Referat über Prostitutionswesen," Vienna, 8 January 1907.

6. Wingfield, *The World of Prostitution*, 212–13; Maureen Healy, *Vienna and the Fall of the Habsburg Empire: Total War and Everyday Life in World War I* (New York: Cambridge University Press, 2004), 148–59.

7. Number taken from Wingfield, *The World of Prostitution*, 138.

8. Karin Jusek, *Auf der Suche nach der Verlorenen: Die Prostitutionsdebatten im Wien der Jahrhundertwende* (Vienna: Löcker Verlag, 1994), 100.

9. Keely Stauter-Halsted, "The Physician and the Fallen Woman: Medicalizing Prostitution in the Polish Lands," *Journal of the History of Sexuality* 20, no. 2 (May 2011): 282.

10. Wingfield, *The World of Prostitution*, 5.

11. Stefan Zweig, *The World of Yesterday*, trans. Anthea Bell (1942; Lincoln: University of Nebraska Press, 2013), 107.

12. For parks, see Josef Schrank, *Die Regelung der Prostitution vom gewerblich-nationalökonomischen Standpunkte betrachtet* (Vienna, 1892), 376. For bridges, see Arthur Schnitzler, "Die Dirne und der Soldat," in *Reigen* (1900; Frankfurt: Fischer Taschenbuch Verlag, 1989).

13. Schrank, *Die Regelung der Prostitution*, 376.

14. ABpdW, P/M, 1918/3, Sittenpolizeiliche Agenden (hereafter S/A), Letter from Anonymous, Vienna, 23 December 1918.

15. Wingfield, *The World of Prostitution*, 145.

16. Wingfield, *The World of Prostitution*, 147–51.

17. "Am Praterstern!" *WN*, 24 July 1926, 3–4.

18. For prostitution in working-class districts, see ABpdW, P/M, 1906/2, Vienna, 16 December 1906; for prostitution in bourgeois districts, see ABpdW, P/M, 1914/2, S/A, Vienna, 3 June 1915; on brothels, see Wingfield, *The World of Prostitution*, 110–36.

19. For prostitution on the Graben, see *Der Floh*, 11 November 1877, 8; for a list of prohibited spaces in Vienna, by district, see OeStA, AVI, MdI, Mädchenhandel u. Prostitution, (hereafter M/P), Teil 2 A 2121, Protokoll, 1900.

20. Schrank, *Die Regelung der Prostitution*, 373.

21. "Die Dirnenrennbahn auf der Kärntnerstrasse," *WN*, 3 July 1926, 1.

22. Michel de Certeau, *The Practice of Everyday Life*, trans. Steven F. Rendall (1984; Berkeley: University of California Press, 2011), 98.

23. Certeau, *The Practice of Everyday Life*, 376.

24. Allan Pred, *Lost Words and Lost Worlds: Modernity and the Language of Everyday Life in Late Nineteenth-Century Stockholm* (New York: Cambridge University Press, 1990), 129; Schrank, *Die Regelung der Prostitution*, 376; "Schutz der Ehre," *Reichspost*, 13 March 1901, 1.

25. ABpdW, P/M, 1914/2, S/A, Vienna, 18 September 1913. See also ABpdW, P/M, 1908, "Die Prostitution vom sozialen und rechtlichen Standpunkte, mit besonderer Berücksichtigung der Wiener Verhältnisse."

26. ABpdW, P/M, 1922–1923, Letter to Sittenamt, Vienna, 25 August 1923.

27. See, for example, ABpdW, P/M, 1915, Gruppe XIII. Abschnitt: 104, Staupe Antonia, 1 April 1911.

28. "Die Dirnenrennbahn auf der Kärntnerstrasse," 1.

29. ABpdW, P/M, 1914/2, S/A, Vienna, 2 August 1912; ABpdW, P/M, 1908, "Die Prostitution vom sozialen und rechtlichen Standpunkte, mit besonderer Berücksichtigung der Wiener Verhältnisse."

30. ABpdW, P/M, 1924–1925, Vienna, 27 May 1925.

31. "Polizeilicher Frauenschutz," AnZ, 6 August 1896, 1–2.

32. ABpdW, P/M, 1914/3, S/A, Pocs Gisela, Vienna, 9 August 1914.

33. "Der Irrtum des Polizeiagenten," NWT, 9 November 1916, 16.

34. By summer 1916, street lighting in Vienna was turned off to conserve electricity. For the weather forecast, see WZ, 18 September 1916, 7. Moon phase data from https://moonpage.com.

35. ABpdW, Sb, 1916, IV, Vienna, 7 September 1916.

36. See ABpdW, P/M, 1917, Vienna, 22 December 1918.

37. J. Robert Wegs, Growing Up Working Class: Continuity and Change Among Viennese Youth, 1890–1938 (University Park: Pennsylvania State University Press, 1989), 108; Sigrid Augeneder, Arbeiterinnen im Ersten Weltkrieg: Lebens- und Arbeitsbedingungen proletarischer Frauen in Österreich (Vienna: Europaverlag, 1987), 33.

38. Healy, Vienna and the Fall of the Habsburg Empire, 43.

39. Healy, 44.

40. ABpdW, Sb, 1916, IV, Vienna, 28 September 1916.

41. "Ein aussichtsloser Kampf," WSMZ, 5 January 1920, 2–3.

42. Robert Rotenberg, Landscape and Power in Vienna (Baltimore, MD: Johns Hopkins University Press, 1995); Eve Blau, The Architecture of Red Vienna 1919–1934 (Cambridge, MA: MIT Press, 1999), 52; Elisabeth Lichtenberger, Vienna: Bridge Between Cultures, trans. Dietline Mühlgassner and Craig Reisser (New York: Belhaven Press, 1993).

43. Traffic regulations for drivers and pedestrians were introduced in 1913. Peter Payer, "The Age of Noise: Early Reactions in Vienna, 1870–1914," Journal of Urban History 33, no. 5 (July 2007): 773–93.

44. Carl Schorske, Fin-de-Siècle Vienna: Politics and Culture (New York: Vintage Books, 1981), 24–115.

45. Julius Meurer, A Handy Illustrated Guide to Vienna and Environs, 2nd ed. (Vienna: A. Hartleben, 1906), 37.

46. Heikki Lempa, Beyond the Gymnasium: Educating the Middle-Class Bodies in Classical Germany (New York: Lexington Books, 2007), 163–93, 176–77.

47. Walter Benjamin, "The Flâneur," in Charles Baudelaire: A Lyric Poet in the Era of High Capitalism, trans. Harry Zohn (New York: Verso, 1983), 36.

48. Charles Baudelaire, "The Painter of Modern Life," in The Painter of Modern Life and Other Essays, trans. Jonathan Mayne (New York: Phaidon, 1964), 9.

49. Keith Tester, "Introduction," in The Flâneur (New York: Routledge, 1994), 7.

50. Benjamin, "The Flâneur," 54, 37.

51. Baudelaire, "The Painter of Modern Life," 9.

52. Tester, "Introduction," 13.

53. Adolf Loos, quoted in Janet Stewart, Fashioning Vienna: Adolf Loos's Cultural Criticism (New York: Taylor & Francis, 2013), 134.

54. *Der Floh*, 10 March 1889, 2.

55. See, for example, "Botanische Ausstellung des Kikeriki: Augentrost. Gigerl vom Ring," *Kikeriki*, 25 June 1905, 5.

56. J. F. Wagner, "'Gigerl' Marsch für Pianoforte" (Vienna: Rebay & Robitschek, ca. 1895).

57. Military marches were an important feature of the Habsburg soundscape, as encapsulated in Joseph Roth's 1932 novel named after one such march: Joseph Roth, *The Radetzky March*, trans. Joachim Neugroschel (1932; New York: The Overlook Press, 1991).

58. See, for example, Janet Wolff, "The Invisible Flâneuse: Women and the Literature of Modernity," *Theory, Culture & Society* 2, no. 3 (November 1985): 37–46; Elizabeth Wilson, "The Invisible Flâneur," *New Left Review* 1, no. 191 (January–February 1992): 90–110.

59. Baudelaire, "The Painter of Modern Life," 11.

60. This "impressionism" was also tied to the Viennese cult around death and decay. William M. Johnston, *The Austrian Mind: An Intellectual and Social History, 1848–1938* (Berkeley: University of California Press, 1972), 169.

61. "Federwolken!" *WC*, 2 December 1900, 3.

62. See Peter K. Andersson, *Silent History: Body Language and Nonverbal Identity, 1860–1914* (Montreal: McGill-Queen's University Press, 2018), 232.

63. Susan Buck-Morss, "The Flâneur, the Sandwichman and the Whore: The Politics of Loitering," *New German Critique* 39 (Autumn 1986): 119.

64. Malvine von Steinau, *Der gute Ton für Damen*, 7th ed. (Vienna: A. Hartleben, 1922), 25. Although this piece of advice is taken from von Steinau's 1922 edition, the similarities between the 1878 edition and this one suggest that the fin de siècle edition most likely contained similar instructions.

65. Von Steinau, *Der gute Ton für Damen*, 7th ed., 26; Malvine von Steinau, *Der gute Ton für Damen*, 2nd ed. (Vienna: A. Hartleben, 1878), 25–26.

66. Andersson, *Silent History*, 109–17.

67. Ilse-Dore Tanner, *Gutes Benehmen: Ein Ratgeber in allen Fragen des guten Tones und der feinen Sitten* (Vienna: W. Vobach, 1923), 27.

68. Tanner, *Gutes Benehmen*, 27.

69. *Vienne en Tramway* (Pathé Frères, 1906).

70. Walkowitz, *City of Dreadful Delight*, 223.

71. Andersson, *Silent History*, 109–17.

72. Andersson, *Silent History*, 73, 83.

73. "29. Straßenzug," *BdH* 11, no. 1 (1900): 9.

74. Andersson, *Silent History*, 131–61.

75. "Uebergriffe der Polizei. Ein Massenmeeting der Wiener Frauen," *NWJ*, 12 March 1901, 4.

76. Marie Lang, quoted in "Uebergriffe der Polizei," 4.

77. My effort to imagine this movement historically through urban space takes inspiration from Marisa J. Fuentes's *Dispossessed Lives*. See Marisa J. Fuentes, *Dispossessed Lives: Enslaved Women, Violence, and the Archive* (Philadelphia: University of Pennsylvania Press, 2016).

78. Wolfgang Maderthaner and Lutz Musner argue that flânerie could not take place beyond the Ring. See Wolfgang Maderthaner and Lutz Musner, *Unruly Masses: The Other Side of Fin-de-Siècle Vienna* (New York: Berghahn Books, 2008), 31–43, 68–76.

79. Between 1869 and 1890, the population in the inner suburbs grew by 200,000 to a

total of 743,000, while the population in the outer suburbs nearly tripled from 220,000 to 600,000. Blau, *The Architecture of Red Vienna 1919–1934*, 65.

80. "Frauenehre und Polizistenehre," *AZ*, 2 November 1899, 2; "Uebergriffe der Polizei."

81. G. Engelsmann, "Feuilleton. Dies und Das," *WSMZ*, 6 November 1899, 1.

82. Marianne Valverde, "The Love of Finery: Fashion and the Fallen Woman in Nineteenth-Century Social Discourse," *Victorian Studies* (Winter 1989): 169–88.

83. Zweig, *The World of Yesterday*, 107.

84. Emilie Exner, quoted in Deborah R. Coen, *Vienna in the Age of Uncertainty: Science, Liberalism, and Private Life* (Chicago: University of Chicago Press, 2007), 199–200.

85. A woman was once arrested for looking out the window in a "conspicuous red blouse." See "Polizeilicher Frauenschutz," *AnZ*, 6 August 1896, 1–2.

86. Quoted in Coen, *Vienna in the Age of Uncertainty*, 198–99.

87. Emilie Exner, quoted in Coen, *Vienna in the Age of Uncertainty*, 200; "Was darf ich tragen?" *BdH* 15, no. 43 (1904): 1078.

88. Details in this paragraph taken from "Frauenehre und Polizistenehre," *AZ*, 2 November 1899, 2.

89. Maderthaner and Musner, *Unruly Masses*, 91–94.

90. "Wieder ein Uebergriff der Polizei," *WMJ*, 5 March 1900, 3.

91. "Wieder ein Uebergriff der Polizei," 3.

92. "Aus dem Gemeinderathe," *BP*, 15 March 1900, 2.

93. "Der Schutz der Persönlichen Freiheit der Frauen," *DF*, 1 June 1900, 172–75.

94. In Czernowitz, it was more common for women to work in brothels than on the street. See Wingfield, *The World of Prostitution in Late Imperial Austria*, 91.

95. OeStA, AVA, JM, Vergehen gegen die öffentliche Sittlichkeit (hereafter VgoS), I A1135, IK.I/40–1917, Letter to k. u. k. Ministry of Justice, Czernowitz, April 1900.

96. See Erna Appelt, "The Gendering of the Service Sector in Austria at the End of the Nineteenth Century," in *Austrian Women in the Nineteenth and Twentieth Centuries: Cross-Disciplinary Perspectives*, ed. David F. Good, Margarete Grandner, and Mary Jo Maynes (Providence, RI: Berghahn Books, 1996): 115–32; Susan Zimmermann, "'Making a Living from Disgrace': The Politics of Prostitution, Female Poverty and Urban Gender Codes in Budapest and Vienna, 1860–1920," in *The City in Central Europe: Culture and Society from 1800 to the Present*, ed. Malcolm Gee, Tim Kirk, and Jill Steward (Brookfield, VT: Ashgate, 1999): 175–96; Ambika Natarajan, "Sex, Surveillance, and the Servant Question in Vienna, 1850–1914" (PhD diss., Oregon State University, 2019); Ambika Natarajan, *Servants of Culture: Paternalism, Policing, and Identity Politics in Vienna, 1700–1914* (New York: Berghahn Books, 2023).

97. Andrea Althaus, "Lebensverhältnisse von Dienstmädchen und Hausgehilfinnen im 19. und 20. Jahrhundert," in *Mit Kochlöffel und Staubwedel: Erzählungen aus dem Dienstmädchenalltag* (Vienna: Böhlau Verlag, 2010), 275.

98. Marina Tichy, *Alltag und Traum: Leben und Lektüre der Wiener Dienstmädchen um die Jahrhundertwende* (Vienna: Böhlau Verlag, 1984), 24.

99. Holly Case, *The Age of Questions: Or, A First Attempt at an Aggregate History of the Eastern, Social, Woman, American, Jewish, Polish, Bullion, Tuberculosis, and Many Other Questions over the Nineteenth Century, and Beyond* (Princeton, NJ: Princeton University Press, 2018); EK, "Zur Dienstbotenfrage," *AnZ*, 25 January 1900, 4; Julius Ofner, "Zur Dienstbotenfrage," *DF*, 15 January 1900, 580.

100. ABpdW, P/M, 1907/1, "Fragebogen. P.B. 1075, Betreff: Enquete der Gesellschaft zur Bekämpfung der Geschlechtskrankheiten," Vienna, 30 August 1907.

101. Ambika Natarajan, "Vagrant Servants as Disease Vectors: Regulation of Migrant

Maidservants in Fin-de-Siècle Vienna," *Austrian History Yearbook* 51 (2020): 152–72, here 153. See also Natarajan, *Servants of Culture.*

102. "Theorie des polizeilichen Uebergriffs," *AZ*, 19 March 1901, 4.

103. ABpdW, P/M, 1912, S/A, Plaschek Anna, Vienna, 27 April 1912.

104. ABpdW, P/M, 1919/1, Tinhof Marie, Vienna, 3 October 1919.

105. EK, "Zur Dienstbotenfrage."

106. Emma Goldman, "The Traffic in Women," 1910, in *Feminism: The Essential Historical Writings*, ed. Miriam Schneir (New York: Vintage Books, 1994): 308–17.

107. Schnitzler, *Reigen*, 36.

108. Hans Heinz Hahnl, "Lust und Frust," in *Wiener Lust: Eine Anthologie österreichischer erotischer Literatur*, ed. Hans Heinz Hahnl (Vienna: Locker Verlag, 1989), 6–7.

109. Johann Rautenstrauch, "Über die Stubenmädchen in Wien" (Vienna, 1781).

110. For example, ÖNB, BAA, August Stauda (photographer), "Wien 8, Josefstädter-straße 12," Photograph (Vienna, 1904).

111. O. Timidior, *Der Hut und seine Geschichte: Eine kulturgeschichtliche Monographie* (Vienna: A. Hartleben, 1914), 96.

112. Many police reports note that sex workers often promenaded "without a hat." See ABpdW, P/M, 1914/2, Alois Hanawik, Vienna, 18 September 1913.

113. ABpdW, P/M, 1907/1, Vienna, 24 January 1907.

114. von Steinau, *Der gute Ton für Damen*, 7th ed., 17.

115. "Typen aus der Welt der Wiener Prostitution. Brigittenauer Dirnen und ihre Zuhälter," *IOKZ*, 2 September 1907, 6.

116. Recently, scholars have started reconceptualizing the Habsburg Empire as a quasi-colonial power pursuing an "internal colonialism" in eastern Europe, "othering" and "ori-entalizing" its lands and peoples. See, for example, Johannes Feichtinger, Ursual Pratsch, and Mortiz Csaky, eds., *Habsburg Postcolonial: Machtstrukturen und kollektives Gedächtnis* (Innsbruck: Studien, 2003); Wolfgang Müller-Funk, Peter Plener, and Clemens Ruthner, eds., *Kakanien Revisited: Das Eigene und das Fremde (in) der österreichisch-ungarischen Monarchie* (Tübingen: Francke, 2002).

117. Larry Wolff, *Inventing Eastern Europe: The Map of Civilization on the Mind of the Enlightenment* (Stanford, CA: Stanford University Press, 1994), 4.

118. Bertha Pappenheim and Sara Rabinowitz, *Zur Lage der jüdischen Bevölkerung in Galizien: Reise-Eindrücke und Vorschläge zur Besserung der Verhältnisse* (Frankfurt am Main: Neuer Frankfurter Verlag, 1904), 24.

119. For the weather forecast on 29 January 1900, see *WA*, 29 January 1900, 6.

120. For job postings outlining duties of chambermaids, see *NFP*, 9 January 1900, 20.

121. Meurer, *A Handy Illustrated Guide*, 37.

122. Gregor Gatscher-Riedl, *K. u. k. Sehnsuchtsort Czernowitz: "Klein-Wien" am Ostrand der Monarchie* (Berndorf: KRAL Verlag, 2017), 161–62.

123. See "Moses Hermann," *BR*, 11 March 1900, 7.

124. Herman Mittelmann, *Illustrierter Führer durch die Bukowina* (Czernowitz: Verlag der Buchhandlung Romuald Schally, 1907/1908), 77; Gatscher-Riedl, *K. u. k. Sehnsuchtsort Czernowitz*, 124.

125. See "Café de l'Europe," in Mittelmann, *Illustrierter Führer durch die Bukowina*, 83.

126. Gatscher-Riedl, *K. u. k. Sehnsuchtsort Czernowitz*, 175.

127. "Ein unerhörter Missgriff der Polizei!" *DF*, 1 March 1901, 738–40.

128. "Ein unerhörter Missgriff der Polizei!"

129. Marie Lang, quoted in "Uebergriffe der Polizei."

130. "Die Wiener Erlebnisse einer Französin," *NWT*, 6 March 1901, 7.

131. "Interpellation des Abgeordneten Dr. Ofner und Genossen an Seine Excellenz den Herrn Minister des Innern, wegen Übergriffe der Polizei" (hereafter Interpellation Ofner), 16. Sitzung, XVII Session, 5 March 1901, ÖNB, ALEX, SPdAdR, 947–49.

132. "Anfrage des Abgeordneten Laurenz Hofer und Genossen an Seine Excellenz den Herrn Ministerpräsidenten als Leiter des Ministeriums des Innern und an Seine Excellenz den Herrn Justizminister" (hereafter Anfrage Hofer), 17. Sitzung, XVII Session, 6 March 1901, ÖNB, ALEX, SPdAdR, 1017–20.

133. "Anfrage Hofer," 1019.

134. "Anfrage Hofer," 1020.

135. "Anfrage des Abgeordneten Dr. Josef Pommer und Genossen an Seine Excellenz den Herrn Ministerpräsidenten als Leiter des Ministeriums des Innern, betreffend einen Fall von groben Missbrauches der Amtsgewalt von Seite einiger Organe der Wiener Polizei" (hereafter Anfrage Pommer), 19. Sitzung, XVII Session, 8. March, 1901, ÖNB, ALEX, SPdAdR, 1087–88.

136. "Ein unererhörter Missgriff der Polizei!"

137. "Schutz der Ehre," *Reichspost*, 13 March 1901, 1.

138. "Die Ritter vom Uebergriff," *AZ*, 14 March 1901, 4.

139. For the weather, see *WA*, 4 March 1901, 6.

140. Meurer, *A Handy Illustrated Guide*, 42.

141. Iris Marion Young, "Throwing Like a Girl: A Phenomenology of Feminine Body Comportment, Motility, and Spatiality," in *On Female Body Experience: "Throwing Like a Girl" and Other Essays* (New York: Oxford University Press, 2005), 39.

142. Stacy Alaimo, "Trans-Corporeal Feminisms and the Ethical Space of Nature," in *Material Feminisms*, ed. Stacy Alaimo and Susan Hekman (Bloomington: Indiana University Press, 2008), 237–64.

143. "Federwolken!" *WC*, 2 December 1900, 3.

144. Saidiya Hartman, *Wayward Lives, Beautiful Experiments: Intimate Histories of Social Upheaval* (New York: W. W. Norton, 2019), 227–28, 237.

145. "Böse Zungen," *Die Bombe*, 17 March 1901, 8.

146. ABpdW, P/M, 1906, I Bäckergasse 16, Vienna, 17 November 1916.

147. *Schaufensterbummel* became a term by 1927. Gerda Buxbaum, *Mode aus Wien: 1815–1938* (Vienna: Reidenz Verlag, 1986), 104.

148. Hertha Römer-Rosenfeld, "Der Reiz der Wiener Auslagen," *BdH* 42, no. 4 (November 1926): ii–iii.

149. *BdH* 41, no. 25 (September 1926): 11.

150. Quoted in Buxbaum, *Mode aus Wien*, 137.

151. Streetwear also appeared in magazines from the fin de siècle, but was more frequently featured later on. Buxbaum, *Mode aus Wien*, 126–42.

152. "Für die Strasse," *BdH*, 22 August 1915, 1.

153. Grete Müller, "Mode: Genre Trotteur," *Die Bühne*, 18 October 1928, 37–38.

154. "Wiener Mode," *BdH* 44, no. 4 (November 1928): 122; "Auf dem Weg zum Büro," *BdH* 36, no. 22/24 (August 1921): 1.

155. "Wiener Wintermode," *BdH* 44, no. 2 (October 1928): 51.

156. Advertisement for Palma-Kautschukabsätze, *BdH* 43, no. 24 (August 1928): iii; advertisement for Burgit Fußbad, *IFHR* 31, no. 6 (1925): 15.

157. Advertisement for Diana Puder, *BdH*, 22 September 1918, 10.

Chapter Two

1. "Besseres Wetter," *IKZ*, 6 August 1932, 2; ABpdW, P/M, 1930–1936, Sittenpolizeiliche Agenden (hereafter S/A), Piowati Gisela, Vienna, 5 August 1932.

2. Although Magnus Hirschfeld's 1910 book *Die Transvestitin: Eine Untersuchung über den erotischen Verkleidungstrieb* explained cross-dressing as an erotic fetish that was not necessarily tied to homosexuality or gender inversion, the category of the "transvestite" remained fuzzy into the 1920s. See Laurie Marhoefer, *Sex and the Weimar Republic: German Homosexual Emancipation and the Rise of the Nazis* (Toronto: University of Toronto Press, 2015), 59–61.

3. "Die Wiener Behörden und die Transvestiten," *Die Stunde*, 3 April 1930, 5.

4. "Die Dirnenrennbahn auf der Kärntnerstrasse," *WN*, 3 July 1926, 1; "Die Gürtel-Prostitution," *WN*, 9 October 1926, 1–2; "Der Homosexuelle 'Adele,'" and "Wiener ein 'Anderer,'" *WNP*, 28 August 1926, 1–2.

5. On the media and homosexuality in fin-de-siècle Vienna, see Scott Spector, "The Wrath of the 'Countess Merviola': Tabloid Exposé and the Emergence of Homosexual Subjects in Vienna in 1907," in *Sexuality in Austria*, ed. Günter Bischof, Anton Pelinka, and Dagmar Herzog (New Brunswick, NJ: Transaction, 2007), 31–47.

6. Piowati was Jewish, and insofar as this occurred in 1932, she may have been denounced for antisemitic reasons. Since her denouncers, Hilda Schuch and Josefine Glinz, both had Jewish surnames, however, this explanation seems unlikely.

7. Otto Weininger, *Sex & Character*, 6th ed. (1903; New York: G. P. Putnam's Sons, 1906), 65.

8. Weininger, *Sex & Character*, 68.

9. "Die Zukunfts-Frauen," *WC*, 10 May 1896, 4–5.

10. Luzifer, "Frauen. Eine naturgeschichtliche Studie," *Figaro*, 11 April 1908, 8.

11. Luzifer, "Frauen," 8.

12. "Imperial-Feigen-Kaffee," *IFHR* 1 (1913); R. Hofstätter, *Die rauchende Frau: Eine klinische psychologische und soziale Studie* (Vienna: Hölder-Pichler-Tempsky, 1924), 190; "Die Naturgeschichte der Frau," *Die Muskete*, 1 July 1924, 6.

13. Grete Müller, "Bub oder Mädel?" *Die Bühne*, 29 November 1928, 4–5.

14. Claire Patek, "Die Frau von heute," *Die Bühne*, 28 April 1927, 17–18.

15. Desiderius Papp, "Besuch in der Bibliothek," *NWJ*, 15 October 1922, 8.

16. Weininger, *Sex & Character*, 9.

17. Weininger, 7.

18. Rosa Mayreder, *Das Haus in der Landskrongasse. Jugenderinnerungen* (Vienna: Mandelbaum Verlag Michael Baiculescu, 1998), 146.

19. Carl Heinrich Stratz, *Die Körperpflege der Frau: Physiologische und ästhetische Diätetik für das weibliche Geschlecht* (Stuttgart: Verlag von Ferdinand Enke, 1918), 194.

20. "Werden die Frauenhände grösser?" *IFHR* 19, no. 17 (1913): 181.

21. Maureen Healy, *Vienna and the Fall of the Habsburg Empire: Total War and Everyday Life in World War I* (New York: Cambridge University Press, 2004), 205.

22. O. Janetschek, *Weib und Genuß: Für reife Menschen* (Vienna: Anzengruber-Verlag, 1922), 70.

23. Jack Halberstam, *Female Masculinity* (Durham, NC: Duke University Press, 1998), 234.

24. Michael Hau, *The Cult of Health and Beauty in Germany: A Social History 1890–1930* (Chicago: University of Chicago Press, 2003), 33.

25. Johann Joachim Winckelmann, *Geschichte der Kunst des Alterthums* (Dresden, 1764); Johann Wolfgang von Goethe, *Italian Journey* (1816; London: Penguin Books, 1970).

26. Alma Mahler-Werfel, "Thursday 6 July, Suite 12, 1899," in *Diaries 1898–1902*, trans. Antony Beaumont (Ithaca, NY: Cornell University Press, 1999), 160–61.

27. Hau, *The Cult of Health*, 65–67.

28. Mayreder, *Das Haus in der Landskrongasse*, 146.

29. Fritz Kehren, *Unter vier Augen: Die hohe Schule der Gattenliebe*, 10th ed. (Přívoz: I. Buchsbaum, 1920), 130.

30. Wolfgang G. Fischer with Dorothea McEwan, *Gustav Klimt & Emilie Flöge: An Artist and His Muse* (London: Lund Humphries, 1992), 35.

31. Carl Heinrich Stratz, *Die Rassenschönheit des Weibes*, 5th ed. (Stuttgart: Verlag von Ferdinand Enke, 1902), 358–60.

32. Stratz, *Die Rassenschönheit des Weibes*, 355; Adolf Loos made a connection between dumplings and soft female curves. See Janet Stewart, "A Taste of Vienna: Food as a Signifier of Urban Modernity in Vienna, 1890–1930," in *The City and the Senses: Urban Culture Since 1500*, ed. Alexander Cowan and Jill Steward (London: Routledge, 2007), 181.

33. "Grazie für jede Frau," *IFHR* 31, no. 2 (1925): 3.

34. "Das gefährliche Alter," *IFHR* 31, no. 19 (1925): 3–4.

35. Hau, *The Cult of Health*, 67.

36. Mahler-Werfel, "Thursday 6 July, Suite 12, 1899," 160–61.

37. F. König, *Ratgeber in gesunden und kranken Tagen* (1910), quoted in Hau, *The Cult of Health*, 64–65.

38. Sabine Wieber, "Sculpting the Sanatorium: Nervous Bodies and Femmes Fragiles in Vienna, 1900," in *Women in German Yearbook: Feminist Studies in German Literature & Culture* 27 (2011): 69.

39. Wieber, "Sculpting the Sanatorium," 64.

40. Ageeth Sluis, *Deco Body, Deco City: Female Spectacle and Modernity in Mexico City, 1900–1939* (Lincoln: University of Nebraska Press, 2016).

41. "Der Poiret-Rummel," *ÖIZ*, 10 December 1911, 267; "Poiret in Wien," *WZ*, 27 November 1911, 3.

42. "Generalprobe Poiret," *NWJ*, 27 November 1911, 1; Poiret's fabrics were partially indebted to the designs of the Wiener Werkstätte. See Heather Hess, "The Lure of Vienna: Poiret and the Wiener Werkstätte," in *Poiret*, ed. Harold Koda and Andrew Bolton (New York: Metropolitan Museum of Art, 2007), 39–40.

43. Adalbert Grafen Sternberg, "Poirets Halbweltkostüme," *NWJ*, 5 December 1911, 2.

44. See, for example, "Vertauschte Rollen," *Der Floh*, 9 April 1911, 4.

45. See, for example, "Der Kampf gegen den Hosenrock," *IKZ*, 11 March 1911, 5.

46. "Paris im Frühjahr 1911," *BdH*, 19 March 1911, 5.

47. "Herr Poiret in Wien," *IKZ*, 29 November 1911, 6.

48. Sternberg, "Poirets Halbweltkostüme," 2.

49. On late-nineteenth-century Viennese dress cuts, see Gerda Buxbaum, *Mode aus Wien: 1815–1938* (Vienna: Residenz Verlag, 1986), 89, 95.

50. Stefan Zweig, *The World of Yesterday*, trans. Anthea Bell (Lincoln: University of Nebraska Press, 2009), 93.

51. Zweig, *The World of Yesterday*, 94.

52. Mayreder, *Das Haus in der Landskrongasse*, 146.

53. Mayreder, 147.

54. Buxbaum, *Mode aus Wien*, 93.

55. On dress reform in Vienna, see Rebecca Houze, "Fashionable Reform Dress and the Invention of 'Style' in Fin de Siècle Vienna," *Fashion Theory* 5, no. 1 (2001): 29–56; Mary L. Wagener, "Fashion and Feminism in 'Fin de Siècle' Vienna," *Woman's Art Journal* 10, no. 2 (Autumn 1989–Winter 1990): 29–33.

56. Breus, "Gutachten von Ärzten über das Miedertragen," *DF*, 1 March 1902, 668.

57. Friedrich Schauta, "Gutachten von Ärzten über das Miedertragen," *DF*, 1 March 1902, 675.

58. *WS*, 11 September 1892, 8.

59. They were published in *Deutsche Kunst und Dekoration* 19 (October 1906–March 1907): 65–73.

60. Houze, "Fashionable Reform Dress," 48–49. See also Valerie Steele, *Fashion and Eroticism: Ideals of Feminine Beauty from the Victorian Era to the Jazz Age* (New York: Oxford University Press, 1985), 6.

61. See, for example, O. H., "Anleitung zum Schneidern," *FS* 22, no. 9 (1913): 3.

62. On *Konfektionen*, see Buxbaum, *Mode aus Wien*, 213–18.

63. On the relationship between Poiret and Viennese fashion, see Wagener, "Fashion and Feminism in 'Fin de Siècle' Vienna," 32; Fischer, with McEwan, *Gustav Klimt & Emilie Flöge*, 81.

64. Iris Marion Young, "Women Recovering Our Clothes," in *On Female Body Experience: "Throwing Like a Girl" and Other Essays* (New York: Oxford University Press, 2005), 63–74.

65. See, for example, Alma Mahler-Werfel, "Wednesday 18 May, Suite 5, 1898," in *Diaries 1898–1902*, 31.

66. Mary Louise Roberts has argued that the new fashion produced "the illusion of freedom" instead of freedom itself. While I do not necessarily disagree with this assessment, I do want to recognize the experience of the historical actors themselves. See Mary Louise Roberts, "Samson and Delilah Revisited: The Politics of Women's Fashion in 1920s France," *American Historical Review* 98, no. 3 (June 1993): 657–84.

67. See, for example, "Was aus unmodernen Kleidern werden kann," *BdH*, 27 December 1914, 8–9.

68. E. H., "Was sollen wir tragen?" *BdH*, 18 October 1914, 3; "Für Straße und Haus," *BdH*, 31 October 1915, 6.

69. On the ton-skirt, see E. H., "Die neue Linie," *BdH*, 3 September 1916, 3. In the summer and fall of 1914, women's fashion no longer modeled itself after Parisian trends as a result of wartime Francophobia. See Regina Forstner, "Die Wiener Damenmode in der zweiten Hälfte des 19. Jahrhunderts bis zum Ende des Ersten Weltkrieges," in *Die Frau im Korsett: Wiener Frauenalltag zwischen Klischee und Wirklichkeit, 1848–1920* (Vienna: Eigenverlag der Museen der Stadt Wien, 1984), 75.

70. For an example of the linear silhouette toward the end of the war years, see E. H., "Frühjahrs-Moden," *BdH*, 10 February 1918, 1.

71. Steele, *Fashion and Eroticism*, 70–71.

72. Steele, 239; G. M., "Interview mit Frau Minna," *Die Bühne*, 15 September 1927, 48–49.

73. Steele, 239.

74. See, for example, Willy Ungar, "Reiches Modenbericht," *DM*, 6 April 1925, 8; G. M., "Kleid und Frisur in Harmonie," *Die Bühne*, 20 September 1928, 33 and 36. On the history of Garçonne fashion in Vienna, see Buxbaum, *Mode aus Wien*, 102–4.

75. This is especially true in personals. See "Korrespondenzen," *BW* 3, no. 16 (1926): 20–21; "Korrespondenzen," *BW* 3, no. 39 (1926): 19–21.

76. Hugo Bettauer, "Von der Mode," *BW* 1, no. 1 (15 May 1924): 16.

77. Charlotte Delroy, "Brassieres, Girdles, Waspies, and Cami-Panties Since 1900," in *Fashioning the Body: An Intimate History of the Silhouette*, ed. Denis Bruna (New Haven, CT: Yale University Press, 2015), 229–41.

78. Delroy, "Brassieres, Girdles, Waspies, and Cami-Panties Since 1900," 232.

79. Advertisement for Diva-Gummi-Fesselformer, *ÖIZ*, 2 October 1927, 20.

80. "Die männliche Linie der Frau," *NWJ*, 8 April 1925, 6.

81. "Der Poiret-Rummel," *ÖIZ*, 10 December 1911, 267.

82. Steele, *Fashion and Eroticism*, 227.

83. "Generalprobe Poiret," *NWJ*, 27 November 1911, 1–2.

84. "Herr Poiret in Wien," *IKZ*, 29 November 1911, 6.

85. "Wienerinnen bei Poiret," *Der Floh*, 19 November 1911, 5.

86. *Die freudlose Gasse*, dir. Georg Wilhelm Pabst (Berlin: Sofar-Film-Produktion, 1925).

87. Healy, *Vienna and the Fall of the Habsburg Empire*, 46.

88. Healy, 82.

89. Figures from Healy, 45.

90. Healy, 41–42.

91. Alice Weinreb, *Modern Hungers: Food and Power in Twentieth-Century Germany* (New York: Oxford University Press, 2017); Alice Weinreb, "Embodying German Suffering: Rethinking Popular Hunger during the Hunger Years (1945–1949)," *Body Politics* 2, no. 4 (2014): 466–67.

92. Weinreb, "Embodying German Suffering," 467.

93. Zweig, *The World of Yesterday*, 35–36.

94. In Arthur Schnitzler's play, *Liebelei*, for example, Sweet Girl Mizi indulges in mocha crème cake. Arthur Schnitzler, *Liebelei* (1895; Frankfurt: Fischer Taschenbuch Verlag, 1989).

95. See Stewart, "A Taste of Vienna," 181.

96. ABpdW, Sb, III, 1916, 23 March.

97. Maria Laßnig, "Kriegsbrot," *BdH*, 21 February 1915, 18.

98. ABpdW, Sb, II, 1915, 22 July.

99. Healy, *Vienna and the Fall of the Habsburg Empire*, 43.

100. On cookbooks, see Healy, 37.

101. Gisela Urban, *Unsere Kriegskost: 290 erprobte österreichische Kriegskochrezepte, unter Berücksichtigung der kriegswirtschaftlichen Verhältnisse und Forderung neu zusammengestellt* (Vienna: St. Stefan Wiener Verlag, 1916).

102. "Wie koche ich jetzt?" *BdH*, 24 October 1915, 2–5.

103. ABpdW, Sb, II, 1915, 30 September.

104. ABpdW, Sb, II, 1915, 7 October.

105. ABpdW, Sb, II, 1915, 7 October.

106. ABpdW, Sb, II, 1915, 14 October.

107. ABpdW, Sb, III, 1916, 3 February.

108. ABpdW, Sb, III, 1916, 6 April.

109. ABpdW, Sb, III, 1916, 2 March.

110. ABpdW, Sb, III, 1916, 20 April.

111. ABpdW, Sb, IV, 1916, 27 July.

112. SFn, Mathilde Hanzel-Hübner (hereafter MHH), NL I/4d/III, Mathilde Hanzel to Ottokar Hanzel, 15 March 1916.

113. SFn, MHH, NL I/4d/III, Mathilde Hanzel to Ottokar Hanzel, 15 March 1916.

114. On *Anstellen*, see Healy, *Vienna and the Fall of the Habsburg Empire*, 73–86.

115. ABpdW, Sb, III, 1916, 27 April.

116. ABpdW, Sb, III, 1916, 9 March.

117. ABpdW, Sb, IV, 1916, 23 November.

118. ABpdW, Sb, III, 1916, 16 March.

119. ABpdW, Sb, IV, 1916, 13 July.

120. ABpdW, Sb, IV, 1916, 20 July.

121. ABpdW, Sb, IV, 1916, 7 September.

122. Healy, *Vienna and the Fall of the Habsburg Empire*, 42, 69–72.

123. Kathleen Canning, "The Body as Method? Reflections on the Place of the Body in Gender History," in *Gender History in Practice: Historical Perspectives on Bodies, Class & Citizenship* (Ithaca, NY: Cornell University Press, 2006), 181.

124. ABpdW, Sb, III, 1916, 18 May.

125. ABpdW, Sb, III, 1916, 1 June.

126. ABpdW, Sb, IV, 1916, 28 September.

127. ABpdW, Sb, IV, 1916, 23 November.

128. SFn, MHH, Box: NL I/4e/V, Mathilde Hanzel to Ottokar Hanzel, no. 65, 5 May 1917.

129. "Gerichte aus Steckrüben," *FM* 7, no. 2 (November 1917): 40–42.

130. ABpdW, Sb, V, 1917, 8 February.

131. ABpdW, Sb, V, 1917, 1 March.

132. ABpdW, Sb, V, 1917, 5 April.

133. Elaine Scarry, *The Body in Pain: The Making and Unmaking of the World* (New York: Oxford University Press, 1985), 12.

134. "Das Wohlfahrtsfleisch," *Wiener Allgemeine Zeitung*, 22 October 1917, 2; ABpdW, Sb, V, 1917, 10 May.

135. Rudolfine Fleischner, "Die Lehren des Hungers," *AnZ*, 18 September 1917, 3.

136. Healy, *Vienna and the Fall of the Habsburg Empire*, 44.

137. Anna Mahler, quoted in Cate Haste, *Passionate Spirit: The Life of Alma Mahler* (New York: Basic Books, 2019), 168.

138. "Das Pferdefleisch," *Neues 8 Uhr-Blatt*, 29 May 1918, 2.

139. Rosa Mayreder, "15. November 1918," in *Tagebücher, 1873–1937*, ed. Harriet Anderson (Frankfurt: Insel Verlag, 1988), 185.

140. ABpdW, Sb, 1918, 23 June.

141. ABpdW, Sb, 1918, 18 June.

142. ABpdW, Sb, 1918, Englische Blätter, 15 November.

143. "Das Kinderelend in Wien, 1919," *Österreich Box, 1896–1995*, Disc 1: Das Ende der Donaumonarchie, 1896–1918, ed. Hannes Leidinger, Verena Moritz, and Karin Moser (Vienna: Filmarchiv Austria, 2009), DVD.

144. SFn, Christine Wastl (hereafter CW), NL 42/II, Christl Wastl to Franzi Wastl, 22 November 1919.

145. "Die freudlose Gasse," *Die Stunde*, 7 November 1925, 9.

146. "Unter dem Mikrophon," *MF* 276 (1931): 12.

147. "Diagonal-Doppelroller," *BW* 45 (1926): 19.

148. "Lebensgefährliche Abmagerungskuren," *DM*, 27 August 1928, 5.

149. Anne Bernfeld, "Nähre dich redlich, aber nicht schädlich!" *DmF* 2 (1926): 17.

150. Sluis, *Deco Body, Deco City*, 295.

151. Oskar Schalek, "Die Stadt schöner Mädchen," *Die schöne Frau* 3, no. 6 (1928): 4.

152. "Lebensgefährliche Abmagerungskuren," 5.

153. "Diagonal-Doppelroller," 19.

154. Annelie Ramsbrock, *The Science of Beauty: Culture and Cosmetics in Modern Germany, 1750–1930*, trans. David Burnett (Washington, DC: Palgrave Macmillan, 2015), 124.

155. "Schlank," *IFHR* 31, no. 8 (1925): 1

156. "Lebensgefährliche Abmagerungskuren," 5; "Mohrrüben machen schlank!" *DF*, 14 August 1926, 22.

157. Luise Kernbichler, "Hungernde Frauen," *Die Unzufriedene*, 18 December 1926, 3.

158. Hau, *The Cult of Health*, 14.

159. "Entefettungs-Tee," *BdH* 39, no. 24 (September 1924): 23.

160. "Lebensgefährliche Abmagerungskuren," 5.

161. Luise Kernbichler, "Hungernde Frauen," *Die Unzufriedene*, 18 December 1926, 3.

162. Erik N. Jensen, *Body by Weimar: Athletes, Gender, and German Modernity* (New York: Oxford University Press, 2010).

163. Hau, *The Cult of Health*, 14.

164. "Fünf Minuten täglich!" and "Die schlanke Linie," *BdH* 36, no. 33/34 (August 1921): 3.

165. Truida, "Wie werde ich wieder jung und schön?" *BW* 22 (9 October 1924).

166. Helmut Gruber, *Red Vienna: Experiment in Working-Class Culture, 1919–1934* (New York: Oxford University Press, 1991), 148.

167. "The SDAP was much more interested in creating and supporting a New Mother, rather than the (single and childless) New Woman." In Britta McEwen, *Sexual Knowledge: Feeling, Fact, and Social Reform in Vienna, 1900–1934* (New York: Berghahn Books, 2012), 93; quote from Zweig, *The World of Yesterday*, 95.

168. OeStA, AVA, UM, Körpersport, 1924–1927, 142, "Hauptverband für Körpersport: Tätigkeitsbericht," 1925.

169. Vicki Baum, "Die Mütter von morgen—die Backfische von heute," in *Bubikopf*, ed. Anna Rheinsberg (Darmstadt: Luchterhand, 1988), 31–35.

170. Sandra Lee Bartky, *Femininity and Domination: Studies in the Phenomenology of Oppression* (New York: Routledge, 1990).

171. "Die Jugend des Körpers," *IFHR* 31, no. 16 (1925): 4.

172. "Gymnastische Uebungen für Frauen und Mädchen," *IFHR* 31, no. 3 (1925): 1–2.

173. OeStA, AVA, UM, Körpersport, 1924–1927, 142, "Hauptverband für Körpersport: Tätigkeitsbericht," 1925.

174. See, for example, "6266," *Wiener Modezeitung* 51 (1932): 6.

175. *Die Büchse der Pandora*, dir. G. W. Pabst (Berlin: Nero-Film, 1929).

176. On 23 November 1941, Piowati was deported to the Kaunas ghetto in occupied Lithuania. She died a few days later. One wonders whether her appearance as a cross-dressing "homosexual" man played a role in the deportation insofar as National Socialism criminalized male homosexuality.

Chapter Three

1. The facility would one day play a crucial role in the Nazis' T-4 euthanasia *Aktion*. WStLA, OWS, KgF, 6, Elisabeth Bergner.

2. Leslie Topp, "Otto Wagner and the Steinhof Psychiatric Hospital: Architecture as Misunderstanding," *The Art Bulletin* (March 2005): 132, 139.

3. Leslie Topp, "The Mad Objects of Fin-de-Siècle Vienna: Journeys, Contexts and Dislocations in the Exhibition 'Madness and Modernity,'" in *Journeys into Madness: Mapping*

Mental Illness in the Austro-Hungarian Empire, ed. Gemma Blackshaw and Sabine Wiener (New York: Berghahn Books, 2012), 16.

4. "The Treatment of the Insane, Then and Now," quoted in Topp, "Otto Wagner and the Steinhof Psychiatric Hospital," 137.

5. Fedor Gerenyi, quoted in Topp, "Otto Wagner and the Steinhof Psychiatric Hospital," 139.

6. Topp, "Otto Wagner and the Steinhof Psychiatric Hospital," 139.

7. Georg Simmel, "The Metropolis and Mental Life," in *The People, Place, and Space Reader*, ed. Jen Jack Gieseking et al. (1903; New York: Routledge, 2014), 223–26; Andreas Killen, *Berlin Electropolis: Shock, Nerves, and German Modernity* (Berkeley: University of California Press, 2006), 4.

8. Killen, *Berlin Electropolis*, 6.

9. Killen, 4.

10. Killen, 5.

11. Carroll Smith-Rosenberg, "The Hysterical Woman: Sex Roles and Role Conflict in 19th Century America," *Social Research* 39, no. 4 (Winter 1972): 652–78.

12. The kleptomania diagnosis was gendered; see Elaine S. Abelson, *Women Ladies Go A-Thieving: Middle-Class Shoplifters in the Victorian Department Store* (New York: Oxford University Press, 1989).

13. Alma Mahler-Werfel, "Friday 29 June, Suite 18, 1900," in *Diaries 1898–1902*, trans. Antony Beaumont (Ithaca, NY: Cornell University Press, 1999), 297.

14. William M. Reddy, *The Navigation of Feeling: A Framework for the History of Emotions* (New York: Cambridge University Press, 2001).

15. "AHR Conversation: The Historical Study of Emotions," *American Historical Review* 117, no. 5 (December 2012): 1497.

16. Barbara H. Rosenwein, "Worrying about Emotions in History," *American Historical Review* 107, no. 3 (June 2002): 842.

17. Norbert Elias, *The Civilizing Process: Sociogenetic and Psychogenetic Investigations*, trans. Edmund Jephcott (1939; Oxford: Blackwell, 2000).

18. For this point, see Edward Ross Dickinson, *Dancing in the Blood: Modern Dance and European Culture on the Eve of the First World War* (Cambridge: Cambridge University Press, 2017), 92.

19. SFn, Mathilde Hanzel-Hübner (hereafter MHH), NL IIIC/4, Diary 1901–1903, 5 May 1902.

20. Malvine von Steinau, *Der gute Ton für Damen*, 2nd ed. (Vienna: A. Hartleben, 1878), 35.

21. Dickinson, *Dancing in the Blood*, 90.

22. Malvine von Steinau, *Der gute Ton für Damen*, 7th ed. (Vienna: A. Hartleben, 1922), 28.

23. For challenges to Elias's thesis, see Reddy, *The Navigation of Feeling*, Rosenwein, "Worrying about Emotions in History"; Barbara H. Rosenwein, *Emotional Communities in the Early Middle Ages* (Ithaca, NY: Cornell University Press, 2006); Nicole Eustace, *Passion Is the Gale: Emotions, Power, and the Coming of the American Revolution* (Chapel Hill: University of North Carolina Press, 2008); Nicole Eustace, *1812: War and the Passions of Patriotism* (Philadelphia: University of Pennsylvania Press, 2012).

24. Susan A. Glenn, *Female Spectacle: The Theatrical Roots of Modern Feminism* (Cambridge, MA: Harvard University Press, 2000), 6.

25. Glenn, *Female Spectacle*, 5–6.

26. Despite her "progressive" politics (she was actively involved in the more radical General Austrian Women's Association from 1910 to 1914), she was privately sympathetic to

National Socialism and its racist ideologies. See Monika Bernold and Johanna Gehmacher, eds., *Auto/Biografie und Frauenfrage. Tagebücher, Briefwechsel, Politische Schriften von Mathilde Hanzel-Hübner (1884–1970)*. *L'Homme Archiv*, Band 1 (Vienna: Böhlau, 2003).

27. Rosenwein, "Worrying about Emotions in History," 821–45; Rosenwein, *Emotional Communities in the Early Middle Ages*.

28. Rosenwein, "Worrying about Emotions in History," 842–43.

29. SFn, MHH, NL IIIC/4, Diary 1901–1903, 26 September 1903.

30. SFn, MHH, NL IIIC/4, Diary 1904, Ostermontag 1904.

31. SFn, MHH, NL IIIC/4, Diary 1905–1910, 28 May 1908.

32. SFn, MHH, NL IIIC/4, Diary 1905–1910, 16 September 1909.

33. SFn, MHH, NL IIIC/4, Diary 1905–1910, 22 May 1907.

34. SFn, MHH, NL IIIC/4, Diary 1901–1903, 2 June 1903.

35. SFn, MHH, NL IIIC/4, Diary 1904, Ostermontag 1904.

36. SFn, MHH, NL IIIC/4, Diary 1905–1910, 16 December 1905.

37. SFn, MHH, NL IIIC/4, Diary 1904, 21 March 1905.

38. SFn, MHH, NL IIIC/4, Diary 1901–1903, 15 September 1904.

39. SFn, MHH, NL IIIC/4, Diary 1905–1910, 30 October 1908.

40. SFn, MHH, NL IIIC/4, Diary 1905–1910, 29 September 1906; SFn, MHH, NL IIIC/4, Diary 1905–1910, 30 December 1908.

41. SFn, MHH, NL IIIC/4, Diary 1905–1910, 7 February 1909.

42. Mahler-Werfel, "Thursday 1 November, Suite 19, 1900," in *Diaries 1898–1902*, 337.

43. Alys X. George, *The Naked Truth: Viennese Modernism and the Body* (Chicago: University of Chicago Press, 2020), 174–75.

44. Georg Fuchs, *Die Schaubühne der Zukunft* (Berlin: Schuster & Loeffler, 1905), 65–66.

45. J. R. Liebenwein, "Gabriele d'Annunzio und Eleonora Duse," *WS*, 12 April 1902, 15–16.

46. George, *The Naked Truth*, 176.

47. George, 169.

48. Hugo von Hofmannsthal, "Über die Pantomime," in *Gesammelte Werke, Bd. 8: Reden und Aufsätze I, 1891–1913*, ed. Bernd Schoeller and Rudolf Hirsch (Frankfurt: Fischer Verlag, 1979), 502–5.

49. Hofmannsthal, quoted in Heinz Hiebler, *Hugo von Hofmannsthal und die Medienkultur der Moderne* (Würzburg: Königshausen und Neumann, 2003), 438.

50. On Grete Wiesenthal, see Reingard Witzmann, ed., *Die neue Körpersprache: Grete Wiesenthal und ihr Tanz* (Vienna: Eigenverlag der Museen der Stadt Wien, 1986).

51. Hofmannsthal, quoted in Mary Fleischer, *Embodied Texts: Symbolist Playwright-Dancer Collaborations* (New York: Rodopi, 2007), 131.

52. Grete Wiesenthal, *Der Aufstieg: Aus dem Leben einer Tänzerin* (Berlin: Ernst Rowohlt Verlag, 1919), 68.

53. Dickinson, *Dancing in the Blood*, 15. On free dance in Vienna, see also Andrea Amort, "Free Dance in Interwar Vienna," in *Interwar Vienna: Culture between Tradition and Modernity*, ed. Deborah Holmes and Lisa Silverman (Rochester, NY: Camden House, 2009), 118–20.

54. Freud would later go on to argue that civilization involves the repression of one's innermost instincts and drives. See Sigmund Freud, *Civilization and Its Discontents*, trans. Joan Riviere (London: Hogarth Press, 1930).

55. On photography and hysteria, see Georges Didi-Huberman, *Invention of Hysteria: Charcot and the Photographic Iconography of the Sâlpetrière*, trans. Alisa Hartz (Cambridge, MA: MIT Press, 2003).

56. Jan Goldstein, "The Hysteria Diagnosis and the Politics of Anticlericalism in Late Nineteenth-Century France," *Journal of Modern History* 54, no. 2 (June 1982): 209–39; Gemma Blackshaw, "The Pathological Body: Modernist Strategising in Egon Schiele's Self-Portraiture," *Oxford Art Journal* 30, no. 3 (2007): 377–401; Nathan J. Timpano, *Constructing the Viennese Modern Body: Art, Hysteria and the Puppet* (New York: Routledge, 2017).

57. Timpano, *Constructing the Viennese Modern Body*, 11.

58. Freud studied under Charcot from October 1885 to February 1886 and was also impacted by this iconography. See Didi-Huberman, *Invention of Hysteria*, 80.

59. Oscar Wilde, *Salomé* (1891); Richard Strauss, *Salome*, op. 54 (1905). On the "perverted" nature of *Salome*, especially to German-speaking audiences, see Sander L. Gilman, "Strauss, the Pervert and Avant-Garde Opera," *New German Critique* 43 (Winter 1988): 35–68. Although Gustav Mahler, the head of the Vienna Court Opera, wanted to stage Strauss's opera, it was rejected by the court censor because of its "perverted sensuality." Its official premiere at the Vienna Court Opera was in 1918.

60. V. S., "Richard Strauß' 'Salome,'" *Der Humorist*, 1 June 1907, 2. Strauss's libretto was a translation of Wilde's text; some of the more sexually salacious parts were removed.

61. Gilman, "Strauss, the Pervert and Avant-Garde Opera," 53.

62. Julius Korngold, "Richard Strauß's 'Salome.' Ein Gespräch," *NFP*, 28 May 1907, 1.

63. Sander L. Gilman, "Strauss and Racial Science," *Opera in a Multicultural World: Coloniality, Culture, Performance*, ed. Mary Ingraham, Joseph So, and Roy Moodley (New York: Routledge, 2016), 127.

64. Kerry Wallach, "Escape Artistry: Elisabeth Bergner and Jewish Disappearance in *Der träumende Mund* (Czinner, 1932)," *German Studies Review* 38, no. 1 (February 2015): 22.

65. Gilman, "Strauss and Racial Science," 134.

66. Susan McClary, *Feminine Endings: Music, Gender, and Sexuality* (Minneapolis: University of Minnesota Press, 1991), 100.

67. Thanks to Pierce Gradone for his help with this musical analysis.

68. McClary, *Feminine Endings*, 100.

69. For a discussion of the "hystero-theatrical gestures" of Salome, see Timpano, *Constructing the Viennese Modern Body*, 105–15.

70. Note the allusion to incest, believed by antisemitic contemporaries to be a Jewish sexual practice.

71. Strauss, quoted in Derrick Puffet, ed., *Richard Strauss: Salome*, Cambridge Opera Books (Cambridge: Cambridge University Press, 1989), 166–67. It is worth noting that both Jewish and Orientalist tropes were drawn on in the construction of Salome-the-hysteric.

72. All quotes in this paragraph are from "Frau Verhunk—Salome. Eine Plauderstunde," *Die Zeit*, 30 May 1907, 5.

73. Udo Kultermann, "The Dance of the Seven Veils: Salome and Erotic Culture around 1900," *Artibus et Historiae* 27, no. 53 (2006): 205–13.

74. Allan's version of the dance was not performed to Strauss's music. "Repetoire des Carl-Theaters," *WZ*, 29 December 1906, 12; "Sensationsdebüts im Apollotheater," *Die Bombe*, 17 February 1900, 6, quote taken from "Miß Maud Allan," *IKZ*, 30 December 1906, 18–19.

75. Judith R. Walkowitz, "The 'Vision of Salome': Cosmopolitanism and Erotic Dancing in Central London, 1908–1918," *American Historical Review* 108, no. 2 (April 2003): 340.

76. "Uebergriffe der Polizei. Ein Massenmeeting der Wiener Frauen," *NWJ*, 12 March 1901, 4.

77. "Ein Walzertraum," *MF* 21 (1926): 2.

78. Arthur Schnitzler, *Liebelei* (1895; Frankfurt: Fischer Taschenbuch Verlag, 1989), 106.

79. On the Sweet Girl, see "Hugo, "Das ist das süße Mädel . . . !" *MF* 103 (1927): 5. For the operetta, see Oscar Straus, *Ein Walzertraum* (Operette in 3 Akten), libretto by Felix Dörmann and Leopold Jacobson (Vienna: Ludwig Doblinger [Bernhard Herzmansky], 1907).

80. "Carl-Theater. Ein Walzertraum," *Der Floh*, 24 February 1907, 3; "Theater, Kunst und Literatur," *SuS*, 20 April 1907, 11.

81. "Im Carl-theater . . . ," *Der Humorist*, 1 May 1907, 2; "Aus den Wiener Theatern," *Die Zeit*, 27 October 1907, 3–4.

82. Quidam, "Karlsbader Sprudel," *Der Humorist*, 20 June 1908, 3.

83. Quidam, "Ischler Plaudereien," *Der Humorist*, 21 July 1908, 3; "Carl-theater," *Der Humorist*, 20 August 1908, 2.

84. "Mizzi Zwerenz gestorben," *Die Weltpresse*, 16 June 1947, 3.

85. Heikki Lempa, *Beyond the Gymnasium: Educating the Middle-Class Bodies in Classical Germany* (New York: Lexington Books, 2007), 118–19, 135–40.

86. George, *The Naked Truth*, 196–203.

87. Grete Wiesenthal, "Sphärischer Tanz (Ein Vortrag)," in *Grete Wiesenthal, die Schönheit der Sprache des Körpers im Tanz*, ed. Leonhard M. Fiedler and Martin Lang (Salzburg: Residenz Verlag, 1985), 147.

88. Wiesenthal, "Sphärischer Tanz (Ein Vortrag)," 149.

89. Grete Wiesenthal, quoted in Amort, "Free Dance in Interwar Vienna," 121–23.

90. Alys George describes Isadora Duncan's influence on Wiesenthal in *The Naked Truth*, 299n107. Mizzi Zwerenz/Franzi was in the audience for Wiesenthal's 1904 performance. See B. S., "Theater und Kunst: Carl-Theater," *NWJ*, 8 January 1904, 6.

91. "Duncan-Gastspiel im Carl-Theater," *NFP*, 8 January 1904, 9.

92. Marie Lang, "Offenbarung," *DF*, 15 February 1902, 636–38.

93. Lang, "Offenbarung," 637.

94. Ludwig Hevesi, "Miß Duncan in der Sezession," in *Acht Jahre Sezession (März 1897–Juni 1905): Kritik, Polemik, Chronik* (Vienna, 1906), 368–70; Sabine Wieber, "Sculpting the Sanatorium: Nervous Bodies and Femmes Fragiles in Vienna 1900," *Women in German Yearbook: Feminist Studies in German Literature & Culture* 27 (2011): 58–86. According to Ann Daly, "Rejecting the extreme and unvarying lightness of ballet, [Duncan] instead emphasized groundedness as its necessary complement and foundation." See Ann Daly, "Isadora Duncan's Dance Theory," *Dance Research Journal* 26, no. 2 (Autumn 1994): 27.

95. Hevesi, "Miß Duncan in der Sezession," 368–70.

96. Lang, "Offenbarung," 636–38.

97. Dickinson, *Dancing in the Blood*, 67.

98. Isadora Duncan, *My Life* (Garden City, NY: Garden City Publishing Co., 1927), 300.

99. "Carl-Theater," *NFP*, 28 March 1903, 10.

100. Duncan, *My Life*, 164, 166.

101. For the term "kinesthetic empathy," see Dee Reynolds and Matthew Reason, eds., *Kinesthetic Empathy in Creative and Cultural Practices* (Chicago: University of Chicago Press, 2012). The quotation is from Isadora Duncan, *Art of the Dance* (New York: Theatre Art Books, 1928), 131.

102. Kimerer L. LaMothe, *Nietzsche's Dancers: Isadora Duncan, Martha Graham, and the Revaluation of Christian Values* (New York: Palgrave Macmillan, 2006), 142.

103. LaMothe, *Nietzsche's Dancers*, 144.

104. On women and modern dance, see Dickinson, *Dancing in the Blood*, 82–86.

105. Lang, "Offenbarung," 637.

106. Isadora Duncan, *Der Tanz der Zukunft: Eine Vorlesung*, trans. Karl Federn (Leipzig: Eugen Diederichs, 1903), 12, 14.

107. Lang, "Offenbarung," 637.

108. Duncan, *Der Tanz der Zukunft*, 27.

109. Duncan, 14–15, 25, 26.

110. *Ein Walzertraum*, dir. Ludwig Berger (Berlin: Universum Film, 1925).

111. Emphasis mine. Hugo, "Das ist das süße Mädel . . . !" *MF* 103 (1927): 5.

112. "'Ein Walzertraum,'" *Die Stunde*, 22 May 1926, 8.

113. George, *The Naked Truth*, 203.

114. Mary Ann Doane, "The Voice in the Cinema: The Articulation of Body and Space," *Yale French Studies* 60 (1980): 33.

115. Helen Day-Mayer, "Documents of Performance: Lillian Gish on Acting on the Silent Screen," *Nineteenth Century Theatre and Film* 29, no. 1 (Summer 2002): 80–82.

116. George, *The Naked Truth*, 168–228.

117. Grete Wiesenthal, quoted in Gisela Bärbel Schmid, "Das unheimliche Erlebnis eines jungen Elegants in einer merkwürdigen visionären Nacht: Zu Hofmannsthals Pantomime *Das fremde Mädchen*," *Hofmannsthal-Blätter* 34 (Autumn 1986): 50.

118. "Hugo von Hofmannsthal im Film," *Kinematographische Rundschau*, 8 June 1913, 61.

119. *Einmal kommt der Tag . . . !* dir. Paul Czinner (Berlin: Elisabeth Bergner Poetic Film Co., 1924). In March 1925, the film was screened in cinemas in districts I, II, III, IV, VI, VII, and IX. See "Spielpläne," *Die Filmwelt* 6 (1925): 14. The film would become popular in Vienna; it was ranked number five in "Welchen Film wollen Sie wieder sehen?" *MF* 24 (1926): 6. In Germany the film was titled *Nju—eine unverstandene Frau*.

120. All quotes in this paragraph from Friedrich Porges, "Elisabeth Bergner im Film," *DF*, 23 August 1924, 9–10.

121. On the gestural soliloquy, see Rebecca Swender, "The Problem of the Divo: New Models for Analyzing Silent-Film Performance," *Journal of Film and Video* 58, no. 1/2 (Spring/Summer 2006): 10.

122. Ofer Ashkenazi, *Weimar Film and Modern Jewish Identity* (New York: Palgrave Macmillan, 2012), 59.

123. Ashkenazi, *Weimar Film*, 60.

124. Werner Michael Schwarz, *Kino und Kinos in Wien: Eine Entwicklungsgeschichte bis 1934* (Vienna: Verlag Turia & Kant, 1992), 69.

125. Schwarz, *Kino und Kinos in Wien*, 34.

126. SFn, Frau Maria Siess verh. Kling (hereafter MSK), NL 32 II, Haushaltsbuch, 1918.

127. Alys X. George, "Hollywood on the Danube? Vienna and Austrian Silent Film of the 1920s," in *Interwar Vienna*, 149–51.

128. Emilie Altenloh, *Zur Soziologie des Kinos* (1914), quoted in Schwarz, *Kino und Kinos in Wien*, 109.

129. Monika Bernold, "Kino(t)raum: Über den Zusammenhang von Familie, Freizeit und Konsum," in *Familie: Arbeitsplatz oder Ort des Glücks? Historische Schnitte ins Private* (Vienna: Picus Verlag, 1990), 137.

130. *Varieté*, dir. E. A. Dupont (Berlin: Universum Film, 1925). In February and March 1926, for example, the film was screened in cinemas in districts V, VII, VIII, IX, XII, XIII,

XV, XVII, and XX, ensuring an audience that included both working-class and bourgeois spectators. See *MF* 9 (1926): 9–14.

131. See Miriam Hansen, "Pleasure, Ambivalence, Identification: Valentino and Female Spectatorship," *Cinema Journal* 25, no. 4 (Summer 1986): 6–32.

132. H. W. S., "Was macht Kinonarren aus uns?" *MF* 91 (1927): 7.

133. Lya de Putti, "Die individuelle Maske," *MF* 97 (1927): 3.

134. Lori Landay, "The Flapper Film: Comedy, Dance, and Jazz Age Kinaesthetics," in *A Feminist Reader in Early Cinema*, ed. Jennifer M. Bean and Diane Negra (Durham, NC: Duke University Press, 2002), 226.

135. Landay, "The Flapper Film," 222.

136. Jonathan Crary, *Techniques of the Observer: On Vision and Modernity in the Nineteenth Century* (Cambridge, MA: MIT Press, 1990).

137. Mary Louise Roberts, *Disruptive Acts: The New Woman in Fin-de-Siècle France* (Chicago: University of Chicago Press, 2002), 2.

138. See, for example, "Die entstellte Freude," *Die Unzufriedene*, 10 May 1924, 4.

139. Else Feldmann, "Vor dem Kino," in *Bubikopf: Aufbruch in den Zwanzigern: Texte von Frauen*, ed. Anna Rheinsberg (Darmstadt: Luchterhand, 1988), 56–59.

140. "Hollywood—der Hafen der verlorenen Mädchen (Fortsetz.)," *BW* 17 (1927): vi.

141. Magda Sonja, "Vom ungemütlichen Filmen," *Die Kinowoche*, 1 October 1919, 2.

142. "Das Glück der Brigitte Helm," *MF* 1 (1926): 8.

143. Vivian Sobchack, "Phenomenology and the Film Experience," in *Viewing Positions: Ways of Seeing Film*, ed. Linda Williams (New Brunswick, NJ: Rutgers University Press, 1995), 53.

144. Ernst Schultze, *Der Kinematograph als Bildungsmittel: Eine kulturpolitische Untersuchung* (Halle: Buchhandlung des Waisenhauses, 1911), 17.

145. On music in Viennese cinemas, see Schwarz, *Kino und Kinos in Wien*, 152–55.

146. See, for example, "'s Kino!" *Die Muskete*, 30 October 1919, 37.

147. "Welchem Filmstar-Typ entspricht ihr aussehen?" *MF* 5 (1926): 4.

148. "Welchem Filmstar sehen sie ähnlich?" *BW* 50 (1926): 20; Chris Rojek, *Celebrity* (London: Reaktion Books, 2001), 109.

149. "Die Sprache der Hände," *MF* 12 (1926): 13.

150. "In 8 Lektionen Filmschauspieler," *BW* 17 (1927): 7.

151. "Welchem Filmstar-Typ entspricht Ihr Aussehen?" 7–8.

152. Oskar Diehl, *Mimik im Film: Leitfaden für den praktischen Unterricht in der Filmschauspielkunst* (Munich: Georg Müller Verlag, 1922), 14–16.

153. *The Smiling Lieutenant*, dir. Ernst Lubitsch (Hollywood, CA: Paramount Pictures, 1931).

154. Advertisement for Odol, *Die Dame* 54, no. 15 (April 1927).

Chapter Four

1. Hilde R., "Courths-Mahler," *BW* 17 (1926): 17.

2. Hugo Bettauer, "Die Courths-Mahler," *DM*, 29 May 1922, 5.

3. Desiderius Papp, "Besuch in der Bibliothek. Die literarische Mode des Tages," *NWJ*, 15 October 1922, 8.

4. Bettauer, "Die Courths-Mahler," 5.

5. She was, according to Bettauer, the "poetess of the German Volk." Courths-Mahler's career in fact continued after 1933. Although her novels were put on the "undesired" list in

the late 1930s, she continued writing and publishing until 1939. See Bettauer, "Die Courths-Mahler," 5. On the characterization of Courths-Mahler's literature as glorifying "bourgeois morality," see M. Kay Flavell, "Kitsch and Propaganda: The Blending of Myth and History in Hedwig Courths-Mahler's *Lissa geht ins Glück* (1936)," *German Studies Review* 8, no. 1 (February 1985): 65–87; Enno Lohmeyer, "Hedwig Courths-Mahler and the Everlasting Desire for Royal Romance," in *Mediating Germany: Popular Culture Between Tradition and Innovation*, ed. Gerd Bayer (Newcastle, UK: Cambridge Scholars Press, 2006), 37–53.

6. Bettauer, "Die Courths-Mahler," 5.

7. Hans Reimann, *Hedwig Courths-Mahler: Schlichte Geschichten fürs traute Heim* (Leipzig: Paul Steegemann Verlag, 1922), 68.

8. Flavell, "Kitsch and Propaganda," 37–53.

9. Reimann, *Hedwig Courths-Mahler*, 101.

10. Reimann, *Hedwig Courths-Mahler*, 9.

11. Reimann, *Hedwig Courths-Mahler*, 149.

12. For another analysis of this image, see Sherwin Simmons, "Chaplin Smiles on the Wall: Berlin Dada and Wish-Images of Popular Culture," *New German Critique* 84 (Autumn 2001): 29–30.

13. Reimann, *Hedwig Courths-Mahler*, 65.

14. Vera von Schmiterlöw, "Die Courths-Mahler war schuld," *MF* 250 (1930): 5.

15. SFn, Marie Theresia Fröhnert (hereafter MTF), NL 80, Marie Landa to Alfred Fröhnert, 8 August 1904.

16. SFn, Mathilde Hanzel-Hübner (hereafter MHH), NL I/2b, Tilde Mell to Mathilde Hübner, 21 January 1904.

17. See Paul M. Horntrich, "Science, Sin, and Sexuality in Roman-Catholic Discourses in the German-Speaking Area, 1870s to 1930s," *Sexuality & Culture* 24 (2020): 2137–60.

18. Alois J. Schweykart, *An die Katholiken Österreichs! Ein Wort der Aufklärung und Abwehr gegen die Angriffe auf die katholische Ehe. Acht Vorträge* (Vienna: Verlag der Buchhandlung "Reichspost" Wien, 1906), 31.

19. Horntrich, "Science, Sin, and Sexuality," 2155.

20. Stefan Zweig, *The World of Yesterday*, trans. Anthea Bell (Lincoln: University of Nebraska Press, 2013), 99.

21. Malvine von Steinau, *Der gute Ton für Damen*, 2nd ed. (Vienna: A. Hartleben, 1878), 61.

22. Alma Mahler-Werfel, "Tuesday 6 November, Suite 20, 1900," in *Diaries 1898–1902*, trans. Antony Beaumont (Ithaca, NY: Cornell University Press, 1999), 342.

23. SFn, MHH, NL IIIC/4, Diary 1904, 18 March 1904.

24. SFn, MHHNL IIIC/4, Diary 1904, 17 April 1904.

25. SFn, MHH, Box: NLIIIC/4, Diary 1904, 20 October 1904.

26. Emanuele L. M. Meyer, *Vom Mädchen zur Frau: Ein zeitgemäßiges Erziehungs- und Ehebuch allen reifen Töchtern, Gattinnen, Müttern und Volkserziehern gewidmet* (Stuttgart: Verlag von Strecker und Schröder, 1912), 114–15.

27. SFn, MHH, NL IIIC/4, Diary 1904, 6 January 1904.

28. SFn, MHH, NL IIIC/4, Diary 1904, 1 February 1904.

29. Harriet Anderson, *Utopian Feminism: Women's Movements in Fin-de-Siècle Vienna* (New Haven, CT: Yale University Press, 1992), 93.

30. Harry Oosterhuis, *Stepchildren of Nature: Krafft-Ebing, Psychiatry, and the Making of Sexual Identity* (Chicago: University of Chicago Press, 2000), 30.

31. Arthur Schnitzler, *Reigen* (1900; Frankfurt: Fischer Taschenbuch Verlag, 1989), 51.

32. Dr. med. Braun, *Häusliches Glück oder: Was ein Mann und ein Mädchen vor und von der Ehe wissen müssen* (Leipzig: Wendel, 1907).

33. SFn, MMH, NL IIIC/4, Diary 1904, 18 January 1904.

34. SFn, MHH, NL IIIC/4, Diary 1904, 17 April 1904.

35. Mahler-Werfel, "Thursday 24 September, Suite 24, 1901," in *Diaries 1898–1902*, 433–34.

36. Mahler-Werfel, "Saturday 9 November, Suite 24 1901," in *Diaries 1898–1902*, 444; Mahler-Werfel, "Wednesday 30 December, Suite 25, 1901," *Diaries 1898–1902*, 466.

37. SFn, MMH, NL IIIC/4, Diary 1905–1919, 9 June 1905.

38. SFn, MHH, NL IIIC/4, Letter Diary "Wir," 5 December 1905.

39. SFn, MHH, NL IIIC/4, Letter Diary "Wir," Ottokar Hanzel to Mathilde Hübner, 19 December 1905.

40. SFn, MHH, NL I/3, Ottokar Hanzel to Mathilde Hübner, 18 July 1907; SFn, MHH, NL I/3, Ottokar Hanzel to Mathilde Hübner, 29 July 1907.

41. Catholic culture did not necessarily seek to negate the body; rather, it sought to control it for a higher end. On Habsburg and Austrian Catholicism, see Anna Coreth, *Pietas Austriaca*, trans. William D. Bowman and Anna Maria Leitgeb (West Lafayette, IN: Purdue University Press, 2004); Daniel L. Unowsky, *The Pomp and Politics of Patriotism: Imperial Celebrations in Habsburg Austria, 1848–1916* (West Lafayette, IN: Purdue University Press, 2005).

42. Cate Haste, *Passionate Spirit: The Life of Alma Mahler* (New York: Basic Books, 2019), 13–14, 20–21.

43. Rosa Mayreder, *Zur Kritik der Weiblichkeit: Essays* (Leipzig: Eugen Diederichs, 1905), 197.

44. Käthe Leichter, *Leben, Werk und Sterben einer österreichischen Sozialdemokratin*, ed. Herbert Steiner (Vienna: Ibera & Molden Verlag, 1997), 303. Steven Beller argues that Leichter's Jewishness gave her license to read such authors in the first place. See Steven Beller, *Vienna and the Jews, 1867–1938: A Cultural History* (1989; New York: Cambridge University Press, 1991), 185–86. Although it is certainly true that assimilated Jews in Vienna were likely to consume "forbidden" literature, I have found that many women read such books.

45. Hannah S. Decker, *Freud, Dora, Vienna 1900* (New York: The Free Press, 1991), 76.

46. "Burgtheater," *NWJ*, 23 February 1906, 9. On the popularity of Prévost among Viennese women, see Papp, "Besuch in der Bibliothek," 8.

47. Käthe van Beeker, "Heimliche Pfade," *BdH* 13, no. 6 (1902–1903): 156.

48. P. Hoche, "Vom Lesen," *WH*, 18 November 1906, 2.

49. Zweig, *The World of Yesterday*, 99.

50. Marina Solina, "Mädchenlektüre," *WHZ*, 22 January 1893, 29–30.

51. Hoche, "Vom Lesen," 1–2.

52. Lotte Glas, "Vom Lesen," *AnZ*, 17 May 1900, 3.

53. See, for example, "An E. J. John," *WH*, 10 March 1907, 12.

54. Ernst Schultze, *Die Schundliteratur: Ihr Vordringen. Ihre Folgen. Ihre Bekämpfung* (Halle: Verlag der Buchhandlung des Waisenhauses, 1911), 11.

55. Marianne Fischer, *Erotische Literatur vor Gericht: Der Schmutzliteraturkampf im Wien des beginnenden 20. Jahrhunderts* (Vienna: Braumüller, 2003), 25.

56. Schultze, *Die Schundliteratur*, 9–10.

57. At the beginning of their courtship, Hanzel-Hübner even compared Ottokar Hanzel to Rodion Raskolnikov, the protagonist of Fyodor Dostoevsky's *Crime and Punishment* (1866). See SFn, MHH, NL IIIC/4, Diary 1905, 10 March 1905. On the popularity of Émile Zola, see Solina, "Mädchenlektüre," 29–30; Gary D. Stark, *Banned in Berlin: Literary*

Censorship in Imperial Germany, 1871–1918 (New York: Berghahn Books, 2009), 193. On Mahler-Werfel's secret library, see Haste, *Passionate Spirit*, 21.

58. Schultze, *Die Schundliteratur*, 9–10.

59. Domestic servants were believed to be the biggest audience of these books. See Tony Kelly, "Über das Lesen der Schauerromane," *DF* 7, no. 12 (September 1902): 319–24.

60. Simone de Beauvoir, *Memoirs of a Dutiful Daughter*, trans. James Kirkup (New York: Harper Perennial, 2005), 109.

61. Britta McEwen, *Sexual Knowledge: Feeling, Fact and Social Reform in Vienna, 1900–1934* (New York: Berghahn Books, 2012), 2.

62. McEwen, *Sexual Knowledge*, 91.

63. Franz X. Eder, "Sexual Cultures in Germany and Austria, 1700–2000," in *Sexual Cultures in Europe: National Histories*, ed. Franz X. Eder, Lesley A. Hall, and Gert Hekma (New York: Manchester University Press, 1999), 145.

64. Sigmund Freud, *A Case of Hysteria (Dora)*, trans. Anthea Bell (1905; New York: Oxford University Press, 2013), 20–21.

65. Nicoletta Pireddu, "Introduction," in Paolo Mantegazza, *The Physiology of Love and Other Writings*, ed. Nicoletta Pireddu, trans. David Jacobson (Toronto: University of Toronto Press, 2007), 17; Oosterhuis, *Stepchildren of Nature*.

66. McEwen, *Sexual Knowledge*, 9–13.

67. Freud, *A Case of Hysteria (Dora)*, 29n1.

68. Papp, "Besuch in der Bibliothek," 8.

69. Stark, *Banned in Berlin*, 193.

70. On the controversy surrounding *Psychopathia Sexualis* see Oosterhuis, *Stepchildren of Nature*, 185–89; Freud, *A Case of Hysteria (Dora)*, 40–41.

71. Krafft-Ebing, quoted in Oosterhuis, *Stepchildren of Nature*, 188.

72. Mahler-Werfel, "Thursday 19 September, Suite 24, 1901," in *Diaries 1898–1902*, 433.

73. Decker, *Freud, Dora, Vienna 1900*, 113.

74. Advertisements for Mantegazza's *Physiology of Love* appeared in popular newspapers and magazines. See for example "Hochinteressante Bücher!" *Die Bombe*, 10 February 1901, 6.

75. Paolo Mantegazza, *The Physiology of Love and Other Writings*, ed. Nicoletta Pireddu, trans. David Jacobson (Toronto: University of Toronto Press, 2007), 184–85.

76. Mantegazza, *The Physiology of Love*, 185.

77. Mantegazza, 185.

78. Mantegazza, 305.

79. Mantegazza, 280.

80. Richard von Krafft-Ebing, *Psychopathia Sexualis*, trans. Charles Gilbert Chaddock (Philadelphia: F. A. Davis, 1892), 2.

81. Pireddu, "Introduction," in *The Physiology of Love*, 19.

82. Mantegazza, *The Physiology of Love*, 159.

83. Mantegazza, 212.

84. Mantegazza, 161.

85. Mantegazza, 161.

86. That said, Decker also observes, "Perhaps the daughters of assimilated Viennese Jews lived in two worlds more than did their middle-class Christian counterparts." Decker, *Freud, Dora, Vienna 1900*, 232n29.

87. Krafft-Ebing, *Psychopathia Sexualis*, 12.

88. SFn, MHH, NL I/2b, Tilde Mell to Mathilde Hübner, 14 August 1907.

89. Mantegazza, *The Physiology of Love*, 136.

90. Mantegazza, 172.

91. Eder, "Sexual Cultures in Germany and Austria, 1700–2000," 144.

92. Krafft-Ebing, *Psychopathia Sexualis*, 13.

93. Krafft-Ebing, 12.

94. Mahler-Werfel, "Sunday 15 September, Suite 24, 1901," in *Diaries 1898–1902*, 432.

95. SFn, MHH, NL I/2b, Tilde Mell to Mathilde Hübner, 1 November 1907.

96. Todd Curtis Kontje, *Women, the Novel, and the German Nation 1771–1871: Domestic Fiction in the Fatherland* (New York: Cambridge University Press, 1998).

97. Kontje, *Women, the Novel, and the German Nation*, 1.

98. On Marlitt as a realist author, see Kirsten Belgum, "E. Marlitt: Narratives of Virtuous Desire," in *A Companion to German Realism 1848–1900*, ed. Todd Kontje (Rochester, NY: Camden House, 2002), 259–82.

99. Alfons Petzgold, "Die Bücher einer Dichterin," *FS* 8 (1910): 1; Belgum, "E. Marlitt: Narratives of Virtuous Desire," 262.

100. Lynne Tatlock, "The Afterlife of Nineteenth-Century Popular Fiction and the German Imaginary: The Illustrated Collected Novels of E. Marlitt, W. Heimburg, and E. Werner," in *Publishing Culture and the "Reading Nation": German Book History in the Long Nineteenth Century*, ed. Lynne Tatlock (Rochester, NY: Camden House, 2010), 118–51.

101. Solina, "Mädchenlektüre," 29–30.

102. Emma Goldman, *Living My Life* (New York: Cosimo, 2008), 116.

103. Urszula Bonter, *Der Populärroman in der Nachfolge von E. Marlitt: Wilhelmine Heimburg, Valeska Gräfin Bethusy-Huc, Eufemia von Adlersfeld-Ballestrem* (Würzburg: Verlag Königshausen & Neumann, 2005).

104. Hedwig Courths-Mahler, "Zum 100. Geburtstag der Marlitt," *DIW* 1, no. 9 (1925): 3.

105. On critiques of Marlitt, see Belgum, "E. Marlitt: Narratives of Virtuous Desire," 262–63.

106. Meyer, *Vom Mädchen zur Frau*, 48–49.

107. Solina, "Mädchenlektüre," 30.

108. Mayreder, *Zur Kritik der Weiblichkeit*, 93.

109. On desire in *Goldelse*, see Kirsten Belgum, *Popularizing the Nation: Audience, Representation, and the Production of Identity in* Die Gartenlaube, *1853–1900* (Lincoln: University of Nebraska Press, 1998), 133–36; Tatlock, "The Afterlife of Nineteenth-Century Popular Fiction and the German Imaginary," 133–36.

110. E. Marlitt, *Gold Elsie*, trans. A. L. Wister (Philadelphia: J. B. Lippincott, 1868), 118–19.

111. Marlitt, *Gold Elsie*, 124–25.

112. Belgum, "E. Marlitt: Narratives of Virtuous Desire," 275; Marlitt, *Gold Elsie*, 327.

113. Marlitt, *Gold Elsie*, 328, 167, 222.

114. Belgum, "E. Marlitt: Narratives of Virtuous Desire," 275–76.

115. SFn, MHH, NL IIIC/4, Diary 1905, 21 March 1905.

116. Ellen Key, *Die Frauenbewegung* (Frankfurt: Rütten & Loening, 1909), 135.

117. Edward Ross Dickinson, *Sex, Freedom, and Power in Imperial Germany, 1880–1914* (New York: Cambridge University Press, 2014), 194.

118. Anderson, *Utopian Feminism*, 231.

119. Agatha Schwartz, *Shifting Voices: Feminist Thought and Women's Writing in Fin-de-Siècle Austria and Hungary* (Montreal: McGill-Queen's University Press, 2008), 107. For a recent book on the work and life of Grete Meisel-Hess, see Helga Thorson, *Grete Meisel-Hess: The New Woman and the Sexual Crisis* (Rochester, NY: Camden House, 2022). Thorson

argues (p. 22) that "Meisel-Hess saw herself not only as a New Woman . . . but also as the writer of the New Woman."

120. Gabriele Reuter, "Verlästerte Bücher," *DF*, 15 July 1902, 231.

121. Vera [Betty Kurth], *Eine für Viele: Aus dem Tagebuche eines Mädchens* (Leipzig: Hermann Seemann Nachfolger, 1902); Anonymous [Margarete Böhme], *Tagebuch einer Verlorenen* (Berlin: F. Fontane, 1905). Several reviewers compared *Eine für Viele* to Meisel-Hess's *Fanny Roth*. See, for example, Helene Stöcker, "Weibliche Erotik (1903)," in *Die Liebe und die Frauen* (Minden in Westfalen: J. C. C. Bruns' Verlag, 1905), 89–94.

122. Hermann Hölzke, "Die Emanzipationsromane," in *Die Deutsche Literatur von den Anfängen der Moderne bis zur Gegenwart* (Leipzig: Gerstenberg, 1913), 184–90.

123. Wengraf, "Frauenbücher," 99.

124. Grete Meisel-Hess, *Fanny Roth: Eine Jungfrauengeschichte* (1902; Berlin: Hermann Seemann Nachfolger Verlagsgesellschaft, 1910). On the influence of Nietzsche on Meisel-Hess, see Ellinor Melander, "Toward the Sexual and Economic Emancipation of Women: The Philosophy of Grete Meisel-Hess," *History of European Ideas* 14, no. 5 (1992): 705–6.

125. Meisel-Hess, *Fanny Roth*, 42, 79, 81, 118–19, 133.

126. Meisel-Hess, 122, 77.

127. On the emancipation novel, see Charlotte Woodford, ed., *Women, Emancipation and the German Novel 1871–1910: Protest Fiction in Its Cultural Context* (New York: Legenda, 2014), 1–2.

128. Grete Meisel-Hess, *The Sexual Crisis: A Critique of Our Sex Life*, trans. Eden and Cedar Paul (New York: Critic and Guide, 1917), 234.

129. Meisel-Hess, *The Sexual Crisis*, 198.

130. Meisel-Hess, *Fanny Roth*, 56–57.

131. Schwartz, *Shifting Voices*, 127.

132. On the influence of Haeckel on Meisel-Hess, see Melander, "Toward the Sexual and Economic Emancipation of Women," 699–700.

133. Meisel-Hess, *The Sexual Crisis*, 170.

134. Meisel-Hess, *Fanny Roth*, 16, 29–30, 107.

135. Meisel-Hess, *The Sexual Crisis*, 301, 198, 200.

136. Audre Lorde, *Uses of the Erotic: The Erotic as Power* (Trumansburg, NY: Out & Out Books, 1978), 4.

137. Kathleen Canning, "Feminist History after the Linguistic Turn: Historicizing Discourse and Experience," *Signs* 19, no. 2 (Winter 1994): 377.

138. Stöcker, "Weibliche Erotik (1903)," 91.

139. Helene Stöcker, "Die modern Frau," *FB* 4 (1893): 1215–17, trans. Angela A. Kurtz. Reprinted in *German History in Documents and Images, Volume 5* (Washington, DC: German Historical Institute), https://ghdi.ghi-dc.org/sub_document.cfm?document_id=706.

140. See Maria Mesner, "Educating Reasonable Lovers: Sex Counseling in Austria in the First Half of the Twentieth Century," in *Sexuality in Austria*, ed. Günther Bischof, Anton Pelinka, and Dagmar Herzog (New Brunswick, NJ: Transaction, 2007), 48–64; Maria Mesner, *Geburten/Kontrolle: Reproduktionspolitik im 20. Jahrhundert* (Vienna: Böhlau, 2010); McEwen, *Sexual Knowledge*; Britta McEwen, "Emotional Expression and the Construction of Heterosexuality: Hugo Bettauer's Viennese Advice Columns," *Journal of the History of Sexuality* 25, no. 1 (January 2016): 114–36.

141. SFn, Lilli Wehle-Weber (hereafter LWW), NL 21/13, "Frau Friedl," 1 October 1926.

142. SFn, LWW, NL 21/13, "Untitled," 3 September 1926.

143. SFn, LWW, NL 21/13, Rhyme Diary 1926, "Verlangen," 15 January 1927.

144. Johann Ferch, *Die Revolutionierung des Liebeslebens* (Berlin: Verlag der „Neuen Weltanschauung," 1919).

145. Ferch, *Die Revolutionierung*, 28.

146. Ferch, 30.

147. Ferch, 31.

148. Ferch, 28.

149. Despite this shared goal, the parties envisioned the regenerative society in different ways. The SDAP envisioned a cooperative society made up of healthy *neue Menschen*, while the CSP sought to remake the First Republic into a bastion of conservative Catholic tradition to fight off "foreign" influence.

150. On popular sexual knowledge for and about women, see McEwen, *Sexual Knowledge*, 91–117.

151. Therese Schlesinger, "Zur Evolution der Erotik," *Die Unzufriedene*, 6 July 1931.

152. Atina Grossmann, "The New Woman and the Rationalization of Sexuality in Wemar Germany," in *Powers of Desire: The Politics of Sexuality*, ed. Ann Snitow, Christine Stansell, and Sharon Thompson (New York: NYU Press, 1983): 155.

153. Rudolf Glaessner, *Reif zur Liebe! Eine ärztliche Aufklärungsschrift über alles Wissenswerte im Liebes- und Geschlechtsleben des Weibes* (Vienna, 1921), 32–33.

154. "Die Kunst zu lieben. Gedanken über die Liebe!" *Wb* 1 (1925): 10.

155. "Sexualerziehung," *SR* 5, no. 17 (January 1924): 5–6.

156. Glaessner, *Reif zur Liebe!* 7.

157. Joseph Carl Schlegel, *Hygiene des Ehelebens: Der Führer zu Liebes- und Eheglück* (Vienna: Schusdeks Verlag, 1929), 81.

158. Bernhard A. Bauer, *Wie bist du, Weib? Betrachtungen über Körper, Seele, Sexualität und Erotik des Weibes* (Vienna: Rikola Verlag, 1923), 262.

159. Emma S., "Muss wahre Liebe sinnlich sein?" *Wb* 12 (1925): 7.

160. Lissy, "Der Geist, der stets verneint," *BW*, 14 September 1924, 16–17. See also McEwen, "Emotional Expression and the Construction of Heterosexuality."

161. "Heisses Blut," *BW*, 26 June 1924, 12.

162. Helly, "Innige Bitte," *BW*, 10 July 1924, 15.

163. On the Socialist Society, see McEwen, *Sexual Knowledge*, 133–36; Mesner, "Educating Reasonable Lovers," 57–59.

164. Wilhelm Reich, *Geschlechtsreife, Enthaltsamkeit, Ehemoral: Eine Kritik der bürgerlichen Sexual-Reform* (Vienna: Münster Verlag, 1931).

165. Wilhelm Reich, "The Socialistic Society for Sexual Advice and Sexual Research," in *The Practice of Contraception: An International Symposium and Survey*, ed. Margaret Sanger and Hannah M. Stone (Baltimore, MD: Waverly Press, 1931), 271.

166. Mesner, "Educating Reasonable Lovers," 58.

167. Sophie Lazarsfeld, *Erziehung zur Ehe* (Vienna: Verlag von Mortiz Perles, 1928), 26.

168. Lazarsfeld, *Erziehung zur Ehe*, 26.

169. For an overview of the League, see McEwen, *Sexual Knowledge*, 128–33; Mesner, "Educating Reasonable Lovers," 55–57.

170. "Sexualerziehung," *SR* 5, no. 17 (January 1924): 5–6.

171. Atina Grossmann, *Reforming Sex: The German Movement for Birth Control and Abortion Reform, 1920–1950* (New York: Oxford University Press, 1995), 35.

172. WStLA, GV, Bund gegen Mutterschaftszwang, 1440/1923, 1919 Statuten.

173. On the SDAP's Marriage Advice Centers, see Karl Kautsky, "Die Eheberatung im

Dienste der Wohlfahrtspflege," *BWSW* 24, no. 248 (March–April 1925): 26. For a historical analysis, see McEwen, *Sexual Knowledge*, 121–28; Mesner, "Educating Reasonable Lovers," 51–57. On the League's Women's Advice Centers, see "Errichtung der Frauenschutz-Beratungsstelle," *SR* 4, no. 13 (January 1923): 1.

174. The first Women's Advice Center opened its doors in the city's district VI, Mariahilf, in 1923. Betty Ferch, "The Birth Control Association of Austria," in *The Practice of Contraception: An International Symposium and Survey*, ed. Margaret Sanger and Hannah M. Stone (Baltimore, MD: Waverly Press, 1931), 268–70.

175. Ferch, "The Birth Control Association of Austria," 269.

176. Dagmar Herzog, *Sexuality in Europe: A Twentieth-Century History* (New York: Cambridge University Press, 2011), 55–56.

177. Quotes from Glaessner, *Reif zur Liebe!* 23.

178. McEwen, *Sexual Knowledge*, 97.

179. Bauer, *Wie bist du, Weib?*

180. Theodoor H. van de Velde, *Die vollkommene Ehe: Eine Studie über ihre Physiologie und Technik* (Leipzig: Montana-Verlag AH Medizinische Abteilung, 1928), 38.

181. Bauer, *Wie bist du, Weib?* 336–47.

182. Van de Velde, *Die vollkommene Ehe*, 136.

183. Van de Velde, 24. See also Bauer, *Wie bist du, Weib?* 327.

184. Van de Velde, *Die vollkommene Ehe*, 140.

185. Van de Velde, 25.

186. Bauer, *Wie bist du, Weib?* 311.

187. Van de Velde, *Die vollkommene Ehe*, 30.

188. Bauer, *Wie bist du, Weib?* 308–9.

189. Van de Velde, *Die vollkommene Ehe*, 23, 142, 144.

190. SFn, MHH, NL IIIC/4, Diary 1901–1903, 7 December 1902.

191. SFn, MHH, NL IIIC/4, Diary 1904, 2 December 1904.

192. Bauer, *Wie bist du, Weib?* 301–6.

193. Van de Velde, *Die vollkommene Ehe*, 43, 151.

194. Van de Velde, 148.

195. Van de Velde, 230.

196. The following analysis examines a period of only a few years because earlier records were set ablaze in the Palace of Justice during the July Revolt in 1927.

197. Ulrike Harmat, "Divorce and Remarriage in Austria-Hungary: The Second Marriage of Franz Conrad von Hötzendorf," *Austrian History Yearbook* 32 (2001): 70.

198. In the Hungarian half of the monarchy, however, divorce for Catholics was legal, thus prompting a wave of divorce tourism. See Sandor Nagy, "One Empire, Two States, Many Laws: Matrimonial Law and Divorce in the Austro-Hungarian Monarchy," *The Hungarian Historical Review* 3, no. 1 (2014): 190–221.

199. If, at the time of the divorce, none of the parties identified as Jewish anymore, then the rules of non-Catholic Christian couples applied.

200. These came to be known as the "Sever-Marriages," which, by 1921, were declared illegal. See Samuel R. Watchtell, "Marriage by Dispensation in Austrian Law," *United States Law Review* 68 (1934): 649–59; Ulrike Harmat, *Ehe auf Widerruf? Der Konflikt um das Eherecht in Österreich 1918–1938* (Frankfurt: V. Klostermann, 1999).

201. Evan Burr Bukey, *Jews and Intermarriage in Nazi Austria* (New York: Cambridge University Press, 2011), 86.

202. Bukey, *Jews and Intermarriage in Nazi Austria*, 86.

203. For another discussion of this phenomenon, see Ernst Hanisch, *Männlichkeiten: Eine andere Geschichte des 20. Jahrhunderts* (Vienna: Böhlau, 2005), 170–79.

204. WStLA, LgZ, Abt. 30Cg/1268, 74/27/7, 5 May 1927.

205. WStLA, LgZ, Abt. 14Cg/494, 1/28/41, 6 November 1930.

206. WStLA, LgZ, Abt. 30Cg/1268, 14 May 1927.

207. WStLA, LgZ, Abt. 30Cg/1268, 186/27/35, 5 February 1929.

208. WStLA, LgZ, Abt. 30Cg/1268, 17 March 1928.

209. WStLA, LgZ, Abt. 14Cg/494, 673/28/1, 28 December 1928.

210. WStLa, LgZ, Abt. 30Cg/1268, 278/28/22, 27 October 1929.

211. WStLA, LgZ, Abt. 30Cg/1268, 188/7/20, 4 May 1928.

212. WStLA, LgZ, Abt. 30Cg/1268, 10 February 1927.

213. WStLA, LgZ, 30Cg/1268, 1 July 1928.

214. WStLA, LgZ, Abt. 14Cg/494, 11 July 1928.

215. WStLA, LgZ, Abt. 30Cg/1268, 28 January 1928.

216. WStLA, LgZ, Abt. 30Cg/1268, 232/28/3, 4 June 1928.

217. Helene Stöcker, "Die modern Frau," *FB* 4 (1893): 1215–17, trans. Angela A. Kurtz. Reprinted in *German History in Documents and Images, Volume 5*.

218. Bauer, *Wie bist du, Weib?* 356.

219. Papp, "Besuch in der Bibliothek," 8.

220. Grossmann, "The New Woman and the Rationalization of Sexuality," 155.

221. Hedwig Courths-Mahler, *Eine ungeliebte Frau* (1918; Cologne: Gustav Lübbe Verlag, 1984), 118.

222. Courths-Mahler, *Eine ungeliebte Frau*, 60, 135–37.

223. Courths-Mahler, 130, 147, 157–58.

224. Courths-Mahler, 49.

225. Dagmar Herzog, "Syncopated Sex: Transforming European Sexual Cultures," *American Historical Review* 114, no. 5 (2009): 1287–1308.

Chapter Five

1. WStLA, LgSt, Sa, II 204/27, 25 May 1927.

2. Dr. Muska was most likely Dr. Anton Musger of district XIII, Hietzing. See "Gesundheitswesen: Musger, Anton, Ob. Stadtarzt," *Wiener Adreßbuch, Lehmanns Wohnungsanzeiger 1927* 68, no. 2 (1927): Part V, 69.

3. Elisabeth Steffl is not listed in the "Midwives" section of the 1927 address book, indicating that she may have been an unlicensed midwife.

4. The law made no mention of quickening or an unformed fetus, implying that pregnancy was understood to begin at conception.

5. WStLA, LgSt, Sa, I 8515/1899, 21 December 1899.

6. The legislation did not change until 1974. That said, the abortion laws may have been more rigorously enforced around 1900 as birth rates declined across Europe.

7. WStLA, LgSt, Sa, I 1137/1902, 19 July 1902.

8. For years, abortion was seen as a form of birth control, despite being illegal in most of Europe. See Dagmar Herzog, *Sexuality in Europe: A Twentieth-Century History* (New York: Cambridge University Press, 2011), 20–21.

9. Richard von Krafft-Ebing, *Psychopathia Sexualis: The Classic Study of Deviant Sex* (1892; New York: Arcade, 2011).

10. Leslie J. Reagan, *When Abortion Was a Crime: Women, Medicine, and Law in the United States, 1867–1973* (Berkeley: University of California Press, 1997), 9.

11. Cornelie Usborne, *Cultures of Abortion in Weimar Germany* (New York: Berghahn Books, 2007), 154–55.

12. Usborne, *Cultures of Abortion*, 127–62.

13. Barbara Duden, *The Woman Beneath the Skin: A Doctor's Patients in Eighteenth-Century Germany*, trans. Thomas Dunlap (Cambridge, MA: Harvard University Press, 1991), 69.

14. Iris Marion Young, "Menstrual Meditations," in *On Female Body Experience: "Throwing Like a Girl" and Other Essays* (New York: Oxford University Press, 2005), 121.

15. Young, "Menstrual Meditations," 104.

16. Young, 121.

17. Alma Mahler-Werfel, "Monday 5 September, Suite 7, 1898," in *Diaries 1898–1902*, trans. Antony Beaumont (Ithaca, NY: Cornell University Press, 2000), 56.

18. WStLA, LgSt, Sa, I 4938/1915, 8 August 1915.

19. WStLA, LgSt, Sa, I 4938/1915, 10 April 1916.

20. Helen King, *Hippocrates' Woman: Reading the Female Body in Ancient Greece* (London: Routledge, 1998); Noga Arokha, *Passions and Tempers: A History of the Humours* (New York: HarperCollins, 2007).

21. Monica H. Green, "Flowers, Poisons and Men: Menstruation in Medieval Western Europe," in *Menstruation: A Cultural History*, ed. Andrew Shail and Gillian Howie (New York: Palgrave Macmillan, 2005), 53.

22. Duden, *The Woman Beneath the Skin*, 118.

23. Usborne, *Cultures of Abortion*, 156–57.

24. Duden, *The Woman Beneath the Skin*, 126, 132, 140.

25. Duden, 157–70.

26. It was believed that the fetus only received a soul at quickening, not conception. Thus, the expulsion of the fetus during early pregnancy was never viewed as an abortion. This changed in the late eighteenth and nineteenth centuries, when physicians came to view conception as the beginning of life. See Merry E. Weisner, "The Midwives of South Germany and the Public/Private Dichotomy," in *The Art of Midwifery: Early Modern Midwives in Europe*, ed. Hilary Marland (New York: Routledge, 1993), 94n48. Yet the public continued to view quickening as the beginning of life. See Reagan, *When Abortion Was a Crime*, 25.

27. Cathy McClive, "The Hidden Truths of the Belly: The Uncertainties of Pregnancy in Early Modern Europe," *Social History of Medicine* 15, no. 2 (August 2002): 209–27.

28. Duden, *The Woman Beneath the Skin*, 160. See also McClive, "The Hidden Truths of the Belly," 209 27.

29. Michael Stolberg, "Menstruation and Sexual Difference in Early Modern Medicine," in *Menstruation: A Cultural History*, ed. Andrew Shail and Gillian Howie (New York: Palgrave Macmillan, 2005), 95–98.

30. Duden, *The Woman Beneath the Skin*, 127.

31. Duden, 113.

32. On the persistence of these beliefs, see Reagan, *When Abortion Was a Crime*; Usborne, *Cultures of Abortion*; Lara Freidenfelds, *The Modern Period: Menstruation in Twentieth-Century America* (Baltimore, MD: Johns Hopkins University Press, 2009); Lara Freidenfelds, *The Myth of the Perfect Pregnancy: A History of Miscarriage in America* (New York: Oxford University Press, 2019).

33. For this interpretation, see Freidenfels, *The Modern Period*, 23–24.

34. Rudolf Glaessner, *Reif zur Liebe! Eine ärztliche Aufklärungsschrift über alles Wissenswerte im Liebes- und Geschlechtsleben des Weibes* (Vienna: Anzengruber-Verlag, 1921), 38.

35. Fürst, "Zur Gesundheitspflege der Frau währen der Menstruation," *HZ*, 15 June 1888, 82.

36. SFn, Mathilde Hanzel-Hübner (hereafter MHH), NL I/2b, Tilde Mell to Mathilde Hübner, 26 April 1911.

37. SFn, MHH, NL IIIC/4, Diary 1901–1903, 9 March 1902.

38. Duden, *The Woman Beneath the Skin*, 140–49.

39. On "blocked menses," see Usborne, *Cultures of Abortion*, 146–51.

40. WStLA, LgSt, Sa, I 5493/1905, 14 October 1905.

41. WStLA, LgSt, Sa, I 8515/1899, 17 March 1902.

42. WStLA, LgSt, Sa, I 1673/1911.

43. Usborne, *Cultures of Abortion*, 154–62.

44. Julia Kristeva, *Powers of Horror: An Essay on Abjection* (New York: Columbia University Press, 1982).

45. On the healthiness of menstrual blood, see Stolberg, "Menstruation and Sexual Difference in Early Modern Medicine," 92.

46. Luce Irigaray, *This Sex Which Is Not One*, trans. Catherine Porter and Carolyn Burke (Ithaca, NY: Cornell University Press, 1985).

47. See Freidenfels, *The Modern Period*, 25. On emmenagogues, see also John M. Riddle, *Eve's Herbs: A History of Contraception and Abortion in the West* (Cambridge, MA: Harvard University Press, 1997); Elisha P. Renne and Etienne van de Walle, eds., *Regulating Menstruation: Beliefs, Practices, and Interpretations* (Chicago: University of Chicago Press, 2001).

48. WStLA, LgSt, Sa, I 4938/1915, 3 May 1916.

49. Michel Foucault, *The Birth of the Clinic: An Archaeology of Medical Perception*, trans. A. M. Sheridan Smith (New York: Vintage Books, 1994), 133, 202–3. On physical diagnosis, see W. F. Bynum, *Science and the Practice of Medicine in the Nineteenth Century* (Cambridge: Cambridge University Press, 1994), 33–42.

50. Wilhelm Hahn, "Die Periode," *HZ*, 15 September 1905, 136–37. The only other reason a woman might miss her menses was anemia, in which case iron pills would be prescribed.

51. Emily Martin, *The Woman in the Body: A Cultural Analysis of Reproduction* (Boston: Beacon Press, 2001), 27–53.

52. Glaessner, *Reif zur Liebe!* 38.

53. OeStA, AVA, MdI, Prostitution, in genere, Teil 2 A 2122, "Belehrung," 1909.

54. For Jahn, see WStLA, OWS, KgF, 36, Rosa Jahn. For Kacafirk, see WStLA, OWS, KgF, 38, Vinzencia Kacafirek.

55. For an example of this logic, see Hahn, "Die Periode," 136–37.

56. Stolberg, "Menstruation and Sexual Difference," 90–101.

57. Tatjana Buklijas, "Culture of Death and Politics of Corpse Supply: Anatomy in Vienna, 1848–1914," *Bulletin of the History of Medicine* 82, no. 3 (Fall 2008): 570–607.

58. David S. Luft, *Eros and Inwardness in Vienna: Weininger, Musil, Doderer* (Chicago: University of Chicago Press, 2003), 22–27. Buklijas argues that unlike the Protestant "North," the Catholic "South" believed that death "was a quick and radical separation of the soul from the body," so that dissection seemed less invasive (Buklijas, "Culture of Death and Politics of Corpse Supply," 576). On the Viennese fascination with death, see also William M. Johnston, *The Austrian Mind: An Intellectual and Social History 1848–1938* (Berkeley: University of California Press, 1972), 165–80.

59. Johnston, *The Austrian Mind*, 165; Stefan Zweig, *The World of Yesterday*, trans. Anthea Bell (1942; Lincoln: University of Nebraska Press, 2013), 39.

60. Johnston, *The Austrian Mind*, 168.

61. Thomas Laqueur, *Making Sex: Body and Gender from the Greeks to Freud* (Cambridge, MA: Harvard University Press, 1990), 207–27.

62. Duden, *The Woman Beneath the Skin*, 17–18.

63. WStLA, LgSt, Sa, I 7820/24, 6 December 1924.

64. WStLA, LgSt, Sa, I 7820/24, 28 May 1925.

65. Sigrun Bohle, *Hebammen: Zur Situation der Geburtshelferinnen im endenden 19. und beginnenden 20. Jahrhundert in Österreich* (master's thesis, University of Vienna, 1985), 100.

66. Marina Hilber, "Antiseptics Leave the Clinic—The Introduction of (Puerperal) Prophylaxis in Austrian Midwifery Education (1870s–1880s)," *Social History of Medicine* 35, no. 1 (2022): 100–101.

67. On obstetrics in Vienna, see Erna Lesky, *The Vienna Medical School of the 19th Century* (Baltimore, MD: Johns Hopkins University Press, 1976), 52–59, 181–92, 423–34.

68. Anna Graf, "Ueber die Pfuscherinnen!" *HZ*, 15 February 1906, 29–30.

69. "Ohne Hebamme," *HZ*, 1 May 1911, 206; Graf, "Ueber die Pfuscherinnen!" "Ohne Hebamme," and "Eine bedrohte Hebamme," *HZ*, 30 January 1899, 13. Bohle cites an article in which quackery was likened to "Hexenkunst." See Bohle, *Hebammen*, 17.

70. On the German context, see Marita Metz-Becker, *Der verwaltete Körper: Die Medikalisierung schwangerer Frauen in den Gebärhäusern des frühen 19. Jahrhunderts* (Frankfurt: Campus Verlag, 1997), 37.

71. After the SDAP's election victory in the Vienna City Council in 1919, it was the SDAP women who first made demands to reform anti-abortion legislation, citing eugenic reasons. The SDAP was not a particularly pro-woman organization, but, with women's suffrage being introduced in 1918, the party made an effort to appeal to women voters.

72. Adelheid Popp, quoted in Karin Lehner, *Verpönte Eingriffe: Sozialdemokratische Reformbestrebungen zu den Abtreibungsbestimmungen in der Zwischenkriegszeit* (Vienna: Picus Verlag, 1989), 101.

73. In this way, the *Fristenmodell* attempted to redefine pregnancy as beginning at quickening, instead of at conception.

74. Lehner, *Verpönte Eingriffe*, 128–33.

75. Julius Tandler, "Mutterschaftszwang und Bevölkerungspolitik" (1924), quoted in Lehner, *Verpönte Eingriffe*, 130–31.

76. Lehner, *Verpönte Eingriffe*, 131–32.

77. Bohle, *Hebammen*, 34–35.

78. Buklijas, "Culture of Death and Politics of Corpse Supply," 598–605.

79. For a discussion of this exhibition, see Alys X. George, *The Naked Truth: Viennese Modernism and the Body* (Chicago: University of Chicago Press, 2020), 44–56.

80. The exhibition was open every day from 9 a.m. until midnight, making it accessible to people from all classes (even those working into the evening). One of the goals of the exhibition was for the Habsburg monarchy to establish itself as a leader of medicine and hygiene on the Continent and attract an international audience. See "Allgemeine hygienische Ausstellung, Wien, Rotunde 1906," *NFP*, 12 May 1906, 18. For article mentioned, see Heinrich Keller, "Die hygienische Ausstellung," *WSMZ*, 14 May 1906, 6.

81. For a description of these exhibitors, see "Der erste Sonntag in der hygienischen Ausstellung," *WSMZ*, 14 May 1906, 6–7. For a description of the interior, as well as of other exhibitors, see "Ein Rundgang durch die hygienische Ausstellung," *NFP*, 12 May 1906, 7–8.

82. Keller, "Die hygienische Ausstellung," 6.

83. Theodor Altschul, *Lehrbuch der Körper- und Gesundheitslehre: Somatologie und Hygiene. Für Mädchenlyzeen und ähnliche Lehranstalten* (Vienna: F. Tempsky, 1908), 82.

84. George, *The Naked Truth*, 45.

85. According to Philipp Sarasin, the idea of having a body, being a subject with a body, emerged within hygiene discourse in the nineteenth century. See Philipp Sarasin, *Reizbare Maschinen: Eine Geschichte des Körpers, 1765–1914* (Frankfurt: Suhrkamp, 2001).

86. Jonathan Crary, *Techniques of the Observer: On Vision and Modernity in the Nineteenth Century* (Cambridge: MIT Press, 1999), 98.

87. See Maria Mesner, "Educating Reasonable Lovers: Sex Counseling in Austria in the First Half of the Twentieth Century," in *Sexuality in Austria*, ed. Günther Bischof, Anton Pelinka, and Dagmar Herzog (New Brunswick, NJ: Transaction, 2007), 48–64.

88. Quoted in Peter M. Judson, *The Habsburg Empire: A New History* (Cambridge, MA: The Belknap Press of Harvard University Press, 2016), 51.

89. Johann Peter Frank, *System einer vollständigen medicinischen Polizey*, Bd. 1 (Mannheim, 1784), 99.

90. On cholera, see Othmar Birkner, *Die bedrohte Stadt: Cholera in Wien* (Vienna: Franz Deuticke, 2002). Tuberculosis killed around 171,302 people in Vienna between 1867 and 1900. See Karin Jusek, *Auf der Suche nach der Verlorenen: Die Prostitutionsdebatten im Wien der Jahrhundertwende* (Vienna: Löcker Verlag, 1994), 124.

91. Heikki Lempa, *Beyond the Gymnasium: Educating the Middle-Class Bodies in Classical Germany* (New York: Lexington Books, 2007), 202.

92. OeStA, AVA, MdI, Tuberkulose, in genere, SA A 3153, Tuberculosis Poster, 1911.

93. See Alain Corbin, *The Foul and the Fragrant: Odor and the French Social Imagination* (Cambridge, MA: Harvard University Press, 1986); Norbert Elias, *The Civilizing Process: Sociogenetic and Psychogenetic Investigations*, trans. Edmund Jephcott (Oxford: Blackwell, 2000); on hygiene in Vienna see Peter Payer, *Der Gestank von Wien: Über Kanalgase, Totendünste und andere üble Geruchskulissen* (Vienna: Döcker Verlag, 1997), 29–40.

94. Peter Stallybrass and Allon White, *The Politics and Poetics of Transgression* (New York: Cornell University Press, 1986), 125–48.

95. On water's healing properties, see Jill Steward, "The Culture of the Water Cure in Nineteenth-Century Austria, 1800–1914," in *Water, Leisure and Culture: European Historical Perspectives*, ed. Susan C. Anderson and Bruce H. Tabb (New York: Berg, 2002), 23–36.

96. Malvine von Steinau, *Der gute Ton für Damen*, 2nd ed. (Vienna: A. Hartleben, 1878), 14.

97. See Marcel Chahrour, "'A Civilizing Mission?' Austrian Medicine and the Reform of Medical Structures in the Ottoman Empire, 1838–1850," *Studies in History and Philosophy of Science of Biological and Medical Sciences* 38, no. 4 (December 2007): 687–705.

98. On the Stadtphysikat and its annual reports on disease, see L. Senfelder, *Geschichte des Wiener Stadtphysikates* (Vienna: Selbstverlag des Verfassers, 1908); Sylvia Gierlinger, *Die Jahresberichte des Wiener Stadtphysikates, 1866–1913* (Vienna: Zentrum für Umweltgeschichte, 2015).

99. On the history of hygiene at the Vienna Medical School, see Lesky, *The Vienna Medical School*, 537–51.

100. Peter Payer, "The Age of Noise: Early Reactions in Vienna, 1870–1914," *Journal of Urban History* 33, no. 5 (July 2007): 775.

101. By 1873 about 90 percent of Vienna's houses were connected to the city's sewer system. See Sándor Békési, "The Beginnings of the 'City Machine,'" in *Science in the Metropolis:*

Vienna in Transnational Context, 1848–1918, ed. Mitchell G. Ash (New York: Routledge, 2021), 76–77; Sylvia Gierlinger and Michael Neundlinger, "Cleaning a Metropolis: The History of Vienna's Sewage System," in *Social Ecology: Society-Nature Relations across Time and Space*, ed. Helmut Haberl, Marina Fischer-Kowalski, Friolin Krausmann, and Verena Winiwarter (Geneva: Springer, 2016), 465–86. The Vienna High Spring Water Source Pipeline/ Hochquellen-Wasserleitung was opened in 1873. On Vienna's parks, see Robert Rotenberg, *Landscape and Power in Vienna* (Baltimore, MD: Johns Hopkins University Press, 1995).

102. On public health in "Red Vienna," see Helmut Gruber, *Red Vienna: Experiment in Working-Class Culture 1919–1934* (New York: Oxford University Press, 1991), 65–73.

103. OeStA, AVA, MdI, Prostitution, in genere, 2 A 2122, TP 95/III, "Belehrung," 1909.

104. OeStA, AVA, JM, Vergehen gegen die öffentliche Sittlichkeit, 1 A 1135, "Aufruf," 18 May 1907.

105. OeStA, AVA, MdI, Ausstellung, Sanitäts, 1911–1918, SA A2941, "Bericht der 'Altona Nachricht,'" 11 July 1911.

106. On VD and World War I, see Nancy M. Wingfield, *The World of Prostitution in Late Imperial Austria* (New York: Oxford University Press, 2017), 213–20.

107. Gustav Riether, "Die Geschlechtskrankheiten der Eltern und ihre Bedeutung für die Nachkommenschaft," *BWSW* 23, no. 243 (May–June 1924): 43–46.

108. Glaessner, *Reif zur Liebe!* 10–11.

109. Fritz Kehren, *Unter vier Augen: Die hohe Schule der Gattenliebe*, 10th ed. (Přívoz: I. Buchsbaum, 1930).

110. On Julius Tandler, see Britta McEwen, *Sexual Knowledge: Feeling, Fact, and Social Reform in Vienna, 1900–1934* (New York: Berghahn Books, 2012), 26–53.

111. McEwen, *Sexual Knowledge*, 33.

112. For an overview of interwar exhibitions on hygiene, health, and the body, see George, *The Naked Truth*, 49–53.

113. "Venus-Gürtel" and "Damen!" *IFHR* 28, no. 24 (1913/14): 244.

114. Hahn, "Die Periode," 136.

115. Glaessner, *Reif zur Liebe!* 38.

116. Werner Fischer-Defoy, *Die körperliche und geistige Hygiene der berufstätigen Frau* (Dresden: Deutscher Verlag für Volkswohlfahrt, 1927), 42.

117. Margarete Rada, *Das reifende Proletariermädchen: Ein Beitrag zur Umweltforschung* (Vienna: Deutscher Verlag für Jugend und Volk, 1931), 68.

118. Karl Kautsky, *Soziale Hygiene der Frau: Eine sozialmedizinische Darstellung des Weiblichen Geschlechtslebens* (Prague: Verlag des Parteivorstandes der Deutschen sozialdemokratischen Arbeiterpartei, 1931), 11–12.

119. Fischer-Defoy, *Die körperliche und geistige Hygiene der berufstätigen Frau*, 42.

120. Otfried O. Fellner, "Hygiene der Frau," *FM* 6 (March 1913): 157.

121. Dora Teleky, "Ueber das Entwicklungsalter der Mädchen," *DmF* 12 (1928): 5–6.

122. Quotes from Fellner, "Hygiene der Frau," 157.

123. Fürst, "Zur Gesundheitspflege der Frau während der Menstruation," *HZ*, 15 June 1888, 82–84.

124. "Verbandstoff-Fabrik von Hartmann & Kiesling, Hollzwoll-Binden für Damen," *HZ*, 15 November 1887, 7.

125. "Venus-Gürtel," *IFHR* 28, no. 24 (1913/14): 244.

126. Quoted in Rada, *Das reifende Proletariermädchen*, 69.

127. Young, "Menstrual Meditations," 109.

128. See, for example, Marius Turda and Paul Weindling, eds., *Blood and Homeland: Eugenics and Racial Nationalism in Central and Southeast Europe, 1900–1940* (Budapest: Central European University Press, 2007).

129. WStLA, LgSt, Sa, I 4224/1914, 6 July 1914.

130. WStLA, LgSt, Sa, I 4938/1915, 8 August 1915.

131. WStLA, LgSt, Sa, I 4938/1915, 17 August 1915.

132. The League Against Forced Motherhood (*Bund gegen den Mutterschaftszwang*) was particularly vocal in the abortion reform movement in the early days of the First Republic. Founded on 30 July 1919, the organization was the brainchild of the sex reformer Johann Ferch and was committed to the repeal of §§ 144–48.

133. Adelheid Popp, "Der Gebärzwang für das Elend," *Die Unzufriedene*, 23 February 1924, 1.

134. Adelheid Popp (1921), quoted in Lehner, *Verpönte Eingriffe*, 63.

135. WStLA, LgSt, Sa, I 3411/1912, 29 August 1912.

136. WStLA, LgSt, Sa, I 4224/1914, 6 May 1914.

137. WStLA, LgSt, Sa, I 1673/1911, 27 February 1911.

138. Friedrich Schauta, *Lehrbuch der Gesamten Gynäkologie. Erster Teil: Geburtshilfe*, 3rd ed. (Vienna: Franz Deuticke, 1906), 572; Reagan, *When Abortion Was a Crime*, 70–79.

139. See, for example, WStLA, LgSt, Sa, I 7820/24, 28 May 1925.

140. WStLA, LgSt, Sa, II 204/27, 25 May 1927.

141. See, for example, WStLA, LgSt, Sa, I 4938/1915, 8 August 1915.

142. Rosa Mayreder, "2 Februar 1913," in *Tagebücher, 1873–1937*, trans. Harriet Anderson (Frankfurt: Insel Verlag, 1988), 136.

143. WStLA, LgSt, Sa, I 4938/1915, 18 August 1915.

144. WStLA, LgSt, Sa, I 4938/1915, 3 May 1916.

145. Schauta, *Lehrbuch der Gesamten Gynäkologie*, 365.

146. WStLA, LgSt, Sa, LG I 4938/1915, 17 August 1915.

147. WStLA, LgSt, Sa, I 4938/1915, 9 May 1916.

148. Usborne, *Cultures of Abortion*, 123.

149. See Joanna Bourke, *The Story of Pain: From Prayer to Painkillers* (New York: Oxford University Press, 2014), 53–87, 131–58, 159–91.

150. Bourke, *The Story of Pain*, 7, 17.

151. Alma Mahler-Werfel, "Thursday, 6 July, Suite 12, 1899," *Diaries, 1898–1902*, 161.

152. WStLA, LgSt, Sa, I 8515/1899, 20 November 1899.

153. WStLA, LgSt, Sa, I 1137/1902, 19 July 1902.

154. WStLA, LgSt, Sa, I 4938/1915, 17 August 1915.

155. WStLA, LgSt, Sa, I 4938/1915, 18 August 1915.

156. WStLA, LgSt, Sa, I 7820/24, 6 December 1924.

157. WStLA, LgSt, Sa, I 4938/1915, 17 August 1915.

158. WStLA, LgSt, Sa, II 2438/31, 17 October 1931.

159. Elizabeth Grosz, "Bodies-Cities," in *Space, Time, and Perversion: Essays on the Politics of Bodies* (New York: Routledge, 1995), 103–10.

Epilogue

1. Walter G., "Probleme des Lebens: Die faule Wienerin," *BW* 25 (1927): 14.

2. Wilma P., "Probleme des Lebens: Ein paar Worte zur 'faulen Wienerin' in Nr. 25," *BW* 29 (1927): 13–14.

3. "Korrespondenzen," *BW* 16 (1926): 20–21.

4. "Unsere Heiratspost: Männlich," *IW*, 27 March 1931, 16.

5. "Korrespondenzen," *BW* 51 (1926): 21.

6. "Unsere Heiratspost," *IW*, 24 August 1928, 12.

7. "Unsere Heiratspost: Weiblich," *IW*, 12 April 1929, 10.

8. "Correspondenzen," *NWJ*, 21 April 1929, 40.

9. Truida, "Was ziehe ich heute Abend an?" *BW* 1 (1926): 21. On the new maternalism, see Ann Taylor Allen, *Feminism and Motherhood in Western Europe, 1890–1970* (New York: Palgrave Macmillan, 2005).

10. *Schrammeln*, dir. Géza von Bolváry (Vienna: Wien-Film Verleih, 1944); *Wiener Mädeln*, dir. Willi Forst (Vienna: Wien-Film Verleih, 1949). See also Sabine Hake, *Popular Cinema of the Third Reich* (Austin: University of Texas Press, 2002), 149–71.

11. Tyler Carrington, *Love at Last Sight: Dating, Intimacy, and Risk in Turn-of-the-Century Berlin* (New York: Oxford University Press, 2019), 101–45.

12. Simone de Beauvoir, *The Second Sex*, trans. Constance Borde and Sheila Malovany-Chevallier (1949; New York: Vintage Books, 2011).

13. de Beauvoir, *The Second Sex*, 3.

Bibliography

Archives and Libraries

Archiv Bundespolizeidirektion Wien (ABpdW)
   Prostitution und Mädchenhandel (P/M)
   Stimmungsberichte (Sb)
Filmarchiv Austria
Austrian Film Museum
Österreichische Nationalbibliothek (ÖNB)
   Austrian Newspapers Online (ANNO)
   Bildarchiv Austria (BAA)
   Historische Rechts- und Gesetztexte Online (ALEX)
   Stenographische Protokolle des Abgeordnetenhauses des Reichsrates (SPdAdR)
Österreichisches Staatsarchiv (OeStA)
   Allgemeines Verwaltungsarchiv (AVA), Justizministerium (JM)
   Allgemeines Verwaltungsarchiv (AVA), Ministerium des Innern (MdI)
   Allgemeines Verwaltungsarchiv (AVA), Unterrichtsministerium (UM)
Sammlung Frauennachlässe (SFn)
Wiener Stadt- und Landesarchiv (WStLA)
   Gelöschte Vereine (GV)
   Otto-Wagner-Spital (OWS), Krankengeschichten Frauen (KgF)
   Landesgericht für Strafsachen (LgSt), Strafakten (Sa)

Newspapers and Journals

Arbeiter-Zeitung (AZ)
Arbeiterinnen-Zeitung (AnZ)
   Freie Stunden. Beilage der
      Arbeiterinnen-Zeitung (FS)
Bukowinaer Rundschau (BR)
Bettauers Wochenschrift (BW)
Blätter für das Wohlfahrtswesen der Stadt
   Wien (BWSW)
Bukowiner Post (BP)
Das Blatt der Hausfrau (BdH)

Der Humorist
Der Kuckuck
Der Morgen: Wiener Montagblatt (DM)
Die Bombe
Die Bühne
Die Dame
Der Floh
Der Filmbote: Zeitschrift für alle Zweige der
   Kinematographie (DF)
Die Frau

Die Frau und Mutter (FM)
Die Kinowoche
Die literarische Welt (DlW)
Die moderne Frau (DmF)
Die Muskete
Die neue Wiener Nachtwelt (WN)
Die Stunde
Die Unzufriedene
Die Weltpresse
Die Zeit
Dokumente der Frauen (DF)
Figaro
Freie Bühne (FB)
Hebammen-Zeitung (HZ)
Illustrierte Oesterreichische Kriminal Zeitung (IOKZ)
Illustriertes Familienblatt: Häuslicher Ratgeber für Österreichs Frauen (IFHR)
Illustrierte Kronen-Zeitung (IKZ)
Illustrierte Wochenpost (IW)
Kikeriki
Mein Film (MF)
Moderne Welt (MW)
Neue Freie Presse (NFP)
Neues 8 Uhr-Blatt

Neues Wiener Journal (NWJ)
Neues Wiener Tageblatt (NWT)
Österreichs Illustrierte Zeitung (ÖIZ)
Österreichs Reichswehr
Reichspost
Sexual-Reform: Zeitschrift für Sexualreform und Neomalthusiansimus (SR)
Sport und Salon: Illustrierte Zeitschrift für die vornehme Welt (SuS)
Wiener Allgemeine Zeitung
Wiener Caricaturen (WC)
Wiener Hausfrau: Wochenschrift für Hauswirtschaft, Mode, Handarbeiten und Unterhaltung (WH)
Wiener Hausfrauen-Zeitung (WHZ)
Wiener Modezeitung
Wiener Montags-Journal (WMJ)
Wiener Nacht-Presse (WNP)
Wiener Salonblatt (WS)
Wiener Sonn- und Montags-Zeitung (WSMZ)
Wiener Zeitung (WZ)
Wiener Abendpost. Beilage zur Wiener Zeitung (WA)
Wir beide: Zeitschrift für Kultur und Erotik (Wb)

Films

Einmal kommt der Tag . . . ! (1924)
Ein Walzertraum (1925)
Die Büchse der Pandora (1929)
Die freudlose Gasse (1925)
Schrammeln (1944)

The Smiling Lieutenant (1931)
Vienne en Tramway (1906)
Varieté (1925)
Wiener Mädeln (1949)

Primary Sources

Adolph Lehmanns Allgemeiner Wohnungsanzeiger nebst Handels- und Gewerbe-Adressbuch für Wien. Vienna, 1890–1934.

Altschul, Theodor. *Lehrbuch der Körper- und Gesundheitslehre: Somatologie und Hygiene. Für Mädchenlyzeen und ähnliche Lehranstalten.* Vienna: F. Tempsky, 1908.

Bauer, Bernhard A. *Wie bist du, Weib? Betrachtungen über Körper, Seele, Sexualität und Erotik des Weibes.* Vienna: Rikola Verlag, 1923.

Baum, Vicki. "Die Mütter von morgen—die Backfische von heute." In *Bubikopf: Aufbruch in den Zwanzigern: Texte von Frauen,* ed. Anna Rheinsberg, 31–35. Darmstadt: Luchterhand, 1988.

Beauvoir, Simone de. *Memoirs of a Dutiful Daughter*. Translated by James Kirkup. New York: Harper Perennial, 2005.

Blei, Franz. *Lehrbücher der Liebe*. Munich: Georg Müller Verlag, 1923.

Bloch, Alice. *Harmonische Schulung des Frauenkörpers: Nach gesundheitlichen Richtlinien in Bildern und Merkworten*, 2nd ed. Stuttgart: Dieck, 1926.

Böhme, Margarete. *Tagebuch einer Verlorenen*. Berlin: F. Fontane, 1905.

Braun, Dr. med. *Häusliches Glück oder: Was ein Mann und ein Mädchen vor und von der Ehe wissen müssen*. Leipzig: Wendel, 1907.

Brücke, Ernst. *Schönheit und Fehler der Menschlichen Gestalt*. Vienna: Wilhelm Braumüller, 1891.

Courths-Mahler, Hedwig. *Eine ungeliebte Frau*. 1918. Cologne: Gustav Lübbe Verlag, 1984.

Diehl, Oskar. *Mimik im Film: Leitfaden für den praktischen Unterricht in der Filmschauspielkunst*. Munich: Georg Müller Verlag, 1922.

Duncan, Isadora. *Art of the Dance*. New York: Theatre Art Books, 1928.

Duncan, Isadora. *My Life*. Garden City, NY: Garden City Publishing Co., 1927.

Duncan, Isadora. *Der Tanz der Zukunft (The Dance of the Future): Eine Vorlesung*. Translated by Karl Federn. Leipzig: Eugen Diederichs, 1903.

Ethische Gesellschaft. *Die Arbeits- und Lebensverhältnisse der Wiener Lohnarbeiterinnen: Ergebnisse und stenographisches Protokoll der Enquete über Frauenarbeit, abgehalten in Wien vom 1. März bis 21. April 1896*. Vienna, 1897.

Feldmann, Else. "Vor dem Kino." In *Bubikopf: Aufbruch in den Zwanzigern: Texte von Frauen*, ed. Anna Rheinsberg, 56–59. Darmstadt: Luchterhand, 1988.

Ferch, Betty. "The Birth Control Association of Austria." In *The Practice of Contraception: An International Symposium and Survey*, ed. Margaret Sanger and Hannah M. Stone, 268–270. Baltimore, MD: Waverly Press, 1931.

Ferch, Johann. *Liebe und Ehe in der arbeitenden Klasse*. Oranienburg: Orania-Verlag, 1913.

Ferch, Johann. *Die Revolutionierung des Liebeslebens*. Berlin: Verlag der "Neuen Weltanschauung," 1919.

Fischer-Defoy, Werner. *Die körperliche und geistige Hygiene der berufstätigen Frau*. Dresden: Deutscher Verlag für Volkswohlfahrt, 1927.

Frank, Johann Peter. *System einer vollständigen medizinischen Polizey*, Bd. 1. Mannheim, 1784.

Freud, Sigmund. *A Case of Hysteria (Dora)*. 1905. Translated by Anthea Bell. New York: Oxford University Press, 2013.

Freud, Sigmund. *Civilization and Its Discontents*. Translated by Joan Riviere. London: Hogarth Press, 1930.

Freud, Sigmund. "Some Psychical Consequences of the Anatomical Distinction Between the Sexes." Vienna, 1925.

Freie Liebe und bürgerliche Ehe: Schwurgerichtsverhandlung gegen die Arbeiterinnen-Zeitung durchgeführt bei dem k.k. Landes- und Schwurgerichte in Wien am 30. September 1895. Vienna: Verlag der Ersten Wiener Volksbuchhandlung, 1895.

Fuchs, Georg. *Die Schaubühne der Zukunft*. Berlin: Schuster & Loeffler, 1905.

Glaessner, Rudolf. *Reif zur Liebe! Eine ärztliche Aufklärungsschrift über alles Wissenswerte im Liebes- und Geschlechtsleben des Weibes*. Vienna, 1921.

Glatterer, Michael. *Im Glaubenslicht: Christliche Gedanken über das Geschlechtsleben*. Innsbruck: Verlag Felician Rauch, 1927.

Goethe, Johann Wolfgang von. *Italian Journey*. 1816. London: Penguin Books, 1970.

Goldman, Emma. *Living My Life*. 1931. New York: Cosimo, 2008.

Goldman, Emma. "The Traffic in Women." 1910. In *Feminism: The Essential Historical Writings*, ed. Miriam Schneir, 308–17. New York: Vintage Books, 1994.

Grand, Sarah. "The New Aspect of the Woman Question." *North American Review* 158 (March 1894): 270.

Guglia, Eigem. *Wien, ein Führer durch Stadt und Umgebung*. Vienna: Gerlach & Wiedling, 1908

Günther, Hans F. K. *Rassenkunde des deutschen Volkes*. Munich: J. F. Lehmanns-Verlag, 1922.

Hahnl, Hans Heinz. "Lust und Frust." In *Wiener Lust: Eine Anthologie österreichischer erotischer Literatur*, ed. Hans Heinz Hahnl, 5–42. Vienna: Löcker Verlag, 1989.

Hainisch, Marianne. *Die Brodfrage der Frau*. Vienna: Gistel, 1875.

Hainisch, Marianne. *Ein Mutterwort über die Frauenfrage*. Vienna, 1892.

Hevesi, Ludwig. *Acht Jahre Sezession (März 1897–Juni 1905): Kritik, Polemik, Chronik*. Vienna, 1906.

Hofmannsthal, Hugo von. *Gesammelte Werke, Bd. 8: Reden und Aufsätze I, 1891–1913*, ed. Bernd Schoeller and Rudolf Hirsch. Frankfurt am Main: Fischer Verlag, 1979.

Hofstätter, R. *Die rauchende Frau: Eine klinische psychologische und soziale Studie*. Vienna: Hölder-Pichler-Tempsky, 1924.

Hölzke, Hermann. *Die Deutsche Literatur von den Anfängen der Moderne bis zur Gegenwart*. Leipzig: Gerstenberg, 1913.

Ibsen, Henrik. *A Doll's House*. 1879.

Janetschek, O. *Weib und Genuß: Für reife Menschen*. Vienna: Anzengruber-Verlag, 1922.

Jerusalem, Else. *Der heilige Skarabäus*. Vienna, 1908.

Kautsky, Karl. *Soziale Hygiene der Frau: Eine sozialmedizinische Darstellung des weiblichen Geschlechtslebens*. Prague: Verlag des Parteivorstandes der Deutschen sozialdemokratischen Arbeiterpartei in der Tschechoslowakischen Republik, 1931.

Kehren, Fritz. *Unter vier Augen: Die hohe Schule der Gattenliebe*. 10th ed. Přívoz: I. Buchsbaum, 1930.

Key, Ellen. *Die Frauenbewegung*. Frankfurt: Rütten & Loening, 1909.

Krafft-Ebing, Richard von. *Psychopathia Sexualis*. Translated by Charles Gilbert Chaddock. Philadelphia: F. A. Davis, 1892.

Lazarsfeld, Sophie. *Die Ehe von heute und morgen*. Munich: Verlag J. F. Bergmann, 1927.

Lazarsfeld, Sophie. *Erziehung zur Ehe*. Vienna: Verlag von Mortiz Perles, 1928.

Leichter, Käthe. *Leben, Werk und Sterben einer österreichischen Sozialdemokratin*, ed. Herbert Steiner. Vienna: Ibera & Molden Verlag, 1997.

Leitich, Ann Tizia. *Die Wienerin*. Stuttgart: Franckh'sche Verlagshandlung, 1939.

Mahler-Werfel, Alma. *Diaries 1898–1902*. Translated by Antony Beaumont. Ithaca, NY: Cornell University Press, 1999.

Mann, Thomas. *The Magic Mountain*. 1924. Translated by John E. Woods. New York: Vintage, 1996.

Mantegazza, Paolo. *The Physiology of Love and Other Writings*. Edited by Nicoletta Pireddu. Translated by David Jacobson. Toronto: University of Toronto Press, 2007.

Marlitt, E. *Gold Elsie*. Translated by A. L. Wister. Philadelphia: J. B. Lippincott, 1868.

Mayreder, Rosa. *Die Ersten fünf Jahre des allg. Österreichischen Frauenvereins*. Berlin: S. N., 1898.

Mayreder, Rosa. *Geschlecht und Kultur: Essays*. Jena: E. Diedrich, 1923.

Mayreder, Rosa. *Das Haus in der Landskrongasse: Jugenderinnerungen*. 1948. Vienna: Mandelbaum Verlag Michael Baiculescu, 1998.

Mayreder, Rosa. *Zur Kritik der Weiblichkeit: Essays*. 1905. Munich: Verlag Frauenoffensive, 1982.

Mayreder, Rosa. *Tagebücher, 1873–1937*. Edited by Harriet Anderson. Frankfurt: Insel Verlag, 1988.

Meisel-Hess, Grete. *Fanny Roth: Eine Jungfrauengeschichte*. 1902. Berlin: Hermann Seemann Nachfolger Verlagsgesellschaft, 1910.

Meisel-Hess, Grete. *The Sexual Crisis: A Critique of Our Sex Life*. Translated by Eden and Cedar Paul. New York: The Critic and Guide Company, 1917.

Meisel-Hess, Grete. *Die sexuelle Krise: Eine sozialpsychologische Untersuchung*. Jena: Diederichs Verlag, 1909.

Meurer, Julius. *A Handy Illustrated Guide to Vienna and Environs*, 2nd ed. Vienna: A. Hartleben, 1906.

Meyer, Emanuele L. M. *Vom Mädchen zur Frau: Ein zeitgemäßiges Erziehungs- und Ehebuch allen reifen Töchtern, Gattinnen, Müttern und Volkserziehern gewidmet*. Stuttgart: Verlag von Strecker und Schröder, 1912.

Mitteilungen der Kulturpolitischen Gesellschaft: Protokolle der Enquete betreffend die Reform des österreichischen Eherechts (vom 27. Jänner bis 24. February 1905) unter dem Vorsitze des Hofrat Dr. Karl von Pelser-Fürnberg. Vienna: Verlag Kulturpolitische Gesellschaft, 1905.

Mittelmann, Herman. *Illustrierter Führer durch die Bukowina*. Czernowitz: Verlag der Buchhandlung Romuald Schally, 1907/1908.

Musil, Robert. *The Man Without Qualities*, vol. 1: *A Sort of Introduction* and *Pseudo Reality Prevails*. 1930. Translated by Sophie Watkins. New York: Vintage, 1996.

Nemes-Nagy, Zoltán von. *Vita sexualis: Das Geschlechtsleben der Menschen*. Vienna: Braunmüller, 1926.

Ouida. "The New Woman." *North American Review* 158 (May 1894): 611.

Pappenheim, Bertha, and Sara Rabinowitz. *Zur Lage der jüdischen Bevölkerung in Galizien: Reise-Eindrücke und Vorschläge zur Besserung der Verhältnisse*. Frankfurt am Main: Neuer Frankfurter Verlag, 1904.

Popp, Adelheid. *Jugend einer Arbeiterin*. 1909. Berlin: Dietz, 1980.

Popp, Adelheid. *Der Weg zur Höhe: Die sozialdemokratische Frauenbewegung Österreichs; ihr Aufbau, ihre Entwicklung und ihr Aufstieg*, 2nd ed. Vienna, 1930.

Rada, Margarete. *Das reifende Proletariermädchen: Ein Beitrag zur Umweltforschung*. Vienna: Deutscher Verlag für Jugend und Volk, 1931.

Rautenstrauch, Johann. "Über die Stubenmädchen in Wien." Vienna, 1781.

Reich, Wilhelm. *Geschlechtsreife, Enthaltsamkeit, Ehemoral: Eine Kritik der bürgerlichen Sexual-Reform*. Vienna: Münster Verlag, 1931.

Reich, Wilhelm. *Sexualerregung und Sexualbefriedigung*. Vienna: Münster Verlag, 1929.

Reich, Wilhelm. "The Socialistic Society for Sexual Advice and Sexual Research." In *The Practice of Contraception: An International Symposium and Survey*, ed. Margaret Sanger and Hannah M. Stone, 271. Baltimore, MD: Waverly Press, 1931.

Reimann, Hans. *Hedwig Courths-Mahler: Schlichte Geschichten fürs traute Heim*. Leipzig: Paul Steegemann Verlag, 1922.

Roth, Joseph. *The Radetzky March*. 1932. Translated by Joachim Neugroschel. New York: The Overlook Press, 1991.

Schauta, Friedrich. *Lehrbuch der Gesamten Gynäkologie. Erster Teil: Geburtshilfe*. 3rd ed. Vienna: Franz Deuticke, 1906.

Schlegel, Joseph Carl. *Hygiene des Ehelebens: Der Führer zu Liebes- und Eheglück*. Vienna: Schusdeks Verlag, 1929.

Schnitzler, Arthur. *Liebelei*. 1895. Frankfurt: Fischer Taschenbuch Verlag, 1989.

Schnitzler, Arthur. *Reigen*. 1900. Frankfurt: Fischer Taschenbuch Verlag, 1989.

Schrank, Josef. *Die Regelung der Prostitution vom gewerblich-nationalökonomischen Standpunkte betrachtet*. Vienna, 1892.

Schultze, Ernst. *Der Kinematograph als Bildungsmittel: Eine kulturpolitische Untersuchung*. Halle: Buchhandlung des Waisenhauses, 1911.

Schultze, Ernst. *Die Schundliteratur: Ihr Vordringen. Ihre Folgen. Ihre Bekämpfung*. Halle: Verlag der Buchhandlung des Waisenhauses, 1911.

Schweykart, Alois J. *An die Katholiken Österreichs! Ein Wort der Aufklärung und Abwehr gegen die Angriffe auf die katholische Ehe. Acht Vorträge*. Vienna: Verlag der Buchhandlung "Reichspost" Wien, 1906.

Senfelder, L. *Geschichte des Wiener Stadtphysikates*. Vienna: Selbstverlag des Verfassers, 1908.

Simmel, Georg. "The Metropolis and Mental Life." 1903. In *The People, Place, and Space Reader*, ed. Jen Jack Gieseking, William Mangold, Cindi Katz, Setha Low, and Susan Saegert, 223–26. New York: Routledge, 2014.

Stöcker, Helene. *Die Liebe und die Frauen*. Minden in Westfalen: J. C. C. Bruns' Verlag, 1905.

Stöcker, Helene. "Die modern Frau." *FB* 4 (1893): 1215–17. Translated by Angela A. Kurtz. Reprinted in *German History in Documents and Images, Volume 5*. Washington, DC: German Historical Institute. https://ghdi.ghi-dc.org/sub_document.cfm?document_id=706.

Stratz, Carl Heinrich. *Die Körperpflege der Frau: Physiologische und ästhetische Diätetik für das weibliche Geschlecht*. Stuttgart: Verlag von Ferdinand Enke, 1918.

Stratz, Carl Heinrich. *Die Rassenschönheit des Weibes*, 5th ed. Stuttgart: Verlag von Ferdinand Enke, 1902.

Straus, Oscar. *Ein Walzertraum* (Operette in 3 Akten). Libretto by Felix Dörmann and Leopold Jacobson. Vienna: Ludwig Doblinger (Bernhard Herzmansky), 1907.

Strauss, Richard. *Salome* (music drama in one act after Oscar Wilde's tragedy, with modifications for use on the English stage by Alfred Kalisch), Op. 54, 1905. Vocal score by Otto Singer. London: Boosey & Hawkes, 1943.

Tanner, Ilse-Dore. *Gutes Benehmen: Ein Ratgeber in allen Fragen des guten Tones und der feinen Sitten*. Vienna: Verlag von W. Vobach, 1923.

Tarnosky, Pauline. *Étude anthropométrique sur les prostituées et les voleuses*. Paris, 1889.

Timidior, O. *Der Hut und seine Geschichte: Eine kulturgeschichtliche Monographie*. Vienna: A. Hartleben, 1914.

Van de Velde, Theodoor H. *Die vollkommene Ehe: Eine Studie über ihre Physiologie und Technik*. Leipzig: Montana-Verlag AH Medizinische Abteilung, 1928.

Vera. *Eine für Viele: Aus dem Tagebuche eines Mädchens*. Leipzig: Hermann Seemann Nachfolger, 1902.

Steinau, Malvine von. *Der gute Ton für Damen*, 2nd ed. Vienna: A. Hartleben, 1878.

Steinau, Malvine von. *Der gute Ton für Damen*, 7th ed. Vienna: A. Hartleben, 1922.

Urban, Gisela. *Unsere Kriegskost: 290 erprobte österreichische Kriegskochrezepte, unter Berücksichtigung der kriegswirtschaftlichen Verhältnisse und Forderung neu zusammengestellt*. Vienna: St. Stefan Wiener Verlag, 1916.

Wagner, J. F. "'Gigerl' Marsch für Pianoforte." Vienna: Rebay & Robitschek, ca. 1895.

Watchtell, Samuel R. "Marriage by Dispensation in Austrian Law." *United States Law Review* 68 (1934): 649–59.

Weininger, Otto. *Sex & Character* [1903], authorized translation from the 6th German edition. New York: G. P. Putnam's Sons, 1906.

Wiesenthal, Grete. *Der Aufstieg: Aus dem Leben einer Tänzerin*. Berlin: Ernst Rohwolt Verlag, 1919.

Wiesenthal, Grete. *Grete Wiesenthal, die Schönheit der Sprache des Körpers im Tanz*, ed. Leonhard M. Fiedler and Martin Lang. Salzburg: Residenz Verlag, 1985.

Wilde, Oscar. *Salome: A Tragedy in One Act*. Translated by Lord Alfred Bruce Douglas. Pictured by Aubrey Beardsley. 1891. Boston: Copeland & Day, 1894.

Winckelmann, Johann Joachim. *Geschichte der Kunst des Alterthums*. Dresden, 1764.

Zweig, Stefan. *Die Welt von Gestern: Erinnerungen eines Europäers*. 1942. Frankfurt: Fischer Taschenbuch Verlag, 1985.

Zweig, Stefan. *The World of Yesterday*. Translated by Anthea Bell. 1942. Lincoln: University of Nebraska Press, 2013.

Secondary Sources

Abelson, Elaine S. *Women Ladies Go A-Thieving: Middle-Class Shoplifters in the Victorian Department Store*. New York: Oxford University Press, 1989.

Adelson, Leslie A. *Making Bodies, Making History: Feminism and German Identity*. Lincoln: University of Nebraska Press, 1993.

Ahmed, Sara. *Strange Encounters: Embodied Others in Post-Coloniality*. New York: Routledge, 2000.

Ahmed, Sara. *Queer Phenomenology: Orientations, Objects, Others*. Durham, NC: Duke University Press, 2006.

"AHR Conversation: The Historical Study of Emotions." *American Historical Review* 117, no. 5 (December 2012): 1487–1531.

Alaimo, Stacy. "Trans-Corporeal Feminisms and the Ethical Space of Nature." In *Material Feminisms*, ed. Stacy Alaimo and Susan Hekman, 237–64. Bloomington: Indiana University Press, 2008.

Alaimo, Stacy. *Undomesticated Ground: Recasting Nature as Feminist Space*. Ithaca, NY: Cornell University Press, 2000.

Allen, Ann Taylor. *Feminism and Motherhood in Western Europe, 1890–1970*. New York: Palgrave Macmillan, 2005.

Althaus, Andrea. "Lebensverhältnisse von Dienstmädchen und Hausgehilfinnen im 19. und 20. Jahrhundert." In *Mit Kochlöffel und Staubwedel: Erzählungen aus dem Dienstmädchenalltag*, 275–92. Vienna: Böhlau Verlag, 2010.

Amort, Andrea. "Free Dance in Interwar Vienna." In *Interwar Vienna: Culture between Tradition and Modernity*, ed. Deborah Holmes and Lisa Silverman, 117–42. Rochester, NY: Camden House, 2009.

Anderson, Harriet. *Utopian Feminism: Women's Movements in Fin-de-Siècle Vienna.* New Haven, CT: Yale University Press, 1992.

Anderson, Susan, and Bruce Tabb, eds. *Water, Leisure, and Culture: European Historical Perspectives.* New York: Berg, 2002.

Andersson, Peter K. *Silent History: Body Language and Nonverbal Identity, 1860–1914.* Montreal: McGill-Queen's University Press, 2018.

Ankum, Katharina von, ed. *Women in the Metropolis: Gender and Modernity in Weimar Culture.* Berkeley: University of California Press, 1997.

Appelt, Erna. "The Gendering of the Service Sector in Austria at the End of the Nineteenth Century." In *Austrian Women in the Nineteenth and Twentieth Centuries: Cross-Disciplinary Perspectives*, ed. David F. Good, Margarete Grandner, and Mary Jo Maynes, 115–32. Providence, RI: Berghahn Books, 1996.

Arokha, Noga. *Passions and Tempers: A History of the Humours.* New York: HarperCollins, 2007.

Ashby, Charlotte, Tag Gronberg, and Simon Shaw-Miller, eds. *The Viennese Café and Fin-de-Siècle Culture.* New York: Berghahn Books, 2013.

Ashkenazi, Ofer. *Weimar Film and Modern Jewish Identity.* New York: Palgrave Macmillan, 2012.

Augeneder, Sigrid. *Arbeiterinnen im Ersten Weltkrieg: Lebens- und Arbeitsbedingungen proletarischer Frauen in Österreich.* Vienna: Europaverlag, 1987.

Auslander, Leora. "Beyond Words." *American Historical Review* 110, no. 4 (October 2004): 1015–45.

Auslander, Leora. *Cultural Revolutions: Everyday Life and Politics in Britain, North America, and France.* Berkeley: University of California Press, 2009.

Bader-Zaar, Birgitta. "Women in Austrian Politics, 1890–1934: Goals and Visions." In *Austrian Women in the Nineteenth and Twentieth Centuries: Cross-Disciplinary Perspectives*, ed. David F. Good, Margarete Grandner, and Mary Jo Maynes, 59–90. Providence, RI: Berghahn Books, 1996.

Barad, Karen. "Posthumanist Performativity: Toward an Understanding of How Matter Comes to Matter." In *Material Feminisms*, ed. Stacy Alaimo and Susan Hekman, 120–54. Bloomington: Indiana University Press, 2008.

Bartky, Sandra Lee. *Femininity and Domination: Studies in the Phenomenology of Oppression.* New York: Routledge, 1990.

Baudelaire, Charles. *The Painter of Modern Life and Other Essays.* Translated by Jonathan Mayne. New York: Phaidon, 1964.

Beauvoir, Simone de. *The Second Sex.* Translated by Constance Borde and Sheila Malovany-Chevallier. New York: Vintage, 2011.

Békési, Sándor. "The Beginnings of the 'City Machine.'" In *Science in the Metropolis: Vienna in Transnational Context, 1848–1918*, ed. Mitchell G. Ash, 67–89. New York: Routledge, 2021.

Belgum, Kirsten. "E. Marlitt: Narratives of Virtuous Desire." In *A Companion to*

German Realism 1848–1900, ed. Todd Kontje, 259–82. Rochester, NY: Camden House, 2002.

Belgum, Kirsten. *Popularizing the Nation: Audience, Representation, and the Production of Identity in* Die Gartenlaube, *1853–1900*. Lincoln: University of Nebraska Press, 1998.

Beller, Steven. *Rethinking Vienna 1900*. New York: Berghahn Books, 2001.

Beller, Steven. *Vienna and the Jews, 1867–1938: A Cultural History*. New York: Cambridge University Press, 1991.

Benjamin, Walter. *Charles Baudelaire: A Lyric Poet in the Era of High Capitalism*. Translated by Harry Zohn. New York: Verso, 1983.

Bernold, Monika. "Kino(t)raum: Über den Zusammenhang von Familie, Freizeit und Konsum." In *Familie: Arbeitsplatz oder Ort des Glücks? Historische Schnitte ins Private*, 135–65. Vienna: Picus Verlag, 1990.

Bernold, Monika. "Representations of the Beginning: Shaping Gender Identities in Written Life Stories of Women and Men." In *Austrian Women in the Nineteenth and Twentieth Centuries: Cross-Disciplinary Perspectives*, ed. David F. Good, Margarete Grandner, and Mary Jo Maynes, 197–212. Providence, RI: Berghahn Books, 1996.

Bernold, Monika, and Johanna Gehmacher, eds. *Auto/Biografie und Frauenfrage. Tagebücher, Briefwechsel, Politische Schriften von Mathilde Hanzel-Hübner (1884–1970)*. *L'Homme Archiv*, Band 1. Vienna: Böhlau Verlag, 2003.

Bakhtin, Mikhail. *Rabelais and His World*. Translated by Hélène Iswolsky. Bloomington: Indiana University Press, 1984.

Birkner, Othmar. *Die bedrohte Stadt: Cholera in Wien*. Vienna: Franz Deuticke, 2002.

Bischof, Günther, Anton Pelinka, and Dagmar Herzog, eds. *Sexuality in Austria*. New Brunswick, NJ: Transaction, 2007.

Bischof, Günter, Anton Pelinka, and Erika Thurner, eds. *Women in Austria*. New Brunswick, NJ: Transaction, 1998.

Blackshaw, Gemma. "The Pathological Body: Modernist Strategising in Egon Schiele's Self-Portraiture." *Oxford Art Journal* 30, no. 3 (2007): 377–401.

Blau, Eve. *The Architecture of Red Vienna 1919–1934*. Cambridge, MA: MIT Press, 1999.

Bohle, Sigrun. *Hebammen: Zur Situation der Geburtshelferinnen im endenden 19. und beginnenden 20. Jahrhundert in Österreich*. MA thesis, University of Vienna, 1986.

Bonter, Urszula. *Der Populärroman in der Nachfolge von E. Marlitt: Wilhelmine Heimburg, Valeska Gräfin Bethusy-Huc, Eufemia von Adlersfeld-Ballestrem*. Würzburg: Verlag Königshausen & Neumann, 2005.

Bordo, Susan. *Unbearable Weight: Feminism, Western Culture, and the Body*. Berkeley: University of California Press, 1995.

Bourdieu, Pierre. *Outline for a Theory of Practice*. Translated by Richard Nice. New York: Cambridge University Press, 1977.

Bourke, Joanna. *The Story of Pain: From Prayer to Painkillers*. New York: Oxford University Press, 2014.

Boutin, Aimee. "Rethinking the Flâneur: Flânerie and the Senses." *Dix-Neuf* 16, no. 2 (July 2012): 124–32.

Boyer, John W. *Culture and Political Crisis in Vienna: Christian Socialism in Power, 1897–1918*. Chicago: University of Chicago Press, 1995.

Boyer, John W. "Freud, Marriage, and Late Viennese Liberalism: A Commentary from 1905." *The Journal of Modern History* 50, no. 1 (March 1978): 72–102.

Boyer, John W. *Karl Lueger (1844–1910): Christlichsoziale Politik als Beruf.* Vienna: Böhlau, 2010.

Boyer, John W. *Political Radicalism in Late Imperial Vienna: Origins of the Christian Social Movement, 1848–1897.* Chicago: University of Chicago Press, 1981.

Brandow-Faller, Megan. *The Female Secession: Art and the Decorative at the Viennese Women's Academy.* University Park: Pennsylvania State University Press, 2020.

Brewster, Ben, and Lea Jacobs. *Theatre to Cinema.* New York: Oxford University Press, 1997.

Buck-Morss, Susan. "The Flâneur, the Sandwichman and the Whore: The Politics of Loitering." *New German Critique* 39 (Autumn 1986): 99–140.

Bukey, Evan Burr. *Jews and Intermarriage in Nazi Austria.* New York: Cambridge University Press, 2011.

Buklijas, Tatjana. "Culture of Death and Politics of Corpse Supply: Anatomy in Vienna, 1848–1914." *Bulletin of the History of Medicine* 82, no. 3 (Fall 2008): 570–607.

Bunzl, Matti. "Desiderata for a History of Austrian Sexualities." *Austrian History Yearbook* 38 (2007): 48–57.

Bunzl, Matti. *Symptoms of Modernity: Jews and Queers in Late Twentieth-Century Vienna.* Berkeley: University of California Press, 2004.

Butler, Judith. *Bodies That Matter: On the Discursive Limits of "Sex."* New York: Routledge, 1993.

Butler, Judith. *Gender Trouble: Feminism and the Subversion of Identity.* New York: Routledge, 1990.

Buxbaum, Gerda. *Mode aus Wien: 1815–1938.* Vienna: Reidenz Verlag, 1986.

Byer, Doris. *Rassenhygiene und Wohlfahrtspflege: Zur Entstehung eines sozialdemokratischen Machtdispositivs in Österreich bis 1934.* Frankfurt: Campus Verlag, 1988.

Bynum, Caroline Walker. *Fragmentation and Redemption: Essays on Gender and the Human Body in Medieval Religion.* New York: Zone Books, 1991.

Bynum, Caroline Walker. *Holy Feast and Holy Fast: The Religious Significance of Food to Medieval Women.* Berkeley: University of California Press, 1987.

Bynum, W. F. *Science and the Practice of Medicine in the Nineteenth Century.* Cambridge: Cambridge University Press, 1994.

Canning, Kathleen. "Feminist History after the Linguistic Turn: Historicizing Discourse and Experience." *Signs* 19, no. 2 (Winter 1994): 368–404.

Canning, Kathleen. *Gender History in Practice: Historical Perspectives on Bodies, Class, and Citizenship.* Ithaca, NY: Cornell University Press, 2006.

Canning, Kathleen. *Languages of Labor and Gender: Female Factory Work in Germany, 1850–1914.* Ithaca, NY: Cornell University Press, 1996.

Carrington, Tyler. *Love at Last Sight: Dating, Intimacy, and Risk in Turn-of-the-Century Berlin.* New York: Oxford University Press, 2019.

Case, Holly. *The Age of Questions: Or, A First Attempt at an Aggregate History of the Eastern, Social, Woman, American, Jewish, Polish, Bullion, Tuberculosis, and Many Other Questions over the Nineteenth Century, and Beyond.* Princeton, NJ: Princeton University Press, 2018.

Cernuschi, Claude. "Pseudo-Science and Mythic Misogyny: Oskar Kokoschka's *Murderer, Hope of Women.*" *The Art Bulletin* 81, no. 1 (March 1999): 126–48.

Certeau, Michel de. *The Practice of Everyday Life.* Translated by Steven F. Rendall. Berkeley: University of California Press, 2011.

Chahrour, Marcel. "'A Civilizing Mission?' Austrian Medicine and the Reform of

Medical Structures in the Ottoman Empire, 1838–1850." *Studies in History and Philosophy of Science of Biological and Medical Sciences* 38, no. 4 (December 2007): 687–705.

Chauncey, George. *Gay New York: Gender, Urban Culture, and the Making of the Gay Male World 1890–1940.* New York: Basic Books, 1994.

Classen, Constance. *The Deepest Sense: A Cultural History of Touch.* Urbana and Chicago: University of Illinois Press, 2012.

Classen, Constance. "Foundations for an Anthropology of the Senses." *International Social Science Journal* 153 (1997): 401–12.

Clough, Patricia T. "The Affective Turn: Political Economy, Biomedia and Bodies." *Theory, Culture & Society* 25, no. 1 (2008): 1–22.

Coen, Deborah R. *Vienna in the Age of Uncertainty: Science, Liberalism, and Private Life.* Chicago: University of Chicago Press, 2007.

Connell, R. W. *Masculinities.* Berkeley: University of California Press, 2005.

Conor, Liz. *The Spectacular Modern Woman: Feminine Visibility in the 1920s.* Bloomington: Indiana University Press, 2004.

Corbin, Alain. *The Foul and the Fragrant: Odor and the French Social Imagination.* Cambridge, MA: Harvard University Press, 1986.

Coreth, Anna. *Pietas Austriaca.* Translated by William D. Bowman and Anna Maria Leitgeb. West Lafayette, IN: Purdue University Press, 2004.

Cornwall, Mark. "Heinrich Rutha and the Unraveling of a Homosexual Scandal in 1930s Czechoslovakia." *GLQ: A Journal of Lesbian and Gay Studies* 8, no. 3 (June 1, 2002): 319–47.

Crary, Jonathan. *Techniques of the Observer: On Vision and Modernity in the Nineteenth Century.* Cambridge, MA: MIT Press, 1990.

Crenshaw, Kimberlé. "Mapping the Margins: Intersectionality, Identity Politics, and Violence against Women of Color." *Stanford Law Review* 43, no. 6 (July 1991): 1241–99.

Csáky, Moritz. *Ideologie der Operette und Wiener Moderne: Ein kulturhistorischer Essay.* Vienna: Böhlau Verlag, 1998.

Cunningham, Patricia A. *Reforming Women's Fashion, 1850–1920: Politics, Health, and Art.* Kent, OH: Kent State University Press, 2003.

Daly, Ann. "Isadora Duncan's Dance Theory." *Dance Research Journal* 26, no. 2 (Autumn 1994): 24–31.

Dassanowsky, Robert von. *Austrian Cinema: A History.* Jefferson, NC: McFarland & Company, 2005.

Davis, Lennard J. *Enforcing Normalcy: Disability, Deafness, and the Body.* New York: Verso, 1995.

Day-Mayer, Helen. "Documents of Performance: Lillian Gish on Acting on the Silent Screen." *Nineteenth Century Theatre and Film* 29, no. 1 (Summer 2002): 80–82.

Decker, Hannah S. *Freud, Dora, Vienna 1900.* New York: The Free Press, 1991.

Delroy, Charlotte. "Brassieres, Girdles, Waspies, and Cami-Panties since 1900." In *Fashioning the Body: An Intimate History of the Silhouette,* ed. Denis Bruna, 229–42. New Haven, CT: Yale University Press, 2015.

Dickinson, Edward Ross. *Dancing in the Blood: Modern Dance and European Culture on the Eve of the First World War.* Cambridge: Cambridge University Press, 2017.

Dickinson, Edward Ross. "'A Dark, Impenetrable Wall of Complete Incomprehension': The Impossibility of Heterosexual Love in Imperial Germany." *Central European History* 40 (2007): 467–97.

Dickinson, Edward Ross. *Sex, Freedom, and Power in Imperial Germany, 1880–1914.* New York: Cambridge University Press, 2014.

Didi-Huberman, Georges. *Invention of Hysteria: Charcot and the Photographic Iconography of the Sâlpetrière.* Translated by Alisa Hartz. Cambridge, MA: MIT Press, 2003.

Diethe, Carol. *Nietzsche's Women: Beyond the Whip.* New York: de Gruyter, 1996.

Dijkstra, Bram. *Idols of Perversity: Fantasies of Feminine Evil in Fin-de-Siècle Culture.* New York: Oxford University Press, 1986.

Doane, Mary Ann. "The Voice in the Cinema: The Articulation of Body and Space." *Yale French Studies* 60 (1980): 35–50.

Dollard, Catherine L. *The Surplus Woman: Unmarried in Imperial Germany, 1871–1918.* New York: Berghahn Books, 2009.

Dreidemy, Lucile. *Der Dollfuß-Mythos: Eine Biographie des Posthumen.* Vienna: Böhlau Verlag, 2014.

Duden, Barbara. *The Woman Beneath the Skin: A Doctor's Patients in Eighteenth-Century Germany.* Translated by Thomas Dunlap. Cambridge, MA: Harvard University Press, 1998.

Eder, Franz X. "'Diese Theorie ist sehr delikat . . . Zur Sexualisierung der 'Wiener Moderne.'" In *Die Wiener Jahrhundertwende,* ed. Jürgen Nautz and Richard Vahrenkamp, 159–78. Vienna: Böhlau Verlag, 1993.

Eder, Franz X. *Kultur der Begierde: Eine Geschichte der Sexualität.* Munich: Beck, 2002.

Eder, Franz X. "'The Nationalists' 'Healthy Sensuality' Was Followed by America's Influence: Sexuality and Media from National Socialism to the Sexual Revolution." In *Sexuality in Austria,* ed. Günther Bischof, Anton Pelinka, and Dagmar Herzog, 102–30. New Brunswick, NJ: Transaction, 2007.

Eder, Franz X. "Sexual Cultures in Germany and Austria, 1700–2000." In *Sexual Cultures in Europe: National Histories,* ed. Franz X. Eder, Lesley A. Hall, and Gert Hekma, 138–72. Manchester: Manchester University Press, 1999.

Ehrmann-Hämmerle, Christa. *Heimat/Front: Geschlechtergeschichte/n des Ersten Weltkriegs in Österreich-Ungarn.* Vienna: Böhlau Verlag, 2014.

Elias, Norbert. *The Civilizing Process: Sociogenetic and Psychogenetic Investigations.* Translated by Edmund Jephcott. Oxford: Blackwell, 2000.

Renne, Elisha P., and Etienne van de Walle, eds. *Regulating Menstruation: Beliefs, Practices, and Interpretations.* Chicago: University of Chicago Press, 2001.

Eustace, Nicole. *1812: War and the Passions of Patriotism.* Philadelphia: University of Pennsylvania Press, 2012.

Eustace, Nicole. *Passion Is the Gale: Emotions, Power, and the Coming of the American Revolution.* Chapel Hill: University of North Carolina Press, 2008.

Evans, Jennifer V. *Life among the Ruins: Cityscape and Sexuality in Cold War Berlin.* New York: Palgrave Macmillan, 2011.

Feichtinger, Johannes, Ursual Pratsch, and Mortiz Csaky, eds. *Habsburg Postcolonial: Machtstrukturen und kollektives Gedächtnis.* Innsbruck: Studien, 2003.

Fischer, Marianne. *Erotische Literatur vor Gericht: Der Schmutzliteraturkampf im Wien des beginnenden 20. Jahrhunderts.* Vienna: Braumüller, 2003.

Fischer, Wolfgang G., with Dorothea McEwan. *Gustav Klimt & Emilie Flöge: An Artist and His Muse.* London: Lund Humphries, 1992.

Flavell, M. Kay. "Kitsch and Propaganda: The Blending of Myth and History in Hedwig Courths-Mahler's *Lissa geht ins Glück* (1936)." *German Studies Review* 8, no. 1 (February 1985): 65–87.

Fleischer, Mary. *Embodied Texts: Symbolist Playwright-Dancer Collaborations.* New York: Rodopi, 2007.

Forstner, Regina. "Die Wiener Damenmode in der zweiten Hälfte des 19. Jahrhunderts bis zum Ende des Ersten Weltkrieges." In *Die Frau im Korsett: Wiener Frauenalltag zwischen Klischee und Wirklichkeit, 1848–1920,* 68–77. Vienna: Eigenverlag der Museen der Stadt Wien, 1984.

Foucault, Michel. *The Birth of the Clinic: An Archaeology of Medical Perception.* Translated by A. M. Sheridan Smith. New York: Vintage Books, 1994.

Foucault, Michel. *Discipline and Punish: The Birth of the Prison.* Translated by Alan Sheridan. New York: Vintage Books, 1995.

Foucault, Michel. *The History of Sexuality, Vol. 1.* Translated by Robert Hurley. New York: Vintage Books, 1990.

Foucault, Michel. *The History of Sexuality, Vol. 2: The Use of Pleasure.* Translated by Robert Hurley. New York: Vintage Books, 1990.

Frank, Alison F. "The Air Cure Town: Commodifying Mountain Air in Alpine Central Europe." *Central European History* 45, no. 2 (June 2012): 185–207.

Frei, Alfred Georg. *Rotes Wien: Austromarxismus und Arbeiterkultur: Sozialdemokratische Wohnungs- und Kommunalpolitik, 1919–1934.* Berlin: DVK Verlag, 1984.

Freidenfelds, Lara. *The Modern Period: Menstruation in Twentieth-Century America.* Baltimore, MD: Johns Hopkins University Press, 2009.

Freidenfelds, Lara. *The Myth of the Perfect Pregnancy: A History of Miscarriage in America.* New York: Oxford University Press, 2019.

Freidenreich, Harriet Pass. *Female, Jewish, and Educated: The Lives of Central European University Women.* Bloomington: Indiana University Press, 2002.

Freidenreich, Harriet Pass. "Die jüdische 'Neue Frau' des frühen 20. Jahrhunderts." In *Deutsch-jüdische Geschichte als Geschlechtergeschichte: Studien zum 19. und 20. Jahrhundert,* ed. Kirsten Heinsohn and Stefanie Schüler-Springorum, 123–32. Göttingen: Wallstein Verlag, 2005.

Freundlich, Emmy. "Die Frauenarbeit im Krieg." In *Die Regelung der Arbeitsverhältnisse im Kriege,* ed. Ferdinand Hanusch and Emanuel Adler. Vienna: Hölder-Pichler-Tempsky, 1927.

Fritzsche, Peter. *Reading Berlin 1900.* Cambridge, MA: Harvard University Press, 1996.

Fuentes, Marisa J. *Dispossessed Lives: Enslaved Women, Violence, and the Archive.* Philadelphia: University of Pennsylvania Press, 2016.

Gal, Susan. "A Semiotics of the Public/Private Distinction." *Differences* 13, vol. 1 (2002): 77–95.

Garland Thomson, Rosemarie. *Extraordinary Bodies: Figures Physical Disability in American Culture and Literature.* New York: Columbia University Press, 1997.

Garland Thomson, Rosemarie. "Feminist Theory, the Body, and the Disabled Figure." In *The Disability Studies Reader,* ed. Lennard J. Davis, 279–92. New York: Routledge, 1997.

Gatscher-Riedl, Gregor. *K. u. k. Sehnsuchtsort Czernowitz: "Klein-Wien" am Ostrand der Monarchie.* Berndorf: KRAL Verlag, 2017.

Gatens, Moira. *Imaginary Bodies: Ethics, Power and Corporeality*. New York: Routledge, 1996.

George, Alys X. "Hollywood on the Danube? Vienna and Austrian Silent Film of the 1920s." In *Interwar Vienna: Culture between Tradition and Modernity*, ed. Deborah Holmes and Lisa Silverman, 143–60. Rochester, NY: Camden House, 2009.

George, Alys X. *The Naked Truth: Viennese Modernism and the Body*. Chicago: University of Chicago Press, 2020.

Gierlinger, Sylvia. *Die Jahresberichte des Wiener Stadtphysikates, 1866–1913*. Vienna: Zentrum für Umweltgeschichte, 2015.

Gierlinger, Sylvia, and Michael Neundlinger. "Cleaning a Metropolis: The History of Vienna's Sewage System." In *Social Ecology: Society-Nature Relations across Time and Space*, ed. Helmut Haberl, Marina Fischer-Kowalski, Friolin Krausmann, and Verena Winiwarter, 465–86. Geneva: Springer, 2016.

Gilman, Sander L. *The Case of Sigmund Freud: Medicine and Identity at the Fin de Siècle*. Baltimore, MD: Johns Hopkins University Press, 1993.

Gilman, Sander L. *Freud, Race, and Gender*. Princeton, NJ: Princeton University Press, 1993.

Gilman, Sander L. "Strauss and Racial Science." In *Opera in a Multicultural World: Coloniality, Culture, Performance*, ed. Mary Ingraham, Joseph So, and Roy Moodley, 122–37. New York: Routledge, 2016.

Gilman, Sander L. "Strauss, the Pervert and Avant-Garde Opera." *New German Critique* 43 (Winter 1988): 35–68.

Gilman, Sander L. "Touch, Sexuality and Disease." In *Medicine and the Five Senses*, ed. W. F. Bynum and Roy Porter, 198–224. New York: Cambridge University Press, 1993.

Glajar, Valentina. "From *Halb-Asien* to Europe: Contrasting Representations of Austrian Bukovina." *Modern Austrian Literature* 34, nos. 1–2 (2001): 15–35.

Glajar, Valentina. *The German Legacy in East-Central Europe, as Recorded in Recent German-Language Literature*. Rochester, NY: Camden, 2004.

Gleber, Anke. "Female Flânerie and the *Symphony of the City*." In *Women in the Metropolis: Gender and Modernity in Weimar Culture*, ed. Katharina von Ankum, 67–88. Berkeley: University of California Press, 1997.

Glenn, Susan A. *Female Spectacle: The Theatrical Roots of Modern Feminism*. Cambridge, MA: Harvard University Press, 2000.

Glettler, Monika. "Minority Culture in a Capital City: The Czechs in Vienna at the Turn of the Century." In *Decadence and Innovation: Austro-Hungarian Life and Art at the Turn of the Century*, ed. Robert B. Pynsent, 49–60. London: Weidenfeld and Nicolson, 1989.

Goldstein, Jan. "The Hysteria Diagnosis and the Politics of Anticlericalism in Late Nineteenth-Century France." *Journal of Modern History* 54, no. 2 (June 1982): 209–39.

Gollance, Sonia. *It Could Lead to Dancing: Mixed-Sex Dancing and Jewish Modernity*. Stanford, CA: Stanford University Press, 2021.

Good, David F. *The Economic Rise of the Habsburg Empire, 1750–1914*. Berkeley: University of California Press, 1984.

Good, David F., Margarete Grandner, and Mary Jo Maynes, eds. *Austrian Women in* the Nineteenth and Twentieth Centuries: Cross-Disciplinary Perspectives. Providence, RI: Berghahn Books, 1996.

Grandner, Margarete, and Edith Saurer, eds. Geschlecht, Religion und Engagement: Die jüdischen Frauenbewegungen im deutschsprachigen Raum. Vienna: Böhlau Verlag, 2005.

Green, Monica H. "Flowers, Poisons and Men: Menstruation in Medieval Western Europe." In Menstruation: A Cultural History, ed. Andrew Shail and Gillian Howie, 51–64. New York: Palgrave Macmillan, 2005.

Grossmann, Atina. "The New Woman and the Rationalization of Sexuality in Weimar Germany." In Powers of Desire: The Politics of Sexuality, ed. Ann Snitow et al., 153–71. New York: Monthly Review Press, 1983.

Grossmann, Atina. Reforming Sex: The German Movement for Birth Control and Abortion Reform, 1920–1950. New York: Oxford University Press, 1995.

Grosz, Elizabeth. Space, Time, and Perversion: Essays on the Politics of Bodies. New York: Routledge, 1995.

Grosz, Elizabeth. Volatile Bodies: Toward a Corporeal Feminism. Bloomington: Indiana University Press, 1994.

Gruber, Helmut. Red Vienna: Experiment in Working-Class Culture, 1919–1934. New York: Oxford University Press, 1991.

Hackett, Amy. "Helene Stöcker: Left-Wing Intellectual and Sex-Reformer." In When Biology Became Destiny: Women in Weimar and Nazi Germany, ed. Renate Bridenthal, Atina Grossmann, and Marion Kaplan, 109–30. New York: Monthly Review Press, 1984.

Hake, Sabine. Popular Cinema of the Third Reich. Austin: University of Texas Press, 2002.

Halberstam, Jack. Female Masculinity. Durham, NC: Duke University Press, 1998.

Halperin, David M. How to Do the History of Homosexuality. Chicago: University of Chicago Press, 2004.

Hamelmann, Gudrun. Helene Stöcker, der "Bund für Mutterschutz," und "Die Neue Generation." Frankfurt: Haag & Herchen, 1992.

Hamer, Thomas Lewis. "Beyond Feminism: The Women's Movement in Austrian Social Democracy, 1890–1926." PhD diss., Ohio State University, 1973.

Hanisch, Ernst. Männlichkeiten: Eine andere Geschichte des 20. Jahrhunderts. Vienna: Böhlau, 2005.

Hansen, Miriam. "Early Silent Cinema: Whose Public Sphere?" New German Critique 29 (Spring/Summer 1983): 147–84.

Hansen, Miriam. "Pleasure, Ambivalence, Identification: Valentino and Female Spectatorship." Cinema Journal 25, no. 4 (Summer 1986): 6–32.

Harmat, Ulrike. "Divorce and Remarriage in Austria-Hungary: The Second Marriage of Franz Conrad von Hötzendorf." Austrian History Yearbook 32 (2001): 69–103.

Harmat, Ulrike. Ehe auf Widerruf? Der Konflikt um das Eherecht in Österreich 1918–1938. Frankfurt: V. Klosterman, 1999.

Haraway, Donna. The Haraway Reader. New York: Routledge, 2003.

Hartman, Saidiya. "Venus in Two Acts." Small Axe 12, no. 2 (June 2008): 1–14.

Hartman, Saidiya. Wayward Lives, Beautiful Experiments: Intimate Histories of Social Upheaval. New York: W. W. Norton, 2019.

Haste, Cate. Passionate Spirit: The Life of Alma Mahler. New York: Basic Books, 2019.

Hau, Michael. *The Cult of Health and Beauty in Germany: A Social History, 1890–1930*. Chicago: University of Chicago Press, 2003.

Hauch, Gabriella. *Frau Biedermeier auf den Barrikaden: Frauenleben in der Wiener Revolution 1848*. Vienna: Verlag für Gesellschaftskritik, 1990.

Hauch, Gabriella. *Frauen bewegen Politik: Österreich 1848–1938*. Innsbruck: StudienVerlag, 2009.

Hauch, Gabriella. "Sisters and Comrades: Women's Movements and the 'Austrian Revolution': Gender in Insurrection, the Räte Movement, Parties and Parliament." In *Aftermaths of War: Women's Movements and Female Activists, 1918–1923*, ed. Ingrid Sharp and Matthew Stibbe, 221–43. Boston: Brill, 2011.

Hauch, Gabriella. *Vom Frauenstandpunkt aus: Frauen im Parlament 1919–1933*. Vienna: Verlag für Gesellschaftskritik, 1995.

Healy, Maureen. "Civilizing the Soldier in Postwar Austria." In *Gender and War in Twentieth-Century Eastern Europe*, ed. Nancy M. Wingfield and Maria Bucur, 47–69. Bloomington: Indiana University Press, 2006.

Healy, Maureen. *Vienna and the Fall of the Habsburg Empire: Total War and Everyday Life in World War I*. New York: Cambridge University Press, 2004.

Heineman, Elizabeth D. *What Difference Does a Husband Make? Women and Marital Status in Nazi and Postwar Germany*. Berkeley: University of California Press, 1999.

Helfert, Veronika. "Between Pacifism and Militancy: Socialist Women in the First Austrian Republic, 1918–1934." *Diplomacy & Statecraft* 31, no. 4 (2020): 648–72.

Helfert, Veronika. *Frauen, wacht auf! Eine Frauen- und Geschlechtergeschichte von Revolution und Rätebewegung in Österreich, 1917–1924*. Göttingen: Vandenhoeck & Ruprecht, 2021.

Helly, Dorothy O., and Susan M. Reverby, eds. *Gendered Domains: Rethinking Public and Private in Women's History: Essays from the 7th Berkshire Conference on the History of Women*. Ithaca, NY: Cornell University Press, 1992.

Herzog, Dagmar. *Sex after Fascism: Memory and Morality in Twentieth-Century Germany*. Princeton, NJ: Princeton University Press, 2005.

Herzog, Dagmar. *Sexuality in Europe: A Twentieth-Century History*. New York: Cambridge University Press, 2011.

Herzog, Dagmar. "Syncopated Sex: Transforming European Sexual Cultures." *American Historical Review* 114, no. 5 (2009): 1287–1308.

Hess, H. "The Lure of Vienna: Poiret and the Wiener Werkstätte." In *Poiret*, ed. Harold Koda and Andrew Bolton, 39–40. New York: The Metropolitan Museum of Art, 2007.

Hiebler, Heinz. *Hugo von Hofmannsthal und die Medienkultur der Moderne*. Würzburg: Königshausen und Neumann, 2003.

Hilber, Marina. "Antiseptics Leave the Clinic—The Introduction of (Puerperal) Prophylaxis in Austrian Midwifery Education (1870s–1880s)." *Social History of Medicine* 35, no. 1 (2022): 97–120.

Hintermayr, Michaela. *Suizid und Geschlecht in der Moderne: Wissenschaft, Medien und Individuum (Österreich 1870–1970)*. Boston: De Gruyter Oldenbourg, 2021.

Holmes, Deborah, and Lisa Silverman, eds. *Interwar Vienna: Culture between Tradition and Modernity*. Rochester, NY: Camden House, 2009.

Horntrich, Paul M. "Science, Sin, and Sexuality in Roman-Catholic Discourses in the German-Speaking Area, 1870s to 1930s." *Sexuality & Culture* 24 (2020): 2137–60.

Houze, Rebecca. "Fashionable Reform Dress and the Invention of 'Style' in Fin de Siècle Vienna." *Fashion Theory* 5, no. 1 (2001): 29–56.

Irigaray, Luce. *This Sex Which Is Not One.* Translated by Catherine Porter and Carolyn Burke. Ithaca, NY: Cornell University Press, 1985.

Janik, Allan, and Stephen Toulmin. *Wittgenstein's Vienna.* New York: Simon and Schuster, 1973.

Jensen, Erik N. *Body by Weimar: Athletes, Gender, and German Modernity.* New York: Oxford University Press, 2010.

Johnson, Julie M. *The Memory Factory: The Forgotten Women Artists of Vienna 1900.* West Lafayette, IN: Purdue University Press, 2012.

Johnston, William M. *The Austrian Mind: An Intellectual and Social History, 1848–1938.* Berkeley: University of California Press, 1972.

Judson, Pieter M. *Exclusive Revolutionaries: Liberal Politics, Social Experience, and National Identity in the Austrian Empire, 1848–1914.* Ann Arbor: University of Michigan Press, 1996.

Judson, Pieter M. "The Gendered Politics of German Nationalism in Austria, 1880–1900." In *Austrian Women in the Nineteenth and Twentieth Centuries: Cross-Disciplinary Perspectives,* ed. David F. Good, Margarete Grandner, and Mary Jo Maynes, 1–17. Providence, RI: Berghahn Books, 1996.

Judson, Pieter M. *The Habsburg Empire: A New History.* Cambridge, MA: Harvard University Press, 2016.

Jusek, Karin J. *Auf der Suche nach der Verlorenen: Die Prostitutionsdebatten im Wien der Jahrhundertwende.* Vienna: Löcker Verlag, 1994.

Kaes, Anton. "The Debate about Cinema: Charting a Controversy (1909–1929)." *New German Critique* 40 (Winter 1987): 7–33.

Kaes, Anton, ed. *Kino-Debatte: Texte zum Verhältnis von Literatur und Film 1909–1929.* Munich: Deutscher Taschenbuch Verlag, 1978.

Kern, Stephen. *The Culture of Time and Space: 1880–1918.* Cambridge, MA: Harvard University Press, 1983.

Killen, Andreas. *Berlin Electropolis: Shock, Nerves, and German Modernity.* Berkeley: University of California Press, 2006.

King, Helen. *Hippocrates' Woman: Reading the Female Body in Ancient Greece.* London: Routledge, 1998.

Kontje, Todd Curtis. *Women, the Novel, and the German Nation 1771–1871: Domestic Fiction in the Fatherland.* New York: Cambridge University Press, 1998.

Koritz, Amy. *Gender Bodies/Performing Art: Dance and Literature in Early-Twentieth-Century Culture.* Ann Arbor: University of Michigan Press, 1995.

Kos, Wolfgang, ed. *Wiener Typen: Klischees und Wirklichkeit.* Vienna: Christian Brandstätter Verlag, 2013.

Krasny, Elke. *Stadt und Frauen: Eine andere Topographie von Wien.* Vienna: Metroverlag, 2008.

Kristeva, Julia. *Powers of Horror: An Essay on Abjection.* New York: Columbia University Press, 1982.

Kuhn, Thomas. *The Structure of Scientific Revolutions.* Chicago: University of Chicago Press, 1962.

Kultermann, Udo. "The Dance of the Seven Veils: Salome and Erotic Culture around 1900." *Artibus et Historiae* 27, no. 53 (2006): 187–215.

Kurimay, Anita. *Queer Budapest, 1873–1961.* Chicago: University of Chicago Press, 2020.

Kuriyama, Shigehisa. "Interpreting the History of Bloodletting." *Journal of the History of Medicine and Allied Sciences* 50, no. 1 (January 1994): 11–46.

Landay, Lori. "The Flapper Film: Comedy, Dance, and Jazz Age Kinaesthetics." In *A Feminist Reader in Early Cinema*, ed. Jennifer M. Bean and Diane Negra, 221–48. Durham, NC: Duke University Press, 2002.

Lafleur, Ingrun. "Adelheid Popp and Working-Class Feminism in Austria." *Frontiers: A Journal of Women's Studies* 1, no. 1 (Autumn 1975): 86–105.

LaMothe, Kimerer L. *Nietzsche's Dancers: Isadora Duncan, Martha Graham, and the Revaluation of Christian Values.* New York: Palgrave Macmillan, 2006.

Laqueur, Thomas. *Making Sex: Body and Gender from the Greeks to Freud.* Cambridge, MA: Harvard University Press, 1990.

Lempa, Heikki. *Beyond the Gymnasium: Educating the Middle-Class Bodies in Classical Germany.* New York: Lexington Books, 2007.

Le Rider, Jacques. *Modernity and the Crises of Identity: Culture and Society in Fin de Siècle Vienna.* Translated by Rosemary Morris. New York: Continuum, 1993.

Lehner, Karin. *Verpönte Eingriffe: Sozialdemokratische Reformbestrebungen zu den Abtreibungsbestimmungen in der Zwischenkriegszeit.* Vienna: Picus Verlag, 1989.

Lesky, Erna. *The Vienna Medical School of the 19th Century.* Baltimore, MD: Johns Hopkins University Press, 1976.

Lichtenberger, Elisabeth. *Vienna: Bridge Between Cultures.* Translated by Dietline Mühlgassner and Craig Reisser. New York: Belhaven Press, 1993.

Lohmeyer, Enno. "Hedwig Courths-Mahler and the Everlasting Desire for Royal Romance." In *Mediating Germany: Popular Culture Between Tradition and Innovation*, ed. Gerd Bayer, 37–53. Newcastle: Cambridge Scholars Press, 2006.

Longhurst, Robyn. *Maternities: Gender, Bodies, and Space.* New York: Routledge, 2008.

Lorde, Audre. *Uses of the Erotic: The Erotic as Power.* Trumansburg, NY: Out & Out Books, 1978.

Lowy, Dina. *The Japanese 'New Woman': Images of Gender and Modernity.* New Brunswick, NJ: Rutgers University Press, 2007.

Lüdtke, Alf. *Alltagsgeschichte: Zur Rekonstruktion historischer Erfahrungen und Lebensweisen.* Frankfurt: Campus Verlag, 1984.

Luft, David S. *Eros and Inwardness in Vienna: Weininger, Musil, Doderer.* Chicago: University of Chicago Press, 2003.

Lybeck, Marti M. *Desiring Emancipation: New Women and Homosexuality in Germany, 1890–1933.* Albany, NY: SUNY Press, 2014.

Maderthaner, Wolfgang, and Lutz Musner. *Unruly Masses: The Other Side of Fin-de-Siècle Vienna.* New York: Berghahn Books, 2008.

Marcus, Laura. *Auto/Biographical Discourses.* New York: Manchester University Press, 1994.

Marks, Patricia. *Bicycles, Bangs, and Bloomers: The New Woman in the Popular Press.* Lexington: University of Kentucky Press, 1990.

Marhoefer, Laurie. *Sex and the Weimar Republic: German Homosexual Emancipation and the Rise of the Nazis.* Toronto: University of Toronto Press, 2015.

Martin, Emily. *The Woman in the Body: A Cultural Analysis of Reproduction.* Boston: Beacon Press, 2001.

Massumi, Brian. *Parables of the Virtual: Movement, Affect, Sensation.* Durham, NC: Duke University Press, 2002.

Matysik, Tracie. *Reforming the Moral Subject: Ethics and Sexuality in Central Europe, 1890–1930.* Ithaca, NY: Cornell University Press, 2008.

Mayer, David. "Acting in Silent Film: Which Legacy of the Theatre?" In *Screening Acting*, ed. Alan Lovell, 10–30. New York: Routledge, 1999.

McClary, Susan. *Feminine Endings: Music, Gender, and Sexuality.* Minneapolis: University of Minnesota Press, 1991.

McClive, Cathy. "The Hidden Truths of the Belly: The Uncertainties of Pregnancy in Early Modern Europe." *Social History of Medicine* 15, no. 2 (August 2022): 209–27.

McClive, Cathy. *Menstruation and Procreation in Early Modern France.* London: Routledge, 2015.

McCormick, Richard W. *Gender and Sex in Weimar Modernity.* New York: Palgrave, 2001.

McDowell, Linda. *Gender, Identity, and Place: Understanding Feminist Geographies.* Minneapolis: University of Minnesota Press, 1999.

McEwen, Britta. "Emotional Expression and the Construction of Heterosexuality: Hugo Bettauer's Viennese Advice Columns." *Journal of the History of Sexuality* 25, no. 1 (January 2016): 114–36.

McEwen, Britta. *Sexual Knowledge: Feeling, Fact, and Social Reform in Vienna, 1900–1934.* New York: Berghahn Books, 2012.

McGrath, William J. *Dionysian Art and Populist Politics in Austria.* New Haven, CT: Yale University Press, 1974.

Melander, Ellinor. "Toward the Sexual and Economic Emancipation of Women: The Philosophy of Grete Meisel-Hess." *History of European Ideas* 14, no. 5 (1992): 695–713.

Merleau-Ponty, Maurice. *Phenomenology of Perception.* Translated by Donald Landes. New York: Routledge, 2001.

Mesner, Maria. "Educating Reasonable Lovers: Sex Counseling in Austria in the First Half of the Twentieth Century." In *Sexuality in Austria*, ed. Günther Bischof, Anton Pelinka, and Dagmar Herzog, 48–64. New Brunswick, NJ: Transaction, 2007.

Mesner, Maria. *Geburten/Kontrolle: Reproduktionspolitik im 20. Jahrhundert.* Vienna: Böhlau, 2010.

Metz-Becker, Marita. *Der verwaltete Körper: Die Medikalisierung schwangerer Frauen in den Gebärhäusern des frühen 19. Jahrhunderts.* Frankfurt: Campus Verlag, 1997.

Moi, Toril. *What Is a Woman and Other Essays.* New York: Oxford University Press, 2001.

Motyl, Katya. "Re-Embodying History's 'Lady': Women's History, Materiality and Public Space in Early Twentieth-Century Vienna." *Gender & History* 33, no. 1 (March 2021): 169–91.

Müller-Funk, Wolfgang, Peter Plener, and Clemens Ruthner, eds. *Kakanien Revisited: Das Eigene und das Fremde (in) der österreichisch-ungarischen Monarchie.* Tübingen: Francke, 2002.

Murphy, Patricia. *The New Woman Gothic: Reconfiguration of Distress.* Columbia: University of Missouri Press, 2016.

Museum der Stadt Wien. *Die Frau im Korsett: Wiener Frauenalltag zwischen Klischee und Wirklichkeit, 1848–1920.* Vienna: Eigenverlag des Museen der Stadt Wien, 1984.

Musner, Lutz. *Der Geschmack von Wien: Kultur und Habitus einer Stadt*. Frankfurt: Campus Verlag, 2009.

Nagy, Sandor. "One Empire, Two States, Many Laws: Matrimonial Law and Divorce in the Austro-Hungarian Monarchy." *The Hungarian Historical Review* 3, no. 1 (2014): 190–221.

Natarajan, Ambika. *Servants of Culture: Paternalism, Policing, and Identity Politics in Vienna, 1799–1914*. New York: Berghahn Books, 2023.

Natarajan, Ambika. "Sex, Surveillance, and the Servant Question in Vienna, 1850–1914." PhD diss., Oregon State University, 2019.

Natarajan, Ambika. "Vagrant Servants as Disease Vectors: Regulation of Migrant Maidservants in Fin-de-Siècle Vienna." *Austrian History Yearbook* 51 (2020): 152–72.

Nunn, Joan. *Fashion in Costume, 1200–2000*. Chicago: New Amsterdam Books, 2000.

O'Brien, Patricia. "The Kleptomania Diagnosis: Bourgeois Women and Theft in Late Nineteenth-Century France." *Journal of Social History* (Fall 1983): 65–77.

Offen, Karen. *European Feminisms, 1700–1950: A Political History*. Stanford, CA: Stanford University Press, 2000.

Oosterhuis, Harry. *Stepchildren of Nature: Krafft-Ebing, Psychiatry, and the Making of Sexual Identity*. Chicago: University of Chicago Press, 2000.

Otto, Elizabeth, and Vanessa Rocco, eds. *The New Woman International: Representations in Photography and Film from the 1870s through the 1960s*. Ann Arbor: University of Michigan Press, 2011.

O'Toole, Tina. *The Irish New Woman*. London: Palgrave Macmillan, 2013.

Payer, Peter. "The Age of Noise: Early Reactions in Vienna, 1870–1914." *Journal of Urban History* 33, no. 5 (July 2007): 773–93.

Payer, Peter. *Der Gestank von Wien: Über Kanalgase, Totendünste und andere üble Geruchskulissen*. Vienna: Döcker, 1997.

Peiss, Kathy. *Cheap Amusements: Working Women and Leisure in Turn-of-the-Century New York*. Philadelphia: Temple University Press, 1986.

Peters, Meindert E. "Reevaluations through Dance: Friedrich Nietzsche's Thought in Isadora Duncan's Speech *The Dance of the Future*." *Dance Research* 37, no. 2 (2019): 206–19.

Pick, Daniel. *Faces of Degeneration: A European Disorder, c. 1848–c. 1918*. New York: Cambridge University Press, 1996.

Pilcher, Jeffrey M. "Review Essay: The Embodied Imagination in Recent Writings on Food History." *American Historical Review* 121, no. 3 (June 2016): 861–87.

Porter, Roy. "History of the Body Reconsidered." In *New Perspectives on Historical Writing*, ed. Peter Burke, 233–60. University Park: Pennsylvania State University Press, 1992.

Pred, Allan. *Lost Words and Lost Worlds: Modernity and the Language of Everyday Life in Late Nineteenth-Century Stockholm*. New York: Cambridge University Press, 1990.

Prokopovych, Markian. "Prostitution in Vienna in the Long Nineteenth Century." In *Trafficking in Women 1924–1926—The Paul McKinsie Reports for the League of Nations*, ed. Jean-Michel Chaumont, Magaly Rodriguez Garcia, and Paul Servais. New York: United Nations Publications, 2016.

Puffet, Derrick, ed. *Richard Strauss: Salome*. Cambridge Opera Books. Cambridge: Cambridge University Press, 1989.

Rabinbach, Anson. *The Crisis of Austrian Socialism: From Red Vienna to Civil War, 1927–1934.* Chicago: University of Chicago Press, 1983.

Rabinbach, Anson. *The Human Motor: Energy, Fatigue, and the Origins of Modernity.* Berkeley: University of California Press, 1992.

Ramsbrock, Annelie. *The Science of Beauty: Culture and Cosmetics in Modern Germany, 1750–1930.* Translated by David Burnett. Washington, DC: Palgrave Macmillan, 2015.

Reagan, Leslie J. *When Abortion Was a Crime: Women, Medicine, and Law in the United States, 1867–1973.* Berkeley: University of California Press, 1997.

Rechter, David. "Galicia in Vienna: Jewish Refugees in the First World War." *Austrian History Yearbook* 28 (1997): 113–30.

Reddy, William M. *The Making of Romantic Love: Longing and Sexuality in Europe, South Asia, and Japan, 900–1200 CE.* Chicago: University of Chicago Press, 2012.

Reddy, William M. *The Navigation of Feeling: A Framework for the History of Emotions.* New York: Cambridge University Press, 2001.

Reden, Alexander Sixtus von, and Josef Schweikhardt. *Eros unterm Doppeladler: Eine Sittengeschichte Altösterreichs.* Vienna: Ueberreute, 1993.

Reynolds, Dee, and Matthew Reason, eds. *Kinesthetic Empathy in Creative and Cultural Practices.* Chicago: University of Chicago Press, 2012.

Rheinsberg, Anna, ed. *Bubikopf: Aufbruch in den Zwanzigern: Texte von Frauen.* Darmstadt: Luchterhand, 1988.

Richardson, Angelique, and Chris Willis, eds. *The New Woman in Fiction and in Fact: Fin-de-Siècle Feminisms.* New York: Palgrave, 2001.

Riddle, John M. *Eve's Herbs: A History of Contraception and Abortion in the West.* Cambridge, MA: Harvard University Press, 1997.

Rigler, Edith. *Frauenleitbild und Frauenarbeit in Österreich: Vom ausgehenden 19. Jahrhundert bis zum Zweiten Weltkrieg.* Vienna: Verlag für Geschichte und Politik, 1976.

Roberts, Mary Louise. *Civilization Without Sexes: Reconstructing Gender in Postwar France, 1917–1927.* Chicago: University of Chicago Press, 1994.

Roberts, Mary Louise. *Disruptive Acts: The New Woman of Fin-de-Siècle France.* Chicago: University of Chicago Press, 2002.

Roberts, Mary Louise. "Samson and Delilah Revisited: The Politics of Women's Fashion in 1920s France." *American Historical Review* 98, no. 3 (June 1993): 657–84.

Rojek, Chris. *Celebrity.* London: Reaktion Books, 2001.

Rose, Alison. *Jewish Women in Fin de Siècle Vienna.* Austin: University of Texas Press, 2008.

Rosenwein, Barbara H. *Emotional Communities in the Early Middle Ages.* Ithaca, NY: Cornell University Press, 2006.

Rosenwein, Barbara H. "Worrying about Emotions in History." *American Historical Review* 107, no. 3 (June 2002): 821–45.

Rotenberg, Robert. *Landscape and Power in Vienna.* Baltimore, MD: Johns Hopkins University Press, 1995.

Rozenblit, Marsha L. *The Jews of Vienna, 1867–1914: Assimilation and Identity.* Albany: State University of New York Press, 1983.

Sandgruber, Roman. *Die Anfänge der Konsumgesellschaft: Konsumgüterverbrauch, Lebensstandard und Alltagskultur in Österreich im 18. und 19. Jahrhundert.* Munich: R. Oldenbourg, 1982.

Sarasin, Philipp. *Reizbare Maschinen: Eine Geschichte des Körpers, 1765–1914*. Frankfurt: Suhrkamp, 2001.

Sato, Barbara. *The New Japanese Woman: Modernity, Media, and Women in Interwar Japan*. Durham, NC: Duke University Press, 2003.

Scarry, Elaine. *The Body in Pain: The Making and Unmaking of the World*. New York: Oxford University Press, 1985.

Schmid, Gisela Bärbel. "Das unheimliche Erlebnis eines jungen Elegants in einer merkwürdigen visionären Nacht: Zu Hofmannsthals Pantomime *Das fremde Mädchen.*" *Hofmannsthal-Blätter* 34 (Autumn 1986): 46–57.

Schoppmann, Claudia. *Verbotene Verhältnisse: Frauenliebe, 1938–1945*. Berlin: Querverlag, 1999.

Schorske, Carl E. *Fin-de-Siècle Vienna: Politics and Culture*. New York: Vintage Books, 1981.

Schulze, Winfried, ed. *Sozialgeschichte, Alltagsgeschichte, Mikro-Historie*. Göttingen: Vandenhoeck & Ruprecht, 1994.

Schwartz, Agatha. "Sexual Cripples and Moral Degenerates: Fin-de-Siècle Austrian Women Writers on Male Sexuality and Masculinity." *Seminar* 44, no. 1 (2008): 53–67.

Schwartz, Agatha. *Shifting Voices: Feminist Thought and Women's Writing in Fin-de-Siècle Austria and Hungary*. Montreal: McGill-Queen's University Press, 2008.

Schwartz, Agatha, ed. *Gender and Modernity in Central Europe: The Austro-Hungarian Monarchy and Its Legacy*. Ottawa: University of Ottawa Press, 2010.

Schwartz, Vanessa R. *Spectacular Realities: Early Mass Culture in Fin-de-Siècle Paris*. Berkeley: University of California Press, 1998.

Schwarz, Werner Michael. *Kino und Kinos in Wien: Eine Entwicklungsgeschichte bis 1934*. Vienna: Verlag Turia & Kant, 1992.

Scott, Joan W. "The Evidence of Experience." *Critical Inquiry* 17, no. 4 (Summer 1991): 773–97.

Scott, Joan W. "Gender: A Useful Category of Historical Analysis." *American Historical Review* 91, no. 5 (December 1986): 1053–75.

Scott, Joan W. *Gender and the Politics of History*. New York: Columbia University Press, 1999.

Sengoopta, Chandak. *Otto Weininger: Sex, Science, and Self in Imperial Vienna*. Chicago: University of Chicago Press, 2000.

Silverman, Debora L. *Art Nouveau in Fin-de-Siècle France: Politics, Psychology, and Style*. Berkeley: University of California Press, 1989.

Silverman, Lisa. *Becoming Austrians: Jews and Culture Between the World Wars*. New York: Oxford University Press, 2012.

Simmons, Sherwin. "Chaplin Smiles on the Wall: Berlin Dada and Wish-Images of Popular Culture." *New German Critique* 84 (Autumn 2001): 3–34.

Sluis, Ageeth. *Deco Body, Deco City: Female Spectacle & Modernity in Mexico City, 1900–1939*. Lincoln: University of Nebraska Press, 2016.

Smith, Bonnie. *The Gender of History: Men, Women, and Historical Practice*. Cambridge, MA: Harvard University Press, 1998.

Smith, Jill Suzanne. *Berlin Coquette: Prostitution and the New German Woman, 1890–1933*. Ithaca, NY: Cornell University Press, 2013.

Smith-Rosenberg, Carroll. *Disorderly Conduct: Visions of Gender in Victorian America*. New York: Knopf, 1985.

Smith-Rosenberg, Carroll. "The Hysterical Woman: Sex Roles and Role Conflict in 19th Century America." *Social Research* 39, no. 4 (Winter 1972): 652–78.

Snyder, Sharon L., and David T. Mitchell. "Re-engaging the Body: Disability Studies and the Resistance to Embodiment." *Public Culture* 13, no. 3 (2001): 367–89.

Sobchack, Vivian. "Phenomenology and the Film Experience." In *Viewing Positions: Ways of Seeing Film*, ed. Lisa Williams, 36–58. New Brunswick, NJ: Rutgers University Press, 1995.

Spector, Scott. *Violent Sensations: Sex, Crime, and Utopia in Vienna and Berlin, 1860–1914*. Chicago: University of Chicago Press, 2016.

Spector, Scott. "The Wrath of the 'Countess Merviola': Tabloid Exposé and the Emergence of Homosexual Subjects in Vienna in 1907." In *Sexuality in Austria*, ed. Günther Bischof, Anton Pelinka, and Dagmar Herzog, 31–47. New Brunswick, NJ: Transaction, 2007.

Spongberg, Mary. *Feminizing Venereal Disease: The Body of the Prostitute in Nineteenth-Century Medical Discourse*. New York: NYU Press, 1997.

Stallybrass, Peter, and Allon White. *The Politics and Poetics of Transgression*. Ithaca, NY: Cornell University Press, 1986.

Stark, Gary D. *Banned in Berlin: Literary Censorship in Imperial Germany, 1871–1918*. New York: Berghahn Books, 2009.

Stauter-Halsted, Keely. *The Devil's Chain: Prostitution and Social Control in Partitioned Poland*. Ithaca, NY: Cornell University Press, 2015.

Stauter-Halsted, Keely. "'A Generation of Monsters': Jews, Prostitution, and Racial Purity in the 1892 L'viv White Slavery Trial." *Austrian History Yearbook* 38 (2007): 25–35.

Stauter-Halsted, Keely. "Moral Panic and the Prostitute in Partitioned Poland: Middle-Class Respectability in Defense of the Modern Nation." *Slavic Review* 68, no. 3 (Fall 2009): 557–81.

Stauter-Halsted, Keely. "The Physician and the Fallen Woman: Medicalizing Prostitution in the Polish Lands." *Journal of the History of Sexuality* 20, no. 2 (May 2011): 270–90.

Steedman, Carolyn. *Labours Lost: Domestic Service and the Making of Modern England*. New York: Cambridge University Press, 2009.

Steele, Valerie. *Fashion and Eroticism: Ideals of Feminine Beauty from the Victorian Era to the Jazz Age*. New York: Oxford University Press, 1985.

Steinberg, Michael. *The Meaning of the Salzburg Festival: Austria as Theater and Ideology, 1890–1938*. Ithaca, NY: Cornell University Press, 1990.

Steward, Jill. "The Culture of the Water Cure in Nineteenth-Century Austria, 1800–1914." In *Water, Leisure and Culture: European Historical Perspectives*, ed. Susan C. Anderson and Bruce H. Tabb, 23–36. New York: Berg, 2002.

Steward, Jill. "The Spa Towns of the Austrian-Hungarian Empire and the Growth of Tourist Culture: 1860–1914." In *New Directions in Urban History: Aspects of European Urban Cultural Life in the Mirror of Art, Health and Tourism*, ed. P. Borsay, G. Hirschfelder, and R.-E. Mohrmann, 87–126. Münster: Waxmann, 2000.

Stewart, Janet. *Fashioning Vienna: Adolf Loos's Cultural Criticism*. New York: Taylor & Francis, 2013.

Stewart, Janet. "A Taste of Vienna: Food as a Signifier of Urban Modernity in Vienna, 1890–1930." In *The City and the Senses: Urban Culture Since 1500*, ed. Alexander Cowan and Jill Steward, 179–97. London: Routledge, 2007.

Stibbe, Matthew, Olga Shnyrova, and Veronika Helfert. "Women and the Socialist Revolution, 1917–1923." In *Women Activists Between War and Peace: Europe, 1918–1923*, ed. Ingrid Sharp and Matthew Stibbe, 123–72. New York: Bloomsbury, 2017.

Stolberg, Michael. "Menstruation and Sexual Difference in Early Modern Medicine." In *Menstruation: A Cultural History*, ed. Andrew Shail and Gillian Howie, 90–101. New York: Palgrave Macmillan, 2005.

Sutherland, Gillian. *In Search of the New Woman: Middle-Class Women and Work in Britain, 1870–1914*. New York: Cambridge University Press, 2015.

Swender, Rebecca. "The Problem of the Divo: New Models for Analyzing Silent-Film Performance." *Journal of Film and Video* 58, no. 1/2 (Spring/Summer 2006): 7–20.

Tálos, Emmerich, and Wolfgang Neugebauer, eds. *Austrofaschismus: Politik—Ökonomie—Kultur 1933–1938*, 5th ed. Vienna: Lit Verlag, 2005.

Tatlock, Lynne. "The Afterlife of Nineteenth-Century Popular Fiction and the German Imaginary: The Illustrated Collected Novels of E. Marlitt, W. Heimburg, and E. Werner." In *Publishing Culture and the "Reading Nation": German Book History in the Long Nineteenth Century*, ed. Lynne Tatlock, 118–54. Rochester, NY: Camden House, 2010.

Taylor, Diana. *The Archive and the Repertoire: Performing Cultural Memory in the Americas*. Durham, NC: Duke University Press, 2003.

Tester, Keith. *The Flâneur*. New York: Routledge, 1994.

Theweleit, Klaus. *Male Fantasies, Volume 1: Women, Floods, Bodies, History*. Minneapolis: University of Minnesota Press, 1987.

Thorpe, Julie. *Pan-Germanism and the Austrofascist State, 1933–38*. Manchester: Manchester University Press, 2011.

Thorson, Helga. *Grete Meisel-Hess: The New Woman and the Sexual Crisis*. Rochester, NY: Camden House, 2022.

Tichy, Marina. *Alltag und Traum: Leben und Lektüre der Wiener Dienstmädchen um die Jahrhundertwende*. Vienna: Böhlau Verlag, 1984.

Timms, Edward. *Karl Kraus, Apocalyptic Satirist: Cultural Catastrophe in Habsburg Vienna*. New Haven, CT: Yale University Press, 1986.

Timpano, Nathan J. *Constructing the Viennese Modern Body: Art, Hysteria, and the Puppet*. New York: Routledge, 2017.

Topp, Leslie. "The Mad Objects of Fin-de-Siècle Vienna: Journeys, Contexts and Dislocations in the Exhibition 'Madness and Modernity.'" In *Journeys into Madness: Mapping Mental Illness in the Austro-Hungarian Empire*, ed. Gemma Blackshaw and Sabine Wiener, 10–26. New York: Berghahn Books, 2012.

Topp, Leslie. "Otto Wagner and the Steinhof Psychiatric Hospital: Architecture as Misunderstanding." *The Art Bulletin*, March 2005, 130–56.

Turda, Marius, and Paul Weindling, eds. *Blood and Homeland: Eugenics and Racial Nationalism in Central and Southeast Europe, 1900–1940*. Budapest: Central European University Press, 2007.

Unowsky, Daniel L. *The Pomp and Politics of Patriotism: Imperial Celebrations in Habsburg Austria, 1848–1916*. West Lafayette, IN: Purdue University Press, 2005.

Usborne, Cornelie. *Cultures of Abortion in Weimar Germany*. New York: Berghahn Books, 2007.

Valverde, Marianne. "The Love of Finery: Fashion and the Fallen Woman in Nineteenth-Century Social Discourse." *Victorian Studies* (Winter 1989): 169–88.

Vicinus, Martha. *Intimate Friends: Women Who Loved Women, 1778–1928.* Chicago: University of Chicago Press, 2006.

Wagener, Mary L. "Fashion and Feminism in 'Fin de Siècle' Vienna." *Woman's Art Journal* (1989): 29–33.

Wagner, Nike. *Karl Kraus und die Erotik der Wiener Moderne.* Frankfurt: Suhrkamp, 1982.

Walkowitz, Judith. *City of Dreadful Delight: Narratives of Sexual Danger in Late-Victorian London.* Chicago: University of Chicago Press, 1992.

Walkowitz, Judith. "The 'Vision of Salome': Cosmopolitanism and Erotic Dancing in Central London, 1908–1918." *American Historical Review* 108, no. 2 (April 2003): 337–76.

Wallach, Kerry. "Escape Artistry: Elisabeth Bergner and Jewish Disappearance in *Der träumende Mund* (Czinner, 1932)." *German Studies Review* 38, no. 1 (February 2015): 17–34.

Wånggren, Lena. *Gender, Technology and the New Woman.* Edinburgh: University of Edinburgh Press, 2017.

Wasserman, Janek. *Black Vienna: The Radical Right in the Red City, 1918–1938.* Ithaca, NY: Cornell University Press, 2014.

Wegs, J. Robert. *Growing Up Working Class: Continuity and Change Among Viennese Youth, 1890–1938.* University Park: Pennsylvania State University Press, 1989.

Weinbaum, Alys Eve, Lynn M. Thomas, Priti Ramamurthy, Uta G. Poiger, Madeleine Yue Dong, and Tani E. Barlow, eds. *The Modern Girl around the World: Consumption, Modernity, and Globalization.* Durham, NC: Duke University Press, 2008.

Weinreb, Alice. "Embodying German Suffering: Rethinking Popular Hunger during the Hunger Years (1945–1949)." *Body Politics* 2, no. 4 (2014): 463–88.

Weinreb, Alice. *Modern Hungers: Food and Power in Twentieth-Century Germany.* New York: Oxford University Press, 2017.

Weisner, Merry E. "The Midwives of South Germany and the Public/Private Dichotomy." In *The Art of Midwifery: Early Modern Widwives in Europe,* Wellcome Institute Series in the History of Medicine, ed. Hilary Marland, 77–94. New York: Routledge, 1993.

Wenninger, Florian, and Lucile Dreidemy, eds. *Das Dollfuß/Schuschnigg-Regime 1933–1938: Vermessung eines Forschungsfeldes.* Vienna: Böhlau Verlag, 2013.

Witzmann, Reingard, ed. *Die neue Körpersprache: Grete Wiesenthal und ihr Tanz.* Vienna: Eigenverlag der Museen der Stadt Wien, 1986.

Wickert, Christl. *Helene Stöcker, 1869–1943: Frauenrechtlerin, Sexualreformerin und Pazifistin.* Bonn: Dietz, 1991.

Wieber, Sabine. "Sculpting the Sanatorium: Nervous Bodies and Femmes Fragiles in Vienna, 1900." *Women in German Yearbook: Feminist Studies in German Literature & Culture* 27 (2011): 58–86.

Wieber, Sabine. "Vienna's Most Fashionable Neurasthenic: Empress Sisi and the Cult of Size Zero." In *Journeys into Madness: Mapping Mental Illness in the Austro-Hungarian Empire,* ed. Gemma Blackshaw and Sabine Wieber, 90–108. New York: Berghahn Books, 2012.

Williams, John Alexander. *Turning to Nature in Germany: Hiking, Nudism, and Conservation, 1900–1940.* Stanford, CA: Stanford University Press, 2007.

Wilson, Elizabeth. "The Invisible Flâneur." *New Left Review* 1, no. 191 (January–February 1992): 90–110.

Wilson, Elizabeth. *The Sphinx in the City: Urban Life, the Control of Disorder, and Women*. Berkeley: University of California Press, 1992.

Wingfield, Nancy M. "Destination: Alexandria, Buenos Aires, Constantinople; White Slavers in Late Imperial Austria." *Journal of the History of Sexuality* 20, no. 2 (May 2011): 291–311.

Wingfield, Nancy M. "The Enemy Within: Regulating Prostitution and Controlling Venereal Disease in Cisleithanian Austria during the Great War." *Central European History* 46, no. 3 (2013): 568–98.

Wingfield, Nancy M. *The World of Prostitution in Late Imperial Austria*. New York: Oxford University Press, 2017.

Witzmann, Reingard, ed. *Die neue Körpersprache: Grete Wiesenthal und ihr Tanz*. Vienna: Eigenverlag der Museen der Stadt Wien, 1986.

Wolff, Janet. "The Invisible Flâneuse: Women and the Literature of Modernity." *Theory, Culture & Society* 2, no. 3 (November 1, 1985): 37–46.

Wolff, Larry. *Child Abuse in Freud's Vienna: Postcards from the End of the World*. New York: NYU Press, 1988.

Wolff, Larry. *The Idea of Galicia: History and Fantasy in Habsburg Political Culture*. Stanford, CA: Stanford University Press, 2010.

Wolff, Larry. *Inventing Eastern Europe: The Map of Civilization on the Mind of the Enlightenment*. Stanford, CA: Stanford University Press, 1994.

Wolfgruber, Gudrun. "Kind- und Jugendfürsorge im Roten Wien zwischen sozialer Kontrolle und Hilfe; dargestellt am Beispiel der Kindesabnahmen." PhD diss., University of Vienna, 1996.

Wood, Nathaniel. *Becoming Metropolitan: Urban Selfhood and the Making of Modern Cracow*. DeKalb: Northern Illinois University Press, 2010.

Wood, Nathaniel. "Sexual Violence, Sex Scandals, and the Word on the Street: The Kolasówna Lustmord in Cracow's Popular Press, 1905–06." *Journal of the History of Sexuality* 20, no. 2 (May 2011): 243–69.

Woodford, Charlotte, ed. *Women, Emancipation and the German Novel 1871–1910: Protest Fiction in Its Cultural Context*. New York: Modern Humanities Research Association and Routledge, 2014.

Young, Iris Marion. *On Female Body Experience: "Throwing Like a Girl" and Other Essays*. New York: Oxford University Press, 2005.

Zettelbauer, Heidrun. *"Die Liebe sei Euer Heldentum": Geschlecht und Nation in völksichen Vereinen der Habsburgermonarchie*. Frankfurt: Campus Verlag, 2005.

Zimmermann, Susan. "'Making a Living from Disgrace': The Politics of Prostitution, Female Poverty and Urban Gender Codes in Budapest and Vienna, 1860–1929." In *The City in Central Europe: Culture and Society from 1800 to the Present*, ed. Malcolm Gee, Tim Kirk, and Jill Steward, 175–96. Brookfield, VT: Ashgate, 1999.

Zweiniger-Bargielowska, Ina. *Managing the Body: Body, Health, and Fitness in Britain 1880–1939*. New York: Oxford University Press, 2011.

Index